Middle School 3-1

중간고사 완벽대비

KB086784

적중100

영어 기출 문제집

중3

미래엔 | 최연희

Best Collection

구성과 특징

교과서의 주요 학습 내용을 중심으로 학습 영역별 특성에 맞춰 단계별로 다양한 학습 기회를 제공하여
단원별 학습능력 평가는 물론 중간 및 기말고사 시험 등에 완벽하게 대비할 수 있도록 내용을 구성

Words & Expressions

Step1   Key Words 단원별 핵심 단어 설명 및 풀이
           Key Expression 단원별 핵심 숙어 및 관용어 설명
           Word Power 반대 또는 비슷한 뜻 단어 배우기
           English Dictionary 영어로 배우는 영어 단어

Step2   실력평가 단원별 수시평가 대비 주관식, 객관식 문제풀이

Step3   서술형 대비 학업성취도 및 수행능력평가 대비 서술형 문제풀이

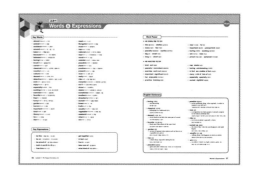

Conversation

Step1   핵심 의사소통 소통에 필요한 주요 표현 방법 요약
           핵심 Check 기본적인 표현 방법 및 활용능력 확인

Step2   대화문 익히기 교과서 대화문 심층 분석 및 확인

Step3   교과서 확인학습 빈칸 채우기를 통한 문장 완성 능력 확인

Step4   기본평가 시험대비 기초 학습 능력 평가

Step5   실력평가 단원별 수시평가 대비 주관식, 객관식 문제풀이

Step6   서술형 대비 학업성취도 및 수행능력평가 대비 서술형 문제풀이

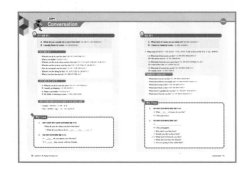

Grammar

Step1   주요 문법 단원별 주요 문법 사항과 예문을 알기 쉽게 설명
           핵심 Check 기본 문법사항에 대한 이해 여부 확인

Step2   기본평가 시험대비 기초 학습 능력 평가

Step3   실력평가 단원별 수시평가 대비 주관식, 객관식 문제풀이

Step4   서술형 대비 학업성취도 및 수행능력평가 대비 서술형 문제풀이

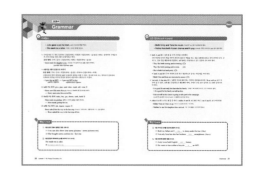

Reading

Step1   구문 분석 단원별로 제시된 문장에 대한 구문별 분석과 내용 설명
           확인문제 문장에 대한 기본적인 이해와 인지능력 확인

Step2   확인학습A 빈칸 채우기를 통한 문장 완성 능력 확인

Step3   확인학습B 제시된 우리말을 영어로 완성하여 작문 능력 키우기

Step4   실력평가 단원별 수시평가 대비 주관식, 객관식 문제풀이

Step5   서술형 대비 학업성취도 및 수행능력평가 대비 서술형 문제풀이
           교과서 구석구석 교과서에 나오는 기타 문장까지 완벽 학습

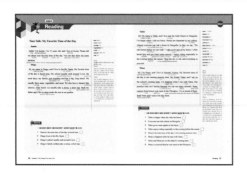

Composition

|영역별 핵심문제|

단어 및 어휘, 대화문, 문법, 독해 등 각 영역별 기출문제의 출제 유형을 분석하여 실전에 대비하고 연습할 수 있도록 문제를 배열

|단원별 예상문제|

기출문제를 분석한 후 새로운 시험 출제 경향을 더하여 새롭게 출제될 수 있는 문제를 포함하여 시험에 완벽하게 대비할 수 있도록 준비

|서술형 실전 및 창의사고력 문제|

학교 시험에서 점차 늘어나는 서술형 시험에 집중 대비하고 고득점을 취득하는데 만전을 기하기 위한 학습 코너

|단원별 모의고사|

영역별, 단계별 학습을 모두 마친 후 실전 연습을 위한 모의고사

교과서 파헤치기

- **단어Test1~3** 영어 단어 우리말 쓰기, 우리말을 영어 단어로 쓰기, 영영풀이에 해당하는 단어와 우리말 쓰기
- **대화문Test1~2** 대화문 빈칸 완성 및 전체 대화문 쓰기
- **본문Test1~5** 빈칸 완성, 우리말 쓰기, 문장 배열연습, 영어 작문하기 복습 등 단계별 반복 학습을 통해 교과서 지문에 대한 완벽한 습득
- **구석구석지문Test1~2** 지문 빈칸 완성 및 전문 영어로 쓰기

이책의 차례

Contents

Lesson **1** **Young Enough to Change the World** 5

Lesson **2** **Timeless Tales of Gods and Heroes** 61

Lesson **3** **Plants That Feed Us** 121

〈Insight on the textbook〉 교과서 파헤치기 01~65

〈책 속의 책〉 정답 및 해설 01~46

Lesson 1

Young Enough to Change the World

🎤 의사소통 기능

- 의향 말하기
  A: What's your plan for this year?
  B: I'm thinking of taking swimming lessons.

- 도움 제안하기
  A: Do you want me to fix it?
  B: Yes, please.

🎤 언어 형식

- 선행사를 포함하는 관계대명사 what
  What you do today can change the world.

- '양보'의 부사절 접속사 although
  Although they are only teenagers, they have actually made a difference in the world.

Words & Expressions

Key Words

- **actually** [ǽktʃuəli] 부 실제로
- **adopt** [ədápt] 동 입양하다
- **although** [ɔːlðóu] 접 ～임에도 불구하고, 비록 ～이지만
- **book review** 서평
- **bring** [briŋ] 동 ～을 가져오다
- **charity** [tʃǽrəti] 명 자선단체, 자선
- **cheetah** [tʃíːtə] 명 치타
- **child-care center** 탁아소, 보육원
- **collect** [kəlékt] 동 모으다, 수집하다
- **deliver** [dilívər] 동 전달하다, 배달하다
- **difficult** [dífikʌlt] 형 어려운
- **donate** [dóuneit] 동 기부하다, 기증하다
- **educate** [édʒukèit] 동 가르치다, 교육하다
- **endangered** [indéindʒərd] 형 멸종 위기의
- **expression** [ikspréʃən] 명 표현
- **fix** [fiks] 동 고치다
- **generation** [dʒènəréiʃən] 명 세대
- **gulf** [gʌlf] 명 만
- **leader** [líːdər] 명 리더, 지도자, 대표
- **marine** [məríːn] 형 해양의
- **mayonnaise** [mèiənéiz] 명 마요네즈

- **neighborhood** [néibərhùd] 명 이웃, 근처
- **non-profit organization** 명 비영리 단체
- **occur** [əkə́ːr] 동 일어나다, 발생하다
- **parking space** 주차 공간
- **probably** [prábəbli] 부 아마도
- **problem** [prábləm] 명 문제
- **raise** [reiz] 동 기르다
- **reduce** [ridjúːs] 동 줄이다
- **rescue** [réskjuː] 명 구조, 구출
- **rubber** [rʌ́bər] 명 고무
- **signature** [sígnətʃər] 명 서명
- **specialist** [spéʃəlist] 명 전문가
- **spill** [spil] 명 유출
- **supply** [səplái] 명 공급
- **teenager** [tíːnèidʒər] 명 십 대, 청소년
- **throat** [θrout] 명 목구멍, 목
- **translate** [trænsléit] 동 번역하다
- **various** [vɛ́riəs] 형 다양한, 여러 가지의
- **volunteer** [vàləntíər] 명 자원봉사자 동 자원하다
- **waste** [weist] 명 쓰레기

Key Expressions

- **a bit** 조금, 약간
- **a few** 어느 정도, 조금
- **any longer** 더 이상, 이제는
- **ask for help** 도움을 청하다
- **ask+목적어+to 동사원형** …가 ～하는 것을 요청하다
- **be able to 동사원형** ～할 수 있다
- **be covered with** ～으로 뒤덮여 있다
- **break down** 고장나다
- **die from** ～으로 죽다
- **do volunteer work** 자원봉사를 하다
- **for example** 예를 들어

- **in addition to** ～ 이외에, ～에 더하여
- **lend 사물 to 사람** ～에게 ～을 빌려주다
- **name+목적어+목적격보어(명사)** ～를 …라고 이름 짓다
- **read A to B** A를 B에게 읽어주다
- **run into** (곤경, 어려움 등을) 만나다[겪다]
- **send A to B** A를 B에게 보내다
- **share A with B** A를 B와 나누다, 공유하다
- **throw up** 토하다
- **translate ～ into 언어** …를 ～으로 번역하다
- **want+목적어+to부정사** ～가 …하는 것을 원하다

Word Power

※ 명사형 어미 -ion/-tion(행위, 성질, 상태)

- ☐ **act**(행동하다)+**-ion** → **action**(행동)
- ☐ **collect**(모으다, 수집하다)+**-ion** → **collection**(수집)
- ☐ **create**(~을 창조하다, 새로 만들어 내다)+**-ion** → **creation**(창조)
- ☐ **educate**(교육하다, 가르치다)+**-ion** → **education**(교육)
- ☐ **generate**(발생시키다, 일으키다)+**-ion** → **generation**((전기 등의) 발생)
- ☐ **protect**(보호하다)+**-ion** → **protection**(보호)
- ☐ **imagine**(상상하다)+**-tion** → **imagination**(상상)
- ☐ **invite**(초대하다)+**-tion** → **invitation**(초대)

※ **make**와 같이 쓰이는 단어의 짝

- ☐ **make a difference** (차이를 낳다, 변화를 가져오다)
- ☐ **make a discovery** (발견하다)
- ☐ **make a wish** (소원을 빌다)

English Dictionary

☐ **charity** 자선단체
→ an organization which raises money in order to help people who are sick or very poor, or who have a disability
아프거나 가난하거나 장애가 있는 사람들을 돕기 위해 돈을 모으는 단체

☐ **deliver** 전달하다, 배달하다
→ to take goods, letters, packages etc. to a particular place or person
물건, 편지, 소포 등을 특정한 장소나 사람에게 가져다주다

☐ **donate** 기부하다, 기증하다
→ to give something, especially money, to a person or an organization in order to help them
도울 목적으로 사람이나 단체에게 물건, 특히 돈을 주다

☐ **educate** 가르치다, 교육하다
→ to teach a child at a school, college, or university
학교 또는 대학에서 아이들을 가르치다

☐ **endangered** 멸종 위기의
→ in danger of extinction
멸종 위기에 있는

☐ **expression** 표현
→ something you say, write, or do that shows what you think or feel
당신이 생각하거나 느끼는 바를 보여주는 말하거나 쓰거나 또는 행동을 하는 것

☐ **fix** 고치다
→ to repair something that is broken or not working properly
고장나거나 적절하게 작동하지 않는 것을 수리하다

☐ **gulf** 만
→ a large area of sea partly enclosed by land
부분적으로 땅으로 둘러싸인 바다의 큰 지역

☐ **marine** 해양의
→ relating to the sea and the creatures that live there
바다와 거기에 살고 있는 생물과 관련된

☐ **occur** 일어나다, 발생하다
→ to happen
발생하다

☐ **reduce** 줄이다
→ to make something smaller or less in size, amount, or price
어떤 것의 크기, 양 또는 가격을 작게 만들다

☐ **signature** 서명
→ your name written in the way you usually write it, for example at the end of a letter, or on a cheque etc, to show that you have written it
예를 들어 편지의 끝이나 수표에 당신이 썼다는 것을 보여주기 위해 보통 쓰는 방식으로 쓰여진 이름

☐ **specialist** 전문가
→ someone who knows a lot about a particular subject, or is very skilled at it
특정한 주제에 대해 많이 알거나 그것에 대해 매우 숙련된 사람

☐ **translate** 번역하다
→ to change written or spoken words into another language
쓰여지거나 말해진 단어들을 다른 언어로 바꾸다

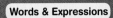

01 접미사를 붙여 명사로 만들 때 다른 접미사를 사용하는 하나를 고르시오.

① succeed ② imagine
③ act ④ educate
⑤ collect

02 밑줄 친 부분과 바꿔 쓸 수 있는 말을 쓰시오.

> I'm feeling a little tired.

① a lot of ② usually
③ much ④ a bit
⑤ just

03 다음 빈칸 (A)~(C)에 들어갈 말이 바르게 짝지어진 것은?

> • The bank refused to lend the money __(A)__ us.
> • Don't be afraid to ask __(B)__ help.
> • The desk was covered __(C)__ papers.

  (A) (B) (C)
① to – for – with
② to – to – by
③ to – for – for
④ for – for – with
⑤ for – to – by

서답형

04 다음 영영풀이가 나타내는 말을 주어진 철자로 시작하여 쓰시오.

> to teach a child at a school, college, or university

➡ e_____

05 다음 제시된 단어를 사용하여 자연스러운 문장을 만들 수 없는 것은? (형태 변화 가능)

> bring　educate　fix　occur

① The police said that the accident _____ at about 4:30 p.m.
② The concert organizers say they will _____ all profits to charity.
③ He was _____ at Bristol University.
④ Ellis is able to quickly find and _____ the problem.
⑤ My parents always encouraged us to _____ our friends home.

06 밑줄 친 부분과 바꿔 쓸 수 있는 말을 고르시오.

> We are decreasing costs and investing for more effective ones.

① increasing ② providing
③ requiring ④ reducing
⑤ preventing

서답형

07 다음 우리말에 맞도록 빈칸에 알맞은 말을 쓰시오.

(1) 물병은 많은 플라스틱 쓰레기를 만든다.
  ➡ Water bottles create too much plastic _____.

(2) 바다에는 많은 해양생물이 있다.
  ➡ There's a lot of _____ life in the oceans.

01 주어진 우리말과 괄호 안의 단어를 활용하여 빈칸에 알맞은 말을 쓰시오.

(1) 나는 당신의 저녁 초대를 거절해야만 해서 유감입니다.

➡ I'm afraid I have to turn down your _____ to dinner. (invite)

(2) 그 도마뱀들은 멸종 위기종으로 분류되었다.

➡ The lizards are classed as an _____ species. (danger)

02 다음 빈칸에 공통으로 들어갈 말을 쓰시오. (대·소문자 무시, 한 단어)

> • _____ it was too cold, kids ran out to play.
> • She didn't eat anything _____ she was too hungry.
> • _____ everyone played well, we lost the game.

03 두 문장이 같은 의미가 되도록 빈칸을 채우시오.

> There are now several different types of cars which are eco-friendly.
> = There are now _____ cars which are eco-friendly.

04 밑줄 친 우리말과 일치하도록 주어진 단어를 이용하여 영작하시오.

(1) 너는 내가 창문을 닫기를 원하니?

➡ _____
(want, close)

(2) 그녀는 자기의 개를 Mary라고 이름 짓기로 결정했다.

➡ _____
(to, name, decide)

(3) 산은 눈으로 뒤덮여 있다.

➡ _____
(cover)

(4) 많은 사람들은 더러운 물을 먹어서 죽는다.

➡ _____
(dirty, from, many)

(5) 나는 방학 동안에 봉사활동을 하려고 계획 중이야.

➡ _____
(during, do, plan)

(6) 그 남자는 담배를 끊으라고 요청받았다.

➡ _____
(smoke, ask, quit, to)

05 다음 빈칸을 〈보기〉에 있는 어휘를 이용하여 채우시오. (단어는 한 번씩만 사용할 것.)

> ┤ 보기 ├
> collect   deliver   raise   translate

(1) The book has been _____ into 27 languages.

(2) One of Tony's hobbies was _____ rare coins.

(3) I have _____ two turtles for one year.

(4) We will _____ your order between noon and 1 p.m.

Conticle
교과서
Conversation

① 의향 말하기

> **A** What's your plan for this year? 올해 너의 계획이 뭐니?
>
> **B** I'm thinking of taking swimming lessons. 나는 수영 강습을 받을까 해.

■ 'I'm thinking of ~.'는 '나는 ~할까 생각 중이다'라는 뜻으로 of 뒤에 동명사를 취해 의도나 계획을 나타낼 때 쓰는 표현이다. 전치사 of 대신 about을 사용하여 'I'm thinking about ~.'으로도 표현한다.

■ 상대방의 의향을 물을 때는 'What do you want to ~?', 'What are you going to ~?', 'What would you like to ~?' 등의 표현을 사용한다.

■ 'I'm thinking of ~.' 대신에 'I'm considering (동)명사 ~.', 'I intend to 동사원형 ~.', 'I'm planning to 동사원형 ~.'을 사용할 수 있다.

의향 말하기

- I'm thinking of (동)명사 ~.
- I'm considering (동)명사 ~.
- I'm planning to 동사원형 ~.
- I intend to 동사원형 ~.

핵심 Check

1. 다음 우리말과 일치하도록 빈칸에 알맞은 말을 쓰시오.

A: What do you want to eat? (너는 무엇을 먹고 싶니?)

B: Well, _____ thinking _____ _____ a sandwich.
(음, 나는 샌드위치를 주문할까 생각 중이야.)

2. 우리말과 일치하도록 주어진 단어를 알맞게 배열하여 문장을 만드시오.

A: What are you going to buy as a present? (선물로 뭐 살 거예요?)

B: _____ (a, I'm, buying, of, thinking, scarf)
(나는 스카프를 살 생각을 하고 있는 걸.)

3. 다음 문장과 같은 의미가 되도록 주어진 단어를 이용하여 쓰시오.

I'm thinking of buying a car.

➡ _____ (consider)

② 도움 제안하기

A **Do you want me to fix it?** 내가 그것을 고쳐 줄까?

B **Yes, please.** 응. 부탁해.

■ 'Do you want me to+동사원형 ~?'은 '당신은 내가 ~해 주기를 원하십니까?'라는 뜻으로 상대방에게 도움이 필요한지 묻는 표현이다.

도움 제안하기

- May I help you? (도와드릴까요?)
- Let me help you. (제가 도와드릴게요.)
- Do you need my help? (도움이 필요합니까?)
- Can I give you a hand? (제가 도와드릴까요?)
- Is there anything I can do? (제가 뭐 도와드릴 일이라도 있나요?)

■ 'Let me help you.'를 'Let me+동사원형 ~ (for you).'로 바꿔 쓸 수도 있다.
- A: I don't know how to use it. (나는 그것을 어떻게 사용하는지 몰라.)
  B: Let me help you. (내가 널 도와줄게.) / Let me show you how to use it. (내가 어떻게 사용하는지 보여줄게.)

핵심 Check

4. 대화가 자연스럽게 연결되도록 순서대로 배열하시오.

(A) It is important to check your bike before riding.

(B) What's wrong? Can I give you a hand?

(C) Yes, please. My bike is broken.

➡ _____

5. 우리말과 일치하도록 주어진 단어를 배열하여 영작하시오.

A: _____ (your, you, you, homework, do, to, me, with, help, want) (너는 내가 너의 숙제를 도와주기를 원하니?)

B: Yes, please.

6. 다음 우리말과 일치하도록 빈칸에 알맞은 말을 쓰시오.

A: I need to get up early tomorrow. (나는 내일 일찍 일어나야 해.)

B: Do _____? (너는 내가 너를 깨워주기를 원하니?)

A: Yes, please. (응. 부탁해.)

Listen & Speak 1 A-1

> G: ❶What are you doing this weekend?
>
> B: ❷I'm thinking of ❸doing some volunteer work at the child-care center.
>
> G: What would you do there?
>
> B: I would ❹probably read some books to the children.
>
> G: That sounds interesting. ❺Can I join you?
>
> B: Of course.

G: 이번 주말에 뭐 하니?
B: 나는 보육원에서 봉사 활동을 좀 하려고 해.
G: 거기서 뭘 할 것 같아?
B: 아마 아이들에게 책을 좀 읽어 줄 것 같아.
G: 그거 흥미로워 보인다. 나도 함께 가도 될까?
B: 물론이지.

❶ 'What are you doing this weekend?'에서 동사는 'be동사+-ing'로 현재진행형의 형태이지만 this weekend라는 미래를 나타내는 어구와 함께 쓰여 가까운 미래를 나타낸다. 'What are you doing this weekend?'는 이번 주말에 무엇을 할지 물어보는 표현으로 'What are you planning to do this weekend?', 'What are you going to do this weekend?'로 바꿔 말할 수 있다.

❷ 'I'm thinking of ~.'는 '나는 ~할까 생각 중이다'라는 뜻으로 of 뒤에 동명사를 취해 의도나 계획을 나타낼 때 쓰는 표현이다.

❸ do volunteer work: 자원봉사를 하다

❹ probably: 아마도 read A to B: A를 B에게 읽어주다(= read B A)

❺ 어떤 일을 하기 전에 'Can I ~?'를 사용하여 상대방에게 허락을 요청할 수 있다. 바꿔 쓸 수 있는 표현으로 'May I ~?', 'Is it okay if I ~?' 등이 있다.

Check(√) True or False

(1) The boy is going to read some books at home.　　　　　T ☐ F ☐

(2) The girl is interested in reading books to the children at the child-care center.　　　　　T ☐ F ☐

 Listen & Speak 2 A-1

> G: Dad, I'm ❶a bit hungry. Is there anything ❷to eat?
>
> M: Do you ❸want me to cook tteokbokki for you?
>
> G: ❹That'd be great. I love tteokbokki.
>
> M: O.K. ❺Give me ❻a few minutes.

G: 아빠, 저 배가 좀 고파요. 먹을 게 있나요?
M: 네게 떡볶이를 만들어 줄까?
G: 그거 정말 좋겠어요. 전 떡볶이를 매우 좋아해요.
M: 알겠다. 잠시만 시간을 주렴.

❶ a bit: 조금, 약간

❷ to eat은 to부정사의 형용사적 용법으로 앞의 대명사 anything을 수식하고 있다.

❸ 여기서 want는 5형식 문장으로 사용되어 목적어(me)와 목적격 보어(to cook tteokbokki)를 취하고 있다.

❹ That'd = That would

❺ give는 4형식 동사로 간접목적어(me)와 직접목적어(a few minutes)를 취하고 있다.

❻ a few: 어느 정도, 조금 a few 뒤에는 셀 수 있는 명사가 올 수 있다.

Check(√) True or False

(3) The girl likes tteokbokki.　　　　　T ☐ F ☐

(4) The man is going to make tteokbokki for the girl.　　　　　T ☐ F ☐

Communicate A

Suho: Anna, do you have any children's books ❶you don't read any longer?

Anna: Sure. Why?

Suho: ❷I'm thinking of sending some books to children in Africa. My aunt ❸told me that they need books ❹to read.

Anna: Good idea, Suho! Wait, aren't your books ❺in Korean?

Suho: Oh, that's a problem.

Anna: Well, ❻how about translating them into English?

Suho: Translating? That's a great idea, Anna.

Anna: Do you ❼want me to help you?

Suho: Sure. If we ❽run into any difficult expressions, ❾let's ask our English teacher for help.

Anna: O.K. ❿It's really great that we can help the children in Africa.

수호: Anna, 너는 더 이상 읽지 않는 아동용 도서들을 가지고 있니?

Anna: 물론이지. 왜?

수호: 나는 아프리카의 아이들에게 책을 좀 보낼 생각을 하고 있어. 우리 이모가 내게 그 아이들이 읽을 책이 필요하다고 말씀하셨어.

Anna: 좋은 생각이야, 수호야! 잠깐만, 네 책들은 한글로 되어 있지 않니?

수호: 오, 그게 문제구나.

Anna: 음. 그것들을 영어로 번역하는 건 어때?

수호: 번역? 그거 좋은 생각이다, Anna.

Anna: 너는 내가 너를 도와주기를 원하니?

수호: 물론이지. 만약 어려운 표현들이 나오면, 영어 선생님께 도움을 요청하자.

Anna: 알겠어. 우리가 아프리카의 아이들을 도울 수 있어서 정말 좋다.

❶ books와 you 사이에 목적격 관계대명사 that[which]이 생략되어 있다. 'you don't read any longer'가 앞의 'any children's books'를 수식하고 있다.

❷ I'm thinking of ~: 나는 ~할까 생각 중이다 send A to B: A를 B에게 보내다

❸ told는 동사 tell의 과거형으로 뒤에 간접목적어 me와 직접목적어 that절을 취하고 있다.

❹ to read는 명사 books를 꾸며주는 to부정사의 형용사적 용법으로 사용되고 있다.

❺ 언어를 나타낼 때 전치사 in을 사용한다.

❻ 'How about 동명사 ~?'는 '~하는 건 어때?'의 의미로 상대방에게 제안할 때 사용한다. translate ~ into 언어: …를 ~로 번역하다, ~를 (~로) 옮기다

❼ want+목적어+to부정사: ~가 …하는 것을 원하다

❽ run into: (곤경, 어려움 등을) 만나다[겪다] expression: 표현

❾ let's+동사원형: ~하자 ask for help: 도움을 청하다

❿ It은 가주어, that절이 진주어로 사용되고 있다.

Check(√) True or False

(5) They have difficult expressions in translating the books in Korean into English.　　T ☐ F ☐

(6) Suho wants to help the children in Africa by sending books.　　T ☐ F ☐

 Progress Check 1

B: ❶What are you doing this weekend?

G: ❷I'm thinking of going for a bike ride.

B: Sounds good. Can I join you?

G: Sure. Let's meet ❸in front of the park at ten.

B: O.K.

B: 이번 주말에 뭐 하니?

G: 자전거를 타러 가려고 해.

B: 좋겠구나. 나도 함께 가도 되니?

G: 물론이야. 공원 앞에서 10시에 보자.

B: 그래.

❶ 'be동사+-ing'로 현재진행형의 형태이지만 this weekend라는 미래를 나타내는 어구와 함께 쓰여 가까운 미래를 나타낸다.

❷ I'm thinking of ~: 나는 ~할까 생각 중이다

❸ in front of: ~ 앞에. 시간 앞에는 전치사 at을 사용한다.

Check(√) True or False

(7) They are going to ride a bike this weekend.　　T ☐ F ☐

(8) The boy doesn't want the girl to ride a bike.　　T ☐ F ☐

Listen & Speak 1 A-2

B: ❶What are you going to read for the ❷book review homework?
G: ❸I'm thinking of reading a book about young leaders.
B: Good idea. I have the perfect book for you.
G: Oh, could you ❹lend it to me?
B: Sure. I'll bring it tomorrow.

❶ 상대방에게 무엇을 할 계획인지(또는 어떤 계획이 있는지) 물어볼 때 'What are you going[planning] to+동사원형 ~?'을 사용할 수 있다.
❷ book review: 서평
❸ 'I'm thinking of ~.'는 '나는 ~할까 생각 중이다'의 의미로 의도나 의향을 표현할 때 사용한다.
❹ lend 사물 to 사람: …에게 ~을 빌려주다(= lend 사람 사물)

Listen & Speak 1 B-1

A: ❶What's your plan for this year?
B: I'm thinking of ❷watching a movie every weekend.

❶ plan: 계획 What's your plan for ~?: ~에 무엇을 할 계획이니? (= What are you planning to do for ~? = What are you going to do for ~?)
❷ watch a movie: 영화를 보다

Listen & Speak 1 B-2

A: What's your plan for this year?
B: I'm thinking of learning ❶how to play baduk.

❶ 'how to 동사원형'은 '~하는 방법'으로 해석하며 learn의 목적어 역할을 하고 있다.

Listen & Speak 2 A-2

B: Sujin, ❶can you help us?
G: Sure. ❷What can I do for you?
B: ❸We're going to ❹ask the school to make a parking space for bicycles.
G: That's a great idea. ❺Do you want me to help you collect signatures from students?
B: That would help us a lot. Thanks!

❶ 'Can you help us?'는 상대방에게 부탁할 때 사용하는 표현으로, 'Do you mind ~ing?', 'Could you do me a favor?', 'Can I ask you to 동사원형 ~?' 등으로 바꿔 쓸 수 있다.
❷ 'What can I do for you?'는 '무엇을 도와드릴까요?'의 의미로 상대방에게 도움을 제공하고자 할 때 사용한다.
❸ 'be going to 동사원형'은 '~할 것이다, ~할 계획이다'의 의미로 의도나 계획에 대해 말할 때 사용하는 표현이다.

❹ ask+목적어+to 동사원형: …가 ~할 것을 요청하다 parking space: 주차 공간, 주차 구역
❺ 'Do you want me to 동사원형 ~?'은 '당신은 내가 ~해 주기를 원하십니까?'라는 뜻으로 상대방에게 도움이 필요한지 묻는 표현이다. collect: 모으다, 수집하다 signature: 서명

Listen & Speak 2 B-1

A: My bike ❶broke down.
B: Do you want me to ❷fix it?
A: Yes, please.

❶ break down: 고장 나다
❷ fix: 고치다 it은 앞의 bike를 받는 대명사이다.

Listen & Speak 2 B-2

A: I didn't ❶bring an umbrella.
B: Do you want me to ❷share my umbrella with you?
A: Yes, please.

❶ bring: ~을 가져오다
❷ share A with B: A를 B와 나누다, 공유하다

Communication B

A: (춤추는 동작을 한다.)
B: ❶Are you thinking of learning taekwondo?
A: No.
C: Are you thinking of ❷learning to dance?
A: Yes. I'm thinking of learning K-pop dancing.
C: Do you want me to ❸teach you?
A: Sure. That'd be great.

❶ 'Are you thinking of learning taekwondo?'에서 'be thinking of(~을 생각 중이다)'는 현재진행형으로 상대방의 의도를 물어보고 있다.
❷ learn이 to부정사를 목적어로 취하고 있다.
❸ teach+간접목적어(you)+직접목적어(K-pop dancing)인데, 직접목적어가 생략되어 있다.

Progress Check 2

M: Can we have pancakes ❶for breakfast?
W: Sure. Oh, we don't have any eggs.
M: Do you want me to go to the store and ❷get some?
W: Thanks, Mike. Can you get blueberry syrup, too?
M: Sure.

❶ for breakfast: 아침식사로
❷ get은 앞의 go와 접속사 and로 연결되어 있다. some은 some eggs를 의미한다.

● 다음 우리말과 일치하도록 빈칸에 알맞은 말을 쓰시오.

Listen & Speak 1 A

1. **G:** What are you _____ _____ weekend?
   B: I'm _____ _____ doing some _____ work at the child-care center.
   G: _____ would you do there?
   B: I would probably _____ some books _____ the children.
   G: That _____ interesting. Can I _____ you?
   B: Of course.

2. **B:** What _____ _____ going _____ for the book review homework?
   G: I'm _____ of reading a book about _____ leaders.
   B: Good idea. I _____ the perfect book for you.
   G: Oh, could you _____ it to me?
   B: Sure. I'll _____ it tomorrow.

Listen & Speak 1 B

1. **A:** _____ your plan for this year?
   B: I'm _____ of watching a movie every weekend.

2. **A:** _____ your _____ for this year?
   B: I'm _____ _____ learning how to play baduk.

3. **A:** _____ your _____ _____ this year?
   B: I'm _____ _____ _____ swimming lessons.

Listen & Speak 2 A

1. **G:** Dad, I'm _____ bit hungry. Is _____ anything _____ eat?
   M: Do you _____ _____ _____ cook tteokbokki for you?
   G: That'd be great. I love tteokbokki.
   M: O.K. Give me a _____ minutes.

2. **B:** Sujin, can you help us?
   G: Sure. _____ _____ _____ _____ for you?
   B: We're going to _____ the school _____ a parking space for bicycles.
   G: That's a great idea. Do you _____ _____ _____ you _____ signatures from students?
   B: That would help us _____ _____. Thanks!

해석

1. **G:** 이번 주말에 뭐 하니?
   B: 나는 보육원에서 봉사 활동을 좀 하려고 해.
   G: 거기서 뭘 할 것 같아?
   B: 아마 아이들에게 책을 좀 읽어 줄 것 같아.
   G: 그거 흥미로워 보인다. 나도 함께 가도 될까?
   B: 물론이지.

2. **B:** 너는 독후감 숙제로 뭘 읽을 거니?
   G: 나는 젊은 지도자들에 관한 책을 읽을까 해.
   B: 좋은 생각이야. 나한테 너에게 딱 맞는 책이 있어.
   G: 오, 내게 빌려줄 수 있어?
   B: 그럼. 내일 그걸 가져올게.

1. **A:** 올해 너의 계획이 뭐니?
   B: 나는 주말마다 영화를 볼까 해.

2. **A:** 올해 너의 계획이 뭐니?
   B: 나는 바둑 두는 걸 배울까 해.

3. **A:** 올해 너의 계획이 뭐니?
   B: 나는 수영 강습을 받을까 해.

1. **G:** 아빠, 저 배가 좀 고파요. 먹을 게 좀 있나요?
   M: 네게 떡볶이를 만들어 줄까?
   G: 그거 정말 좋겠어요. 전 떡볶이를 매우 좋아해요.
   M: 알겠다. 잠시만 시간을 주렴.

2. **B:** 수진아, 우리를 좀 도와줄 수 있니?
   G: 물론이야. 무엇을 해 줄까?
   B: 우리는 학교에 자전거 주차 공간을 만들어 달라고 요청하려 해.
   G: 그거 멋진 생각이다. 학생들에게 사인을 받는 것을 도와줄까?
   B: 그건 우리에게 큰 도움이 될 거야. 고마워!

Listen & Speak 2 B

1. A: My bike _____ down.

   B: Do you _____ _____ _____ fix it?

   A: Yes, please.

2. A: I didn't _____ an umbrella.

   B: Do you want me to _____ my _____ _____ you?

   A: Yes, please.

3. A: _____ box is _____ heavy.

   B: Do you _____ _____ _____ _____ you _____ it?

   A: Yes, please.

4. A: My _____ is too short.

   B: Do you _____ _____ _____ _____ a picture of you?

   A: Yes, please.

해석

1. A: 내 자전거가 고장 났어.
   B: 내가 그것을 고쳐 줄까?
   A: 응, 부탁해.

2. A: 나 우산을 안 가져왔어.
   B: 내가 우산을 너와 함께 쓸까?
   A: 응, 부탁해.

3. A: 이 상자는 너무 무거워.
   B: 내가 그것을 나르는 걸 도와줄까?
   A: 응, 부탁해.

4. A: 내 팔이 너무 짧아.
   B: 내가 네 사진을 찍어줄까?
   A: 응, 부탁해.

Communicate A

Suho: Anna, do you have any children's books _____ _____ read _____ _____?

Anna: Sure. Why?

Suho: _____ _____ _____ _____ some books to children in Africa. My aunt _____ _____ _____ they need books _____ read.

Anna: Good idea, Suho! Wait, _____ your books in Korean?

Suho: Oh, that's a problem.

Anna: Well, how _____ _____ them _____ English?

Suho: _____? That's a great idea, Anna.

Anna: _____ _____ - _____ - _____ - _____ - _____?

Suho: Sure. If we _____ _____ any difficult _____, let's ask our English teacher for help.

Anna: O.K. It's really great _____ _____ can _____ the children in Africa.

수호: Anna, 너는 더 이상 읽지 않는 아동용 도서들을 가지고 있니?
Anna: 물론이지. 왜?
수호: 나는 아프리카의 아이들에게 책을 좀 보낼 생각을 하고 있어. 우리 이모가 내게 그 아이들이 읽을 책이 필요하다고 말씀하셨어.
Anna: 좋은 생각이야, 수호야! 잠깐만, 네 책들은 한글로 되어 있지 않니?
수호: 오, 그게 문제구나.
Anna: 음. 그것들을 영어로 번역하는 건 어때?
수호: 번역? 그거 좋은 생각이다, Anna.
Anna: 너는 내가 너를 도와주기를 원하니?
수호: 물론이지. 만약 어려운 표현들이 나오면, 영어 선생님께 도움을 요청하자.
Anna: 알겠어. 우리가 아프리카의 아이들을 도울 수 있어서 정말 좋다.

Communicate B

A: (춤추는 동작을 한다.)

B: Are you _____ _____ _____ taekwondo?

A: No.

C: _____ _____ _____ of learning _____ _____?

A: Yes. _____ _____ of _____ K-pop dancing.

C: Do you _____ _____ _____ teach you?

A: Sure. That'd be great.

해석
A: (춤추는 동작을 한다.)
B: 너 태권도 배우려고 하니?
A: 아니야.
C: 춤추는 걸 배우려고 하니?
A: 그래. K-pop 춤을 배우려고 해.
C: 내가 가르쳐 줄까?
A: 그래. 그거 좋겠다.

Progress Check 1

B: _____ are you _____ this weekend?

G: _____ _____ _____ going for a bike ride.

B: Sounds good. Can I join you?

G: Sure. _____ meet in front of the park at ten.

B: O.K.

B: 이번 주말에 뭐 하니?
G: 자전거를 타러 가려고 해.
B: 좋겠구나. 나도 함께 해도 되니?
G: 물론이야. 공원 앞에서 10시에 보자.
B: 그래.

Progress Check 2

M: _____ _____ have pancakes _____ breakfast?

W: Sure. Oh, we _____ have any eggs.

M: Do you _____ _____ _____ _____ to the store and _____ some?

W: Thanks, Mike. Can you get blueberry syrup, too?

M: Sure.

M: 아침으로 팬케이크를 먹을까요?
W: 좋아요. 오, 달걀이 없네요.
M: 가게에 가서 좀 사올까요?
W: 고마워요, Mike. 블루베리 시럽도 사와 줄래요?
M: 물론이죠.

[01~02] 다음 대화를 읽고 물음에 답하시오.

B: What are you going to read for the book review homework?
G: I'm thinking of reading a book about <u>young leaders</u>.
B: Good idea. I have the perfect book for you.
G: Oh, could you lend it to me?
B: Sure. I'll bring it tomorrow.

01 밑줄 친 부분과 바꿔 쓸 수 있는 것을 고르시오.

① I'll reading a book about young leaders.
② I am planning reading a book about young leaders.
③ I intend to reading a book about young leaders.
④ I'm considering reading a book about young leaders.
⑤ I'm interested in reading a book about young leaders.

02 대화의 내용과 일치하지 <u>않는</u> 것을 고르시오.

① 남자아이는 젊은 지도자들에 대한 책을 가지고 있다.
② 남자아이는 내일 젊은 지도자들에 대한 책을 가지고 올 것이다.
③ 여자아이는 서평 숙제를 할 예정이다.
④ 여자아이는 숙제를 위해 책을 다시 읽어야 한다.
⑤ 남자아이는 여자아이에게 책을 빌려줄 것이다.

03 주어진 문장 이후에 올 대화의 순서를 바르게 배열한 것을 고르시오.

Sujin, can you help us?

(A) That's a great idea. Do you want me to help you collect signatures from students?
(B) Sure. What can I do for you?
(C) We're going to ask the school to make a parking space for bicycles.
(D) That would help us a lot. Thanks!

① (B) – (A) – (C) – (D)　　② (B) – (C) – (A) – (D)
③ (C) – (A) – (B) – (D)　　④ (C) – (B) – (A) – (D)
⑤ (C) – (D) – (B) – (A)

[01~03] 다음 대화를 읽고 물음에 답하시오.

G: Dad, I'm a bit hungry. (①) Is there anything to eat?

M: (②) Do you want me ___(A)___ tteokbokki for you? (③)

G: (④ I love tteokbokki.

M: O.K. Give me a few minutes. (⑤)

01 위 대화의 ①~⑤ 중 주어진 문장이 들어갈 알맞은 곳은?

| That'd be great. |

①   ②   ③   ④   ⑤

02 빈칸 (A)에 알맞은 말을 고르시오.

① cook   ② to cook

③ cooking   ④ have cooked

⑤ to be cooked

03 대화의 내용과 일치하지 않는 것을 모두 고르시오.

① 아빠는 떡볶이를 좋아한다.

② 여자아이는 자기를 위해 아빠가 떡볶이를 만들어 주는 것을 원한다.

③ 여자아이는 배고파서 먹을 것이 있는지 물었다.

④ 아빠는 떡볶이를 만드는 데 오랜 시간이 걸린다.

⑤ 여자아이는 약간 배고프다.

[04~05] 다음 중 짝지어진 대화가 <u>어색한</u> 것은?

04 ① A: What are you planning to do this weekend?

B: I'm going to visit my grandmother.

② A: What are you going to buy as a present?

B: I'm thinking of this book.

③ A: What are you planning to bring to the field trip?

B: I can't wait for the field trip.

④ A: What club are you going to join?

B: I'm thinking of joining Surprising Magic.

⑤ A: I'm considering buying a car.

B: That's a good idea.

05 ① A: Do you want me to give you a ride to school?

B: No, thanks.

② A: Do you need my help?

B: That would be great.

③ A: Do you want me to help you?

B: No, thanks. It'll be okay.

④ A: I can't find the train station. I'm so late.

B: Let me help you.

⑤ A: Do you want me to set the table?

B: Yes, please. I'll do it.

중요

06 주어진 문장 이후에 올 대화의 순서를 바르게 배열한 것을 고르시오.

> Can we have pancakes for breakfast?

> (A) Sure.
> (B) Thanks, Mike. Can you get blueberry syrup, too?
> (C) Sure. Oh, we don't have any eggs.
> (D) Do you want me to go to the store and get some?

① (B) – (A) – (C) – (D)
② (B) – (C) – (A) – (D)
③ (C) – (A) – (B) – (D)
④ (C) – (B) – (A) – (D)
⑤ (C) – (D) – (B) – (A)

07 대화의 빈칸에 들어갈 말을 고르시오.

> A: I didn't bring an umbrella.
> B: _____
> A: Yes, please.

① Do you want me to share my umbrella with you?
② Do you want me to help you carry it?
③ I'm thinking of eating pizza this weekend.
④ I'm thinking of going for a bike ride.
⑤ Do you want me to take a picture of you?

[08~09] 다음 대화를 읽고 물음에 답하시오.

> G: What are you doing this weekend?
> B: I'm thinking of doing some volunteer work at the child-care center.
> G: What would you do there?

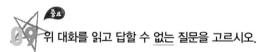

> B: I would probably read some books to the children.
> G: That sounds interesting. Can I join you?
> B: Of course.

08 위 대화의 밑줄 친 문장과 바꿔 쓸 수 없는 것을 모두 고르시오.

① I'd like to do some volunteer work at the child-care center.
② I intend to do some volunteer work at the child-care center.
③ I'm considering doing some volunteer work at the child-care center.
④ I'm planning to do some volunteer work at the child-care center.
⑤ I'm concerned about doing some volunteer work at the child-care center.

중요

09 위 대화를 읽고 답할 수 없는 질문을 고르시오.

① Where is the boy planning to go this weekend?
② How does the boy feel about reading books to the children?
③ Does the boy have a plan this weekend?
④ What will the girl do with the boy this weekend?
⑤ What is the boy going to do at the child-care center?

서답형

10 빈칸을 괄호 안에 주어진 단어를 알맞게 배열하여 채우시오.

> A: What's your plan for this year?
> B: _____ (of, how, I'm, play, to, learning, baduk, thinking)

➡ _____

[01~02] 다음 대화를 읽고 물음에 답하시오.

> B: Sujin, can you help us?
>
> G: Sure. What can I do for you?
>
> B: We're going to ask the school _____(A)_____ (make) a parking space for bicycles.
>
> G: That's a great idea. (B)학생들에게 사인을 받는 것을 도와줄까?
>
> B: That would help us a lot. Thanks!

01 빈칸 (A)를 괄호 안의 단어를 이용하여 어법에 맞게 채우시오.

➡ _____

02 밑줄 친 우리말과 일치하도록 주어진 단어를 이용하여 쓰시오.

➡ _____
_____ (collect, want, help)

[03~05] 다음 대화를 읽고 물음에 답하시오.

> Suho: Anna, (a)너는 더 이상 읽지 않는 아동용 도서들을 가지고 있니?(any, have, don't, children's, longer, do, read, any, you, you, books)
>
> Anna: Sure. Why?
>
> Suho: (b)나는 아프리카의 아이들에게 책을 좀 보낼 생각을 하고 있어. My aunt told me that they need books to read.
>
> Anna: Good idea, Suho! Wait, aren't your books in Korean?
>
> Suho: Oh, that's a problem.
>
> Anna: Well, how about translating them _____(A)_____ English?
>
> Suho: Translating? That's a great idea, Anna.
>
> Anna: Do you want me to help you?

> Suho: Sure. If we run _____(B)_____ any difficult expressions, let's ask our English teacher for help.
>
> Anna: O.K. It's really great that we can help the children in Africa.

03 빈칸 (A)와 (B)에 공통으로 들어갈 말을 쓰시오.

➡ _____

04 밑줄 친 (a)의 우리말과 일치하도록 괄호 안에 주어진 단어를 알맞게 배열하시오.

➡ _____
_____

05 밑줄 친 (b)의 우리말을 주어진 단어를 이용해 영작하시오.

➡ _____
_____ (to, think, in)

06 빈칸을 괄호 안에 주어진 단어를 알맞게 배열하여 채우시오.

> G: Dad, I'm a bit hungry. Is there anything to eat?
>
> M: _____
> (want, for, tteokbokki, me, do, you, you, cook, to)
>
> G: That'd be great. I love tteokbokki.
>
> M: O.K. Give me a few minutes.

➡ _____

Grammar

① **관계대명사 what**

> • This is **what** you can do for the environment. 이것이 환경을 위해 당신이 할 수 있는 것이다.
> • **What** I want to eat for dinner is *Bulgogi*. 내가 저녁으로 먹기 원하는 것은 불고기이다.

■ what은 선행사를 포함하는 관계대명사이다.

- She did **what** she could. 그녀는 그녀가 할 수 있는 (모든) 것을 했다.
  = She did **(all) the thing(s) that** she could.
- **What** Betty told me last week was true. Betty가 지난주에 나에게 말했던 것은 사실이었다.
  = **The thing that** Betty told me last week was true.

■ 관계대명사 what은 명사절을 이끈다.

- **What** the boss announced was surprising. 사장님이 발표한 것은 놀라웠다. (주어)
- I can't believe **what** Jane achieved in such a short time. 그렇게 단시간에 Jane이 해낸 것을 나는 믿을 수 없다. (목적어)
- We like the smell of **what** is baked in the oven now. 우리는 지금 오븐 속에서 구워지는 것의 냄새를 좋아한다. (전치사의 목적어)
- This is **what** I mentioned at the meeting. 이것이 회의에서 내가 언급한 것이다. (보어)

■ 의문대명사 what과 문장의 구조는 동일하며, 구분은 해석으로 한다. 관계대명사 what은 '~하는 것'으로, 의문대명사 what은 '무엇(을/이) ~하는지'로 해석한다.

- I wondered **what** my little daughter hid in her hand. 나는 내 어린 딸이 손에 무엇을 감췄는지 궁금했다. (의문대명사)
- **What** she hid there is a ring. 그녀가 그곳에 숨겨둔 것은 반지이다. (관계대명사)

■ 관계대명사 what의 관용적인 표현들

- You should not judge a man by **what he has**. 사람을 그의 재산으로 판단하면 안 된다.
- Abe is **what is called** a poisonous snake. Abe는 말하자면 독사이다.
- **What's better[worse]** is that she became rich. 더욱 좋은[나쁜] 것은 그녀가 부자가 되었다는 것이다.

핵심 Check

1. 다음 우리말에 맞게 괄호 안의 단어를 바르게 배열하시오.

   (1) 그 가게에서 만드는 것은 과자이다. (the shop, what, cookies, are, made, in, are)

   ➡ _____

   (2) Sandra는 그녀가 아는 것을 나에게 말해 주었다. (what, me, told, knew, she, Sandra)

   ➡ _____

② '양보' 의미의 접속사 although

- **Although** Pam got up late this morning, she didn't miss the train.
  오늘 아침에 비록 Pam이 늦게 일어났지만, 그녀는 기차를 놓치지 않았다.

- **Although** it rained a lot yesterday, the playground is good to play soccer
  now. 비록 어제 비가 많이 왔지만, 지금 운동장은 축구 경기를 하기에 좋다.

■ although는 '비록 ~이지만, ~임에도 불구하고'의 뜻을 가진 접속사로서, 주절의 의미와 상반되는 내용의 종속절을 이끌며, 이를 '양보'의 부사절이라고 부른다.

- **Although** Mansu made much money, he was not satisfied. 비록 만수는 많은 돈을 벌었지만, 만족하지 않았다.

- **Although** Baeksu couldn't make much money, he was satisfied. 비록 백수는 많은 돈을 벌 수 없었지만, 그는 만족했다.

■ although 외에 though, even though 등이 있고, 등위 접속사 but도 같은 의미이다.

- **Although** Alice studied hard, she didn't get good grades. 비록 Alice는 열심히 공부했지만, 좋은 성적을 받지 못했다.

  → **(Even) Though** Alice studied hard, she didn't get good grades.

  → Alice studied hard, **but** she didn't get good grades.

■ despite, in spite of 등은 '~에도 불구하고'라는 '양보' 의미의 전치사(구)로, 접속사 although는 '주어+동사'가 있는 절을, 전치사(구)는 명사나 명사 어구 등이 뒤에 오며, 부사구를 이끈다.

- **Although** the crowd was noisy, Chad concentrated on the game. 비록 관중들이 시끄러웠지만, Chad는 경기에 집중했다.

  → **Despite** the noisy crowd, Chad concentrated on the game. 시끄러운 관중에도 불구하고, Chad는 경기에 집중했다.

  → **In spite of** the noisy crowd, Chad concentrated on the game.

■ 부사절을 이끄는 접속사에는 다음과 같은 것들도 있다.

- **Because** his mom caught a cold, Jason made her dinner. Jason의 엄마가 감기에 걸리셔서 그는 엄마께 저녁을 만들어 드렸다. (이유)

- **If** you know the answer, Dad, please let me know. 아버지, 답을 아신다면 알려주세요. (조건)

- **While** the guests are eating, you shouldn't speak. 손님들이 식사하는 동안, 너는 말을 해서는 안 된다. (시간)

- **While** the walls are dark navy, the ceiling is sky blue. 벽이 짙은 네이비색인데 반해, 천장은 하늘빛 파란색이다. (반대)

핵심 Check

2. 다음 괄호 안에서 알맞은 단어를 고르시오.

(1) (Despite / Although) her hard work, Susan failed the test.

(2) She didn't make it to the party (because / although) she had much time.

01 다음 문장에서 어법상 <u>어색한</u> 단어를 한 개씩만 찾아 고치시오.

(1) The guards judged the lady by which she held in her hand.

_____ ➡ _____

(2) The children still liked their teacher despite she had hit them.

_____ ➡ _____

(3) Even though Sarah was proud of her son, she did praise him.

_____ ➡ _____

(4) All what Bart Simpson told me at the party was a lie.

_____ ➡ _____

02 다음 중 어법상 바르지 <u>않은</u> 것은?

① Samuel doesn't gain weight even though he eats a lot.
② Despite the sound of the firework, the baby didn't wake up.
③ Although Mary broke the promise, Tom got upset.
④ In spite of his unfriendly reaction, the old lady smiled at him.
⑤ Though many people praise her, she doesn't feel happy.

03 다음 빈칸에 들어갈 말로 알맞은 것은?

_____ his mother's death, Robert kept smiling.

① Because   ② Though   ③ Within
④ Despite   ⑤ While

04 다음 문장의 밑줄 친 부분을 한 단어로 바꾸시오.

Barbara donated <u>the things that</u> she bought at the mall to an orphanage.

➡ _____

01 다음 빈칸에 알맞은 것은?

> Is that _____ she wants to buy?

① which　　② those
③ where　　④ what
⑤ for what

02 다음 빈칸에 알맞은 말이 순서대로 바르게 짝지어진 것은?

> • _____ Jane drinks coffee, she doesn't like the flavor of roasted coffee beans.
> • _____ I want from my daddy is money.

① Despite – What
② Even though – That
③ Though – What
④ Although – When
⑤ Because – That

03 다음 중 어법상 어색한 문장을 모두 골라 기호를 쓰시오.

> ⓐ The girls are supposed to do which their parents ask them to do.
> ⓑ Taking some light exercise is a good habit what makes you energetic.
> ⓒ The thing cannot be cured must be endured.
> ⓓ That will make them think about what they should or shouldn't do.
> ⓔ I can't believe that I've just seen.
> ⓕ Making a schedule for your vacation, you should consider what you can do.
> ⓖ That you teach can be different from those you know.

➡ _____

04 다음 중 나머지 네 개의 문장들과 뜻이 같지 <u>않은</u> 문장을 찾으시오.

① Although Jessy has reading difficulties, she knows many languages.
② In spite of her reading troubles, Jessy knows many languages.
③ Even though Jessy has trouble reading, she knows a lot of languages.
④ Jessy has reading difficulties, so she knows many languages.
⑤ Though she can't read well, Jessy knows lots of languages.

05 다음 문장에서 어법상 <u>틀린</u> 부분을 찾아 바르게 고쳐 쓰시오.

> Brown's father failed in business, and that was worse, he broke up with his girl friend.

_____ ➡ _____

06 다음 두 문장의 의미가 같도록 빈칸에 알맞은 말을 쓰시오.

> I missed the school bus, but I arrived on time.
> → _____ _____ I missed the school bus, I arrived on time.

07 다음 빈칸에 알맞은 것은?

> I read the boring magazine _____ my teacher warned me not to.

① because of　　② with
③ for　　④ though
⑤ since

08 다음 밑줄 친 what 중에서 나머지 넷과 같은 용법으로 쓰이지 않은 것은?

① __What__ she said inspired the audience.
② Becky received __what__ her son had sent her.
③ I like __what__ is shown by the magician.
④ She asked me __what__ I was going to do.
⑤ Those are __what__ they suggested.

09 다음 중 밑줄 친 부분의 쓰임이 어색한 것은?

① My mom didn't believe my brother __although__ he was telling the truth.
② __Although__ Jeff caught a cold, he came to school.
③ He was tired __although__ he stayed up all night the day before.
④ __Although__ Henry is quite old enough, he acts like a baby.
⑤ __Although__ it wasn't cold outside, Merrian wore a fur coat.

10 다음 빈칸에 접속사 Although가 들어가기에 어색한 것은?

① _____ Mike has a good job, he always complains about his work.
② _____ Norah caught a bad cold, she had to take the exam.
③ _____ Baker family had very little money, they were happy.
④ _____ Sam was tired, he tried to exercise regularly.
⑤ _____ Susan has much money, she buys expensive goods.

11 다음 빈칸에 들어갈 말로 적절하지 않은 것은?

A: Was your homework completed?
B: No, it wasn't. Although my homework wasn't finished, _____.

① my friends kept asking me to go out
② there was plenty of work to do
③ I should do my homework right now
④ my parents made me run an errand
⑤ Betty's asking me to show her mine

12 다음 중 어법상 어색한 문장을 모두 고르면?

① The fans liked what BTS showed them.
② This is not the thing which the president was speaking about.
③ All my friends loved the movie that the director had filmed.
④ This is not the book what Karen wanted to read.
⑤ Which the coach told them at the winning ceremony made them cry.

13 다음 우리말을 바르게 영작한 것은?

비록 Taylor는 울고 싶었지만, 그녀는 미소를 짓고 있었다.

① In spite that Taylor felt inclined to cry, she was smiling.
② Even though Taylor felt like crying, but she was smiling.
③ Although Taylor felt like crying, she was smiling.
④ As Taylor felt inclined to cry, she was smiling.
⑤ Taylor felt like crying despite of the situation where she was smiling.

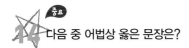

14 다음 중 어법상 옳은 문장은?

① Is this cat what she is looking for?

② Tom bought a new car his daughter to drive.

③ Every student knows what the teacher is giving them a special lesson.

④ The baby boys liked the toy what their aunt bought yesterday.

⑤ What the girl said him was touching.

15 다음 중 어법상 옳은 문장은?

① Even if the fact that I woke up earlier than usual, I was late for work.

② I couldn't get up despite Mom shook me so many times this morning.

③ Despite of the giant storm, my wife's airplane landed safely yesterday.

④ My daughter had nothing but water even though her hunger.

⑤ She felt sick in spite of the fact that she took the prescribed pill.

서답형

16 다음 우리말을, 주어진 단어들을 배열하여 영작할 때, what 은 몇 번째로 오는가?

사장님이 하고 있는 말씀에 집중하라. (to, is, pay, the, saying, attention, boss, what)

➡ _____

17 밑줄 친 what의 용법이 나머지 넷과 다른 하나는?

① The beggar got <u>what</u> they threw her.

② That volunteer work at the orphanage was <u>what</u> she wanted to do.

③ Sandra accepted <u>what</u> he offered.

④ I wondered <u>what</u> she would give me.

⑤ That's <u>what</u> I meant to say.

18 다음 중 어법상 <u>어색한</u> 문장은?

① What Miso liked to have is pizza.

② Frank made what his father designed.

③ Sean loved what he was doing.

④ Tony played the game what he was good at.

⑤ He showed her what Dr. Bae had invented.

19 다음 중 어법상 옳은 문장은?

① In spite she has much money, Amy still isn't happy.

② Although his laziness, Marco passed the test with honors.

③ Though Olivia studied hard, she get an F in her monthly report card.

④ Even though worked hard, Andrew couldn't find the solution to his problem.

⑤ They couldn't hear the radio even though they turned it up.

서답형

20 다음 우리말을 영작할 때, 빈칸에 들어갈 알맞은 말을 쓰시오.

이제 Smith는 과거의 그가 아니다.
= Now, Smith is not _____ he _____.

21 다음 중 어법상 옳은 문장은?

① Bill forgot the thing what she had done.

② I know the reason which it's so hot.

③ She realized the way which her husband hid the pocket money.

④ Grandpa took me what my parents had met for the first time.

⑤ The artist did what she could do best.

01 다음 그림을 보고, 빈칸에 들어갈 알맞은 말을 〈보기〉에서 골라 쓰시오.

┌─── 보기 ───
fall / playing / their / it / love / read / is / other / soccer / asleep / colors / books / each
└─────────

(1)

Although he tried not to _____ _____, there still were many _____ to _____.

(2)

Although _____ _____ raining, the boys are _____ _____ on the playground.

(3)

Although _____ _____ are different, they _____ _____ _____.

02 다음 문장에서 어법상 어색한 부분을 찾아 바르게 고쳐 다시 쓰시오.

(1) I don't believe that Eva said to me.

➡ _____

(2) Show me that you put in your pocket.

➡ _____

(3) Though her fear of his attitude, she looked him right in the eye.

➡ _____

_____

(4) What Josh asked me to help her was not natural.

➡ _____

03 주어진 두 문장을 관계대명사 what을 이용하여, 하나의 문장으로 만드시오.

(1) • Sam bought the things.
　　• They were mystery books.

➡ _____

(2) • Harold couldn't believe the thing.
　　• The reporters referred to it.

➡ _____

_____

(3) • The thing was discussed.
　　• It was surprising.

➡ _____

_____

04 다음 우리말과 일치하도록 괄호 안에 주어진 단어들을 바르게 배열하시오. (필요시 동사의 형태를 변형할 것.)

비록 Jackie는 배가 고프지 않았지만, 그녀는 그 요리사가 그녀에게 만들어준 것을 먹었다.
(Jackie, what, for, not, hungry, be, she, Although, the, eat, cook, have, her, make)

➡ _____

_____

05 다음 〈보기〉에 주어진 표현들을 사용하여, 각 문장의 후반부에 접속사 although를 넣어 한 문장으로 완성하시오.

> • Charlie played soccer all day long.
> • He stayed up all night.
> → Charlie stayed up all night although he played soccer all day long.

┤ 보기 ├
> • Michael doesn't read the books at all.
> • Kelly was late for the wedding.
> • Mongol is a small country.
> • Walter was a careful driver.

(1) It maintains an old tradition.

➡ _____

_____

(2) She was so easygoing.

➡ _____

_____

(3) He caused a serious car accident.

➡ _____

_____

(4) He regularly buys many books.

➡ _____

_____

06 우리말과 일치하도록 괄호 안에 주어진 어휘를 활용, 글자 수에 맞게 영작하시오.

(1) Mary가 동굴 안에서 발견한 것이 마을 사람들을 놀라게 했다. (find, cave, surprise, villagers, 9 단어)

➡ _____

_____

(2) 미술관의 정책에도 불구하고, 아이들은 조용하지 않았다. (quiet, were, despite, the kids, the museum, the policy, 11 단어)

➡ _____

_____

(3) Candy가 시장에서 산 것들은 모두 비싸지 않은 것이었다. (buy, inexpensive, at, all, 9 단어)

➡ _____

_____

07 다음 문장에서 어법상 어색한 한 단어만을 찾아 바르게 고쳐 다시 쓰시오.

(1) Sue finally accepted that Tom gave.

➡ _____

(2) Though his wealth, he was lonely.

➡ _____

(3) That is far different from which Sunny has been waiting for.

➡ _____

_____

(4) What I met her yesterday is true.

➡ _____

(5) Which people believed in the past is called superstition.

➡ _____

_____

08 다음 우리말과 일치하도록 괄호 안에 주어진 단어들을 빈칸에 바르게 배열하시오.

> 비록 Audrey Hepburn은 25년 전에 세상을 떠났지만, 그녀의 아름다운 정신은 우리와 함께 영원히 남아 있을 것이다.
> (beautiful, ago, Audrey Hepburn, us, remain, away, 25 years, will, although, passed, spirit, with, her)
> → _____ forever.

➡ _____

_____

Teens in Action

Many young people are <u>making the world a better place</u>. For example,
make+목적어+목적격 보어: '~을 …로 만들다'
Carter and Olivia Ries <u>have become</u> leaders in saving animals.
현재완료(have+p.p.): 과거의 일이 현재까지 영향을 미쳐 현재와 관련이 있을 때 사용
Although they are only teenagers, they have actually made a difference
in the world. How <u>were they able to</u> do that? Let's hear from Carter.
be able to: can과 의미가 비슷한 표현, be동사는 주어와 시제에 따라서 형태가 바뀐다.
When I was five, my little sister Olivia and I each adopted a
접속사: '~할 때'라는 의미로 뒤에 주어와 동사가 온다.
cheetah. Did we raise cheetahs at home? No, we donated to a charity
that protects wild cheetahs in South Africa. Our parents told us that
= which. 주격 관계대명사로서 앞에 나오는 선행사인 a charity를 수식
if we did not protect them, we might not be able to see cheetahs in the
'~한다면', 조건절을 이끌고 있고 글의 전체 시제에 맞춰 과거형 동사가 쓰였다.
near future.

We soon became interested in <u>helping</u> other endangered animals.
동명사(전치사의 목적어)
<u>A few</u> years later, with help from our parents, we created a non-profit
'어느 정도, 조금'. a few+셀 수 있는 명사, a little+셀 수 없는 명사
organization to protect them. We <u>wanted the next generation to be</u>
want+목적어+to부정사: '~가 …하는 것을 원하다'
able to see these animals, so we <u>named our organization One More</u>
name+목적어+목적격 보어: '~를 …라고 이름 짓다'
<u>Generation</u>. We also studied endangered animals and educated our
friends about them.

어휘
for example 예를 들어
leader 리더, 지도자, 대표
although ～임에도 불구하고, 비록 ～이지만
teenager 십 대, 청소년
actually 실제로
be able to ～할 수 있다
adopt 입양하다
cheetah 치타
raise 기르다
donate 기부하다, 기증하다
charity 자선단체, 자선
endangered 멸종 위기의
non-profit organization 비영리 단체
generation 세대
educate 가르치다, 교육하다

 확인문제

● 다음 문장이 본문의 내용과 일치하면 T, 일치하지 않으면 F를 쓰시오.

1 Carter and Olivia Ries are only teenagers, but they have actually made a difference in the world. ☐

2 Carter and Olivia have actually made no difference in the world. ☐

3 Carter and Olivia each adopted a cheetah. ☐

4 Carter and Olivia raised cheetahs at home. ☐

5 Carter and Olivia became interested in helping endangered animals. ☐

6 Carter and Olivia created a profit-making organization to protect endangered animals. ☐

Then one day, a terrible oil spill occurred in the Gulf of Mexico. A
occur+r+-ed
lot of sea animals were completely covered with oil, and they were
수동태(주어+be동사 + p.p.): '~으로 뒤덮여 있다, ~으로 뒤집어쓰다'
dying. We had to do something. We started collecting animal rescue
= to collect
supplies such as pet carrying cages and rubber gloves from everyone
= like
in our neighborhood. Four months later, our family drove to the Gulf
후에
of Mexico to deliver what we collected and helped to save the animals.
to 부정사의 부사적 용법(목적) what: 관계대명사('~하는 것')   help의 목적어
While we were working there, we learned something very useful.
접속사: '~하는 동안'   -thing으로 끝나는 부정대명사는 형용사가 뒤에서 수식
When we put mayonnaise into a turtle's throat, the turtle threw up. That

way, we were able to get oil out of turtles. I never knew mayonnaise
~으로부터
could be used to save animals!

On our last day, we met a marine life specialist. She told us that
전치사 on은 날짜나 요일, 또는 특정한 날에 사용
plastic waste is more dangerous to sea animals than oil spills are. A lot
종속절의 내용이 일반적인 사실이므로 현재시제를 사용   '~보다 더 위험한'
of sea animals and sea birds die from eating plastic waste. After we
'~으로 죽다', 뒤에는 명사나 동명사를 쓴다.
came home, we created an educational project about how to reduce
how to ~: '어떻게 ~할지, ~하는 방법', 'how+주어+should ~' 구문으로 바꿔 쓸 수 있다.
plastic waste. In addition to this, our organization continues to do

various projects to save animals. Although we started small, we are
접속사: '비록 ~이지만'   start small: 작은 것부터 시작하다
making a big difference. What you do today can change the world, so
관계대명사 what을 포함한 명사절 주어
take that first step!

spill 유출

occur 일어나다, 발생하다

gulf 만

rescue 구조, 구출

supply 공급 (pl. supplies 물품, 보급품)

rubber 고무

neighborhood 이웃, 근처

deliver 전달하다, 배달하다

mayonnaise 마요네즈

throat 목구멍, 목

throw up 토하다

marine 해양의

specialist 전문가

waste 쓰레기

reduce 줄이다

in addition to ~ 이외에, ~에 더하여

various 다양한, 여러 가지의

 확인문제

● 다음 문장이 본문의 내용과 일치하면 T, 일치하지 않으면 F를 쓰시오.

1 When a terrible oil spill occurred in the Gulf of Mexico, many sea animals were
completely covered with oil. ☐

2 Carter's family drove to the Gulf of Mexico to deliver what they bought. ☐

3 Carter's family helped to save the animals covered with oil. ☐

4 Carter's family were able to get oil out of turtles with their hands. ☐

5 Plastic waste is more dangerous to sea animals than oil spills are. ☐

6 Carter's organization started big, so they are making a big difference. ☐

● 우리말을 참고하여 빈칸에 알맞은 말을 쓰시오.

1 Teens _____ _____

2 Many young people are making the world _____ _____ _____.

3 For example, Carter and Olivia Ries have become leaders _____ _____ _____.

4 _____ they are only teenagers, they _____ _____ _____ _____ in the world.

5 _____ were they _____ _____ do that?

6 Let's _____ _____ Carter.

7 When I was five, my little sister Olivia and I _____ _____ a cheetah.

8 Did we _____ cheetahs _____ _____?

9 No, we _____ _____ _____ _____ _____ that protects wild cheetahs in South Africa.

10 Our parents told us that if we did not protect them, we _____ _____ _____ _____ _____ _____ _____ in the near future.

11 We soon _____ _____ _____ helping other _____.

12 A few years later, with help from our parents, we _____ _____ _____ _____ to protect them.

13 We wanted _____ _____ _____ to be able to see these animals, so we named our organization One More Generation.

14 We also studied endangered animals and _____ _____ _____ about them.

15 Then one day, _____ _____ _____ _____ occurred in the Gulf of Mexico.

---

1 활약하는 십 대들

2 많은 젊은 사람들이 세상을 더 좋은 곳으로 만들고 있다.

3 예를 들어, Carter Ries와 Olivia Ries는 동물을 구하는 일에 리더가 되어 왔다.

4 비록 그들은 십 대일 뿐이지만, 실제로 세상에 변화를 일으켜 왔다.

5 그들은 어떻게 그것을 할 수 있었을까?

6 Carter의 이야기를 들어보자.

7 내가 다섯 살이었을 때, 나의 여동생 Olivia와 나는 각자 치타를 입양했다.

8 우리가 치타를 집에서 길렀을까?

9 아니, 우리는 남아프리카 공화국에 있는 야생 치타를 보호하는 자선단체에 기부했다.

10 부모님께서는 우리에게 우리가 그들을 보호하지 않으면, 가까운 미래에 치타를 볼 수 없을지도 모른다고 말씀하셨다.

11 우리는 곧 다른 멸종 위기의 동물들을 도와주는 것에 관심을 갖게 되었다.

12 몇 년 후에, 부모님의 도움으로, 우리는 그들을 보호하기 위해 비영리 단체를 만들었다.

13 우리는 다음 세대가 이러한 동물들을 볼 수 있기를 원했기에, 우리 단체를 One More Generation이라고 이름 붙였다.

14 우리는 또한 멸종 위기의 동물들을 연구했고 친구들에게 그들에 대해 가르쳐 주었다.

15 그러던 어느 날, 끔찍한 석유 유출 사건이 멕시코만에서 발생했다.

16 A lot of sea animals _____ _____ _____ _____
_____, and they were dying.

17 We _____ _____ _____ something.

18 We started collecting _____ _____ _____ such as
pet carrying cages and rubber gloves from everyone _____
_____ _____.

19 Four months later, our family drove to the Gulf of Mexico
to deliver _____ _____ _____ and helped _____
_____ _____ _____.

20 While we were working there, we learned _____ _____
_____.

21 When we put mayonnaise into a turtle's throat, the turtle _____
_____.

22 That way, we were able to _____ oil _____ _____ turtles.

23 I never knew mayonnaise _____ _____ _____ to save
animals!

24 On our last day, we met a _____ _____ _____.

25 She told us that plastic waste is _____ _____ to sea animals
_____ oil spills arc.

26 A lot of sea animals and sea birds _____ _____ _____
plastic waste.

27 After we came home, we _____ _____ _____
about how to reduce plastic waste.

28 _____ _____ _____ this, our organization continues to do
various projects to save animals.

29 Although we started small, we are _____ _____
_____.

30 _____ you do today can change the world, so _____
_____ _____ _____!

16 많은 해양 동물들이 완전히 기름을 뒤집어썼고, 죽어가고 있었다.

17 우리는 무엇인가를 해야만 했다.

18 우리는 애완동물 수송용 우리와 고무장갑과 같은 동물 구조 물품들을 동네의 모든 사람으로부터 모으기 시작했다.

19 4개월 후에, 우리 가족은 우리가 모았던 것들을 전달하기 위해서 멕시코만으로 운전해 갔으며 동물들을 구하는 일을 도왔다.

20 거기서 일하는 동안에, 우리는 매우 유용한 것을 배웠다.

21 마요네즈를 거북이의 목구멍에 집어넣으면, 거북이가 토했다.

22 그런 식으로, 우리는 거북이들에게서 기름을 빼낼 수 있었다.

23 나는 마요네즈가 동물을 구하는 데 사용될 수 있다는 것을 전혀 알지 못했다!

24 마지막 날에, 우리는 해양 생물 전문가를 만났다.

25 그녀는 우리에게 석유 유출보다 플라스틱 쓰레기가 해양 동물에게 더 위험하다고 말했다.

26 많은 해양 동물과 바다 새들이 플라스틱 쓰레기를 먹어서 죽는다.

27 집으로 돌아온 후, 우리는 플라스틱 쓰레기를 줄일 수 있는 방법에 관한 교육 프로젝트를 만들었다.

28 이것 외에도, 우리 단체는 동물들을 구하기 위한 다양한 프로젝트들을 계속하고 있다.

29 비록 우리는 작은 것부터 시작했지만, 큰 변화를 만들어 내고 있는 중이다.

30 당신이 오늘 하는 일이 세상을 바꿀 수 있기에, 첫발을 내디뎌라!

● 우리말을 참고하여 본문을 영작하시오.

1 활약하는 십 대들
➡ _____

2 많은 젊은 사람들이 세상을 더 좋은 곳으로 만들고 있다.
➡ _____

3 예를 들어, Carter Ries와 Olivia Ries는 동물을 구하는 일에 리더가 되어 왔다.
➡ _____

4 비록 그들은 십 대일 뿐이지만, 실제로 세상에 변화를 일으켜 왔다.
➡ _____

5 그들은 어떻게 그것을 할 수 있었을까?
➡ _____

6 Carter의 이야기를 들어보자.
➡ _____

7 내가 다섯 살이었을 때, 나의 여동생 Olivia와 나는 각자 치타를 입양했다.
➡ _____

8 우리가 치타를 집에서 길렀을까?
➡ _____

9 우리는 남아프리카 공화국에 있는 야생 치타를 보호하는 자선단체에 기부했다.
➡ _____

10 부모님께서는 우리에게 우리가 그들을 보호하지 않으면, 가까운 미래에 치타를 볼 수 없을지도 모른다고 말씀하셨다.
➡ _____
_____

11 우리는 곧 다른 멸종 위기의 동물들을 도와주는 것에 관심을 갖게 되었다.
➡ _____

12 몇 년 후에, 부모님의 도움으로, 우리는 그들을 보호하기 위해 비영리 단체를 만들었다.
➡ _____

13 우리는 다음 세대가 이러한 동물들을 볼 수 있기를 원했기에, 우리 단체를 One More Generation 이라고 이름 붙였다.
➡ _____
_____

14 우리는 또한 멸종 위기의 동물들을 연구했고 친구들에게 그들에 대해 가르쳐 주었다.
➡ _____

15 그러던 어느 날, 끔찍한 석유 유출 사건이 멕시코만에서 발생했다.
➡ _____

16 많은 해양 동물들이 완전히 기름을 뒤집어썼고, 죽어가고 있었다.

➡ _____

17 우리는 무엇인가를 해야만 했다.

➡ _____

18 우리는 애완동물 수송용 우리와 고무장갑과 같은 동물 구조 물품들을 동네의 모든 사람으로부터 모으기 시작했다.

➡ _____

_____

19 4개월 후에, 우리 가족은 우리가 모았던 것들을 전달하기 위해서 멕시코만으로 운전해 갔으며 동물들을 구하는 일을 도왔다.

➡ _____

_____

20 거기서 일하는 동안에, 우리는 매우 유용한 것을 배웠다.

➡ _____

21 마요네즈를 거북이의 목구멍에 집어넣으면, 거북이가 토했다.

➡ _____

22 그런 식으로, 우리는 거북이들에게서 기름을 빼낼 수 있었다.

➡ _____

23 나는 마요네즈가 동물을 구하는 데 사용될 수 있다는 것을 전혀 알지 못했다!

➡ _____

24 마지막 날에, 우리는 해양 생물 전문가를 만났다.

➡ _____

25 그녀는 우리에게 석유 유출보다 플라스틱 쓰레기가 해양 동물에게 더 위험하다고 말했다.

➡ _____

26 많은 해양 동물과 바다 새들이 플라스틱 쓰레기를 먹어서 죽는다.

➡ _____

27 집으로 돌아온 후, 우리는 플라스틱 쓰레기를 줄일 수 있는 방법에 관한 교육 프로젝트를 만들었다.

➡ _____

28 이것 외에도, 우리 단체는 동물들을 구하기 위한 다양한 프로젝트들을 계속하고 있다.

➡ _____

29 비록 우리는 작은 것부터 시작했지만, 큰 변화를 만들어 내고 있는 중이다.

➡ _____

30 당신이 오늘 하는 일이 세상을 바꿀 수 있기에, 첫발을 내디뎌라!

➡ _____

[01~03] 다음 글을 읽고 물음에 답하시오.

Many young people are making the world a better place. ⓐ , Carter and Olivia Ries have become leaders in saving animals. Although they are only teenagers, they have ⓑactually made a difference in the world. ⓒHow were they able to do that? Let's hear from Carter.

중요

01 위 글의 빈칸 ⓐ에 들어갈 알맞은 말을 고르시오.

① As a result
② Moreover
③ However
④ For example
⑤ In addition

02 위 글의 밑줄 친 ⓑactually와 뜻이 같은 말을 모두 고르시오.

① in fact
② especially
③ in reality
④ extremely
⑤ probably

서답형

03 위 글의 밑줄 친 ⓒ를 다음과 같이 바꿔 쓸 때 빈칸에 들어갈 알맞은 단어를 쓰시오.

➡ How was it _____ for them to do that?

[04~06] 다음 글을 읽고 물음에 답하시오.

When I was five, my little sister Olivia and I each adopted a cheetah. Did we raise cheetahs at home? No, we donated ⓐ a charity that protects wild cheetahs in South Africa. Our parents told us that if we did not protect ①them, we might not be able to see cheetahs in the near future.

We soon became interested ⓑ helping ②other endangered animals. A few years later, with help from our parents, we created a non-profit organization to protect ③them. We wanted the next generation to be able to see ④these animals, so we named our organization One More Generation. We also studied endangered animals and educated our friends about ⑤them. <I: Carter>

04 위 글의 빈칸 ⓐ와 ⓑ에 들어갈 전치사가 바르게 짝지어진 것은?

	ⓐ	ⓑ		ⓐ	ⓑ
①	on	at	②	to	by
③	to	in	④	for	by
⑤	on	in			

중요

05 밑줄 친 ①~⑤ 중에서 가리키는 대상이 나머지 넷과 다른 것은?

① ② ③ ④ ⑤

중요

06 According to the passage, which is NOT true about Carter and Olivia?

① They raised cheetahs at home.
② They became interested in helping other endangered animals.
③ They created a non-profit organization with help from their parents.
④ They named their organization One More Generation.
⑤ They educated their friends about endangered animals.

[07~09] 다음 글을 읽고 물음에 답하시오.

Then one day, a terrible oil spill occurred in the Gulf of Mexico. A lot of sea animals were completely covered with oil, and they were dying. We had to do something. We started collecting animal rescue supplies such as pet carrying cages and rubber gloves from everyone in our neighborhood. Four months later, our family drove to the Gulf of Mexico to deliver what we collected and helped ⓐ to save the animals. While we were working there, we learned something very useful. When we put mayonnaise into a turtle's throat, the turtle threw up. That way, we were able to get oil out of turtles. I never knew mayonnaise could be used ⓑto save animals!   <I: Carter>

07 다음 보기에서 위 글의 밑줄 친 ⓐto save, ⓑto save와 to 부정사의 용법이 같은 것을 각각 모두 고르시오.

① It is worthwhile to save such animals.

② He was happy to save such animals.

③ It is too late to save such animals.

④ My dream is to save such animals.

⑤ She must be considerate to save such animals.

➡ ⓐ와 같은 것: _____

ⓑ와 같은 것: _____

08 위 글의 주제로 알맞은 것을 고르시오.

① an oil spill and serious water pollution

② the cause of a terrible oil spill in the Gulf of Mexico

③ the activities to save animals dying from an oil spill

④ collecting animal rescue supplies

⑤ the way to use mayonnaise to save animals

09 위 글에서 알 수 있는 Carter의 심경 변화로 가장 알맞은 것을 고르시오.

① delighted   → puzzled

② sympathetic   → surprised

③ depressed   → nervous

④ regretful   → confused

⑤ relieved   → astonished

[10~12] 다음 글을 읽고 물음에 답하시오.

On our last day, we met a marine life specialist. She told us that plastic waste is more dangerous to sea animals than oil spills are. (A)많은 해양 동물과 바다 새들이 플라스틱 쓰레기를 먹어서 죽는다. After we came home, we created an educational project about how to reduce plastic waste. ___ⓐ___ this, our organization continues to do various projects to save animals. (B)Since we started small, we are making a big difference. What you do today can change the world, so take that first step!

10 위 글의 빈칸 ⓐ에 들어갈 알맞은 말을 모두 고르시오.

① Besides   ② In contrast to

③ Instead of   ④ In addition to

⑤ As a result of

서답형

11 위 글의 밑줄 친 (A)의 우리말에 맞게 주어진 어휘를 이용하여 13 단어로 영작하시오.

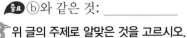
a lot of, from

➡ _____

_____

서답형
12 위 글의 밑줄 친 (B)에서 흐름상 어색한 부분을 찾아 고치시오.

_____ ➡ _____

[13~15] 다음 글을 읽고 물음에 답하시오.

Many young people are making the world a better place. For example, Carter and Olivia Ries have become leaders in ⓐsaving animals. Although they are only teenagers, they have actually made a difference in the world. How were they able to ⓑdo that? Let's hear from Carter.

13 아래 〈보기〉에서 위 글의 밑줄 친 ⓐsaving과 문법적 쓰임이 다른 것의 개수를 고르시오.

┌─── 보기 ├───
① Look at the running boys.
② People have fears about barking dogs.
③ He is good at playing tennis.
④ Reading letters from pen pals is pleasant.
⑤ She tried to calm a crying child down.
└──────────────

① 1개   ② 2개   ③ 3개   ④ 4개   ⑤ 5개

서답형
14 밑줄 친 ⓑ를 다음과 같이 바꿔 쓸 때 빈칸에 들어갈 알맞은 말을 한 단어 쓰시오.

➡ make a _____ in the world

15 위 글의 다음에 올 내용으로 가장 알맞은 것을 고르시오.

① the introduction about many leaders in the world
② the story about many interesting animals
③ the process of creating a non-profit organization
④ many challenges to make a difference in the world
⑤ the story of Carter who has made a difference in the world

[16~17] 다음 글을 읽고 물음에 답하시오.

On our last day, we met a marine life specialist. She told us that plastic ⓐwaste is more dangerous to sea animals than oil spills are. A lot of sea animals and sea birds die from eating plastic waste. After we came home, we created an educational project about how to reduce plastic waste. In addition to this, our organization continues to do various projects to save animals. Although we started small, we are making a big difference. What you do today can change the world, so take that first step!

16 위 글의 밑줄 친 ⓐwaste와 같은 의미로 쓰인 것을 고르시오.

① These meetings are a complete waste of time.
② Don't waste a good opportunity.
③ We should reduce household waste.
④ You should utilize your waste talents.
⑤ I have no time to waste.

17 위 글에 어울리는 속담으로 가장 알맞은 것을 고르시오.

① Look before you leap.
② It never rains but it pours.
③ Haste makes waste.
④ A bird in the hand is worth two in the bush.
⑤ Well begun is half done.

[18~20] 다음 글을 읽고 물음에 답하시오.

When I was five, my little sister Olivia and I each ___ⓐ___ a cheetah. Did we raise cheetahs at home? No, we donated to a charity that protects wild cheetahs in South Africa. (①) Our parents told us that if we did not protect them, we might not be able to see cheetahs in the near future. (②)

We soon became interested in helping other endangered animals. (③) We wanted the next generation to be able to see these animals, so we named our organization One More Generation. (④) We also studied endangered animals and educated our friends about them. (⑤)   <I: Carter>

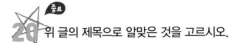

18 주어진 영영풀이를 참고하여 빈칸 ⓐ에 철자 a로 시작하는 단어를 쓰시오. (시제를 어법에 맞게 쓰시오.)

> take into one's family

➡ _____

19 위 글의 흐름으로 보아, 주어진 문장이 들어가기에 가장 적절한 곳은?

> A few years later, with help from our parents, we created a non-profit organization to protect them.

①   ②   ③   ④   ⑤

20 위 글의 제목으로 알맞은 것을 고르시오.

① The Easiest Way to Adopt a Cheetah
② The Way to Raise Cheetahs at Home
③ How to See Cheetahs Now and for Ever
④ The Background of the Creation of One More Generation
⑤ How to Create a Non-profit Organization

[21~23] 다음 글을 읽고 물음에 답하시오.

Then one day, a terrible oil spill occurred in the Gulf of Mexico. A lot of sea animals were completely covered with oil, and they were dying. We had to do something. We started collecting animal rescue supplies such as pet carrying cages and rubber gloves from everyone in our neighborhood. Four months later, our family drove to the Gulf of Mexico to deliver ___ⓐ___ we collected and helped to save the animals. While we were working there, we learned something very useful. When we put mayonnaise into a turtle's throat, the turtle ⓑthrew up. That way, we were able to get oil out of turtles. I never knew mayonnaise could be used to save animals!

21 위 글의 빈칸 ⓐ에 들어갈 알맞은 말을 고르시오.

① that   ② when   ③ as
④ what   ⑤ which

22 위 글의 밑줄 친 ⓑthrew up과 바꿔 쓸 수 있는 한 단어를 쓰시오.

➡ _____

23 According to the passage, which is NOT true?

① One day, there was a terrible oil spill in the Gulf of Mexico.
② A lot of sea animals were dying as they were completely covered with oil.
③ Carter's family collected animal rescue supplies from their neighbors.
④ Carter's family flew to the Gulf of Mexico to deliver what they collected.
⑤ Carter's family learned when they put mayonnaise into a turtle's throat, the turtle threw up.

[01~03] 다음 글을 읽고 물음에 답하시오.

When I was five, my little sister Olivia and I each adopted a cheetah. Did we raise cheetahs at home? No, we donated to a charity that protects wild cheetahs in South Africa. Our parents told us that if we did not protect them, ⓐ<u>we might not be able to see cheetahs in the near future.</u>

We soon became interested in helping other endangered animals. A few years later, ⓑ<u>부모님의 도움으로, 우리는 그들을 보호하기 위해 비영리 단체를 만들었다.</u> We wanted the next generation to be able to see these animals, so we named our organization One More Generation. We also studied endangered animals and educated our friends about them.

<I: Carter>

01 위 글의 밑줄 친 ⓐ를 참조하여, 다음 빈칸에 알맞은 단어를 넣어 cheetah에 대한 소개를 완성하시오.

> Cheetahs are _____ animals.

02 위 글의 밑줄 친 ⓑ의 우리말에 맞게 주어진 어휘를 이용하여 13 단어로 영작하시오.

> with, to protect

➡ _____

_____ 또는

_____

_____

03 After Carter and Olivia adopted cheetahs, how did they raise them? Answer in English in a full sentence. (12 words)

➡ _____

_____

[04~06] 다음 글을 읽고 물음에 답하시오.

ⓐ<u>Then one day, a terrible oil spill was occurred in the Gulf of Mexico.</u> A lot of sea animals were completely covered with oil, and they were dying. We had to do something. We started collecting animal rescue supplies such as pet carrying cages and rubber gloves from everyone in our neighborhood. Four months later, our family drove to the Gulf of Mexico to deliver ⓑ<u>what</u> we collected and helped to save the animals. While we were working there, we learned something very useful. When we put mayonnaise into a turtle's throat, the turtle threw up. That way, we were able to get oil out of turtles. I never knew mayonnaise could be used to save animals!

04 위 글의 밑줄 친 ⓐ에서 어법상 틀린 부분을 찾아 고치시오.

_____ ➡ _____

05 위 글의 밑줄 친 ⓑwhat과 바꿔 쓸 수 있는 말을 세 단어로 쓰시오.

➡ _____

06 What did the writer's family learn while they were working in the Gulf of Mexico? Fill in the blanks (A) and (B) with suitable words.

> They learned that a turtle (A)_____
> _____ when they put (B)_____ into the turtle's throat.

[07~09] 다음 글을 읽고 물음에 답하시오.

When I was five, my little sister Olivia and I each adopted a cheetah. Did we raise cheetahs at home? No, we donated to a charity that protects wild cheetahs in South Africa. Our parents told us that if we did not protect them, we might not be able to see cheetahs in the near future.

We soon became interested in helping other endangered animals. A few years later, with help from our parents, we created a non-profit organization to protect them. @We wanted the next generation to be able to see these animals, so we named our organization One More Generation. We also studied endangered animals and educated our friends about them.   <I: Carter>

07 다음 문장에서 위 글의 내용과 <u>다른</u> 부분을 찾아서 고치시오. (두 군데)

Carter and Olivia adopted a cheetah and donated it to a charity that protects wild cheetahs in South Africa.

_____ ⇒ _____, _____ ⇒ _____

08 Who helped Carter and Olivia create a non-profit organization to protect the endangered animals? Fill in the blanks with suitable words.

_____ helped them.

09 위 글의 밑줄 친 @를 다음과 같이 바꿔 쓸 때 빈칸에 들어갈 알맞은 말을 두 단어로 쓰시오.

⇒ _____ we wanted the next generation to be able to see these animals, we named our organization One More Generation.

[10~12] 다음 글을 읽고 물음에 답하시오.

On our last day, we met a marine life specialist. She told us that plastic waste is more dangerous to sea animals than oil spills @are. A lot of sea animals and sea birds die from eating plastic waste. After we came home, we created an educational project about how to reduce plastic waste. In addition to ⓑthis, our organization continues to do various projects to save animals. Although we started small, we are making a big difference. What you do today can change the world, so take that first step!
                        <we: Carter's family>

10 위 글의 밑줄 친 @are 뒤에 생략된 말을 쓰시오.

⇒ _____

11 위 글의 밑줄 친 ⓑthis가 가리키는 내용을 우리말로 쓰시오.

⇒ _____

_____

12 본문의 내용과 일치하도록 다음 빈칸 (A)와 (B)에 알맞은 단어를 쓰시오.

Carter's family came to know that plastic waste is more dangerous to sea animals than oil spills are, so they created an educational project about how to _____ _____ _____.

교과서

구석구석

해석

After You Read B

A: Why don't you join One More Generation?
Why don't you 동사원형 ~? = How[What] about ~ing?: ~하는 게 어때?

B: What is that?

A: It is a non-profit organization that protects endangered animals.
= which(주격 관계대명사)

B: What does One More Generation mean?

A: The organization wants the next generation to be able to see those animals.
want+목적어+to부정사   = endangered animals

B: That's a great organization. I'll join it.
= One More Generation

구문해설 · non-profit organization: 비영리 단체   · endangered: 멸종 위기의   · generation: 세대

A: One More Generation 에 가입하는 것이 어때?

B: 그게 무엇이니?

A: 그것은 멸종 위기의 동물들을 보호하는 비영리 단체야.

B: One More Generation 이 무슨 뜻이니?

A: 그 단체는 다음 세대가 그러한 동물들을 볼 수 있기를 원해.

B: 그것은 멋진 단체구나. 나는 거기에 가입할게.

Link Science – Share

Asian black bears have a white V-shape on their chests. They mostly live in forests in Asia. They've become endangered because people hunt them
이유를 나타내는 접속사(= as. since) = Asian black bears
for their body parts and destroy forests. We'll tell you what you can do for
hunt와 접속사 and로 연결   tell의 간접목적어   직접목적어
them. First, use less paper to protect forests. Second, you should not buy any
to부정사의 부사적 용법(~하기 위해서)   ~하지 말아야 한다
Asian black bear products.

구문해설 · V-shape: V 모양의, V자 형의   · chest: 가슴   · mostly: 주로   · live in: ~에서 살다
· endangered: 멸종 위기에 처한

아시아흑곰은 가슴에 흰색의 V 모양을 갖고 있습니다. 그들은 주로 아시아의 숲에서 삽니다. 그들은 사람들이 그들의 신체 부분을 얻으려고 사냥을 하고 숲을 파괴하기 때문에 멸종 위기에 처했습니다. 우리는 그들을 위해 여러분이 무엇을 할 수 있는지 말하고자 합니다. 첫째, 숲을 보호하기 위해서 종이를 덜 사용하세요. 둘째, 어떤 아시아의 흑곰 제품도 사지 말아야 합니다.

Write

Air pollution is one of the most serious environmental problems these days.
(~들 중) 하나
Although cars make our lives convenient, they produce a lot of smoke that
비록 ~할지라도(접속사)   = cars   = much   주격 관계대명사
pollutes the air. That is a big problem. Here is what we can do. We can
관계대명사(선행사 포함)
take the bus or subway more. We can also buy local products because they do
take+교통수단: ~을 타다
not need to be shipped very far. Even simple actions like these can help.
배송되다   심지어(부사)   ~와 같은   도움이 되다

구문해설 · air pollution: 공기오염(공해)   · serious: 심각한   · these days 요즘
· convenient: 편리한   · local product: 현지 상품

공해는 요즘 가장 심각한 환경 문제들 중의 하나이다. 비록 자동차가 우리의 생활을 편리하게 하지만, 자동차는 공기를 오염시키는 매연을 많이 만들어낸다. 그것은 커다란 문제이다. 우리가 할 수 있는 일이 있다. 우리는 버스나 지하철을 더 많이 이용할 수 있다. 우리는 또한 현지에서 생산된 상품은 매우 멀리 배송될 필요가 없기 때문에 지역의 제품들을 구매할 수 있다. 이런 일들과 같은 간단한 행동들조차 환경에는 도움이 될 수 있다.

Words & Expressions

01 밑줄 친 부분과 바꿔 쓸 수 있는 말을 고르시오.

> Do you think they can <u>repair</u> the damage?

① harm
② control
③ fix
④ destroy
⑤ supply

02 빈칸에 들어갈 말이 나머지와 다른 하나를 고르시오.

① In addition _____ discounts, they offer a free gift.
② I share a bedroom _____ my brother.
③ He read the letter aloud _____ us.
④ Can you send it _____ me by fax?
⑤ Can you lend some money _____ me until tomorrow?

03 다음 짝지어진 두 단어의 관계가 같도록 빈칸에 알맞은 말을 쓰시오.

> marry : marriage = protect : _____

04 다음 빈칸에 공통으로 들어갈 말을 쓰시오.

> • I can't tell you how much difference exercise has _____ in my life.
> • They _____ a big discovery of water on the Mars.

Conversation

[05~06] 다음 대화를 읽고 물음에 답하시오.

B: What are you doing this weekend? (①)
G: (②) _____ (A) _____
B: (③) Sounds good. (④) Can I join you?
G: Sure. (⑤)
B: O.K.

05 ①~⑤ 중 주어진 문장이 들어갈 곳은?

> Let's meet in front of the park at ten.

①   ②   ③   ④   ⑤

06 빈칸 (A)에 알맞은 말을 고르시오.

① You want me to take a picture.
② I'm reading a book.
③ I am playing soccer with my friends.
④ I'm thinking of watching a movie every weekend.
⑤ I'm thinking of going for a bike ride.

[07~08] 다음 대화를 읽고 물음에 답하시오.

A: My bike broke ___(A)___ .
B: Do you want me ___(B)___ (fix) it?
A: Yes, please.

07 빈칸 (A)에 알맞은 말을 고르시오.

① down   ② with   ③ up
④ on   ⑤ off

08 괄호 안의 단어를 어법에 맞게 빈칸 (B)에 쓰시오

➡ _____

[09~12] 다음 대화를 읽고 물음에 답하시오.

Suho: Anna, do you have any children's books you don't read any longer?

Anna: Sure. Why?

Suho: I'm thinking of sending some books to children in Africa. My aunt told me that they need books (a)to read.

Anna: Good idea, Suho! Wait, aren't your books in Korean?

Suho: Oh, that's a problem.

Anna: Well, how about translating them into English?

Suho: Translating? That's a great idea, Anna.

Anna: 너는 내가 너를 도와주기를 원하니?

Suho: Sure.   (A)   we run into any difficult expressions, let's ask our English teacher for help.

Anna: O.K. It's really great that we can help the children in Africa.

09 빈칸 (A)에 알맞은 말을 고르시오.

① Although   ② Wherever
③ If   ④ Because
⑤ Since

10 밑줄 친 (a)와 같은 용법으로 쓰이지 않은 것을 고르시오.

① Every student wrote down one thing to achieve this year.
② I'd like to open a flea market at school to help poor people.
③ I need a warm jacket to wear at night.
④ I need some books to read on the plane.
⑤ I have many letters to write.

11 대화에서 다음 영영풀이에 해당하는 단어를 찾아 쓰시오.

to change written or spoken words into another language

➡ _____

12 밑줄 친 우리말을 주어진 단어를 이용하여 영작하시오.
(want, help)

➡ _____

Grammar
---

13 다음 중 어법상 옳은 문장은 모두 몇 개인지 고르시오.

ⓐ In spite of Brian was a great poet, he wasn't famous at that time.
ⓑ Despite Jenny is so old, she still leads an active life.
ⓒ Though the danger sign, my friends and I swam in the river.
ⓓ The families enjoyed the day at the park even though the bad weather.
ⓔ Although the heavy snow, the game was not canceled.
ⓕ The employees drink coffee every day although it makes them anxious.

① 0개   ② 1개   ③ 2개   ④ 3개   ⑤ 4개

14 다음 빈칸에 알맞은 말이 바르게 짝지어진 것은?

• The photographer showed me _____ were taken in front of the Blue House.
• Cathy didn't have breakfast _____ she was very hungry.

① what – though   ② that – though
③ whose – although   ④ what – since
⑤ that – since

15 다음 그림을 보고 빈칸에 맞는 단어를 채우시오.

(1)

➡ _____ _____ I have been reading *The Old Man and the Sea* for three days, I don't understand it at all.

(2)

➡ The pyramids showed _____ the ancient Egyptians believed 4,000 years ago.

16 다음 중 밑줄 친 부분이 가장 자연스러운 것을 고르시오.

① <u>Although</u> Clara felt uncomfortable with the waist, she came home early.
② <u>Although</u> Tammy was climbing up the mountain, it started to rain.
③ <u>Although</u> my daddy has strong immunity, he caught a bad cold
④ <u>Although</u> Marc was 11 months old, he couldn't understand the situation.
⑤ <u>Although</u> they agree or disagree isn't important.

17 다음 두 문장을 관계대명사를 이용하여, 하나의 문장으로 만드시오.

(1) • This is not the thing.
   • Hermione has always wanted it.
   ➡ _____

(2) • The neighbors know the things.
   • They happened two months ago.
   ➡ _____
   _____

18 다음 두 문장의 의미가 같도록 빈칸에 알맞은 말을 쓰시오.

(1) Helen's family was poor, but they always helped others.
   ➡ _____ _____ _____ _____
   _____, they always helped others.
(2) Figure skating was an unpopular sport, but Yu-na changed people's perception.
   ➡ _____ _____ _____ _____
   _____ _____ _____, Yu-na changed people's perception.

19 다음 그림을 표현하는 문장을 〈보기〉의 단어를 사용하여 쓰시오. (It으로 시작)

┤ 보기 ├
I / that / myself / it / sweated / fanned / so / even / a / hot / was / lot / I / though

➡ _____
_____

Reading

[20~21] 다음 글을 읽고 물음에 답하시오.

When I was five, my little sister Olivia and I each adopted a cheetah. Did we raise cheetahs at home? No, we donated to a charity ⓐthat protects wild cheetahs in South Africa. Our parents told us ⓑthat if we did not protect them, we might not be able to see cheetahs in the near future.

We soon became interested in helping other endangered animals. A few years later, with help from our parents, we created a non-profit organization to protect them. We wanted the next generation to be able to see these animals, so we named our organization One More Generation. We also studied endangered animals and educated our friends about them.

<I: Carter>

20 다음 〈보기〉에서 위 글의 밑줄 친 ⓐthat, ⓑthat과 문법적 쓰임이 같은 것을 각각 <u>모두</u> 고르시오.

┌─ 보기 ┐
① There was no hope that she would recover her health.
② This is all that matters.
③ The trouble is that we are short of money.
④ He is so poor that he cannot buy it.
⑤ The people that I spoke to were very helpful.
└────────┘

➡ ⓐthat과 같은 것: _____ , _____
　 ⓑthat과 같은 것: _____

21 다음 중 Carter와 Olivia가 한 일이 <u>아닌</u> 것을 고르시오.
① 각자 치타를 입양했다.
② 남아프리카 공화국에 있는 야생 치타를 보호하는 자선단체에 치타를 기부했다.
③ 멸종 위기의 동물들을 도와주는 것에 관심을 갖게 되었다.
④ 멸종 위기의 동물들을 보호하기 위해 비영리 단체를 만들었다.
⑤ 친구들로부터 멸종 위기의 동물들에 대해 배웠다.

[22~24] 다음 글을 읽고 물음에 답하시오.

Then one day, a terrible oil spill occurred in the Gulf of Mexico. (①) A lot of sea animals were completely covered with oil, and they were dying. (②) We had to do something. (③) Four months later, our family drove to the Gulf of Mexico to deliver what we collected and helped to save the animals. (④) While we were working there, we learned something very useful. (⑤) When we put mayonnaise ____ⓐ____ a turtle's throat, the turtle threw up. That way, we were able to get oil ____ⓑ____ turtles. I never knew mayonnaise could be used to save animals!

22 위 글의 빈칸 ⓐ와 ⓑ에 들어갈 전치사가 바르게 짝지어진 것은?

　　ⓐ　　ⓑ　　　　　　ⓐ　　ⓑ
① on – out of　　　② into – by
③ for – from　　　④ on – from
⑤ into – out of

23 위 글의 흐름으로 보아, 주어진 문장이 들어가기에 가장 적절한 곳은?

┌──────────────────────────┐
We started collecting animal rescue supplies such as pet carrying cages and rubber gloves from everyone in our neighborhood.
└──────────────────────────┘

①　　　②　　　③　　　④　　　⑤

24 다음 중 위 글의 내용에 대한 이해가 옳지 <u>않은</u> 사람을 고르시오.

① 미수: One day, a terrible oil spill occurred in the writer's neighborhood.

② 경혜: Lots of sea animals were dying because they were completely covered with oil.

③ 호영: Four months later, the writer's family delivered what they had collected from their neighbors.

④ 규철: The writer's family learned that the turtle threw up when they put mayonnaise into its throat.

⑤ 성진: The writer never knew mayonnaise could be used to save animals.

[25~27] 다음 글을 읽고 물음에 답하시오.

On our last day, we met a ___ⓐ___ life specialist. She told us that plastic waste is more dangerous to sea animals than oil spills are. A lot of sea animals and sea birds die from eating plastic waste. After we came home, we created an educational project about how to reduce plastic waste. In addition to this, our organization continues to do various projects to save animals. Although we started small, we are ___ⓑ___. ©당신이 오늘 하는 일이 세상을 바꿀 수 있다, so take that first step!

<we: Carter's family>

25 주어진 영영풀이를 참고하여 빈칸 ⓐ에는 철자 m으로 시작하는 단어를, 빈칸 ⓑ에는 big을 포함한 4 단어를 쓰시오.

ⓐ of the sea or relating to the sea

ⓑ carrying out an action, the result of which is a significant change

➡ ⓐ _____ ⓑ _____

26 위 글의 밑줄 친 ©의 우리말에 맞게 한 단어를 보충하여, 주어진 어휘를 알맞게 배열하시오.

the world / can / do / change / you / today

➡ _____

27 위 글의 주제로 알맞은 것을 고르시오.

① the effect of dangerous oil spills on marine environment

② the number of sea animals and sea birds eating plastic waste

③ making a big difference by doing various projects to save animals

④ various ways of changing the world

⑤ the difficulty of taking the first step to save animals

[28~29] 다음 대화를 읽고 물음에 답하시오.

A: ⓐWhy don't you join One More Generation?
B: What is ①that?
A: ②It is a non-profit organization that protects endangered animals.
B: What does One More Generation mean?
A: ③The organization wants ④the next generation to be able to see those animals.
B: That's a great organization. I'll join ⑤it.

28 위 글의 밑줄 친 ⓐ를 다음과 같이 바꿔 쓸 때 빈칸에 들어갈 알맞은 말을 두 단어로 쓰시오.

➡ _____ _____ joining One More Generation?

29 밑줄 친 ①~⑤ 중에서 가리키는 대상이 나머지 넷과 <u>다른</u> 것은?

①   ②   ③   ④   ⑤

01 출제율 90%

다음 짝지어진 단어의 관계가 같도록 빈칸에 알맞은 말을 쓰시오.

> occur : happen = expert : s_____

02 출제율 95%

다음 빈칸에 공통으로 들어갈 말을 쓰시오.

(1)

> • What do you do if children _____ for help with their homework?
> • Is it all right if I _____ you to type this letter?

(2)

> • Here are a couple of tips they shared _____ me.
> • He was covered _____ dust while walking along the road.

03 출제율 95%

빈칸 (A)와 (B)에 들어갈 말로 알맞은 것끼리 짝지어진 것을 고르시오.

> • _____(A)_____ the people killed, one more was wounded.
> • _____(B)_____ she has lots of money, she isn't happy.

　　　　　(A)　　　　　　(B)
① However　　　– Although
② However　　　– Despite
③ In addition to – Although
④ In addition to – Despite
⑤ In addition to – In spite of

04 출제율 90%

다음 주어진 우리말에 맞게 빈칸을 채우시오. (철자가 주어진 경우 주어진 철자로 시작할 것)

(1) 제 고양이를 치료할 수 있겠어요?
　➡ Will you be able _____ c_____ my cat?

(2) 그 차는 곧 고장이 날 것 같다.
　➡ The car is likely to b_____ _____ soon.

(3) 그들은 재정적인 어려움을 만난 후에 작년에 회사를 팔기로 동의했다.
　➡ They agreed to sell the company last year after they r_____ _____ financial problems.

(4) 매년 수많은 사람들이 기아로 죽어간다.
　➡ Many thousands of people _____ _____ starvation every year.

[05~06] 다음 대화를 읽고 물음에 답하시오.

> M: Can we have pancakes for breakfast?
> W: (①) Sure. Oh, we don't have any eggs. (②)
> M: 가게에 가서 좀 사올까요? (③)
> W: Thanks, Mike. (④)
> M: Sure. (⑤)

05 출제율 100%

①~⑤ 중 주어진 문장이 들어갈 곳은?

> Can you get blueberry syrup, too?

①　　　　②　　　　③　　　　④　　　　⑤

06 밑줄 친 우리말과 일치하도록 주어진 단어를 이용해 문장을 만드시오.

➡ _____

_____ (some, want, store, get)

07 다음 대화의 빈칸에 들어갈 알맞은 말을 고르시오.

> **A:** My bike broke down.
> **B:** _____
> **A:** Yes, please.

① Do you want me to share my umbrella with you?

② Do you want me to help you carry the box?

③ Do you want me to take a picture of you?

④ Do you want me to go to the store and get some curry?

⑤ Do you want me to fix it?

[08~10] 다음 대화를 읽고 물음에 답하시오.

> **G:** ⓐ[What / How] are you doing this weekend? (①)
> **B:** (②) I'm thinking ___(A)___ doing some volunteer work at the child-care center. (③)
> **G:** What would you do there?
> **B:** I would ⓑ[probable / probably] read some books ___(B)___ the children. (④)
> **G:** That sounds interesting. (⑤)
> **B:** Of course.

08 ①~⑤ 중 주어진 문장이 들어갈 곳은?

> Can I join you?

① ② ③ ④ ⑤

09 위 대화의 괄호 ⓐ와 ⓑ에서 적절한 것을 골라 쓰시오.

➡ ⓐ _____ ⓑ _____

10 위 대화의 빈칸 (A)와 (B)에 알맞은 전치사를 쓰시오.

➡ (A) _____ (B) _____

[11~12] 다음 대화를 읽고 물음에 답하시오.

> **B:** What are you going ___ⓐ___ for the book review homework? (①)
> **G:** (②) I'm ___ⓑ___ of ___ⓒ___ a book about young leaders. (③)
> **B:** Good idea. (④)
> **G:** Oh, could you ___ⓓ___ it to me? (⑤)
> **B:** Sure. I'll ___ⓔ___ it tomorrow.

11 빈칸 ⓐ~ⓔ에 들어가지 <u>않는</u> 말을 고르시오.

① reading　　② to read　　③ lend
④ considering　　⑤ bring

12 ①~⑤ 중 주어진 문장이 들어갈 곳은?

> I have the perfect book for you.

① ② ③ ④ ⑤

13 다음 주어진 문장의 밑줄 친 <u>what</u>과 같은 용법으로 쓰인 것을 <u>모두</u> 고르시오.

> <u>What</u> upset her was his attitude.

① <u>What</u> has she come here for?
② <u>What</u> do you think the speaker meant to deliver?
③ Those are <u>what</u> she has taught for almost 20 years so far.
④ I wonder <u>what</u> you were interested in.
⑤ <u>What</u> was regarded moral in the past is not always seen as such today.

14 다음 문장의 빈칸에 들어가기에 적절한 접속사를 〈보기〉에서 골라 쓰시오.

┌─── 보기 ───┐
if   although   since
└──────────┘

(1) _____ you see a blue sky, let me know it so that I'll dry the laundries.
(2) _____ the problems seemed to be very simple, it took me quite a long time to solve them.
(3) _____ Paul doesn't want to go, I will not go to the meeting, either.
(4) John alone ate pork belly enough for five people _____ he was on a diet.
(5) _____ it rains tomorrow, I will stay home watching TV with my dog.
(6) Sumin often gets lost _____ she is so poor at finding right ways.

15 다음 중 어색한 문장을 <u>모두</u> 고르시오.

① Kelly is the only person which made Karl happy.
② Jane gave him what she had in her purse something valuable.

③ Despite Munch painted *The Scream* in 1893, it still impresses many people.
④ The kids believed what the magician showed them on the stage.
⑤ Though John took care of his sister, his father gave him the cold shoulder.
⑥ It was the books what he bought for Sarah yesterday.
⑦ All the citizens understood what the mayor announced.

16 다음 빈칸에 접속사 since, although 중에서 각각 알맞은 것을 골라 쓰시오.

(1) Alice was late for school _____ she got up early in the morning.
(2) Patrick got an A on the mathematics test _____ he studied very hard.
(3) _____ Daniel always has many friends around, he sometimes looks lonely.

[17~19] 다음 글을 읽고 물음에 답하시오.

Then one day, a (A)[terrible / terrific] oil spill occurred in the Gulf of Mexico. A lot of sea animals were completely covered with oil, and they were dying. We had to do something. We started collecting animal rescue supplies such as pet ⓐcarrying cages and rubber gloves (B) [for / from] everyone in our neighborhood. Four months later, our family drove to the Gulf of Mexico to deliver what we collected and helped to save the animals. While we were working there, we learned (C)[something very useful / very useful something]. When we put mayonnaise into a turtle's throat, the turtle threw up. That way, we were able to get oil out of turtles. I never knew mayonnaise could be used to save animals!   <I: Carter>

17 출제율 90%

위 글의 괄호 (A)~(C)에서 문맥이나 어법상 알맞은 낱말을 골라 쓰시오.

➡ (A) _____ (B) _____

    (C) _____

18 출제율 95%

위 글의 밑줄 친 ⓐcarrying과 문법적 쓰임이 같은 것을 모두 고르시오.

① I don't like a <u>boring</u> story.
② He bought a pair of <u>running</u> shoes.
③ He is a <u>walking</u> dictionary.
④ I need to buy a <u>sleeping</u> bag.
⑤ She is in the <u>waiting</u> room now.

19 출제율 100%

다음 중 글쓴이의 가족이 한 일이 <u>아닌</u> 것을 고르시오.

① 동물 구조 물품들을 동네의 모든 사람으로부터 모으기 시작했다.
② 애완동물 수송용 우리를 만들었다.
③ 그들이 모은 것들을 전달하기 위해서 멕시코만으로 운전해 갔다.
④ 멕시코만에서 동물들을 구하는 일을 도왔다.
⑤ 거북이들에게서 기름을 빼내 주었다.

[20~22] 다음 글을 읽고 물음에 답하시오.

On our (A)[last / latest] day, we met a marine life specialist. (①) She told us that plastic waste is more dangerous to sea animals than oil spills are. (②) A lot of sea animals and sea birds die (B)[for / from] eating plastic waste. (③) (C)[In addition to / In spite of] this, our organization continues to do various projects to save animals. (④) Although we started small, we are making a big difference. (⑤) What you do today can change the world, so take that first step!

20 출제율 90%

위 글의 괄호 (A)~(C)에서 문맥이나 어법상 알맞은 낱말을 골라 쓰시오.

➡ (A) _____ (B) _____

    (B) _____

21 출제율 95%

위 글의 흐름으로 보아, 주어진 문장이 들어가기에 가장 적절한 곳은?

> After we came home, we created an educational project about how to reduce plastic waste.

①   ②   ③   ④   ⑤

22 출제율 100%

According to the passage, which is NOT true?

① On their last day, Carter's family met a marine life specialist.
② A marine life specialist said that plastic waste is more dangerous to sea animals than oil spills are.
③ Many sea animals and sea birds die from eating plastic waste.
④ Carter's family created an educational project about how to reduce oil spills.
⑤ Carter's family started small, but they are making a big difference.

[01~02] 다음 대화를 읽고 물음에 답하시오.

> G: Dad, I'm a bit hungry. Is there anything to eat?
> M: _____(A)_____
> G: That'd be great. I love tteokbokki.
> M: O.K. Give me a little minutes.

01 위의 대화에서 어법상 <u>어색한</u> 것을 찾아 바르게 고치시오.

_____ ➡ _____

02 주어진 단어를 이용하여 빈칸 (A)에 도움을 제안하는 문장을 써 넣으시오. (9 단어)

➡ _____

(want, for, cook)

03 밑줄 친 문장과 같은 의미가 되도록 주어진 단어를 이용하여 쓰시오.

> G: What are you doing this weekend?
> B: <u>I'm thinking of doing some volunteer work at the child-care center.</u>
> G: What would you do there?
> B: I would probably read some books to the children.
> G: That sounds interesting. Can I join you?
> B: Of course.

➡ _____
_____ (consider)
➡ _____
_____ (plan)
➡ _____
_____ (intend)

04 다음 문장을 〈보기〉와 같이 접속사 Although를 사용하여 다시 쓰시오.

> ┤ 보기 ├
> Math problems are difficult, but I like to try to solve them.
> →Although math problems are difficult, I like to try to solve them.

(1) James made a few mistakes, but he succeeded in the project.

➡ _____
_____

(2) Mr. Park left for the station earlier than usual, but he missed the train.

➡ _____
_____

(3) Angela caught a bad cold, but she exercised in the morning.

➡ _____
_____

(4) Jinho prepared for the civil service exam for 4 years, but he failed it.

➡ _____
_____

05 다음 우리말과 같은 뜻이 되도록 주어진 단어들을 이용하여, 제시된 글자 수에 맞게 영작하시오.

(1) 여러분이 하는 것이 여러분이 말하는 것보다 훨씬 중요하다. (speak, than, much, important, 11 단어)

➡ _____

(2) Paula는 그녀가 가진 것을 최대한 활용해야 한다. (most, make, must, of, have, 9 단어)

➡ _____

06 다음 두 문장의 의미가 같도록 빈칸에 들어갈 알맞은 말을 쓰시오.

> Lucy didn't notice the thing that Joseph had done.
> = Lucy didn't notice _____ Joseph had done.

[07~09] 다음 글을 읽고 물음에 답하시오.

> On our last day, we met a marine life specialist. She told us that ⓐplastic waste is more dangerous to sea animals than oil spills are. A lot of sea animals and sea birds die from eating plastic waste. After we came home, we created an educational project about ⓑhow to reduce plastic waste. In addition to this, our organization continues to do various projects to save animals. Although we started small, we are making a big difference. What you do today can change the world, so take that first step!
>
> <we: Carter's family>

07 위 글의 밑줄 친 ⓐ와 같은 의미가 되도록 빈칸에 들어갈 알맞은 말을 쓰시오.

➡ oil spills are _____ dangerous to sea animals than plastic waste is

08 위 글의 밑줄 친 ⓑ를 다음과 같이 바꿔 쓸 때 빈칸에 들어갈 알맞은 말을 두 단어로 쓰시오.

➡ how _____ reduce

09 Why does Carter encourage you to take the first step? Fill in the blanks with suitable words.

> It's because what we do today can _____ _____ _____.

[10~12] 다음 글을 읽고 물음에 답하시오.

> When I was five, my little sister Olivia and I each (A)[adapted / adopted] a cheetah. Did we (B)[raise / rise] cheetahs at home? No, we donated to a charity that (C)[prevents / protects] wild cheetahs in South Africa. Our parents told us that if we did not protect them, we might not be able to see cheetahs in the near future.
>
> We soon became interested in helping other endangered animals. A few years later, with help from our parents, we created a non-profit organization to protect them. We wanted the next generation ⓐ able to see these animals, so we named our organization One More Generation. We also studied endangered animals and educated our friends about them.
>
> <I: Carter>

10 위 글의 빈칸 ⓐ에 be를 알맞은 형태로 쓰시오.

➡ _____

11 위 글의 괄호 (A)~(C)에서 문맥이나 어법상 알맞은 낱말을 골라 쓰시오.

➡ (A) _____ (B) _____ (C) _____

12 Carter와 Olivia가 치타 외의 다른 멸종 위기의 동물들을 도와주는 것에 관심을 갖게 된 이후에 한 활동 세 가지를 우리말로 쓰시오.

➡ (1) _____
_____
_____
(2) _____
(3) _____

01 다음은 Kate의 가족이 이번 주말에 할 계획이다. 이에 대한 정보와 주어진 〈조건〉에 맞게 글을 완성하시오.

Kate, 언니 – 수영하러 가기 엄마 – 미술관 방문하기 아빠 – 집에서 책 읽기

조건

1. think of, consider, plan의 어형을 변화시켜 이용할 것
2. 각 문장에 1의 표현을 반드시 차례로 한 번씩만 이용할 것

Kate and her family members have some plans for this weekend. Kate and her sister like to swim. So _____. Kate's mother is not good at swimming but interested in art. _____. Kate's father _____.

02 다음 그림을 보고 〈보기〉에 주어진 어휘를 활용하여, 접속사 although가 들어가는 문장을 쓰시오.

보기

be different / love each other

➡ _____
_____

03 다음 내용을 바탕으로 환경 문제와 그 해결 방안을 제시하는 짧은 글을 쓰시오.

Problem
• A lot of plastic waste goes into the ocean.   • Sea animals eat it.
Solution
• reuse and recycle   • bring our own bottle and shopping bag

Plastic pollution is one of the most serious environmental problems these days. Although plastic makes our lives convenient, a lot of (A)_____ goes into the ocean and many (B)_____ eat it. That is a big problem. Here is what we can do. We can (C)_____ plastic products. We can also bring our own (D)_____ and (E)_____. Even simple actions like these can help.

단원별 모의고사

01 빈칸 (A)와 (B)에 들어갈 말로 알맞은 것끼리 짝지어진 것을 고르시오.

> • It became an Olympic sport, but _____(A)_____ it isn't that new.
> • _____(B)_____ he is very young, he can solve this math problem.

     (A)   (B)
① actually – Although
② actually – Since
③ actually – Unless
④ though – Although
⑤ though – Since

[02~03] 빈칸에 들어갈 말로 알맞은 것을 고르시오.

02
> There was an oil _____ and the oil destroyed the nature.

① rescue   ② supply   ③ gulf
④ spill   ⑤ cut

03
> A: How much did you _____?
> B: I sent $100 to charity.

① donate   ② occur   ③ volunteer
④ purchase   ⑤ adopt

04 다음 우리말에 맞도록 빈칸에 알맞은 말을 쓰시오. (철자가 주어진 경우 주어진 철자로 시작할 것.)

(1) 우리는 멸종 위기의 동물들을 보호해야만 한다.
➡ We have to protect e_____ animals.

(2) 당신의 전문 지식을 일주일에 몇 시간씩 비영리 기구에 기부해 봐.
➡ _____ your expertise to a _____ for a few hours a week.

(3) 그 구조 시도는 악천후로 좌절되었다.
➡ The r_____ attempt was frustrated by bad weather.

(4) 그 문제는 아마도 다양한 방법으로 해결될 수 있을 것이다.
➡ The _____ will be p_____ solved in v_____ ways.

05 대화가 자연스럽게 연결되도록 (A)~(D)를 적절하게 배열한 것은?

> (A) O.K. Give me a few minutes.
> (B) That'd be great. I love tteokbokki.
> (C) Dad, I'm a bit hungry. Is there anything to eat?
> (D) Do you want me to cook tteokbokki for you?

① (B) – (A) – (C) – (D)
② (B) – (C) – (A) – (D)
③ (C) – (A) – (B) – (D)
④ (C) – (B) – (A) – (D)
⑤ (C) – (D) – (B) – (A)

[06~07] 다음 대화를 읽고 물음에 답하시오.

A: **What are you going to do this year?**
B: 나는 주말마다 영화를 볼까 해.

06 밑줄 친 문장과 같은 의미가 되도록 할 때 빈칸에 들어갈 알맞은 말을 주어진 철자로 시작하여 쓰시오.

What's your _____ for this year?

➡ p_____

07 밑줄 친 우리말과 일치하도록 주어진 단어를 이용하여 영작하시오.

➡ _____

(every, think, watch a movie)

08 빈칸 ⓐ~ⓔ에 들어가지 않는 말을 고르시오.

A: This box is ____ⓐ____ .
B: Do you ____ⓑ____ me ____ⓒ____ you ____ⓓ____ ____ⓔ____ ?
A: Yes, please.

① want   ② carry   ③ them
④ to help   ⑤ too heavy

[09~12] 다음 대화를 읽고 물음에 답하시오.

Suho: Anna, do you have any children's books you don't read any (A)[better / longer]?
Anna: Sure. ⓐHow?
Suho: ⓑI'm thinking of sending some books to children in Africa. My aunt told me (B)[what / that] they need books to read.
Anna: Good idea, Suho! ⓒWait, aren't your books in Korean?

Suho: ⓓOh, that's a problem.
Anna: Well, how about _____ them into English?
Suho: _____? That's a great idea, Anna.
Anna: ⓔDo you want me to help you?
Suho: Sure. If we run into any difficult (C) [expressions / experiences], let's ask our English teacher for help.
Anna: O.K. It's really great that we can help the children in Africa.

09 위 대화의 빈칸에 공통으로 들어갈 단어를 주어진 철자로 시작하여 쓰시오. (대·소문자 무시)

➡ _____

10 위 대화의 괄호 (A)~(C)에서 적절한 것을 골라 쓰시오.

➡ (A) _____ (B) _____ (C) _____

11 ⓐ~ⓔ 중 문맥상 또는 어법상 어색한 것을 고르시오.

① ⓐ   ② ⓑ   ③ ⓒ   ④ ⓓ   ⑤ ⓔ

12 대화의 내용과 일치하지 않는 것을 모두 고르시오.

① Anna는 더 이상 안 읽는 아동용 도서를 가지고 있지 않다.
② 수호와 Anna는 한국어로 된 책을 영어로 번역할 것이다.
③ 수호와 Anna는 아프리카의 아이들에게 줄 책을 모으기 위해 선생님에게 도움을 청할 것이다.
④ 수호는 아프리카의 아이들에게 줄 책을 구하고 있다.
⑤ 수호의 이모는 아프리카의 아이들이 읽을 책이 필요하다고 말했다.

13 두 문장을 같은 의미의 한 문장이 되도록 관계대명사 what을 사용하여 빈칸을 알맞게 채우시오.

(1) • I can't read the strange letters.
  • Sullivan wrote them in his note.
  = I can't read _____.

(2) • Gale says the thing.
  • It is not important.
  = _____ is not important.

14 다음 〈보기〉에 주어진 두 문장을, 각각의 조건에 맞게 한 문장으로 바꾸어 영작할 때, 빈칸에 적절한 말을 쓰시오.

┌─ 보기 ├─
• Peter가 지난 수업에 결석을 했다.
• Peter가 오늘 본 시험에서 만점을 받았다.
(단, score, from, get, absence를 활용할 것)
└─

(1) 접속사 but 사용
  = _____ _____ _____ _____
  the last class, _____ _____
  _____ _____ _____ _____
  on the exam today.

(2) 접속사 Although 사용
  = _____ _____ _____ _____
  _____ the last class, _____
  _____ _____ _____ _____
  on the exam today.

(3) 전치사 despite, 대명사 his 사용
  = _____ _____ _____ from the
  last class, _____ _____ _____
  _____ on the exam today.

15 우리말과 일치하도록 괄호 안의 어구를 바르게 배열하시오. (대문자로 주어진 말로 문장을 시작할 것)

(1) 이것이 바로 Frank가 지난 일요일에 일본인 어부로부터 구매한 것이다. (from, last Sunday, Frank, a, what, This, fisherman, is, purchased, Japanese)
➡ _____
_____

(2) 그는 많이 아팠지만, 직장에 갔다. (although, to, He, very, work, sick, was, he, went)
➡ _____
_____

(3) John이 그 복사기를 수리했는데도, 다음날 그것이 작동하지 않았다. (it, next, fixed, Although, photocopier, the, John, work, the, didn't, day)
➡ _____
_____

16 다음 문장을 〈보기〉와 같이 다시 쓰되, 접속사 though의 위치는 문두에 쓰지 말고, 특히 명사와 대명사도 〈보기〉를 참고하여 알맞게 바꿔 쓰시오.

┌─ 보기 ├─
Math problems are difficult, but I like to try to solve them.
→ I like to try to solve math problems, though they are difficult.
└─

(1) Jason didn't have to read the magazine, but he bought it.
➡ _____
_____

(2) This watch is much older than my grandfather, but it still works well.
➡ _____
_____

(3) Ray has been my classmate for 4 years, but I don't know much about her.
➡ _____
_____

(4) The strawberry looked fine on the surface, but it had a nasty smell.

➡ _____

_____

(5) Many people climbed up on the paper desk, but it didn't break.

➡ _____

_____

17 다음 중 빈칸에 들어갈 것이 다른 하나는?

① Peter sold _____ his family regarded as a treasure to the collector.

② Uncle Joe forgot to tell me _____ he had heard about my lost cat.

③ Did Luke show the police officer _____ I had given him?

④ Mary didn't like the doll _____ her uncle had brought.

⑤ I'll tell you _____ you wanted to hear.

18 다음 밑줄 친 우리말에 맞게 괄호 안에 주어진 단어를 알맞게 배열하시오.

- Reporter: Who or what would you like to give credit to for winning the award tonight?
- Winner: 오늘의 저를 만든 것은 내 어머니의 사랑입니다.

(I, my, me, mother's, made, today, what, who, is, am, love)

➡ _____

[19~21] 다음 글을 읽고 물음에 답하시오.

When I was five, my little sister Olivia and I each adopted a cheetah. Did we raise cheetahs at home? No, ⓐ우리는 남아프리카 공화국에 있는 야생 치타를 보호하는 자선단체에 기부했다. Our parents told us that ⓑif we did not protect them, we might not be able to see cheetahs in the near future.

We soon became interested in helping other endangered animals. A few years later, with help from our parents, we created a non-profit organization to protect them. We wanted the next generation to be able to see these animals, so we named our organization One More Generation. We also studied endangered animals and educated our friends about them.

<I: Carter>

19 위 글의 밑줄 친 ⓐ의 우리말에 맞게 주어진 어휘를 알맞게 배열하시오.

wild cheetahs / donated / in / protects / South Africa / we / to / that / a charity

➡ _____

_____

20 위 글의 밑줄 친 ⓑ를 unless를 사용하여 고치시오.

➡ _____

21 Carter와 Olivia가 그들이 만든 비영리 단체의 이름을 One More Generation이라고 지은 이유를 우리말로 쓰시오.

➡ _____

_____

[22~23] 다음 글을 읽고 물음에 답하시오.

Then one day, a terrible oil spill occurred in the Gulf of Mexico. A lot of sea animals were completely covered with oil, and they were dying. We had to do something. We started collecting animal rescue supplies such as pet carrying cages and rubber gloves from everyone in our neighborhood. Four months later, our family drove to the Gulf of Mexico to deliver what we collected and helped to save (A)the animals. While we were working there, we learned something very useful. When we put mayonnaise into a turtle's throat, the turtle threw up. That way, we were able to get oil out of turtles. I never knew mayonnaise could ____ⓐ____ to save animals!

22 위 글의 빈칸 ⓐ에 use를 알맞은 형태로 쓰시오.

➡ _____

23 다음 빈칸 (A)와 (B)에 알맞은 단어를 넣어 (A)the animals 에 대한 소개를 완성하시오.

> They were dying because they were completely covered with (A)_____ due to a terrible oil spill which occurred in (B)_____ _____ _____ _____.

[24~26] 다음 글을 읽고 물음에 답하시오.

Air pollution is one of the most serious environmental problems these days. Although cars make our lives convenient, (A)they produce a lot of smoke that pollutes the air. That is a big problem. Here is what we can do. We can take the bus or subway more. We can also buy local products because (B)they do not need to ____ⓐ____ very far. Even simple actions like these can help.

24 위 글의 빈칸 ⓐ에 ship을 알맞은 형태로 쓰시오.

➡ _____

25 위 글의 밑줄 친 (A)they, (B)they가 가리키는 것을 본문에 서 찾아 쓰시오.

➡ (A)they가 가리키는 것: _____,
(B)they가 가리키는 것: _____

26 According to the passage, which is NOT true?

① Air pollution is one of the most serious environmental problems these days.
② Cars make our lives convenient.
③ Cars produce a lot of smoke that pollutes the air.
④ We can buy local products to solve environmental problems.
⑤ Local products need to be shipped very far.

[27~29] 다음 글을 읽고 물음에 답하시오.

Asian black bears have a white V-shape on their chests. They mostly live in forests in Asia. They've become endangered because people hunt them for their body parts and destroy forests. ⓐWe'll tell you what you can do for them. First, use less paper to protect forests. Second, you should not buy any Asian black bear products.

27 위 글의 밑줄 친 ⓐ를 다음과 같이 바꿔 쓸 때 빈칸에 들어갈 알맞은 말을 두 단어로 쓰시오.

➡ We'll tell you what _____ _____ for them.

28 본문의 내용과 일치하도록 다음 빈칸 (A)~(C)에 알맞은 단어를 쓰시오.

You should use less (A)_____ to protect forests because Asian black bears mostly live in (B)_____ in Asia, and you should not buy any Asian black bear products because people hunt them for their (C)_____ _____.

29 위 글을 읽고 아시아흑곰에 대해 알 수 없는 것을 고르시오.

① What is special about them?
② Where do they live?
③ Why are they endangered?
④ What should we do for them?
⑤ What products can be made from Asian black bears?

[30~31] 다음 글을 읽고 물음에 답하시오.

Plastic pollution is one of the most serious environmental problems these days. Although plastic makes our lives convenient, a lot of plastic waste goes into the ocean and many sea animals eat it. ⓐThat is a big problem. Here is what we can do. We can reuse and recycle plastic products. We can also bring our own bottle and shopping bag. Even simple actions like these can help.

30 위 글의 밑줄 친 ⓐThat이 가리키는 것을 본문에서 찾아 쓰시오.

➡ _____

_____

31 What are the two solutions to the plastic pollution? Fill in the blanks (A)~(D) with suitable words.

One of the solutions is (A)_____ _____ and (B)_____ _____ plastic products and to bring our own (C)_____ and (D)_____ _____.

Lesson 2

Timeless Tales of Gods and Heroes

 의사소통 기능

- 이유 묻기

  What makes you want to go there?

- 허락 요청하기

  A: Do you mind if I sit here?

  B: No, not at all. Go ahead.

 언어 형식

- It ~ that 강조 구문

  It is we **that** are the finest smiths.

- '계속적 용법'의 관계대명사

  Thor soon found Loki, **who** was drinking at home.

Words & Expressions

Key Words

- □ **accept** [æksépt] 동 받아들이다, 수락하다
- □ **adventure** [ædvéntʃər] 명 모험
- □ **angrily** [ǽŋgrəli] 부 화가 나서
- □ **bet** [bet] 동 단언하다, 돈을 걸다
- □ **bloom** [blu:m] 동 꽃이 피다, 꽃을 피우다
- □ **borrow** [bárou] 동 빌리다
- □ **carriage** [kǽridʒ] 명 마차, 객차
- □ **challenge** [tʃǽlindʒ] 명 도전, 결투 신청
- □ **choose** [tʃu:z] 동 선택하다
- □ **cloth** [klɔːθ] 명 옷감, 천
- □ **control** [kəntróul] 동 조절하다
- □ **decide** [disáid] 동 결정하다
- □ **decision** [disíʒən] 명 결정, 판결
- □ **dwarf** [dwɔːrf] 명 난쟁이
- □ **elf** [elf] 명 요정
- □ **enemy** [énəmi] 명 적, 적군
- □ **fine** [fain] 형 질 좋은, 좋은
- □ **flowing** [flóuiŋ] 형 흐르는 듯한, 유창한
- □ **golden** [góuldən] 형 금빛의
- □ **giant** [dʒáiənt] 명 거인
- □ **hammer** [hǽmər] 명 망치
- □ **harvest** [háːrvist] 명 수확, 추수 동 수확하다, 거둬들이다
- □ **immediately** [imíːdiətli] 부 즉시, 곧
- □ **kingdom** [kíŋdəm] 명 왕국, 왕조
- □ **magical** [mǽdʒikəl] 형 마법 같은
- □ **mind** [maind] 형 언짢아하다, 상관하다
- □ **miss** [mis] 동 놓치다
- □ **moreover** [mɔːróuvər] 부 게다가
- □ **mysterious** [mistíəriəs] 형 신비로운
- □ **myth** [miθ] 명 신화
- □ **order** [ɔ́ːrdər] 동 주문하다
- □ **outside** [áutsáid] 부 바깥에
- □ **piece** [piːs] 명 조각, 일부, 한 가지
- □ **poem** [póuəm] 명 시
- □ **powerful** [páuərfəl] 형 강력한
- □ **precious** [préʃəs] 형 귀중한, 값어치 있는
- □ **produce** [prədjúːs] 동 만들어 내다, 제조하다
- □ **promise** [prámis] 동 약속하다
- □ **protect** [prətékt] 동 지키다, 보호하다
- □ **prove** [pruːv] 동 증명하다
- □ **pull** [pul] 동 당기다
- □ **reply** [riplái] 동 대답하다
- □ **scared** [skɛərd] 형 두려워하는, 겁먹은
- □ **seafood** [síːfud] 명 해산물
- □ **skin** [skin] 명 가죽
- □ **smith** [smiθ] 명 대장장이, 금속 세공인
- □ **soon** [suːn] 부 곧
- □ **southeastern** [sàuθíːstərn] 형 동남의
- □ **spear** [spiər] 명 창
- □ **target** [táːrgit] 명 목표, 표적
- □ **terrible** [térəbl] 형 끔찍한
- □ **throw** [θrou] 동 던지다
- □ **treasure** [tréʒər] 명 보물
- □ **trick** [trik] 명 장난, 묘기
- □ **turn** [təːrn] 명 차례
- □ **undo** [əndú] 동 원상태로 돌리다
- □ **weather** [wéðər] 명 날씨
- □ **wisdom** [wízdəm] 형 지혜, 슬기, 현명함

Key Expressions

- □ **be famous for ~** ~로 유명하다
- □ **be gone** 사라지다, 없어지다
- □ **be into** ~에 관심이 많다
- □ **come along** 함께 가다, 동행하다
- □ **come up with** ~을 생각해 내다
- □ **fall asleep** 잠들다
- □ **give up** 포기하다
- □ **had better ~** ~하는 편이 더 낫다

- □ **How do you like ~?** ~가 마음에 드니?
- □ **I bet ~.** 틀림없이 ~이다.
- □ **in that case** 그렇다면, 그런 경우에는
- □ **of one's own** 자기 자신의
- □ **play tricks (on)** 농간을 부리다, 장난을 치다
- □ **take root** 뿌리를 내리다
- □ **turn into ~** ~로 되다

Word Power

※ 서로 비슷한 뜻을 가진 어휘

- ☐ **harvest** 수확, 추수 : **yield** 수확
- ☐ **moreover** 게다가 : **furthermore** 게다가
- ☐ **precious** 귀중한, 값어치 있는 : **priceless** 대단히 귀중한

- ☐ **reply** 응답하다 : **respond** 응답하다
- ☐ **immediately** 즉시 : **instantly** 즉시
- ☐ **protect** 보호하다 : **shield** 보호하다

※ 서로 반대의 뜻을 가진 어휘

- ☐ **accept** 받아들이다 ↔ **refuse** 거절하다
- ☐ **powerful** 강력한 ↔ **weak** 약한
- ☐ **pull** 당기다 ↔ **push** 밀다

- ☐ **scared** 겁먹은 ↔ **brave** 용감한
- ☐ **precious** 소중한 ↔ **worthless** 가치 없는
- ☐ **reply** 응답하다 ↔ **question** 질문하다

※ 형용사 – 부사

- ☐ **actual** 사실의 – **actually** 사실
- ☐ **careful** 조심스러운 – **carefully** 신중하게
- ☐ **easy** 쉬운 – **easily** 쉽게
- ☐ **immediate** 즉각적인 – **immediately** 즉각적으로
- ☐ **mysterious** 신비로운 – **mysteriously** 신비롭게도

- ☐ **angry** 화난 – **angrily** 화가 나서
- ☐ **complete** 완전한 – **completely** 완전하게
- ☐ **happy** 행복한 – **happily** 행복하게
- ☐ **lucky** 운이 좋은 – **luckily** 운 좋게도
- ☐ **powerful** 강력한 – **powerfully** 강력하게

※ take와 함께 쓰이는 표현

- ☐ **take a break** 쉬다
- ☐ **take a seat** 자리에 앉다
- ☐ **take care** 조심하다

- ☐ **take a look** 보다
- ☐ **take a test** 시험을 보다
- ☐ **take notes** 필기하다

- ☐ **take a picture** 사진을 찍다
- ☐ **take a walk** 산책하다
- ☐ **take root** 뿌리를 내리다

English Dictionary

- ☐ **bet** 돈을 걸다
  → to risk money on the result of a race, game, competition, or other future event
  경주, 경기, 시합, 또는 다른 미래의 사건의 결과에 돈을 거는 위험을 감수하다

- ☐ **carriage** 마차, 수레
  → a vehicle with wheels that is pulled by a horse
  말이 끄는 바퀴 달린 탈것

- ☐ **challenge** 도전
  → something new and difficult which requires great effort and determination
  엄청난 노력과 결심을 요구하는 새롭고 어려운 어떤 것

- ☐ **enemy** 적
  → someone who hates you and wants to harm you
  당신을 싫어하고 해치고 싶어 하는 사람

- ☐ **hammer** 망치
  → a tool with a heavy metal part on a long handle, used for hitting nails into wood
  나무에 못을 박을 때 사용하는 긴 손잡이에 무거운 금속이 있는 도구

- ☐ **smith** 대장장이
  → someone who makes and repairs things made of iron
  철로 된 물건을 만들거나 수리하는 사람

- ☐ **spear** 창
  → a pole with a sharp pointed blade at one end, used as a weapon in the past
  과거에 무기로 사용된 한쪽 끝에 뾰족하고 날카로운 날이 달린 긴 막대기

- ☐ **treasure** 보물
  → a group of valuable things such as gold, silver, jewels. etc.
  금. 은. 보석 같은 귀중한 것들

- ☐ **trick** 장난, 속임수
  → something you do to surprise someone and to make other people laugh
  누군가를 놀라게 하고 다른 사람들을 웃게 하려고 하는 어떤 것

- ☐ **wisdom** 지혜
  → the ability to use your experience and knowledge in order to make sensible decisions or judgments
  분별 있는 결정이나 판단을 하기 위해 경험과 지식을 사용하는 능력

01 다음 영영풀이에 해당하는 말로 가장 적절한 것은?

> a vehicle with wheels that is pulled by a horse

① game ② race
③ spear ④ carriage
⑤ blade

02 주어진 문장의 밑줄 친 부분과 같은 의미로 쓰인 것은?

> I want to order a coke and a sandwich.

① They used to order me to bring some food for them.
② It was time that she should put her life in order.
③ We need to obey social order to live in harmony.
④ She gave orders for the work to be started.
⑤ He will order himself a noodle soup as usual.

03 다음 중 밑줄 친 부분의 뜻풀이가 바르지 않은 것은?

① How do you like the new car? (~가 마음에 드니?)
② This place is famous for its scenery. (~으로 유명하다)
③ I bet she won't come. (틀림없이 ~이다)
④ You had better keep practicing it. (~하는 편이 낫다)
⑤ The man turned into an old man. (~에게로 돌아섰다)

04 다음 우리말에 맞게 빈칸에 알맞은 말을 쓰시오.

> 그가 이미 한 일을 원상태로 되돌릴 수 없어.
> ➡ You can't _____ what he already did.

05 다음 짝지어진 단어의 관계가 같도록 빈칸에 알맞은 말을 주어진 철자로 시작하여 쓰시오.

> reply : respond = precious : p_____

[06~07] 다음 영영풀이에 해당하는 말을 쓰시오.

06

> to prevent something or someone from being harmed or damaged

➡ _____

07

> the gathering of a crop

➡ _____

08 다음 단어의 뜻풀이로 가장 적절한 것은?

> spear

① to plant seeds in the ground
② a pole with a sharp pointed blade at one end, used as a weapon in the past
③ to say someone that you will definitely do something
④ a collection of valuable old objects
⑤ to agree to take an offer

01 다음 빈칸에 알맞은 말을 〈보기〉에서 찾아 쓰시오. 필요하다면 어형을 바꾸시오.

보기

play   give   like   come

(1) He didn't _____ up the work when he was busy taking care of her mother.

(2) If you want to _____ along with us, you have to pay.

(3) Kathy always _____ tricks on her friends.

(4) How do you _____ your new digital camera?

02 다음 빈칸에 들어갈 말을 순서대로 쓰시오.

(A) She loves cats so much that she has five cats _____ her own.

(B) I will try to come _____ with some ideas to solve the problem.

(C) Is the street famous _____ plays and performances?

03 다음 우리말과 일치하도록 주어진 단어를 바르게 배열하시오.

(1) 아이들은 그 방에서 잠들 거야.
(the / will / children / asleep / in / room / fall)

➡ _____

(2) 너는 집에 일찍 가는 편이 나아.
(early / better / had / go / you / home)

➡ _____

(3) 게다가, 그는 겁먹었어.
(scared / was / moreover / he)

➡ _____

04 다음 우리말에 맞게 빈칸에 알맞은 말을 쓰시오.

우리가 꿈꾸던 휴가가 악몽으로 변했어요.
➡ Our dream holiday _____ _____ a nightmare.

05 다음 영영풀이에 해당하는 말을 〈보기〉에서 골라 바르게 쓰시오.

보기

throw   ask   poem

(1) _____ : a piece of writing in which the words are chosen for their beauty and sound and are carefully arranged

(2) _____ : to tell someone that you want them to do it

(3) _____ : to move your hand or arm quickly and let go of an object, so that it moves through the air

06 다음 밑줄 친 부분과 의미가 통하는 하나의 단어를 쓰시오.

While you are moving, please handle the violin with care.

➡ _____

Conhecimento 교과서

Conversation

① 이유 묻기

> • **What makes you want to go there?** 무엇 때문에 거기에 가고 싶으세요?

■ 상대방이 왜 그렇게 말하는지, 혹은 왜 그렇게 생각하는지 등에 대해 이유를 물을 때는 의문사 why를 써서 'Why do you say that?(왜 그렇게 말하니?)'처럼 물어볼 수도 있지만 의문사 what을 사용해서 'What makes you say that?'이라고 물어보기도 한다.

■ 의문사 what을 사용하여 이유를 물어볼 때는 '무엇이 ~하도록 만드느냐?'의 의미로 'What makes you+동사원형 ~?'의 형태가 된다. 행위의 이유를 물어보는 것이므로 '무엇'이라고 해석할 수도 있지만 '왜'라고 해석하기도 한다. 이유를 물어볼 때는 주로 다음과 같은 표현들을 사용할 수 있다.

■ 의문사로 시작하는 이유를 묻는 말 앞에 'Can you tell me'나 'I'd like to know', 'I wonder' 등을 붙여, 간접의문문의 형식으로 좀 더 격식을 갖춰 물어볼 수도 있다. 이유를 말할 때에는 문장 앞에 'I think'나 'In my opinion' 등을 덧붙일 수도 있다.

이유 묻기

- What makes you ~? 무엇이 ~하도록 만드니?
- What makes you want to ~? 무엇이 ~하고 싶도록 만드니?
- What makes you think so? 무엇 때문에 그렇게 생각하니?
- Why is that? 왜 그렇지?
- Why do you ~? 왜 ~하니?
- Why do you think so? 왜 그렇게 생각하니?
- Can you tell me (the reason) why ~? ~의 이유를 설명해 주겠니?

이유 말하기

- I did it because ~. ~ 때문에 그것을 했어요.
- Because ~. 왜냐하면 ~ 때문이야.
- That's because ~. 그것은 ~ 때문입니다.
- Because of ~. ~ 때문이야.

핵심 Check

1. 다음 우리말과 일치하도록 주어진 단어를 이용해 빈칸에 알맞은 말을 쓰시오.

A: I want to visit Iceland.

B: 왜 거기에 가고 싶으니? (make)

A: I want to see the northern lights.

➡ _____ _____ _____ want to go there?

2 허락 요청하기

A Do you mind if I sit here? 여기에 앉아도 될까요?

B No, not at all. Go ahead. 물론입니다. 앉으세요.

■ 다른 사람이 같이 있는 상황에서 어떤 일을 하기 전에 상대방에게 허락을 요청할 때는 허락을 요청하는 조동사를 사용하여 'May I ~?', 'Can I ~?', 또는 'Is it okay if I ~?' 등을 사용할 수 있다. 이런 표현 이외에도 좀 더 공손하게 나타내는 표현으로는 'Do you mind if ~?'를 사용할 수 있다.

■ 그 외에 상대방의 허락을 구하는 말은 'Would you mind if ~?', 'I'm wondering if I could ~.', 'Is it okay (with you) if I ~?', 'Would it be all right if I ~?' 등으로 표현할 수도 있다.

■ 'Do you mind if ~?'에서 'mind'는 '꺼리다, 신경 쓰다'라는 의미이기 때문에 'Yes'라고 답변하면 '꺼린다, 신경 쓴다'는 의미가 되어, 허락하지 않는 것을 나타낸다. 상대방에게 괜찮다고 허락할 때는 '신경 쓰지 않으니까 하고 싶은 대로 하세요.'라는 의미로 'Not at all.', 'Of course not.' 'Certainly not.', 'No problem.', 'Sure.', 'Go ahead.' 등을 사용한다. 상대방에게 허락해 주지 않을 경우에는 'I'm afraid I do.(죄송하지만, 안됩니다.)'라고 대답한다.

허락 요청하기와 대답하기

• Do you mind if I ~? ~해도 되겠습니까?

허락할 때 No, not at all. / Certainly not. / Of course not.
　　　　No, I don't. / No problem. / Sure. / Go ahead. 네, 괜찮습니다.
금지할 때 Yes, I do. / Sorry, but ~. / I'm afraid I ~. 미안하지만 안 됩니다.

• May I ~? ~해도 됩니까?　　　　허락할 때 Yes, you may. 네, 괜찮습니다.

• Can I ~? ~해도 될까요?　　　　허락할 때 Yes, you can. 네, 괜찮습니다.

• Is it okay if I ~? ~해도 괜찮을까요?　허락할 때 Yes, it is. / Sure. / Of course.

핵심 Check

2. 다음 빈칸에 들어가기에 적절하지 <u>않은</u> 것은?

G: Dad, do you mind if I change the channel?

M: _____

G: Thank you. I need to watch a program about Norway.

M: Norway? Why?

G: Well, we're learning about Norway in class.

M: Oh, I see.

① No, not at all.　　　② Certainly not.　　　③ No, I don't.

④ Go ahead.　　　　⑤ I'm afraid I do.

Listen and Speak 1 A-1

W: Is it your first time ❶to visit Korea, Mike?

M: Yes, it is. ❷I've always wanted to come to Seoul.

W: ❸What made you come here?

M: I'm really into Korean TV shows. ❹I'm going to go to the places I saw on TV.

W: Have fun!

W: 한국엔 처음 방문하는 거야, Mike?
M: 맞아. 나는 언제나 서울에 오고 싶었어.
W: 이곳에 온 이유가 뭐니?
M: 나는 한국의 TV 프로그램들을 정말 좋아해. TV에서 봤던 장소들에 갈 거야.
W: 재미있게 지내!

❶ to부정사의 형용사적 용법으로 time 수식
❷ 과거부터 지금까지 쭉 원해 왔다는 의미의 현재완료
❸ 이유를 묻는 표현(= What brought you here?, Why did you come here?)
❹ be going to V: V할 예정이다

Check(√) True or False

(1) Mike is not interested in Korea.   T ☐ F ☐

(2) Mike wants to visit the places that he saw on TV.   T ☐ F ☐

(3) The woman is wondering how many places Mike will visit.   T ☐ F ☐

Listen and Speak 2 A-1

G: Dad, ❶do you mind if I change the channel?

M: ❷No, not at all.

G: Thank you. I need to watch a program about Norway.

M: Norway? Why?

G: Well, we're learning about Norway in class.

M: Oh, I ❸see.

G: 아빠, 제가 채널을 돌려도 될까요?
M: 물론이지.
G: 고마워요. 노르웨이에 대한 프로그램을 봐야 해서요.
M: 노르웨이? 왜?
G: 그게, 수업 시간에 노르웨이에 대해 배우고 있거든요.
M: 오, 그렇구나.

❶ 허락을 요청하는 표현(= I'm wondering if I could change the channel.)
❷ 'Do you mind ~?'에 대한 허락 표현(= Certainly not., Of course not., Go ahead.)
❸ '이해하다'라는 의미로 쓰임. (= understand)

Check(√) True or False

(4) Dad is watching TV now.   T ☐ F ☐

(5) The girl wants to learn about Norway for fun.   T ☐ F ☐

(6) Dad doesn't get the reason why she needs to change the channel.   T ☐ F ☐

Listen and Speak 1 A-2

B: April is the ❶worst month of the year.

G: ❷What makes you say so?

B: Flowers are blooming, but I ❸have to stay inside ❹to study for my exams.

G: Oh, ❺I know what you mean.

❶ bad의 최상급
❷ 이유를 묻는 표현(=Why is that?)
❸ '~해야 한다'
❹ to부정사의 부사적 용법 중 목적 (~하기 위해서)
❺ 상대의 말에 공감하거나 이해할 때 쓰는 표현

 Listen and Speak 2 A-2

M: Jane, ❶do you mind if I open the window?

W: Sorry, but I have a cold, and it's ❷pretty windy today.

M: O.K. No problem. ❸Would you like some hot tea? It'd be good for your cold.

W: That would be great. Thanks.

❶ 허락을 요청하는 표현
❷ '꽤'라는 의미의 부사
❸ 'Would you like ~?' 권유하는 말

 Communicate A

Jaden: Hi, Yuri, What're you doing?

Yuri: Hi, Jaden. I'm reading a book on Norse ❶ myths. I'm really into them these days.

Jaden: ❷What makes you like them so much?

Yuri: The stories are very interesting, and there are lots of movies about Norse myths.

Jaden: Are they ❸any good?

Yuri: Yes. There's actually a new movie about ❹ Thor, a famous god in Norse myths.

Jaden: Oh, I know him. He's my favorite online game character.

Yuri: ❺In that case, we should go see the movie together.

Jaden: ❻Do you mind if I borrow your book when you're finished? I want to read it before we see the movie.

Yuri: ❼No, not at all. I'm sure you'll like this book, too.

❶ myth: 신화(= mythology)
❷ 이유를 묻는 표현
❸ any: 부사로 부정문이나 의문문에서 형용사나 부사를 강조함
❹ 토르(북유럽 신화에서 천둥, 전쟁, 농업을 주관하는 신)
❺ 그렇다면, 그런 경우에는
❻ 'Do you mind if ~?' 허락을 요청하는 표현
❼ 'Do you mind if ~?'에 대한 긍정의 대답

 Progress Check 1

B: April is the best month of the year.

G: ❶What makes you say so?

B: The weather is not cold, and flowers are ❷ blooming.

G: I love April because my birthday is in April.

B: Really? We should ❸throw you a party.

❶ 이유를 묻는 표현
❷ bloom: (꽃이) 피다
❸ throw a party: 파티를 열다

 Progress Check 2

M: Excuse me, ❶do you mind if I take this chair? We need ❷one more.

W: ❸I'm sorry, but I'm waiting for my friend. She'll be here soon.

M: Oh, I see. Never mind.

W: You can ❹ask the waiter to bring more chairs.

❶ 'Do you mind if ~?' 허락을 요청하는 표현
❷ one more: 하나 더
❸ 허락을 요청하는 물음에 대한 거절의 표현
❹ ask+목적어+to부정사: 목적어에게 V하도록 요청하다

● 다음 우리말과 일치하도록 빈칸에 알맞은 말을 쓰시오.

Listen & Speak 1 A-1

W: Is _____ your first time _____ _____ Korea, Mike?

M: Yes, it _____. I've always _____ _____ _____ _____ Seoul.

W: _____ _____ you come here?

M: I'm really _____ Korean TV shows. I'm going to _____ _____ the places _____ _____ on TV.

W: _____ fun!

해석

W: 한국엔 처음 방문하는 거야, Mike?
M: 응. 나는 언제나 서울에 오고 싶었어.
W: 이곳에 온 이유가 뭐니?
M: 나는 한국의 TV 프로그램들을 정말 좋아해. TV에서 봤던 장소들에 갈 거야.
W: 재미있게 지내!

Listen & Speak 1 A-2

B: April is _____ _____ _____ _____ the year.

G: _____ makes you _____ so?

B: Flowers are _____, but I have to _____ _____ to study for my exams.

G: Oh, I know _____ _____ _____.

B: 4월은 1년 중 최악의 달이야.
G: 왜 그렇게 생각해?
B: 꽃은 피는데, 나는 시험 공부를 하느라 집에 있어야 해.
G: 오, 무슨 소린지 알겠어.

Listen & Speak 2 A-1

G: Dad, do you mind _____ _____ the channel?

M: No, _____ _____ _____.

G: Thank you. I need _____ _____ a program _____ Norway

M: Norway? _____?

G: Well, we're _____ _____ Norway in class.

M: Oh, I _____.

G: 아빠, 제가 채널을 돌려도 될까요?
M: 물론이지.
G: 고마워요. 노르웨이에 대한 프로그램을 봐야 해서요.
M: 노르웨이? 왜?
G: 그게, 수업 시간에 노르웨이에 대해 배우고 있거든요.
M: 오, 그렇구나.

Listen & Talk 2 A-2

M: Jane, do you _____ _____ _____ _____ the window?

W: Sorry, but I _____ _____ _____, and it's _____ windy today.

M: O.K. No problem. _____ _____ some hot tea? It'd be good for your cold.

W: That _____ _____ great. Thanks.

M: Jane, 내가 창문을 열어도 되겠니?
W: 미안, 내가 감기에 걸려서, 그리고 오늘 바람이 꽤 많이 불거든.
M: 그래. 괜찮아. 따뜻한 차 좀 줄까? 감기에 도움이 될 거야.
W: 그거 좋겠다. 고마워.

Communicate A

Jaden: Hi, Yuri, What're you _____?

Yuri: Hi, Jaden. I'm _____ a book _____ Norse myths. I'm really _____ _____ these days.

Jaden: _____ makes you _____ _____ so much?

Yuri: The stories are very _____, and there are _____ _____ movies about Norse myths.

Jaden: Are they _____ _____?

Yuri: Yes. There's actually a new movie _____ Thor, a _____ _____ in Norse myths.

Jaden: Oh, I know him. He's my _____ online game _____.

Yuri: _____ _____ _____, we should _____ _____ the movie together.

Jaden: Do you mind _____ _____ _____ your book when you're _____? I want to read _____ _____ we see the movie.

Yuri: No, not at all. I'm sure you'll _____ _____ _____, _____.

Progress Check 1

B: April is the best month _____ _____ _____.

G: What _____ you _____ so?

B: The weather is not cold, and _____ _____ _____.

G: I love April _____ my birthday is in April.

B: Really? We should _____ you _____ _____.

Progress Check 2

M: Excuse me, do you _____ _____ _____ _____ this chair? We need one _____.

W: I'm sorry, but I'm _____ _____ my friend. She'll be here _____.

M: Oh, I see. _____ _____.

W: You can _____ the waiter _____ _____ more chairs.

해석

Jaden: 안녕, 유리야. 뭐 하고 있니?
유리: 안녕, Jaden. 난 북유럽 신화들에 관한 책을 읽고 있어. 요즘 이 신화들에 정말 푹 빠졌어.
Jaden: 네가 그것들을 그렇게 좋아하게 만드는 게 뭐니?
유리: 이야기들이 정말 흥미롭고, 북유럽 신화에 대한 영화들도 많이 있거든.
Jaden: 영화들이 좀 괜찮니?
유리: 응. 사실 북유럽 신화에서 유명한 신인 Thor에 관한 새 영화가 나왔어.
Jaden: 오, 그를 알아. 그는 내가 제일 좋아하는 온라인 게임 캐릭터야.
유리: 그렇다면, 우린 같이 그 영화를 보러 가야겠다.
Jaden: 네가 네 책을 다 읽으면 내가 빌려도 될까? 우리가 그 영화를 보기 전에 그걸 읽고 싶어.
유리: 그럼, 당연하지. 너도 이 책을 좋아할 것이라고 확신해.

B: 4월은 1년 중 최고의 달이야.
G: 왜 그렇게 생각해?
B: 날씨도 춥지 않고, 꽃도 피어나잖아.
G: 나는 내 생일이 4월에 있어서 4월을 아주 좋아해.
B: 정말? 우리 너를 위해 파티를 열어야겠다.

M: 실례합니다. 제가 이 의자를 가져가도 괜찮을까요? 하나가 더 필요해서요.
W: 죄송합니다만, 제 친구를 기다리고 있어요. 곧 올 거예요.
M: 오, 그렇군요. 신경 쓰지 마세요.
W: 웨이터에게 의자를 더 가져다 달라고 부탁해 보세요.

01 다음 대화의 빈칸에 알맞은 것은?

> A: April is the worst month of the year.
> B: _____
> A: Flowers are blooming, but I have to stay inside to study for my exams.

① Who says like that?　② What makes you go there?
③ Why do you think it does?　④ What makes you say so?
⑤ How can you say like that?

02 다음 대화의 밑줄 친 부분과 바꾸어 쓸 수 있는 것은?

> M: Jane, <u>do you mind if I open the window?</u>
> W: Sorry, but I have a cold, and it's pretty windy today.

① do you want me to open the window?
② I'm wondering if I can open the window.
③ do you mind opening the door?
④ would it be alright if you open the window?
⑤ can I close the window?

[03~04] 다음 대화의 빈칸에 알맞은 것을 고르시오.

> G: Dad, do you mind ___(A)___ I change the channel?
> M: No, not at all.
> G: Thank you. I need to watch a program about Norway.
> M: Norway? Why?
> G: Well, we're learning about Norway in class.
> M: Oh, I see.

03 다음 중 빈칸 (A)에 들어갈 말로 가장 적절한 것은?

① what　② that　③ if　④ why　⑤ how

04 What is the girl learning about in class? Answer in English with a full sentence.

➡ _____

01 다음 대화의 빈칸에 들어갈 말로 가장 적절한 것은?

> A: I want to visit Iceland.
> B: _____
> A: I want to see the northern lights.

① What made you go there?
② Why do you want to see her?
③ What makes you want to go there?
④ How do you get there?
⑤ What brings you here?

[02~04] 다음 대화를 읽고 물음에 답하시오.

> G: @Dad, do you mind if I change the channel?
> M: No, not at all.
> G: Thank you. I need to watch a program about Norway.
> M: Norway? Why?
> G: Well, we're learning about Norway in class.
> M: Oh, I see.

02 밑줄 친 @의 의미로 가장 적절한 것은?

① 통보하기 　② 길 묻기 　③ 허락 구하기
④ 동의하기 　⑤ 거절하기

 위 대화의 내용과 일치하지 <u>않는</u> 것은?

① The girl needs to change the channel.
② The man doesn't allow his daughter to change the channel.
③ There is a reason why the girl needs to change the channel.
④ The man is wondering why his daughter needs to watch the program.
⑤ The man understands why his daughter wants to change the channel.

서답형

04 Write the reason why the girl needs to change the channel. Use the phrase 'It's because.'

➡ _____

_____

[05~06] 다음 대화를 읽고 물음에 답하시오.

> (A) What makes you say so?
> (B) Oh, I know what you mean.
> (C) April is the worst month of the year.
> (D) Flowers are @blooming, but I have to stay inside to study for my exams.

서답형

05 자연스러운 대화가 되도록 (A)~(D)를 바르게 배열하시오.

➡ _____

06 다음 중 밑줄 친 @를 대신하여 쓸 수 있는 말은?

① beautiful 　　② exciting
③ opening 　　④ coloring
⑤ closing

다음 대화의 빈칸에 들어갈 말로 알맞지 <u>않은</u> 것은?

> A: Do you mind if I sit here?
> B: _____
> A: Oh, thanks.

① Certainly not.
② No, not at all.
③ Sure, go ahead.
④ Yes, I do.
⑤ Of course not.

[08~10] 다음 대화를 읽고 물음에 답하시오.

M: Jane, ⓐdo you mind if I open the window?

W: Sorry, but I have a cold, and ⓑ오늘은 바람이 꽤 불어.

M: O.K. No problem. Would you like some hot tea? It'd be good for your cold.

W: That would be great. Thanks.

08 다음 중 밑줄 친 ⓐ를 대신하여 쓸 수 있는 것은?

① do you want to open the window?

② is it okay to close the window?

③ can you open the window?

④ don't you want to close the window?

⑤ would it be alright if I open the window?

서답형

09 주어진 단어를 활용하여 밑줄 친 우리말 ⓑ를 영어로 쓰시오.

(it / pretty)

➡ _____

중요

10 What is the man likely to do after the conversation?

① He will bring Jane a blanket.

② He will open the window.

③ He will make some hot tea for Jane.

④ He will bring some cold tea.

⑤ He will go see a doctor.

[11~13] 다음 대화를 읽고 물음에 답하시오.

Jaden: Hi, Yuri, ①What're you doing?

Yuri: Hi, Jaden. I'm reading a book on Norse myths. I'm really into them these days.

Jaden: What makes you like them so much?

Yuri: ②The stories are very interesting, and there are lots of movies about Norse myths.

Jaden: ③Are they any good?

Yuri: Yes. There's actually a new movie about Thor, a famous god in Norse myths.

Jaden: Oh, ④I know him. He's my favorite online game character.

Yuri: In that case, we should go see the movie together.

Jaden: Do you mind if I borrow your book when you're finished? I want to read it before we see the movie.

Yuri: ⑤I'm afraid I do. I'm sure you'll like this book, too.

서답형

11 ①~⑤ 중 대화의 흐름상 어색한 것을 바르게 고쳐 쓰시오.

_____ ➡ _____

서답형

12 According to the dialogue, what does Jaden want to do before he sees the movie? Answer in English with a full sentence.

➡ _____

_____

중요

13 위 대화의 내용과 일치하는 것은?

① Yuri is not interested in Norse myths at all.

② There are few movies about Norse myths.

③ Yuri is watching a movie about Thor.

④ Jaden likes Norse myths so much.

⑤ Jaden wants Yuri to lend her book to him.

[01~02] 다음 대화를 읽고 물음에 답하시오.

> W: Is it your first time to visit Korea, Mike?
> M: Yes, it is. I've always wanted to come to Seoul.
> W: What made you come ⓐhere?
> M: I'm really into Korean TV shows. I'm going to go to the places I saw on TV.
> W: Have fun!

01 밑줄 친 ⓐ가 가리키는 것을 위 대화에서 찾아 쓰시오.

➡ _____

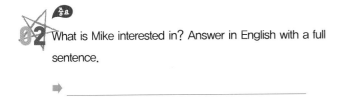

What is Mike interested in? Answer in English with a full sentence.

➡ _____

[03~04] 다음 대화를 읽고 물음에 답하시오.

> M: Excuse me, _____(A)_____?
> We need one more.
> W: I'm sorry, but I'm waiting for my friend. She'll be here soon.
> M: Oh, I see. Never mind.
> W: You can ask the waiter to bring more chairs.

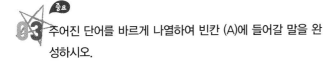

주어진 단어를 바르게 나열하여 빈칸 (A)에 들어갈 말을 완성하시오.

(mind / chair / take / if / you / do / this / I)

➡ _____

04 What is the man likely to do after the conversation?

➡ _____

05 자연스러운 대화가 되도록 (A)~(D)를 바르게 나열하시오.

> (A) O.K. No problem. Would you like some hot tea? It'd be good for your cold.
> (B) Jane, do you mind if I open the window?
> (C) That would be great. Thanks.
> (D) Sorry, but I have a cold, and it's pretty windy today.

➡ _____

[06~07] 다음 대화를 읽고 물음에 답하시오.

> B: April is the best month of the year.
> G: What ____ⓐ____ you ____ⓑ____ so?
> B: The weather is not cold, and flowers are blooming.
> G: I love April because my birthday is in April.
> B: Really? We should ____ⓒ____ you a party.

06 주어진 단어를 빈칸 ⓐ~ⓒ에 각각 쓰시오. 필요하다면 어형을 바꾸시오.

(throw / say / make)

➡ ⓐ _____ ⓑ _____ ⓒ _____

07 Write the reason why the boy thinks April is the best month of the year. Use the phrase 'It's because.'

➡ _____

Grammar
교과서

① It is[was] ~ that 강조구문

- **It was** a hammer **that** they liked most. 그들이 가장 좋아했던 것은 (바로) 망치였다.
- **It was** in Seoul **that** the concert by BTS took place.
  방탄 소년단의 콘서트가 개최된 것은 (바로) 서울에서였다.

■ It+be동사+[명사]+that+불완전한 절: 주어, 목적어인 명사를 강조한다.

- **Steve** invented **the machine**.
  → It was **Steve** that invented the machine. 그 기계를 발명한 것은 (바로) Steve였다.
  → It was **the machine** that Steve invented. Steve가 발명한 것은 (바로) 그 기계였다.

■ It+be동사+[부사(구/절)]+that+완전한 절: 부사(구/절)를 강조한다.

- I met her at the party when she was visiting New York.
  → It was **at the party** that I met her when she was visiting New York.
    그녀가 New York을 방문 중이었을 때, 내가 그녀를 만난 것은 (바로) 파티에서였다.
  → It was **when she was visiting New York** that I met her at the party.
    파티에서 내가 그녀를 만난 것은, (바로) 그녀가 New York을 방문 중이었을 때였다.

■ 'It ~ that' 강조구문에서 강조 대상이 명사일 경우, that을 관계대명사 who(사람일 경우) 또는 which(사물이나 동물일 경우)로 대체할 수 있다.

- Dr. King took care of my ants.
  → **It was** Dr. King **that[who]** took care of my ants. 나의 개미들을 돌봤던 이는 (바로) King 박사였다.
  → **It was** my ants **that[which]** Dr. King took care of. King 박사가 돌봤던 것은 (바로) 나의 개미들이었다.

핵심 Check

1. 다음 괄호 안에서 알맞은 단어를 고르시오.

   (1) It was Susan's car (who / which) Rooney bought last week.

   (2) It was at the theater (that / which) Mom met Daddy for the first time.

② '계속적 용법'의 관계대명사 which / who

- The first treasure was for Odin, **who** had only one eye.
  첫 번째 보물은 Odin을 위한 것이었는데, 그는 눈이 하나뿐이었다.

- This is the novel *Animal Farm*, **which** everyone should read.
  이것은 소설 동물 농장인데, 모든 사람이 이 책을 읽어야 한다.

■ 계속적 용법은 형태상으로 콤마(,)를 쓰며, 관계대명사가 받는 '선행사의 범위'가 다르다.

  • I have two friends **who** are good at playing soccer. - 콤마(×), 축구를 잘하는 친구 두 명(친구들이 더 많을
  수 있다)을 지칭 → 제한적 용법

  • I have two friends, **who** are good at playing soccer. - 콤마(○), 친구들이 두 명 있는데(친구들은 두 명뿐),
  그들은 축구를 잘한다. → 계속적 용법

■ 계속적 용법의 관계대명사는 '접속사+대명사'로 전환 가능하다. (and, but, for, though 등)

  • I purchased a monitor, **which** was broken.

    = I purchased a monitor, **but** it was broken. 나는 모니터 한 대를 구매했지만, 그것은 고장났다.

  • My son has always had many worries, **most of which** were silly.

    = My son has always had many worries, **and most of them** were silly.
    내 아들은 늘 많은 걱정을 해왔는데, 그것들 대부분은 한심한 것들이었다.

■ 선행사는 앞에 나온 명사, 대명사뿐 아니라, 구, 절, 앞 문장 전체 등이 모두 가능하다.

  • Michelle tried to solve the problem, **which** I was proud of.

    = Michelle tried to solve the problem, **and** I was proud of **that**. Michelle은 그 문제를 해결하려고 애썼는데,
    나는 그것을 자랑스럽게 여겼다. → 선행사는 앞 문장 전체(Michelle이 노력한 일)이며, '접속사 and와 대명사 it/that'으
    로 받을 수 있다.

  • It is good for the students not to give up their dream, **which** a few think to be natural.

    = It is good for the students not to give up their dream, though a few think it to be natural. 학생
    들이 자신들의 꿈을 포기하지 않는 것은 좋은 일이다. 비록 소수의 학생들이 그것[꿈을 포기하지 않는 것]이 당연하다
    고 생각하지만 → 선행사는 not to give up their dream이며, 문맥상 '접속사 though와 대명사 it'으로 받을 수 있다.

■ that, what은 계속적 용법으로 쓸 수 없고, '전치사+관계대명사'는 관계부사로 바꿀 수 있다.

  • We visited the house, **which** Einstein once lived in. 우리는 그 집을 방문했는데, 그 집은 Einstein이 한 때 살았었다.

    = We visited the house, **in which** Einstein once lived. (= , **where**)

핵심 Check

2. 다음 괄호 안에서 알맞은 단어를 고르시오.

(1) She worked hard day and night, (that / which) made her a success.

(2) His parents only praise his sisters, (which / who) makes him angry.

01 다음 문장에서 어법상 <u>어색한</u> 단어를 한 개씩만 찾아 고치시오.

(1) Let me see the pictures which you took them in London.

_____ ➡ _____

(2) Karl and his wife, whom I met in Seoul, is going to leave today.

_____ ➡ _____

(3) Robert mentioned her problem, that made her sad.

_____ ➡ _____

(4) Lucy's younger sister, Sue, who age is 3, is a clever girl.

_____ ➡ _____

02 다음 중 어법상 바르지 <u>않은</u> 것은?

① It was David who broke the computer yesterday.
② It was in October that the girl first saw the fireworks.
③ It was four years ago that Chris wrote that novel.
④ It is when people praise his talent that the actor feels happy.
⑤ It was the bus that Sam lost his watch.

03 다음 빈칸에 들어갈 말로 알맞은 것은?

I like the girl, _____ has recently changed her hair style.

① she   ② which   ③ that
④ who   ⑤ what

04 다음 문장의 밑줄 친 부분을 강조하여 문장을 다시 쓰시오.

Veronika has always wanted to have <u>those necklaces</u>.

➡ _____

01 다음 중 어법상 어색한 것을 모두 골라 기호를 쓰고 알맞게 고치시오.

> ⓐ My mom grows some herb plants in the living room, which produce good scent.
> ⓑ Those are the houses, where they lived in.
> ⓒ My cat, Mimi, has odd eyes, that have beautiful blue and brown colors.
> ⓓ Tom bought a horse, which run quite fast.
> ⓔ I don't know the way which she got accepted to Harvard University.

➡ _____

_____

02 다음 중 밑줄 친 부분의 쓰임이 나머지와 다른 것은?

① It was the bathroom light <u>that</u> Maggie turned off this morning.
② It is my cat Lulu <u>that</u> always cries out too loud for my family to sleep.
③ I supported Paul's plan <u>that</u> Kevin should join his rugby club.
④ It was at the market <u>that</u> Elsa bought the stationery.
⑤ It was Juliet <u>that</u> met the mayor at the party last weekend.

서답형

03 다음 대화의 문맥에 맞게 괄호 안에 주어진 단어를 강조하는 'It ~ that' 구문의 문장을 영작하시오. (7 단어)

> Father: Did you tear the newspaper?
> Jonathan: No, _____. (Tom)

➡ _____

04 다음 중 어법상 어색한 문장은?

① His wife, whom he loves dearly, is young and beautiful.
② I don't know where my bag is, which was put on the table a minute ago.
③ Sarah had her car fixed by the mechanic, who cost her lots of money.
④ The crowd applauded the little girl playing the piano, which was touching.
⑤ Sumin helped the old lady cross the street, who had trouble walking fast.

서답형

05 다음 '가'와 '나'에서 서로 관련된 표현을 찾아 관계대명사 또는 관계부사를 사용하여 한 문장으로 완성하시오. ('나'의 순서대로)

가	• I learned Chinese from Lily. • All villagers in town like the bridge. • They will go to Jagalchi market. • There lived a hero named Hercules.
나	• It was built 100 years ago. • She made me speak freely in Beijing. • He was the son of Zeus. • They will buy fresh seafood there.

➡ (1) _____

_____

(2) _____

_____

(3) _____

_____

(4) _____

_____

[06~07] 다음 중 'It ~ that'의 쓰임이 나머지 넷과 <u>다른</u> 것은?

06 ① It was my twin brother that you saw in that picture.

② It was 20 years ago that Mr. Berkins came here to settle down.

③ It is certain that Sandra fell in love with the stranger at a glance.

④ It was on her way home that Sophia bought the food which made her sick.

⑤ It was a shirt that Matthew's aunt made for his graduation ceremony.

07 ① It is playing the online game that Nicholas usually enjoys in his free time.

② It was no wonder that Brandon got fired from his company.

③ It was in Daniel's garage that the secret meeting was held.

④ It was Comet Halley that I happened to witness last night.

⑤ It was an hour ago that the train Tom was on left for New York.

08 다음 중 어법상 <u>어색한</u> 문장은?

① The professor called Sam Hamington, who didn't answer right away.

② Bill Gates invented the operating program, which made him rich.

③ The Simpsons moved to Springfield, where their first baby Bart was born.

④ Cooper met his wife in 2002, which the world cup was held in Seoul.

⑤ My parents like this restaurant, which is known for the special pork dish.

09 다음 문장의 빈칸 (A)~(C)에 들어갈 말로 가장 적절한 것은?

• The car had a wheel, ___(A)___ let it run faster than people thought.

• Tiffany's aunt lives in Los Angeles, ___(B)___ became a jewelry designer last year.

• My family was having a party with a couple from another city, ___(C)___ had two daughters.

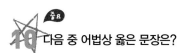

	(A)	(B)	(C)
①	which	who	which
②	who	who	who
③	that	who	which
④	that	which	who
⑤	which	who	who

10 다음 중 어법상 옳은 문장은?

① Jordan is a famous athlete, who often come to Korea to eat *Bulgogi*.

② There is a chair in the room, of which is made of iron.

③ It was raining, that made me stay all day long.

④ The film, which I borrowed from the library, was so boring.

⑤ The president announced that he would resign, who was shocking to me.

서답형

11 다음 우리말을 조건에 맞게 영작하시오.

나의 삼촌들은 Sarah를 아는데, 그녀는 중국어를 원어민처럼 말한다.
(like, speak, a native 사용, 반드시 총 10단어로 영작할 것)

➡ _____

_____

서답형

12 다음 그림을 보고 아래의 대화가 자연스럽게 이뤄지도록 주어진 단어를 모두 활용하여 문장을 완성하시오. (단어들 중 1 단어만 변형할 것.)

> Mom: Has anyone done something to my flower? I think someone must have watered them too much.
>
> Kathy: _____. (Jonathan / responsible / care / for / it / the flower / take / is / is / of / who)

➡ _____

_____

13 다음 중 밑줄 친 that의 쓰임이 나머지와 다른 하나는?

① It was in this spaghetti that Peter put the Vietnamese spice by mistake.

② It was his mom's laptop that Yumi's little brother broke this morning.

③ It is in 2019 that the movie *Parasite* won the Best Picture Award.

④ It is my puppy Momo that wakes my daddy up every day.

⑤ His wife concealed the fact that he was seriously ill.

14 다음 중 어법상 올바른 문장의 개수는?

> ⓐ I met the girl living next door, and who had the refrigerator fixed.
>
> ⓑ Brian asked his sister to clean her desk, which were messy with pieces of paper.
>
> ⓒ Sophia watched the boys dancing on the street, that led her to decide to be a dancer.

> ⓓ The man helped an old lady to cross the street, who was a rare thing nowadays.
>
> ⓔ It was her boss which got Emily to pick up the delivered box.
>
> ⓕ It was my puppy that bit Abigail's toe.
>
> ⓖ Stephen was wounded in the leg, which was the reason he wasn't on time.

① 1개　② 2개　③ 3개　④ 4개　⑤ 5개

15 다음 중 밑줄 친 that을 다른 단어로 대체하여 바꿔 쓸 수 없는 문장은?

① It was the drug dealer that met the FBI agent last night.

② It is no wonder that the team finally made a successful contract.

③ It was the robot arm that carried out the difficult operation.

④ That is the house that I spoke of the other day.

⑤ This is not the book that I am looking for.

16 다음 중 어법상 어색한 문장을 모두 고르시오.

① We respect Mother Theresa, who devoted her whole life to poor people.

② I visited a traditional market in Busan, which sell fresh seafood.

③ Soyeon recently attended Mr. King's lecture, who was impressive.

④ Cathy is proud of her mother, who is good at dancing.

⑤ My sister read the letter, that made all of us cry.

01 다음 문장의 밑줄 친 부분을 강조하여, 각각 It으로 시작하는 문장으로 바꾸어 쓰시오.

> Lucas is going to wear a mask at the
> (A)   (B)   (C)
> party this weekend.

⇒ (A) _____

_____

(B) _____

_____

(C) _____

_____

02 다음 문장에 대한 각 질문에 'It ~ that' 강조 구문을 사용하여 답하시오. 답할 수 없는 질문은 '답변 불가'라고 쓰시오.

> Ellen had Grace's car repaired at the shop three weeks ago.

(1) Who repaired Grace's car?

⇒ _____

(2) Who got Grace's car repaired?

⇒ _____

_____

(3) When did Ellen have Grace's car repaired?

⇒ _____

_____

(4) For how many weeks did it take to repair Grace's car?

⇒ _____

_____

(5) Where was Grace's car repaired three weeks ago?

⇒ _____

_____

03 다음 각 문장에서 어법상 어색한 부분을 모두 찾아 바르게 고치시오. 단, 강조구문 자체가 어색할 경우, 전체를 다시 쓰시오.

(1) It was the auditorium that the girls were watching a musical.

⇒ _____

(2) It was my coworker's mistake who she didn't recognize.

⇒ _____

(3) It was chairman of the council who Anthony was.

⇒ _____

(4) It was the evening that the band gave a street performance at Hongdae street.

⇒ _____

(5) It was carefully that he rescued the injured.

⇒ _____

04 다음 문장을 관계대명사의 계속적 용법을 이용하여 한 문장으로 만드시오.

(1) • All the people there were so selfish.
    • It made the two parties even farther away.

⇒ _____

_____

(2) • Thomas is widely known for dancing.
    • But it is not true.

⇒ _____

_____

(3) • Emma fell in love with Alex.
    • Emma met him only once.

⇒ _____

_____

05 강조구문을 이용하여 다음 주어진 문장과 뜻이 같도록 빈칸을 알맞게 채우시오.

> January 20, 1993 was the day Audrey Hepburn was dead.
> → It was _____ dead.

➡ _____

06 다음 각 문장에서 어법상 <u>어색한</u> 부분을 한 곳씩 찾아 <u>모두</u> 고치시오.

(1) Genie's father allowed her to meet the handsome guy, that made her so happy.

_____ ➡ _____

(2) Susan was practicing the ballet movement, who was very important to her.

_____ ➡ _____

(3) The customs officers don't have all the baggage checked, but which is ordinary.

_____ ➡ _____

(4) The English teacher praised Dylan, which he made feel good.

_____ ➡ _____

07 다음 〈보기〉와 같이 두 문장이 같은 의미가 되도록 관계대명사 또는 관계부사를 활용하여 영작하시오.

> ┤ 보기 ├
> I met Irene, but she said nothing about it.
> → I met Irene, who said nothing about it.

(1) The teacher blamed Susan, though she didn't mean to be late.

➡ _____
_____

(2) Jackson's father looked a lot younger than she thought, but Jackson was ashamed of it.

➡ _____
_____

(3) Almost everyone in the factory stops working at noon, and they go out for lunch then.

➡ _____

(4) Isabella received a letter of apology from her boyfriend, but she hasn't opened it yet.

➡ _____

(5) Bentley's family went to Mexico, and they saw some Mayan ruins there.

➡ _____
_____

08 다음 그림을 보고, 우리말에 맞게 괄호 안의 단어를 활용하여 영작하시오.

> Camila는 아빠와 함께 15장이 넘는 팬케이크를 만들었는데, 그것은 너무나 재미있었다.
> (make, be, over, so, with, dad, pancake, her, fun, which 등 반드시 사용, 변형 가능, 총 12단어)

➡ _____
_____

Treasures for Three Gods

Important Norse Gods

고유명사 뒤에 쉼표와 함께 쓰이는 who: 관계대명사의 계속적
용법으로 바로 앞의 사람에 대한 추가적인 설명을 덧붙일 때 쓴다.

Odin, <u>who</u> is the highest god, gave up his eye for wisdom. Thor is

Odin's son and the strongest god of all. Frey, <u>who is the god of the</u>

Frey controls the weather.라는 문장에 He is the god of the harvest.를 삽입한 형태.

<u>harvest</u>, controls the weather. Loki is a god who plays tricks on <u>others</u>.

= other people

Thor <u>woke</u> and <u>knew</u> immediately <u>something was wrong</u>. His wife's

　　V1　　　V2　　　　　　앞에 접속사 that 생략

beautiful golden hair <u>was gone</u>. He knew only Loki could do <u>such</u> a

사라졌다　　knew 뒤에는 접속사 that이 생략　such. so. really: 다른 어구를 강조하는
역할을 한다.

terrible thing. Thor soon found Loki, <u>who</u> was drinking at home.

= and he

"You'd better undo what you did, or you'll be sorry," Thor said

You had better의 축약된 표현.　what은 선행사를 포함하는　명령문 뒤에 쉼표와 함께　'후회하다'
'~하는 편이 좋다.'　관계대명사: '~한 것'　쓰이는 or: '그렇지 않으면'

angrily to Loki.

Loki was scared. He promised <u>that</u> he would get golden hair for

명사절을 이끄는 접속사

Thor's wife.

Loki knew only the sons of Ivaldi could make fine golden hair. He

went to <u>them</u> and said, "I heard Brokk and his brother are the finest

the sons of Ivaldi　　'…라고 하던데': 전해 들은 것을 전달하는 표현

smiths. Is that true?"

treasure 보물

give up 포기하다

wisdom 지혜, 슬기, 현명함

harvest 수확, 수확물; 수확하다, 거둬들이다

trick 장난, 묘기

play tricks on ~에게 농간을 부리다, ~에게 장난을 치다

wake 잠에서 깨다 (wake–woke–woken)

immediately 즉시, 곧

golden 금빛의

had better (= 'd better) ~하는 편이 좋다

undo 원상태로 돌리다

scared 두려워하는, 겁먹은

promise 약속하다

📎 확인문제

● 다음 문장이 본문의 내용과 일치하면 T, 일치하지 않으면 F를 쓰시오.

1 Odin gave up his eye for wisdom. ☐

2 Frey is a god who plays tricks on others. ☐

3 Thor's wife's beautiful golden hair was gone. ☐

4 Thor didn't know who could do such a terrible thing. ☐

5 Loki promised that he would get golden hair for Thor's wife. ☐

6 Loki didn't know who could make fine golden hair. ☐

"No, it is we who are the finest smiths," the sons of Ivaldi replied.
'It is ~ that …'을 사용한 강조 구문. It is와 that[who/which] 사이에 강조하고자 하는 말을 넣는다.

"They're making three treasures for Odin, Thor, and Frey," said Loki.

"Do you think you can make treasures better than theirs?"
'Brokk 형제의 보물들'을 가리키는 소유대명사

"Of course we can," they answered.

"O.K., then you should also make three treasures for them," said

Loki. "The gods will decide on the best treasure."
decide on: '~에 관해 결정을 하다'   the: 최상급 형용사 앞에 붙는 한정사

Loki also told them that one of the treasures had to be golden hair.
'주어+tell+목적어+that 구문'   must의 과거형

They went to work immediately.
= at once

Loki then went to see Brokk and his brother. "Ivaldi's sons are

making three treasures for Odin, Thor, and Frey," said Loki. "I bet that
= I am certain (that): '내 의견으로는 틀림없이 ~할 것이다'

you can never make treasures as fine as theirs."
as … as ~: '~만큼 …한', 형용사 원급을 사용하여 두 대상을 비교하는 구문

Brokk became angry and accepted the challenge. He and his brother
angrily(×)

produced three treasures of their own.
'그들 자신의'

Loki went to see the three gods with all the treasures. Brokk came
~을 가지고

along. Loki showed them the treasures from Ivaldi's sons. The first
수여동사

treasure was for Odin, who had only one eye. It was a spear that never
선행사에 대한 추가적인 정보를 주는 절에 사용하며, '접속사+대명사(and he)'의 의미   주격 관계대명사, 앞에 오는 명사 a spear를 수식

missed its target. The second treasure was a big ship that could turn
주격 관계대명사, 앞에 오는 명사 a big ship을 수식

into a piece of cloth. It was for Frey.

fine	질 좋은, 좋은
smith	대장장이, 금속 세공인 (= blacksmith)
reply	대답하다
bet	단언하다
accept	받아들이다, 수락하다
challenge	도전, 결투 신청
produce	만들어 내다, 제조하다
come along	함께 가다, 동행하다
spear	창
target	목표, 표적
piece	조각, 일부, 한 가지

 확인문제

● 다음 문장이 본문의 내용과 일치하면 T, 일치하지 않으면 F를 쓰시오.

1 The sons of Ivaldi replied that they were the finest smiths. ☐

2 The sons of Ivaldi should make three treasures for Loki. ☐

3 Loki told the sons of Ivaldi that one of the treasures had to be golden hair. ☐

4 Brokk and his brother refused to accept the challenge. ☐

5 Loki went to see the three gods with all the treasures. ☐

6 The first treasure for Odin was a big ship that could turn into a piece of cloth. ☐

The third treasure was for Thor. Loki showed Thor the flowing
<u>수여동사</u>   <u>I.O.</u>

golden hair for his wife. Thor put the hair on his wife's head, and it
<u>D.O.</u>   the hair를 가리킨다.

took root and became real hair.
'뿌리를 내렸다'

It was now Brokk's turn to show the gods his gifts. He gave Odin
turn을 꾸며 주며, '보여 줄 차례'라는 의미.   show+I.O.(the gods)+D.O.(his gifts)'   <u>I.O.</u>

a gold arm ring that produced eight more gold rings every ninth night.
<u>D.O.</u>: ~에게 ···를 주다'   '아홉 번째 밤이 될 때마다' = every nine nights

Brokk then gave Frey a pig. It could pull his carriage faster than any
                                                '비교급+than any (other)+단수 명사'(최상급의 뜻).
                                                any: 비교 대상이 같은 그룹에 속해 있지 않은 경우

horse.   any other: 비교 대상이 같은 그룹에 속한 경우

"My third treasure is for you, Thor," said Brokk. "This is the hammer
                                                                콤마(,) which로 연결되는 관계대명사절: 앞의 명사.

Mjolnir, which you'll love. If you throw it, it'll always come back to
앞 문장 전체에 대한 추가적인 설명을 할 때 사용된다.   if는 조건을 나타내는 접속사, 미래시제 대신 현재시제를 사용한다.

you. Moreover, nothing can ever break it."

It was an easy decision to choose the greatest treasure. It was Mjolnir
가주어   진주어   It was ~that 강조구문

that the three gods liked most. They thought the hammer would

protect the gods from their enemies.
protect A from B: B로부터 A를 보호하다

"Brokk and his brother," said Odin, "are the better smiths."
                            of the two가 생략되어 있고, of the two가 있는 경우 비교급 앞에 the를 쓴다.

Brokk proved that Loki was wrong, and the three gods now had

precious treasures.

---

flowing 흐르는 듯한, 유창한, 미끈하게 처진

take root 뿌리를 내리다, 정착하다

pull 끌다, 당기다

carriage 마차, 객차

hammer 망치

moreover 게다가

decision 결정, 판결

protect 지키다, 보호하다

enemy 적, 적군 (pl. enemies)

prove 증명하다

precious 귀중한, 값어치 있는

📎 **확인문제**

● 다음 문장이 본문의 내용과 일치하면 T, 일치하지 <u>않으면</u> F를 쓰시오.

1 Loki showed Thor the flowing golden hair for his wife. ☐

2 Brokk gave Odin a gold arm ring that produced nine more gold rings every eighth

   night. ☐

3 The pig that Brokk gave Frey could pull his carriage faster than any horse. ☐

4 If Thor throws Mjolnir, it will never come back to him. ☐

5 The three gods liked Mjolnir most. ☐

6 Brokk proved that Loki was right. ☐

● 우리말을 참고하여 빈칸에 알맞은 말을 쓰시오.

1 _____ for Three Gods

2 **Important** _____ **Gods**

3 Odin, who is the _____ god, _____ _____ his eye for wisdom.

4 Thor is Odin's son and _____ _____ _____ of all.

5 Frey, who is the god of the harvest, _____ _____ _____ .

6 Loki is a god who _____ _____ others.

7 Thor woke and knew immediately _____ _____ _____ .

8 His wife's beautiful golden hair _____ _____ .

9 He knew only Loki could do _____ _____ _____ .

10 Thor soon found Loki, _____ _____ _____ at home.

11 "_____ _____ _____ what you did, or you'll be sorry," Thor said angrily to Loki.

12 Loki was _____ .

13 He promised that he _____ _____ golden hair for Thor's wife.

14 Loki knew only the sons of Ivaldi could make _____ _____ _____ .

15 He went to them and said, "I heard Brokk and his brother are _____ _____ _____ . Is that true?"

16 "No, _____ _____ we _____ are the finest smiths," the sons of Ivaldi replied.

1 세 명의 신을 위한 보물

2 북유럽 신화의 주요 신들

3 Odin은 가장 높은 신이며, 지혜를 위해 한쪽 눈을 포기했다.

4 Thor는 Odin의 아들이며 모든 신들 중에서 가장 강한 신이다.

5 Frey는 수확의 신으로 날씨를 다스린다.

6 Loki는 다른 신들에게 농간을 부리는 신이다.

7 Thor는 잠에서 깨어 즉시 무엇인가가 잘못되었다는 것을 알았다.

8 그의 아내의 아름다운 금발머리가 사라졌다.

9 그는 오직 Loki만이 이런 끔찍한 일을 할 수 있다는 것을 알고 있었다.

10 Thor는 곧 Loki를 찾았는데, 그는 집에서 술을 마시고 있었다.

11 "네가 한 짓을 되돌려 놓는 것이 좋을 거야, 그렇지 않으면 후회하게 될 거다." Thor는 노하여 Loki에게 말했다.

12 Loki는 겁이 났다.

13 그는 Thor의 아내를 위해 금발머리를 얻어 오겠다고 약속했다.

14 Loki는 Ivaldi의 아들들만이 훌륭한 금발머리를 만들 수 있다는 것을 알고 있었다.

15 그는 그들에게 가서 "내가 듣기로 Brokk와 그의 남동생이 가장 훌륭한 대장장이라고 하던데. 그것이 사실인가?"라고 말했다.

16 "아니요, 가장 훌륭한 대장장이는 바로 우리들이요." Ivaldi의 아들들이 대답했다.

17 "They're making _____ _____ for Odin, Thor, and Frey," said Loki.

18 "Do you think you can make treasures _____ _____ _____?"

19 "_____ _____ we can," they answered.

20 "O.K., then you should also _____ three treasures _____ _____," said Loki.

21 "The gods will _____ _____ the best treasure."

22 Loki also told them that one of the treasures _____ _____ _____ golden hair.

23 They went to work _____.

24 Loki then _____ _____ _____ Brokk and his brother.

25 "Ivaldi's sons _____ _____ three treasures _____ Odin, Thor, and Frey," said Loki.

26 "_____ _____ that you can never make treasures _____ _____ _____ _____."

27 Brokk became angry and _____ _____ _____.

28 He and his brother produced three treasures _____ _____ _____.

29 Loki went to see the three gods _____ _____ _____ _____.

30 Brokk _____ _____.

31 Loki _____ them the treasures _____ Ivaldi's sons.

32 The first treasure was _____ Odin, who had _____ _____.

33 _____ _____ a spear _____ never missed its target.

---

17 "그들은 Odin과 Thor와 Frey를 위해서 보물을 만들고 있네." Loki는 말했다.

18 "너희들이 그들의 보물보다 더 나은 보물을 만들 수 있다고 생각하는가?"

19 "물론 할 수 있소." 그들이 대답했다.

20 "좋아, 그러면 너희도 그들을 위해 세 개의 보물을 만들어야 한다." Loki가 말했다.

21 "그 신들이 가장 훌륭한 보물을 결정할 것이다."

22 Loki는 또한 그들에게 보물 중 하나는 금발머리이어야 한다고 말했다.

23 그들은 즉시 일에 착수했다.

24 Loki는 그 다음에 Brokk와 그의 남동생을 보러 갔다.

25 "Ivaldi의 아들들이 Odin과 Thor, 그리고 Frey를 위해 세 개의 보물을 만들고 있어." Loki가 말했다.

26 "너희들은 절대 그들의 보물만큼 훌륭한 보물을 만들 수 없다는 것을 내 장담하지."

27 Brokk는 화가 나서 그 도전을 받아들였다.

28 그와 그의 남동생은 그들만의 세 가지 보물을 만들었다.

29 Loki는 모든 보물을 가지고 세 신을 만나러 갔다.

30 Brokk가 같이 갔다.

31 Loki는 그들에게 Ivaldi의 아들들이 만든 보물들을 보여 주었다.

32 첫 번째 보물은 Odin을 위한 것으로, 그는 눈이 한쪽밖에 없었다.

33 그것은 목표물을 절대로 빗나가지 않는 창이었다.

34 The second treasure was a big ship that could _____ _____ a piece of cloth.

35 It was _____ Frey.

36 _____ _____ _____ was for Thor.

37 Loki showed Thor the _____ _____ _____ for his wife.

38 Thor _____ the hair _____ his wife's head, and it _____ _____ and became real hair.

39 It was now _____ _____ to show the gods his gifts.

40 He gave Odin a gold arm ring that produced _____ _____ gold rings _____ _____ _____.

41 Brokk then gave _____ _____ _____.

42 It could pull his carriage _____ _____ _____ _____.

43 "_____ _____ _____ is for you, Thor," said Brokk.

44 "This is the hammer Mjolnir, _____ you'll love.

45 If you throw it, it'll always _____ _____ _____ you.

46 Moreover, nothing can ever _____ _____."

47 It was an easy decision to choose _____ _____ _____.

48 It was Mjolnir that _____ _____ _____ _____ _____.

49 They thought the hammer would _____ the gods _____ their enemies.

50 "Brokk and his brother," said Odin, "are _____ _____ _____."

51 Brokk _____ that Loki was wrong, and the three gods now had _____ _____.

34 두 번째 보물은 천 조각으로 변할 수 있는 큰 배였다.

35 그것은 Frey를 위한 것이었다.

36 세 번째 보물은 Thor를 위한 것이었다.

37 Loki는 Thor에게 그의 아내를 위한 매끈하게 늘어진 금발머리를 보여 주었다.

38 Thor가 그 머리카락을 그의 아내의 머리에 얹었더니 그것이 뿌리를 내려서 진짜 머리카락이 되었다.

39 이제 Brokk가 신들에게 그의 선물들을 보여 줄 차례였다.

40 그는 Odin에게 아홉 번째 밤이 될 때마다 8개의 금팔찌를 더 만들어 내는 금팔찌를 주었다.

41 그러고 나서 Brokk는 Frey에게 돼지를 한 마리 주었다.

42 그것은 어떤 말보다도 그의 마차를 더 빨리 끌 수 있었다.

43 "나의 세 번째 보물은 당신을 위한 것입니다. Thor." Brokk가 말했다.

44 "이것은 몰니르라는 망치인데 당신은 마음에 드실 겁니다.

45 그것을 던지면, 그것은 항상 당신에게 되돌아 올 것입니다.

46 게다가, 그 무엇도 이것을 부술 수 없지요."

47 가장 훌륭한 보물을 선택하는 것은 쉬운 결정이었다.

48 세 명의 신들이 가장 마음에 든 것은 몰니르였다.

49 그들은 그 망치가 신들을 그들의 적들로부터 보호해 줄 것이라고 생각했다.

50 "Brokk와 그의 남동생이 더 훌륭한 대장장이다." Odin이 말했다.

51 Brokk는 Loki가 틀렸다는 것을 증명해 냈고, 세 신들은 이제 소중한 보물을 가지게 되었다.

● 우리말을 참고하여 본문을 영작하시오.

1 세 명의 신을 위한 보물

➡ _____

2 북유럽 신화의 주요 신들

➡ _____

3 Odin은 가장 높은 신이며, 지혜를 위해 한쪽 눈을 포기했다.

➡ _____

4 Thor는 Odin의 아들이며 모든 신들 중에서 가장 강한 신이다.

➡ _____

5 Frey는 수확의 신으로 날씨를 다스린다.

➡ _____

6 Loki는 다른 신들에게 농간을 부리는 신이다.

➡ _____

7 Thor는 잠에서 깨어 즉시 무엇인가가 잘못되었다는 것을 알았다.

➡ _____

8 그의 아내의 아름다운 금발머리가 사라졌다.

➡ _____

9 그는 오직 Loki만이 이런 끔찍한 일을 할 수 있다는 것을 알고 있었다.

➡ _____

10 Thor는 곧 Loki를 찾았는데, 그는 집에서 술을 마시고 있었다.

➡ _____

11 "네가 한 짓을 되돌려 놓는 것이 좋을 거야, 그렇지 않으면 후회하게 될 거다." Thor는 노하여 Loki에게 말했다.

➡ _____

12 Loki는 겁이 났다.

➡ _____

13 그는 Thor의 아내를 위해 금발머리를 얻어 오겠다고 약속했다.

➡ _____

14 Loki는 Ivaldi의 아들들만이 훌륭한 금발머리를 만들 수 있다는 것을 알고 있었다.

➡ _____

15 그는 그들에게 가서 "내가 듣기로 Brokk와 그의 남동생이 가장 훌륭한 대장장이라고 하던데, 그것이 사실인가?"라고 말했다.

➡ _____

16 "아니요, 가장 훌륭한 대장장이는 바로 우리들이요." Ivaldi의 아들들이 대답했다.

➡ _____

17 "그들은 Odin과 Thor와 Frey를 위해서 보물을 만들고 있네." Loki는 말했다.

➡ _____

18 "너희들이 그들의 보물보다 더 나은 보물을 만들 수 있다고 생각하는가?"

➡ _____

19 "물론 할 수 있소." 그들이 대답했다.

➡ _____

20 "좋아, 그러면 너희도 그들을 위해 세 개의 보물을 만들어야 한다." Loki가 말했다.

➡ _____

21 "그 신들이 가장 훌륭한 보물을 결정할 것이다."

➡ _____

22 Loki는 또한 그들에게 보물 중 하나는 금발머리이어야 한다고 말했다.

➡ _____

23 그들은 즉시 일에 착수했다.

➡ _____

24 Loki는 그 다음에 Brokk와 그의 남동생을 보러 갔다.

➡ _____

25 "Ivaldi의 아들들이 Odin과 Thor, 그리고 Frey를 위해 세 개의 보물을 만들고 있어." Loki가 말했다.

➡ _____

26 "너희들은 절대 그들의 보물만큼 훌륭한 보물을 만들 수 없다는 것을 내 장담하지."

➡ _____

27 Brokk는 화가 나서 그 도전을 받아들였다.

➡ _____

28 그와 그의 남동생은 그들만의 세 가지 보물을 만들었다.

➡ _____

29 Loki는 모든 보물을 가지고 세 신을 만나러 갔다.

➡ _____

30 Brokk가 같이 갔다.

➡ _____

31 Loki는 그들에게 Ivaldi의 아들들이 만든 보물들을 보여 주었다.

➡ _____

32 첫 번째 보물은 Odin을 위한 것으로, 그는 눈이 한쪽밖에 없었다.

➡ _____

33 그것은 목표물을 절대로 빗나가지 않는 창이었다.

➡ _____

34 두 번째 보물은 천 조각으로 변할 수 있는 큰 배였다.

➡ _____

35 그것은 Frey를 위한 것이었다.

➡ _____

36 세 번째 보물은 Thor를 위한 것이었다.

➡ _____

37 Loki는 Thor에게 그의 아내를 위한 매끈하게 늘어진 금발머리를 보여 주었다.

➡ _____

38 Thor가 그 머리카락을 그의 아내의 머리에 얹었더니 그것이 뿌리를 내려서 진짜 머리카락이 되었다.

➡ _____

39 이제 Brokk가 신들에게 그의 선물들을 보여 줄 차례였다.

➡ _____

40 그는 Odin에게 아홉 번째 밤이 될 때마다 8개의 금팔찌를 더 만들어 내는 금팔찌를 주었다.

➡ _____

41 그러고 나서 Brokk는 Frey에게 돼지를 한 마리 주었다.

➡ _____

42 그것은 어떤 말보다도 그의 마차를 더 빨리 끌 수 있었다.

➡ _____

43 "나의 세 번째 보물은 당신을 위한 것입니다, Thor." Brokk가 말했다.

➡ _____

44 "이것은 묠니르라는 망치인데 당신은 마음에 드실 겁니다.

➡ _____

45 그것을 던지면, 그것은 항상 당신에게 되돌아 올 것입니다.

➡ _____

46 게다가, 그 무엇도 이것을 부술 수 없지요."

➡ _____

47 가장 훌륭한 보물을 선택하는 것은 쉬운 결정이었다.

➡ _____

48 세 명의 신들이 가장 마음에 든 것은 묠니르였다.

➡ _____

49 그들은 그 망치가 신들을 그들의 적들로부터 보호해 줄 것이라고 생각했다.

➡ _____

50 "Brokk와 그의 남동생이 더 훌륭한 대장장이야." Odin이 말했다.

➡ _____

51 Brokk는 Loki가 틀렸다는 것을 증명해 냈고, 세 신들은 이제 소중한 보물을 가지게 되었다.

➡ _____

[01~04] 다음 글을 읽고 물음에 답하시오.

Important _ⓐ_ Gods

Odin, who is the highest god, gave up his eye for wisdom.

Thor is Odin's son and the strongest god of all.

Frey, who is the god of the harvest, controls the weather.

Loki is a god who plays tricks _ⓑ_ others.

Thor woke and knew immediately something was wrong. His wife's beautiful golden hair was gone. He knew only Loki could do such a terrible thing. Thor soon found Loki, who was drinking at home.

"You'd better undo what you did, or you'll be sorry," Thor said angrily to Loki.

Loki was scared. He promised that he would get golden hair _ⓒ_ Thor's wife.

서답형

01 주어진 영영풀이를 참고하여 빈칸 ⓐ에 철자 N으로 시작하는 단어를 쓰시오.

> 1. belonging or relating to Scandinavian countries in medieval times
> 2. of or relating to Norway or its people or culture or language

➡ _____

02 위 글의 빈칸 ⓑ와 ⓒ에 들어갈 전치사가 바르게 짝지어진 것은?

   ⓑ   ⓒ   ⓑ   ⓒ
① for – to   ② in – for
③ on – for   ④ for – from
⑤ on – from

중요

03 이야기의 구성 단계 중에서 본문의 내용이 속하는 단계를 고르시오.

① 발단   ② 전개
③ 위기   ④ 설정
⑤ 결말

04 According to the passage, which is NOT true?

① Odin is the highest god and gave up his eye for wisdom.
② Thor, who is Odin's son, is the strongest god of all.
③ Frey is the god of the harvest and controls the weather.
④ Thor's wife's beautiful golden hair was gone.
⑤ Thor promised that he would get his wife golden hair.

[05~07] 다음 글을 읽고 물음에 답하시오.

Loki knew only the sons of Ivaldi could make fine golden hair. He went to ①them and said, "I heard Brokk and his brother are the finest smiths. Is that true?"

ⓐ"No, it is we who is the finest smiths," the sons of Ivaldi replied.

"②They're making three treasures for Odin, Thor, and Frey," said Loki. "Do you think you can make treasures better than theirs?"

"Of course ③we can," they answered.

"O.K., then ④you should also make three treasures for them," said Loki. "The gods will decide on the best treasure."

Loki also told ⑤them that ⓑ보물 중 하나는 금발머리이어야 한다. They went to work immediately.

05 밑줄 친 ①~⑤ 중에서 가리키는 대상이 나머지 넷과 다른 것은?

①   ②   ③   ④   ⑤

06 위 글의 밑줄 친 @에서 어법상 틀린 부분을 찾아 고치시오.

_____ ➡ _____

07 위 글의 밑줄 친 ⓑ의 우리말에 맞게 9단어로 영작하시오.

➡ _____

[08~10] 다음 글을 읽고 물음에 답하시오.

Loki then went to see Brokk and his brother. "Ivaldi's sons are making three treasures for Odin, Thor, and Frey," said Loki. "(A)I bet that you can never make treasures ___@___ fine ___ⓑ___ theirs."
Brokk became angry and accepted (B)the challenge. He and his brother produced three treasures of their own.

08 위 글의 빈칸 @와 ⓑ에 공통으로 들어갈 알맞은 단어를 쓰시오.

➡ _____

09 위 글의 밑줄 친 (A)I bet that과 바꿔 쓸 수 없는 말을 모두 고르시오.

① It is certain that   ② I am sure that

③ It is doubtful if   ④ It is unlikely that

⑤ I am certain that

10 위 글의 밑줄 친 (B)the challenge가 가리키는 내용을 동명사를 포함하여 영어로 쓰시오.

➡ _____

[11~14] 다음 글을 읽고 물음에 답하시오.

Loki went to see the three gods with all the treasures. Brokk came along. Loki showed them the treasures from Ivaldi's sons. The first treasure was for Odin, who had only one eye. It was a spear that never missed its target. The second treasure was a big ship that could turn into a piece of cloth. It was for Frey. The third treasure was for Thor. Loki showed Thor the flowing golden hair for his wife. Thor put the hair on his wife's head, and it took root and became real hair.
It was now Brokk's turn to show the gods his gifts. He gave Odin a gold arm ring that produced eight more gold rings (A)every ninth night. Brokk then gave Frey a pig. It could pull his carriage faster than any horse.
"My third treasure is for you, Thor," said Brokk. "This is the hammer Mjolnir, ___@___ you'll love. If you throw it, it'll always come back to you. ___ⓑ___, nothing can ever break it."
It was an easy decision to choose the greatest treasure. It was Mjolnir that the three gods liked most. They thought the hammer would protect the gods from their enemies.
"Brokk and his brother," said Odin, "are the better smiths."
Brokk proved that Loki was wrong, and the three gods now had precious treasures.

11 빈칸 @에 들어갈 알맞은 말을 쓰시오.

➡ _____

서답형

12 빈칸 ⓑ에 들어갈 알맞은 말을 고르시오.

① However ② Moreover

③ Therefore ④ In other words

⑤ For example

서답형

13 위 글의 밑줄 친 (A)를 다음과 같이 바꿔 쓸 때 빈칸에 들어갈 알맞은 단어를 쓰시오.

➡ every _____ nights

14 위 글의 제목으로 알맞은 것을 고르시오.

① How to Make Treasures for Three Gods

② What Treasures Did Ivaldi's Sons Make?

③ What Is the Greatest Treasure Shown to the Gods?

④ What Treasures Did Brokk and His Brother Make?

⑤ Who Made Treasures in the Norse Myths?

[15~17] 다음 글을 읽고 물음에 답하시오.

Important Norse Gods

Odin, who is the highest god, gave up his eye for wisdom.

Thor is Odin's son and the strongest god of all.

Frey, who is the god of the harvest, controls the weather.

Loki is a god who plays tricks on others.

Thor woke and knew (A)immediately something was wrong. His wife's beautiful golden hair was gone. He knew only Loki could do such a terrible thing. Thor soon found Loki, who was drinking at home.

"You'd better _____ⓐ_____, or you'll be sorry," Thor said angrily to Loki.

Loki was scared. He promised that he would get golden hair for Thor's wife.

15 위 글의 빈칸 ⓐ에 들어갈 알맞은 말을 고르시오.

① repeat what you did

② not play tricks on others

③ undo what you did

④ have the hair removed

⑤ not drink heavily

16 위 글의 밑줄 친 (A)immediately와 바꿔 쓸 수 없는 말을 고르시오.

① instantly ② at once

③ right away ④ gradually

⑤ without delay

17 Which question CANNOT be answered after reading the passage?

① Who is the highest god?

② Who is the strongest god of all?

③ Who is the god of the harvest?

④ What does Frey control?

⑤ Why does Loki play tricks on others?

[18~20] 다음 글을 읽고 물음에 답하시오.

Loki knew only the sons of Ivaldi could make fine golden hair. He went to them and said, "I heard Brokk and his brother are the finest smiths. Is that true?"

"No, ⓐit is we who are the finest smiths," the sons of Ivaldi replied.

"They're making three treasures for Odin, Thor, and Frey," said Loki. "Do you think you can make treasures better than theirs?"

"Of course we can," they answered.

"O.K., then you should also make three treasures for them," said Loki. "The gods will decide on the best treasure."

ⓑLoki also told them that one of the treasure had to be golden hair. They went to work immediately.

18 위 글의 밑줄 친 ⓐit과 문법적 쓰임이 같은 것을 고르시오.

① Was it yesterday that you met him?
② Have you seen it already?
③ It is said that the earth is round.
④ How's it going with you?
⑤ I think it necessary that you should do it at once.

서답형

19 위 글의 밑줄 친 ⓑ에서 어법상 틀린 부분을 찾아 고치시오.

_____ ➡ _____

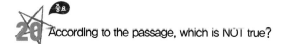

20 According to the passage, which is NOT true?

① Loki knew that the sons of Ivaldi could make fine golden hair.
② The sons of Ivaldi didn't agree that Brokk and his brother were the finest smiths.
③ Loki said that Brokk and his brother were making three treasures for him.
④ The sons of Ivaldi said that they could make treasures better than Brokk and his brother's.
⑤ The sons of Ivaldi went to work on the spot.

[21~24] 다음 글을 읽고 물음에 답하시오.

Loki went to see the three gods with all the treasures. Brokk came along. Loki showed them the treasures from Ivaldi's sons. The first treasure was for Odin, who had only one eye. It was a spear that never ⓐmissed its target. The second treasure was a big ship that could turn into a piece of cloth. It was for Frey. The third treasure was for Thor. Loki showed Thor the flowing golden hair for his wife. Thor put the hair on his wife's head, and it took root and became real hair.

It was now Brokk's turn to show the gods his gifts. He gave Odin a gold arm ring that produced eight more gold rings every ninth night. Brokk then gave Frey a pig. ⓑIt could pull his carriage faster than any horse.

"My third treasure is for you, Thor," said Brokk. "This is the hammer Mjolnir, which you'll love. If you throw it, it'll always come back to you. (①) Moreover, nothing can ever break it." (②)

It was an easy decision to choose the greatest treasure. (③) They thought the hammer would protect the gods from their enemies. (④)

"Brokk and his brother," said Odin, "are the better smiths." (⑤)

Brokk proved that Loki was wrong, and the three gods now had precious treasures.

21 위 글의 밑줄 친 ⓐmissed와 같은 의미로 쓰인 것을 고르시오.

① He completely missed the joke.
② It was an opportunity not to be missed.
③ You missed a good party last night.
④ She will be greatly missed when she leaves.
⑤ The bullet missed her by about six inches.

22 위 글의 밑줄 친 ⓑ와 의미가 같지 <u>않은</u> 문장을 <u>모두</u> 고르시오.

① No horse could pull his carriage so fast as it.

② Any horse could pull his carriage as fast as it.

③ No horse could pull his carriage faster than it.

④ Any horse could pull his carriage faster than it.

⑤ No horse could pull his carriage as fast as it.

23 위 글의 흐름으로 보아, 주어진 문장이 들어가기에 가장 적절한 곳은?

> It was Mjolnir that the three gods liked most.

①　　　②　　　③　　　④　　　⑤

24 According to the passage, which is NOT true?

① The first treasure from Ivaldi's sons for Odin was a spear.

② The treasures for Frey were a big ship and a gold arm ring.

③ The treasure from Ivaldi's sons for Thor was the flowing golden hair for his wife.

④ The treasure from Brokk for Thor was Mjolnir.

⑤ The three gods liked Mjolnir most.

[25~27] 다음 글을 읽고 물음에 답하시오.

Loki knew only the sons of Ivaldi could make fine golden hair. He went to them and said, "I heard ①<u>Brokk and his brother</u> are the finest smiths. Is that true?"

"No, it is we who are the finest smiths," the sons of Ivaldi replied.

"②<u>They</u>'re making three treasures for Odin, Thor, and Frey," said Loki. "Do you think you can make treasures better than theirs?"

"Of course we can," they answered.

"O.K., then you should also make three treasures for them," said Loki. "The gods will decide on the best treasure."

Loki also told them that one of the treasures had to be golden hair. They went to work immediately.

Loki then went to see Brokk and his brother. "③<u>Ivaldi's sons</u> are making three treasures for Odin, Thor, and Frey," said Loki. "I bet that ④<u>you</u> can never make treasures as fine as theirs."

Brokk became angry and accepted the challenge. He and his brother produced three treasures of ⑤<u>their</u> own.

서답형

25 밑줄 친 ①~⑤ 중에서 가리키는 대상이 나머지 넷과 <u>다른</u> 것은?

①　　　②　　　③　　　④　　　⑤

26 위 글에서 알 수 있는 Loki의 성격으로 가장 알맞은 것을 고르시오.

① sincere　　② cunning　　③ arrogant

④ generous　　⑤ patient

서답형

27 다음 빈칸 (A)와 (B)에 알맞은 단어를 넣어 Loki가 Ivaldi의 아들들에게 Brokk와 그의 남동생을 언급한 이유를 완성하시오.

> Loki wanted (A)_____ _____ _____, which only the sons of Ivaldi could make. Thus, he mentioned Brokk and his brother to make the sons of Ivaldi feel a sense of rivalry and accept (B)_____ _____.

[01~03] 다음 글을 읽고 물음에 답하시오.

Important Norse Gods

Odin, who is the highest god, gave up his eye for wisdom.

ⓐThor is Odin's son and the strongest god of all.

Frey, who is the god of the harvest, controls the weather.

Loki is a god who plays tricks on others.

Thor woke and knew immediately something was wrong. His wife's beautiful golden hair was (A)[disappeared / gone]. He knew only Loki could do ⓑsuch a terrible thing. Thor soon found Loki, who was drinking at home.

"You'd better undo ⓒwhat you did, or you'll be sorry," Thor said (B)[angry / angrily] to Loki.

Loki was (C)[scaring / scared]. He promised that he would get golden hair for Thor's wife.

01 위 글의 괄호 (A)~(C)에서 어법상 알맞은 낱말을 골라 쓰시오.

➡ (A) _____ (B) _____ (C) _____

02 밑줄 친 ⓐ를 다음과 같이 바꿔 쓸 때 빈칸에 들어갈 알맞은 말을 두 단어로 쓰시오.

➡ Thor is Odin's son and _____ _____ any other god.

03 위 글의 밑줄 친 ⓑ와 ⓒ가 공통으로 가리키는 내용을 우리말로 쓰시오.

➡ _____

[04~06] 다음 글을 읽고 물음에 답하시오.

Loki knew only the sons of Ivaldi could make fine golden hair. He went to them and said, "I heard Brokk and his brother are the finest smiths. Is that true?"

"No, it is we who are the finest smiths," the sons of Ivaldi replied.

"They're making three treasures for Odin, Thor, and Frey," said Loki. "Do you think you can make treasures better than (A)theirs?"

"Of course we can," they answered.

"O.K., then you should also make three treasures for them," said Loki. "The gods will decide ___ⓐ___ the best treasure."

Loki also told them that one of the treasures had to be golden hair. They went to work immediately.

04 빈칸 ⓐ에 들어갈 알맞은 전치사를 쓰시오.

➡ _____

05 위 글의 밑줄 친 (A)theirs가 가리키는 것을 영어로 쓰시오.

➡ _____

06 위 글의 내용을 다음과 같이 정리하고자 한다. 빈칸에 compete를 알맞은 형태로 쓰시오.

> The Loki triggered* the _____ spirit of the sons of Ivaldi to have them make fine golden hair. *trigger: 촉발시키다

[07~09] 다음 글을 읽고 물음에 답하시오.

Loki went to see the three gods with all the treasures. Brokk came along. Loki showed them the treasures from Ivaldi's sons. The first treasure was for Odin, who had only one eye. It was a spear that never missed its target. The second treasure was a big ship that could turn into a piece of cloth. It was for Frey. The third treasure was for Thor. Loki showed Thor the flowing golden hair for his wife. Thor put the hair on his wife's head, and it took root and became real hair.

It was now Brokk's turn to show the gods his gifts. He gave Odin a gold arm ring that produced eight more gold rings every ninth night. Brokk then gave Frey a pig. It could pull his carriage faster than any horse.

"My third treasure is for you, Thor," said Brokk. "This is the hammer Mjolnir, which you'll love. If you throw it, it'll always come back to you. Moreover, nothing can ever break it."

It was an easy decision to choose the greatest treasure. It was Mjolnir that the three gods liked most. They thought the hammer would protect the gods from their enemies.

"Brokk and his brother," said Odin, "are the better smiths."

Brokk proved that Loki was wrong, and the three gods now had precious treasures.

07 다음 빈칸 (A)~(C)에 알맞은 단어를 넣어 Ivaldi의 아들들이 세 명의 신을 위해 만든 보물들을 소개하시오.

> Ivaldi's sons made (A)_____ _____ for Odin, (B)_____ _____ _____ for Frey, and (C)_____ _____ _____ _____ for Thor's wife.

08 What treasure did the three gods like most? Answer in English in a full sentence. (4 words)

➡ _____

09 Between 'Ivaldi's sons' and 'Brokk and his brother', which did Odin think were the better smiths? Answer in English in a full sentence.

➡ _____

_____

[10~12] 다음 글을 읽고 물음에 답하시오.

Important Norse Gods

Odin, who is the highest god, gave up his cyc for wisdom.

Thor is Odin's son and the strongest god of all.

Frey, who is the god of the harvest, controls the weather.

Loki is a god who plays tricks on others.

Thor woke and knew immediately something was wrong. His wife's beautiful golden hair was gone. He knew only Loki could do such a terrible thing. Thor soon found Loki, ⓐwho was drinking at home.

"You'd better undo what you did, or you'll be sorry," Thor said angrily to Loki.

Loki was scared. He promised that ⓑhe would get golden hair for Thor's wife.

10 본문의 내용과 일치하도록 다음 빈칸에 알맞은 단어를 쓰시오.

> Odin is the highest god and got his wisdom at the expense of _____ _____.

11 위 글의 밑줄 친 ⓐ를 접속사를 사용하여 두 단어로 고치시오.

➡ _____

12 위 글의 밑줄 친 ⓑ를 4형식 문장으로 고치시오.

➡ _____

교과서

구석구석

After You Read A

(1) Loki took the beautiful golden hair of Thor's wife, so Thor became angry
그래서
at him. Loki promised to get golden hair for Thor's wife.
getting(×)

(2) Loki asked the sons of Ivaldi to make three treasures for Odin, Thor, and
ask+목적어+to부정사
Frey. He also had Brokk and his brother produce three treasures for the
have+사람+동사원형: A가 B를 하도록 시키다
gods. Loki bet that Ivaldi's sons would make better treasures.
단언했다

(3) Loki showed the three gods the treasures from Ivaldi's sons.
→ (3형식) showed the treasures from Ivaldi's sons to the three gods
They were a spear, a big ship, and golden hair. The treasures from Brokk
The treasures from Ivaldi's sons
and his brother were a gold arm ring, a pig, and a hammer.

(4) The gods liked the hammer most. They each had their own precious
The gods   They와 동격
treasures.

구문해설 • golden: 금빛의 • promise: 약속하다 • bet: 단언하다 • produce: 만들어 내다, 제조하다
• spear: 창 • hammer: 망치 • precious: 귀중한, 값어치 있는

Link – Create

I have always been friends with Sif, who is the wife of the strongest god. A
└ 현재완료(계속) ┘   관계대명사(계속적 용법)
few days ago, I cut her golden hair just for fun, and her husband became angry
at me. I came up with a good idea to get her hair back. I asked the sons of
부정사 형용사적 용법 (idea 수식)
Ivaldi to make fine golden hair.
목적격보어

구문해설 • just for fun: 단지 재미로 • come up with: ~을 생각해 내다 • get back: 되돌리다

Culture Project

The Strongest Gods and Heroes in the World
strong의 최상급
Hercules, who was the son of Zeus, is famous for his many adventures.
주격 관계대명사(계속적 용법)
Brave and powerful Hercules killed the Nemean lion and wore the lion's skin
네메아의 사자   wear의 과거(and로 killed와 병렬)
as a coat. He also fought the many-headed Hydra. I think it is Hercules who is
전치사(~으로)   It ~ that[who] 강조   = that
the strongest hero in the world.

구문해설 • be famous for ~으로 유명하다 • brave: 용감한 • powerful: 강력한 • skin: 가죽, 피부
• many-headed: 머리가 여럿달린 • Hydra: 히드라(머리가 9개 달린 뱀)

해석

(1) Loki가 Thor의 아내의 아름다운 금발머리를 가져가서, Thor는 그에게 화가 났다. Loki는 Thor의 아내를 위해 금발머리를 얻어 오겠다고 약속했다.

(2) Loki는 Ivaldi의 아들들에게 Odin과 Thor와 Frey를 위해서 보물을 만들어 달라고 부탁했다. 그는 또한 Brokk와 그의 남동생에게 신들을 위한 세 개의 보물을 만들게 시켰다. Loki는 Ivaldi의 아들들이 더 훌륭한 보물을 만들 것이라고 장담했다.

(3) Loki는 세 명의 신들에게 Ivaldi의 아들들이 만든 보물들을 보여 주었다. 그것들은 창과 큰 배와 금발머리였다. Brokk와 그의 남동생이 만든 보물들은 금팔찌와 돼지 한 마리와 망치였다.

(4) 신들이 가장 마음에 든 것은 망치였다. 그들은 각자 그들의 소중한 보물을 가지게 되었다.

나는 가장 강한 신의 아내인 Sif와 항상 친구로 지내왔다. 며칠 전에 나는 그녀의 금발을 단지 재미로 잘랐고 그녀의 남편은 나에게 화가 났다. 나는 그녀의 머리를 되돌릴 좋은 생각이 났다. 나는 Ivaldi의 아들들에게 훌륭한 금발머리를 만들어 달라고 부탁했다.

세상에서 가장 강한 신들과 영웅들

제우스의 아들인 헤라클레스는 그의 많은 모험들로 유명하다. 용감하고 강한 헤라클레스는 네메아의 사자를 죽이고, 그 가죽을 외투로 입었다. 그는 또한 머리가 여러 개 달린 히드라와 싸웠다. 나는 헤라클레스가 세상에서 가장 강한 영웅이라고 생각한다.

100 Lesson 2. Timeless Tales of Gods and Heroes

영역별 핵심문제

01 다음 빈칸에 공통으로 들어갈 말로 가장 적절한 것은?

- It will _____ root.
- I _____ a walk every morning.
- Why don't you _____ a break?

① get   ② make   ③ take
④ help   ⑤ have

02 다음 중 짝지어진 단어의 관계가 다른 하나는?

① immediate – immediately
② actual – actually
③ easy – easily
④ friend – friendly
⑤ precious – preciously

03 다음 중 밑줄 친 단어의 뜻풀이가 잘못된 것은?

① You need to accept her apology. (받아들이다)
② She will prove it true. (증명하다)
③ We need more cloth to make it. (옷)
④ The book is full of mysterious stories. (신비로운)
⑤ She made the decision. (결정)

04 다음 영영풀이에 해당하는 단어를 쓰시오.

to choose to do something, after having thought carefully about other possibilities

➡ _____

05 주어진 문장의 밑줄 친 단어와 같은 의미로 쓰인 것은?

The sale prices were too good to miss.

① We will miss you when you leave.
② Don't miss meals when you study.
③ We may miss your joke.
④ You should not miss the opportunity.
⑤ When did you first miss the watch?

06 다음 문장의 빈칸에 들어갈 말을 〈보기〉에서 골라 알맞은 형태로 쓰시오.

┌─ 보기 ┤
be gone / come along / turn into
└─

(1) The money in the safe _____ _____ the other day.
(2) Please _____ _____ with me. I need some help with my bag.
(3) The milk _____ _____ cheese, so I ate it.

07 주어진 단어를 활용하여 다음 우리말을 영어로 쓰시오.

(1) 너는 어떻게 그 아이디어를 생각해 냈니? (come)
➡ _____
(2) 너의 여동생에게 장난치지 마라. (play / little)
➡ _____
(3) 그는 대장장이로 유명해요. (famous)
➡ _____

Conversation

08 주어진 단어를 활용하여 다음 밑줄 친 우리말을 영어로 쓰시오.

> A: Oh, you have a guitar. I really like to play it. 내가 그것을 연주해 봐도 되겠니? (mind / play) (7 words)
> B: Sure, go ahead.

➡ _____

09 Choose an UNnatural dialogue.

① A: Do you mind if I use your phone?
  B: Certainly not.
② A: What made you come here?
  B: I came here to visit my uncle.
③ A: Is it okay if I turn the radio on?
  B: Of course.
④ A: I think the movie is a disaster.
  B: Why do you say so?
⑤ A: Would you mind if I go home early?
  B: Sure, I do.

10 자연스러운 대화가 되도록 (A)~(E)를 바르게 나열한 것은?

> (A) The weather is not cold, and flowers are blooming.
> (B) What makes you say so?
> (C) Really? We should throw you a party.
> (D) April is the best month of the year.
> (E) I love April because my birthday is in April.

① (B) – (C) – (A) – (E) – (D)
② (D) – (B) – (A) – (E) – (C)
③ (D) – (E) – (B) – (A) – (C)
④ (E) – (A) – (B) – (C) – (D)
⑤ (E) – (B) – (A) – (D) – (C)

[11~12] 다음 대화를 읽고 물음에 답하시오.

> M: Excuse me, _____(A)_____ We need one more.
> W: I'm sorry, but I'm waiting for my friend. She'll be here soon.
> M: Oh, I see. Never mind.
> W: You can ask the waiter to bring more chairs.

11 다음 중 빈칸 (A)에 들어갈 말로 적절하지 않은 것은?

① do you mind if I take this chair?
② is it okay if I take this chair?
③ would you like to take this chair?
④ I'm wondering if I can take this chair.
⑤ would it be alright if I take this chair?

12 Write the reason why the woman doesn't allow the man to take the chair. Use the phrase 'It's because.'

➡ _____
  _____

13 다음 대화를 읽고 답할 수 있는 것은?

> W: Is it your first time to visit Korea, Mike?
> M: Yes, it is. I've always wanted to come to Seoul.
> W: What made you come here?
> M: I'm really into Korean TV shows. I'm going to go to the places I saw on TV.
> W: Have fun!

① Where is Mike from?
② Where are Mike and the woman now?
③ What is Mike interested in?
④ How many places is Mike going to visit?
⑤ How long is Mike going to stay in Korea?

Grammar

14 다음 중 어법상 올바른 문장은?

① The person on the far left of the picture is my father, which is the smartest one in the world.

② Samantha had three sons, that all became politicians.

③ Paparazzi, what is the plural form of paparazzo, is now an ordinary term around the world.

④ A word derived from a person's name is sandwich, which was the name of the 4th Earl of Sandwich.

⑤ My friends were envious of my bag what my aunt bought me from Italy.

15 다음 중 우리말을 영작한 것이 어색한 것을 고르면?

① 어젯밤 만화방에서 Peter를 만난 사람은 바로 Victoria였다.
→ It was Victoria that met Peter at the comic book cafe last night.

② 엄마가 아빠를 처음 만난 것은 바로 엄마가 고등학교 신입생 때였다.
→ It was when she was a highschool freshman that Mom first met Dad.

③ Steve Jobs가 Apple Computer를 설립한 해는 1976년이었다.
→ It was 1976 that Steve Jobs founded Apple Computer.

④ 그 버스를 고장낸 것은 Damian이었다.
→ It was Damian that broke the bus.

⑤ 오늘 아침에 그녀가 교장선생님께 받은 것은 바로 하버드 대학교 입학 통지서였다.
→ It was an acceptance letter to Harvard that she received from the principal this morning.

16 다음 중 성격이 다른 한 문장을 고르시오.

① It was my daddy and I that saw a clown juggling at the amusement park.

② It was a clown that was juggling with red balls on the platform.

③ It was on the platform that a clown was performing the show.

④ It was exciting that my daddy and I watched a clown at the amusement park.

⑤ It was my daddy that was holding me up to watch the clown.

17 다음 중 밑줄 친 부분의 쓰임이 〈보기〉와 같지 않은 것은?

┌ 보기 ┐
Joey hired new employees in spite of the financial crisis, which worsened the situation.
└────┘

① The seafood, which you ordered for me, tasted fantastic.

② Tom saw the sports complex building, which had a central heating system.

③ Charlie had difficulty choosing which employee he would give awards to.

④ Simon was trying to stay awake, which was to no avail in the end.

⑤ We bought the blue car which Mom had always wanted to get.

[18~19] 주어진 우리말을 알맞게 영작할 때 어법상 <u>어색한</u> 문장을 하나 고르시오.

18

> Pual은 Ailey가 어제 산 책과 매우 비슷한 책을 한 권 가지고 있다.

① Paul has a book, and it is very similar to the one what Ailey bought yesterday.
② Paul has a book, which is very similar to the one which Ailey bought yesterday.
③ Paul has a book very similar to the one that Ailey bought yesterday.
④ Paul has a book, which is very similar to what Ailey bought yesterday.
⑤ Paul has a book, and it is very similar to the one that Ailey bought yesterday.

19

> Stella가 운동을 싫어한다는 것을 그녀의 다섯 명의 친구들 모두 알고 있다.

① Stella doesn't like exercise, and all of her five friends know it.
② Stella doesn't like exercise, which all of her five friends know.
③ All of her five friends know that Stella doesn't like exercise.
④ Stella doesn't like exercise, and all five of whose friends know it.
⑤ Stella has five friends, all of whom know she doesn't like exercise.

20 다음 중 밑줄 친 <u>that</u>의 쓰임이 나머지와 <u>다른</u> 하나는?

① It was on the white snow <u>that</u> my pet dogs left their footprints.
② It is so important <u>that</u> you should never forget it.
③ It was last year <u>that</u> you graduated from Munwha elementary school.
④ It was the persuasion skill <u>that</u> made me a lot of money.
⑤ It was the shrimp pizza <u>that</u> my daddy often cooked for me.

21 다음 중 어법상 <u>어색한</u> 문장은?

① This is Sam's book published a month ago, which I've read 4 times.
② Has anyone seen my pen, which was on the desk?
③ Patrick was talking about New York, which is his wife's home city.
④ Everybody voted for Clara, which she was proud of.
⑤ The kids in your kindergarten like Sonia's English class, which are fun.

Reading

[22~23] 다음 글을 읽고 물음에 답하시오.

Loki knew only the sons of Ivaldi could make fine golden hair. He went to them and said, "I heard Brokk and his brother are the finest ____ⓐ____. Is that true?"

"No, it is we who are the finest ____ⓑ____," the sons of Ivaldi replied.

"They're making three treasures for Odin, Thor, and Frey," said Loki. "Do you think you can make treasures better than theirs?"

"Of course we can," they answered.

"O.K., then you should also make three treasures for them," said Loki. "The gods will decide on the best treasure."

Loki also told them that one of the treasures had to be golden hair. They went to work immediately.

22 주어진 영영풀이를 참고하여 빈칸 ⓐ와 ⓑ에 공통으로 들어갈 단어를 철자 s로 시작하여 쓰시오.

> people who work in metal, especially those who shape metal by hammering

➡ _____

23 위 글의 주제로 알맞은 것을 고르시오.

① to introduce the superior ability of the finest craftsmen
② to utilize others' competitive spirit to achieve one's purpose
③ to determine who can make three treasures
④ to take advantage of one's generosity
⑤ to emphasize the importance of hard work

[24~27] 다음 글을 읽고 물음에 답하시오.

Loki went to see the three gods with all the treasures. Brokk came along. Loki showed them the treasures from Ivaldi's sons. The first treasure was for Odin, who had only one eye. It was a spear that never missed its target. The second treasure was a big ship that could turn into a piece of cloth. It was for Frey. The third treasure was for Thor. Loki showed Thor the flowing golden hair for his wife. Thor put the hair on his wife's head, ⓐand it took root and became real hair.

It was now Brokk's turn ⓑto show the gods his gifts. He gave Odin a gold arm ring that produced eight more gold rings every ninth night. Brokk then gave Frey a pig. It could pull his carriage faster than any horse.

"My third treasure is for you, Thor," said Brokk. "This is the hammer Mjolnir, which you'll love. If you throw it, it'll always come back to you. Moreover, nothing can ever break it."

It was an easy decision ⓒto choose the greatest treasure. ⓓ세 명의 신들이 가장 마음에 든 것은 몰니르였다. They thought the hammer would protect the gods from their enemies.

"Brokk and his brother," said Odin, "are the better smiths."

Brokk proved that Loki was wrong, and the three gods now had precious treasures.

24 위 글의 밑줄 친 ⓐand it을 한 단어로 바꿔 쓰시오.

➡ _____

25 다음 〈보기〉 중에서 위 글의 밑줄 친 ⓑto show, ⓒto choose와 to부정사의 용법이 같은 것을 각각 모두 고르시오.

> ① I want to show it to you.
> ② There are plenty of restaurants to choose from.
> ③ Why is it difficult to show your heart?
> ④ My role is to show a person the way to the station.
> ⑤ He is the last person to choose it.

➡ ⓑ와 같은 것: _____
　 ⓒ와 같은 것: _____

26 위 글의 밑줄 친 ⓓ의 우리말에 맞게 한 단어를 보충하여, 주어진 어휘를 알맞게 배열하시오.

> the three gods / Mjolnir / most / liked / was / it

➡ _____

27 다음 중 대장장이와 신의 이름과 선물의 연결이 옳지 <u>않은</u> 것을 고르시오.

smiths	for whom	what

① Ivaldi's sons – Odin – a spear
② Ivaldi's sons – Frey – a big ship
③ Brokk bros. – Odin – a gold arm ring
④ Brokk bros. – Frey – a carriage
⑤ Brokk bros. – Thor – Mjolnir

[28~29] 다음 글을 읽고 물음에 답하시오.

(1) Loki took the beautiful golden hair of Thor's wife, so Thor became angry at him. Loki promised to get golden hair for Thor's wife.
(2) Loki asked the sons of Ivaldi to make three treasures for Odin, Thor, and Frey. He also had Brokk and his brother produce three treasures for the gods. Loki bet that Ivaldi's sons would make better treasures.
(3) Loki showed the three gods the treasures from Ivaldi's sons. They were a spear, a big ship, and golden hair. The treasures from Brokk and his brother were a gold arm ring, a pig, and a hammer.
(4) The gods liked the hammer most. They each had their own precious treasures.

28 이야기의 구성 단계 중에서 본문 (3)번의 내용이 속하는 단계를 고르시오.

① 발단   ② 전개
③ 위기   ④ 절정
⑤ 결말

29 위 글을 읽고 알 수 없는 것을 고르시오.

① 등장인물이 누구인가?
② 사건의 발단은 무엇인가?
③ 등장인물이 무엇을 했는가?
④ 어떻게 이야기가 끝났는가?
⑤ 대장장이들은 각각 어떤 보상을 받는가?

[30~31] 다음 글을 읽고 물음에 답하시오.

I have always been friends with Sif, who is the wife of the strongest god. A few days ago, I cut her golden hair just for fun, and her husband became angry at me.
I came up with ⓐa good idea to get her hair back. I asked the sons of Ivaldi to make fine golden hair.

30 다음 각각의 신들의 특징을 참고하여 위 글의 'I'는 다음 중 어떤 신에 해당할지를 고르시오.

- Odin: the highest god who gave up his eye for wisdom
- Thor: Odin's son and the strongest god of all
- Frey: the god of the harvest who controls the weather
- Loki: a god who plays tricks on others

① Odin   ② Thor   ③ Frey
④ Loki   ⑤ None

31 위 글의 밑줄 친 ⓐa good idea가 가리키는 것을 동명사를 사용하여 영어로 쓰시오.

➡ _____

01 다음 중 주어진 단어의 관계와 같은 관계에 있는 것을 모두 고르시오.

> gold – golden

① wide – widen ② broad – broaden
③ deep – deepen ④ earth – earthen
⑤ wood – wooden

02 다음 중 주어진 문장의 빈칸에 들어갈 말과 같은 말이 들어가는 것은?

> Did you _____ the test?

① We should not _____ a noise in the library.
② She wants to help you _____ a decision.
③ Accidents used to _____ place at this place.
④ I don't understand why you _____ angry a lot.
⑤ Do you _____ along with your friends?

03 다음 단어의 영영풀이로 적절한 것은?

> piece

① strange and not known about or understood
② fail to notice something
③ say or write an answer to something
④ something removed from a dead animal to make things such as coats and bags
⑤ an amount of something that has been broken off, or cut off

[04~05] 다음 대화를 읽고 물음에 답하시오.

W: Is it your first time to visit Korea, Mike?
M: Yes, it is. I've always wanted to come to Seoul.
W: _____(A)_____
M: I'm really into Korean TV shows. I'm going to go to the places I saw on TV.
W: Have fun!

04 빈칸 (A)에 들어갈 말로 가장 적절한 것은?

① How did you get here?
② When did you come here?
③ Where did you visit in Seoul?
④ What made you come here?
⑤ Who brings you here?

05 Choose the one that is true according to the dialogue.

① Mike has been to Korea several times.
② Mike has wanted to visit Korea again.
③ Mike will go around the places he saw on TV.
④ Mike will be guided around Seoul by the woman.
⑤ Mike used to watch Korean TV shows when he was in Korea.

06 단어 why를 활용하여 밑줄 친 (A)와 같은 의미의 문장을 쓰시오.

> B: April is the best month of the year.
> G: (A)What makes you say so?
> B: The weather is not cold, and flowers are blooming.

➡ _____

07 다음 대화의 빈칸에 들어갈 말로 적절하지 <u>않은</u> 것은?

> A: Do you mind if I sit here?
> B: _____
> A: Okay. Never mind.

① Yes, I do. This seat is taken.
② I'm afraid I'm waiting for my friend.
③ Sorry, but I need this chair.
④ No, not at all.
⑤ Sorry, but I do.

[08~10] 다음 대화를 읽고 물음에 답하시오.

> **Jaden:** Hi, Yuri, What're you doing?
> **Yuri:** Hi, Jaden. I'm reading a book on Norse myths. I'm really into them these days. (①)
> **Jaden:** (A)왜 그것들을 그렇게 좋아하는 거야?
> **Yuri:** The stories are very interesting, and there are lots of movies about Norse myths. (②)
> **Jaden:** Are they any good?
> **Yuri:** Yes. There's actually a new movie about Thor, a famous god in Norse myths. (③)
> **Jaden:** Oh, I know him. He's my favorite online game character. (④)
> **Yuri:** In that case, we should go see the movie together.
> **Jaden:** Do you mind if I borrow your book when you're finished? (⑤)
> **Yuri:** No, not at all. I'm sure you'll like this book, too.

08 ①~⑤ 중 주어진 말이 들어가기에 가장 적절한 곳은?

> I want to read it before we see the movie.

① ② ③ ④ ⑤

09 주어진 어구를 활용하여 밑줄 친 우리말 (A)를 영어로 쓰시오.

> (what / them / so much)

➡ _____

10 위 대화를 읽고 답할 수 있는 것은?

① How many books on Norse myths has Yuri read?
② What is Jaden interested in these days?
③ When are they going to see the movie?
④ How many times has Jaden played the online game?
⑤ What movie are they going to see?

11 다음 중 어법상 <u>어색한</u> 문장은?

① Glenn put on the coat, which his wife bought for him.
② He transferred his son to new school, who had trouble getting along with others.
③ Laura had her umbrella stolen, which she put in front of the door.
④ The customer ordered the clerk to bring her a chair, which was for VIP.
⑤ There are some strange words in the book, that are quite difficult to translate.

12 다음 각 문장에 사용된 어법 사항을 〈보기〉에서 기호를 골라 괄호 안에 쓰시오.

> ┌─ 보기 ┤
> ⓐ It ~ that 강조구문 문장
> ⓑ It(가주어) ~ that(진주어) 구문 문장

(1) It is only through practice that you can achieve your goal. (　　　)
(2) It is wonderful that the whole family gets together on New Year's Day. (　　　)

(3) It is when my daughters smile at me that I feel the happiest. (　　)

(4) I can't remember when it was that I visited my grandma in Incheon. (　　)

(5) It is Harold's Idea that all the employees gather at the gate. (　　)

(6) What was it that motivated Gerald to major in genetic engineering? (　　)

① It was Emma who broke Joe's computer.

② It was coffee which Emma spilled.

③ It was her credit card that Emma gave Joe.

④ It was Emma that paid for the repair of computer.

⑤ It was at the shop which Joe's computer was repaired.

출제율 100%

13 다음 중 밑줄 친 관계대명사가 가리키는 것으로 바르지 않은 것은?

① Elizabeth is a teacher at Balsan middle school, which is located in Ilsan.
(→ Balsan middle school)

② The old lady should take the subway line 3, which crosses the Han River.
(→ the subway line 3)

③ Norah is a nurse at the general hospital, which was her first work place.
(→ the general hospital)

④ Fred was not afraid of sea water, which allowed him to be a professional diver.
(→ sea water)

⑤ The host of the show forgot the boy band's name, which started with F.
(→ the boy band's name)

출제율 90%

14 다음의 내용을 'It ~ that' 강조구문으로 쓴 문장들 중 어법상 어색한 것을 고르시오.

Emma accidentally spilled her coffee, which broke Joe's computer down. She gave Joe her credit card and he had the computer repaired at the shop.

출제율 95%

15 다음 밑줄 친 ⓐ~ⓓ를 각각 순서대로 'It'으로 시작하는 강조 구문으로 바꿔 쓰시오.

Tom bought a tablet at the mall 3 weeks ago.
　　ⓐ　　　　ⓑ　　　ⓒ　　　　ⓓ

➡ ⓐ _____

ⓑ _____
_____

ⓒ _____

ⓓ _____

출제율 90%

16 다음 주어진 세 문장을 관계대명사의 계속적 용법과 제한적 용법을 활용하여, 〈조건〉에 맞게 한 문장으로 표현하시오.

• Our school introduced a new system.
• The new system would help improve the students' math grade.
• Our school students' math grade had always been under average.

┌ 조건 ┐
that과 which를 반드시 사용할 것. 본문에 있는 표현만을 활용할 것. (변형불가)

➡ _____
_____

[17~20] 다음 글을 읽고 물음에 답하시오.

Loki knew only the sons of Ivaldi could make fine golden hair. He went to them and said, "I heard Brokk and his brother are the finest smiths. Is @that true?"

"No, ⓑ가장 훌륭한 대장장이는 바로 우리들이요," the sons of Ivaldi replied.

"They're making three treasures for Odin, Thor, and Frey," said Loki. "Do you think you can make treasures better than theirs?"

"Of course we can," they answered.

"O.K., then you should also make three treasures for them," said Loki. "The gods will decide on the best treasure."

Loki also told them that one of the treasures had to be golden hair. They went to work immediately.

출제율 90%

17 위 글의 밑줄 친 @that이 가리키는 것을 본문에서 찾아 쓰시오.

➡ _____

출제율 90%

18 위 글의 밑줄 친 ⓑ의 우리말에 맞게 주어진 어휘를 이용하여 8 단어로 영작하시오.

who, finest

➡ _____

출제율 95%

19 Why did Loki go to the sons of Ivaldi first, not to Brokk and his brother? Fill in the blanks with the suitable words.

Because Loki knew that the sons of Ivaldi were the only smiths who could make _____ _____ _____.

출제율 100%

20 Which question CANNOT be answered after reading the passage?

① Why did Loki go to the sons of Ivaldi?
② What did Loki say to the sons of Ivaldi?
③ What did the sons of Ivaldi think about their craftsmanship?
④ Did the sons of Ivaldi think they could make treasures better than Brokk and his brother's treasures?
⑤ What treasures did the sons of Ivaldi make for the three gods?

[21~24] 다음 글을 읽고 물음에 답하시오.

Loki went to see the three gods with all the treasures. Brokk came along. Loki showed them the treasures from Ivaldi's sons. The first treasure was for Odin, who had only one eye. It was a spear that never missed its target. The second treasure was a big ship that could turn into a piece of cloth. It was for Frey. The third treasure was for Thor. Loki showed Thor the flowing golden hair for his wife. Thor put the hair on his wife's head, and it took root and became real hair.

It was now Brokk's turn to show the gods his gifts. He gave Odin a gold arm ring that produced eight more gold rings every ninth night. Brokk then gave Frey a pig. It could pull his carriage faster than any horse.

"My third treasure is for you, Thor," said Brokk. "This is the hammer Mjolnir, @which you'll love. If you throw it, it'll always come back to you. Moreover, nothing can ever break it."

It was an easy decision to choose the greatest treasure. It was Mjolnir that the three gods liked most. They thought the hammer would protect the gods from their enemies.

"Brokk and his brother," said Odin, "are the better smiths."

Brokk proved that Loki was wrong, and the three gods now had ⓑprecious treasures.

출제율 95%

21 위 글의 종류로 알맞은 것을 고르시오.

① article　　　　② essay
③ biography　　　④ myth
⑤ review

출제율 100%

22 위 글의 주제로 알맞은 것을 고르시오.

① the wonderful skill of Ivaldi's sons
② treasures for three gods and choosing the greatest treasure among them
③ the way to become a better smith
④ the brilliant skill of Brokk and his brother
⑤ the close relationship between gods and the smiths

출제율 90%

23 위 글의 밑줄 친 ⓐwhich you'll love를 접속사를 사용하여 고치시오.

➡ _____

출제율 95%

24 위 글의 밑줄 친 ⓑ가 가리키는 것을 본문에서 찾아 쓰시오.

➡ Odin의 소중한 보물:

_____

➡ Frey의 소중한 보물:

_____

➡ Thor의 소중한 보물:

_____

[25~27] 다음 글을 읽고 물음에 답하시오.

Long ago, there were no ①kings in the southeastern part of Korea. One day, a strange voice was heard from Gujibong, which was a small hill. ⓐIt said that a new country would be built there. When people were singing and dancing for their future king, a golden box came from the sky. They found ②six golden eggs in the box. Twelve days later, the six eggs turned into ③six boys. The boys became ④the kings of the six Gayas. It was King Kim Suro who was the strongest of ⑤them. His kingdom became the center of the six Gayas.

출제율 95%

25 밑줄 친 ①~⑤ 중에서 가리키는 대상이 나머지 넷과 다른 것은?

①　　②　　③　　④　　⑤

출제율 90%

26 위 글의 밑줄 친 ⓐIt이 가리키는 것을 본문에서 찾아 쓰시오.

➡ _____

출제율 95%

27 위 글을 읽고 알 수 없는 것을 고르시오.

① Where were the six Gayas located?
② What was Gujibong?
③ Where did a golden box come from?
④ How did the six eggs turn into six boys?
⑤ Who was the strongest of the kings of the six Gayas?

01 주어진 단어를 문맥에 맞게 빈칸에 쓰시오. 필요하다면 어형을 바꾸시오.

> angry / happy / easy

(1) 그는 그녀를 화가 나서 쳐다보았다.

➡ He looked at her _____.

(2) 그것은 쉬운 결정이었어.

➡ It was an _____ decision.

(3) 나는 기꺼이 너를 도울 거야.

➡ I will _____ help you.

[02~03] 다음 대화를 읽고 물음에 답하시오.

W: Is it your first time to visit Korea, Mike?

M: Yes, it is. I've always wanted to come to Seoul.

W: ⓐWhat made you to come here?

M: I'm really into Korean TV shows. I'm going to go to the places I saw on TV.

W: Have fun!

02 밑줄 친 ⓐ를 어법에 맞게 바르게 고쳐 쓰시오.

➡ _____

03 What is Mike going to do in Seoul? Answer in English with a full sentence.

➡ _____

04 다음 문장을 읽고, 글의 빈칸에 들어갈 알맞은 말을 괄호 안에서 골라 순서대로 쓰시오. (필요할 경우 변형가능.)

> Lucas usually listens to the international radio channels online from various countries and enjoys talking to the foreigner about each other's life and culture. He wants to go to a foreign language high school, _____ _____ _____ _____ _____ _____.
>
> (mean, culture, like, which, he, foreign)

05 다음 주어진 단어를 알맞게 배열하여 문맥에 맞게 대화를 완성하시오. (단, 부사구를 강조하는 문장으로 쓰시오.)

> Reporter: What do you believe the biggest contribution to your winning this award tonight is?
>
> Winner: It _____.
>
> (award / that / because / won / was / of / my mother / I / the)

➡ _____

[06~08] 다음 글을 읽고 물음에 답하시오.

> Thor woke and knew immediately ⓐsomething was wrong. His wife's beautiful golden hair was gone. He knew only Loki could do ⓑ이런 끔찍한 일. Thor soon found Loki, who was drinking at home.
>
> "ⓒYou'd better undo what you did, or you'll be sorry," Thor said angrily to Loki.
>
> Loki was scared. He promised that he would get golden hair for Thor's wife.

06 위 글의 밑줄 친 ⓐ가 가리키는 것을 본문에서 찾아 쓰시오.

➡ _____

07 위 글의 밑줄 친 ⓑ의 우리말에 맞게 4 단어로 영작하시오.

➡ _____

08 위 글의 밑줄 친 ⓒ를 다음과 같이 바꿔 쓸 때 빈칸에 들어갈 알맞은 말을 쓰시오.

➡ I _____ you to undo what you did,
= You _____ undo what you did,
= It would be better for you _____ _____ what you did,

[09~10] 다음 글을 읽고 물음에 답하시오.

Loki went to see the three gods with all the treasures. Brokk came along. Loki showed them the treasures from Ivaldi's sons. The first treasure was for Odin, who had only one eye. It was a spear that never missed its target. The second treasure was a big ship that could turn into a piece of cloth. It was for Frey. The third treasure was for Thor. Loki showed Thor the flowing golden hair for his wife. Thor put the hair on his wife's head, and it took root and became real hair.

It was now Brokk's turn to show the gods his gifts. He gave Odin a gold arm ring that produced eight more gold rings every ninth night. Brokk then gave Frey a pig. It could pull his carriage faster than any horse.

"My third treasure is for you, Thor," said Brokk. "This is the hammer Mjolnir, which you'll love. If you throw it, it'll always come back to you. Moreover, nothing can ever break it."

It was an easy decision to choose the greatest treasure. It was Mjolnir that the three gods liked most. They thought the hammer would protect the gods from their enemies.

"Brokk and his brother," said Odin, "are the better smiths."

Brokk proved that Loki was wrong, and the three gods now had precious treasures.

09 다음 빈칸 (A)~(C)에 알맞은 단어를 넣어 Ivaldi의 아들들이 세 명의 신을 위해 만든 보물들을 소개하시오.

The treasure for Odin was a spear that never (A)_____ its target, and the treasure for Frey was a big ship that could turn into (B)_____ _____ _____ _____. The treasure for Thor was the flowing golden hair for his wife, and when Thor put the hair on his wife's head, it took root and became (C)_____ _____.

10 다음 빈칸 (A)~(C)에 알맞은 단어를 넣어 Brokk와 그의 남동생이 세 명의 신을 위해 만든 보물들을 소개하시오.

Brokk and his brother made (A)_____ _____ _____ _____ for Odin, (B)_____ _____ for Frey, and (C)_____ _____ _____ for Thor.

01 다음 상황을 읽고 대화의 빈칸에 알맞은 말을 쓰시오.

Jessica is learning about Norway in class, so she needs to watch a program about Norway. She goes out to the living room and sees her father watching TV. She asks her father if she changes the channel. Her father allows her to do so.

G: Dad, do you mind _____?

M: No, _____.

G: Thank you. I need to _____.

M: Norway? Why?

G: Well, we're _____.

M: Oh, I see.

02 다음 내용을 바탕으로 가야의 건국 신화를 쓰시오.

1. There were no kings in the southeastern part of Korea. One day, a strange voice was heard from Gujibong. "I'll build a new country."
2. People were singing and dancing for their future king.
3. A golden box came from the sky.
4. There were six golden eggs in the box.
5. The six eggs turned into six boys. The boys became the kings of the six Gayas.
6. King Kim Suro was the strongest of them.

Long ago, there were no kings in the (A)_____ of Korea. One day, a strange voice was heard from (B)_____, which was a small hill. It said that a new country would be built there. When people were (C)_____ for their future king, a golden box came from the sky. They found (D)_____ in the box. Twelve days later, the six eggs turned into six boys. The boys became the kings of the (E)_____. It was (F)_____ who was the strongest of them. His kingdom became the center of the six Gayas.

단원별 모의고사

1 다음 주어진 단어의 관계와 다른 하나는?

> immediate – immediately

① actual – actually
② careful – carefully
③ gentle – gently
④ comfortable – comfortably
⑤ fast – fastly

2 빈칸에 공통으로 들어갈 말을 쓰시오.

> • Can you _____ a picture of us?
> • Frank, _____ care not to cut your fingers.
> • Would you please _____ a look at this?

➡ _____

3 다음 우리말의 의미에 맞게 빈칸에 알맞은 말을 쓰시오.

(1) 그녀는 잠자리에 들어 즉시 잠들었다.
  ➡ She went to bed and _____ _____.

(2) 바깥은 완전히 어두웠다. 나는 아무것도 볼 수 없었다.
  ➡ It was _____ _____ _____. I could not see anything.

[04~05] 다음 대화를 읽고 물음에 답하시오.

B: April is the worst month of the year.
G: (A)What makes you say so?
B: Flowers are blooming, but I have to stay inside to study for my exams.
G: Oh, I know what you mean.

4 Write the reason why the boy has to stay inside in April. Use the phrase 'It's because.'

➡ _____

5 위 대화의 밑줄 친 (A)를 대신하여 쓸 수 있는 것은?

① What brings you here?
② How could you say like that?
③ What did you say?
④ Why is that?
⑤ Can you tell me how you say so?

6 다음 중 대화의 내용이 어색한 것은?

① A: Can I borrow your book?
  B: Yes, you can. Use it as much as you want.
② A: I think they won't come to the party.
  B: Why do you think so?
③ A: Can you tell me why you were late?
  B: It's because I woke up late.
④ A: Do you mind if I park my car here?
  B: Certainly not. Parking here is not allowed.
⑤ A: What makes you drink so much water?
  B: Because I feel thirsty a lot.

7 자연스러운 대화가 되도록 (A)~(D)를 바르게 나열하시오.

> (A) You can ask the waiter to bring more chairs.
> (B) Excuse me, do you mind if I take this chair? We need one more.
> (C) Oh, I see. Never mind.
> (D) I'm sorry, but I'm waiting for my friend. She'll be here soon.

➡ _____

[08~11] 다음 대화를 읽고 물음에 답하시오.

Jaden: Hi, Yuri, What're you doing?

Yuri: Hi, Jaden. I'm reading a book on Norse myths. I'm really into them these days.

Jaden: What makes you like them so much?

Yuri: The stories are very interesting, and there are lots of movies about Norse myths.

Jaden: Are they any good?

Yuri: Yes. There's actually a new movie about Thor, a famous god in Norse myths.

Jaden: Oh, I know him. He's my favorite online game character.

Yuri: In that case, we should go see (A)the movie together.

Jaden: Do you mind if I borrow your book when you're finished? I want to read it before we see the movie.

Yuri: _____ⓐ_____. I'm sure you'll like this book, too.

08 빈칸 ⓐ에 들어갈 말로 알맞지 <u>않은</u> 것은?

① No, not at all.   ② Of course not.
③ Certainly not.   ④ Sure, go ahead.
⑤ Of course, I do.

09 밑줄 친 (A)가 의미하는 것을 위 대화에서 찾아 다섯 단어의 영어로 쓰시오.

➡ _____

10 위 대화의 내용과 일치하지 <u>않는</u> 것은?

① Yuri is reading a book.
② Yuri thinks the stories of Norse myths are interesting.
③ Thor is one of gods in Norse myths.
④ Jaden doesn't know who Thor is.
⑤ Yuri suggests that Jaden go see the movie with her.

11 What does Jaden want to do before he sees the movie? Answer in English with a full sentence.

➡ _____

12 다음 상황을 읽고 빈칸에 알맞은 말을 5 단어로 쓰시오.

You visit your friend's place. He has a new piano in his room. You want to play the piano. So you say, "Do you mind _____?"

➡ _____

13 다음 내용을 읽고, 질문에 대한 답을 조건에 맞게 영작하시오.

• Today, Raina and April watched *Frozen 2*.
• The movie is the second episode of *Frozen*.
• TY sang its Korean version of the OST.

(1) What movie did Raina and April watch today, and what was it specifically? ('계속적' 용법의 관계대명사 which, the movie, they 등을 반드시 사용할 것, 총 12 단어 - 영화 제목은 1 단어로 취급)

➡ _____
_____

(2) What was sung by the singer TY? (the Korean version, *Frozen 2*, which 등을 반드시 사용할 것, 'It ~ that 강조구문' 형식으로 영작할 것, 총 17 단어)

➡ _____
_____

14 다음 밑줄 친 부분과 어법상 쓰임이 같은 것은?

> The students chose to go on a field trip to Gyeongju, <u>which</u> is a historic city in Korea.

① What he says doesn't annoys me, but the way in <u>which</u> he says it annoys me.
② The manager announced <u>which</u> of the applicants his company would hire.
③ I'll do volunteer work, <u>which</u> is baking cookies for people in need.
④ If there are three ways for you to use in that situation, <u>which</u> do you prefer?
⑤ This is the town in <u>which</u> Robert's daughters were born.

15 다음 그림과 우리말 설명을 보고 괄호 안에 주어진 단어를 활용하여 영작하시오.

> 엄마는 나에게 상자에 쓰지 않는 물건들을 담으라고 부탁하셨는데, 우리는 그것들을 자선단체에 기부할 것이다.
> (me / donate / the unused things / Mom / in / will / charity / asked / put / the boxes / we / to)

(1) 접속사 and를 이용하시오. (필요시 단어 추가)

➡ _____

_____

(2) 콤마와 관계대명사를 이용하시오. (필요시 단어 추가)

➡ _____

16 주어진 문장의 밑줄 친 부분을 강조하는 문장으로 어법상 옳은 것은?

> Philip didn't help the rich old man <u>with the desire in mind</u>.

① It was with the desire in mind which Philip didn't help the rich old man.
② It was the desire in mind that Philip didn't help the rich old man with.
③ It wasn't with the desire in mind that Philip didn't help the rich old man.
④ It wasn't with the desire in mind that Philip helped the rich old man.
⑤ It was with the desire in mind that Philip helped the rich old man.

17 다음 각각의 그림을 보고 우리말과 조건에 맞게 영작하시오. (어형 변화 가능)

(1)

> 내가 혼자서 이를 닦았는데, 엄마는 그것을 칭찬하셨다.
> (my, I, Mom, praise, brush, myself, teeth, for, which 활용, 총 9 단어)

➡ _____

_____

(2)

Jason의 개 Brown은 너무 영리해서 많은 그릇을 닦을 수 있는데, 이것이 세상을 놀라게 할 것이다.

(dishes, smart, surprise, dog, he, wash, so, which, many, that, is, can 활용, 총 17단어)

➡ _____

_____

[18~21] 다음 글을 읽고 물음에 답하시오.

Loki went to see the three gods with all the treasures. Brokk came along. Loki showed them the treasures from Ivaldi's sons. The first treasure was for Odin, who had only one eye. ①It was a spear that never missed its target. The second treasure was a big ship that could turn into a piece of cloth. It was for Frey. The third treasure was for Thor. Loki showed Thor the flowing golden hair for his wife. Thor put the hair on his wife's head, and it took root and became real hair.

It was now Brokk's turn ⓐto show the gods his gifts. He gave Odin a gold arm ring that produced eight more gold rings every ninth night. ②Brokk then gave Frey a pig. It could pull his carriage faster than any horse.

"My third treasure is for you, Thor," said Brokk. "This is the hammer Mjolnir, which you'll love. ③If you throw it, it'll always come back to you. Moreover, nothing can ever break it."

④It was an easy decision to choose the greatest treasure. It was Mjolnir that the three gods liked most. They thought the hammer would protect the gods from their enemies.

"⑤Brokk and his brother," said Odin, "are the better smiths."

Brokk proved that Loki was wrong, and the three gods now had precious treasures.

18 위 글의 밑줄 친 ⓐ를 3형식 문장으로 고치시오.

➡ _____

19 다음 빈칸 (A)~(C)에 알맞은 단어를 넣어 Brokk와 그의 남동생이 세 명의 신을 위해 만든 보물들의 특징을 소개하시오.

The treasure for Odin was a gold arm ring that produced (A)_____ _____ _____ _____ every ninth night, and the treasure for Frey was a pig which could pull his carriage (B)_____ than any horse. The treasure for Thor was the hammer Mjolnir, which would always (C)_____ _____ to him whenever he threw it and could never be broken by anything.

20 다음 중 위 글의 밑줄 친 ①~⑤에 대한 설명이 옳지 않은 것을 고르시오.

① 'It was ~ that ...'을 사용한 강조 구문이다.

② 3형식으로 고치면, Brokk then gave a pig to Frey이다.

③ If는 조건의 부사절을 이끄는 접속사로, 주절의 시제가 미래의 일이더라도 if절에서는 현재시제를 사용한다.

④ It은 가주어이고 to choose the greatest treasure가 진주어이다.

⑤ 뒤에 of the two가 생략되어 있고, of the two가 있는 경우에는 비교급 앞에 the를 쓴다.

21 Which question CANNOT be answered after reading the passage?

① What was the treasure from Ivaldi's sons for Odin?

② What was the treasure from Ivaldi's sons for Frey?

③ For whom was the third treasure from Ivaldi's sons?

④ Why did the three gods like Mjolnir most?

⑤ What was the treasure that Loki liked most?

[22~23] 다음 글을 읽고 물음에 답하시오.

This morning, I found my wife's beautiful golden hair was gone. I knew only Loki could do such a terrible thing. I got very ⓐ_____ and shouted at him. Loki promised that he would get golden hair for my wife. I guess he may go to the sons of Ivaldi, ⓑwho are the finest smiths.

22 위 글의 빈칸 ⓐ에 들어갈 알맞은 말을 고르시오.

① excited   ② bored

③ relieved   ④ upset

⑤ indifferent

23 위 글의 밑줄 친 ⓑwho와 바꿔 쓸 수 있는 말을 고르시오.

① because he   ② but they

③ and he   ④ for they

⑤ though they

[24~25] 다음 글을 읽고 물음에 답하시오.

Long ago, there were no kings in the southeastern part of Korea. One day, a strange voice was heard from Gujibong, which was a small hill. It said that a new country would be built there. When people were singing and dancing for their future king, a golden box came from the sky. They found six golden eggs in the box. Twelve days later, the six eggs turned into six boys. The boys became the kings of the six Gayas. It was King Kim Suro who was the strongest of them. His kingdom became the center of the six Gayas.

24 위 글의 종류로 알맞은 것을 고르시오.

① a fable

② nonfiction

③ the fantasy novel

④ science fiction

⑤ the birth myth of a nation

25 본문의 내용과 일치하도록 다음 빈칸 (A)와 (B)에 알맞은 단어를 쓰시오.

King Kim Suro was born from one of the (A)_____ _____ that came from the sky in a golden box. Twelve days later, the six eggs turned into six boys, who became the kings of the (B)_____ _____. King Kim Suro was the strongest of them.

MEMO

Lesson 3

Plants That Feed Us

 의사소통 기능

- 안부 묻고 답하기
  A: Is something wrong?
  B: I have a bad fever.

- 조언 구하기
  What do you think I should do?

언어 형식

- 분사
  He ate a basket of tomatoes in front of many people **watching** him.

- 동사의 강조
  Spinach **does have** a lot of nutrients.

교과서
Words & Expressions

Key Words

- **absorb** [əbsɔ́ːrb] 동 흡수하다
- **actually** [ǽktʃuəli] 부 실제로
- **article** [áːrtikl] 명 기사, 논문
- **battleship** [bǽtlʃip] 명 전함
- **bean** [biːn] 명 콩
- **bloom** [bluːm] 동 꽃을 피우다
- **British** [brítiʃ] 형 영국의
- **capital** [kǽpətl] 명 수도
- **cartoon** [kɑːrtúːn] 명 만화
- **character** [kǽriktər] 명 등장인물
- **characteristic** [kæriktərístik] 명 특성, 특징 형 특징적인
- **consider** [kənsídər] 동 고려하다, 여기다
- **contain** [kəntéin] 동 포함하다, 담고 있다
- **crush** [krʌʃ] 동 으스러뜨리다
- **defeat** [difíːt] 동 물리치다, 패배시키다
- **discover** [diskʌ́vər] 동 발견하다
- **erase** [iréis] 동 지우다
- **expect** [ikspékt] 동 기대하다
- **face** [feis] 동 향하다
- **fighter** [fáitər] 명 전투기, 투사
- **German** [dʒɔ́ːrmən] 형 독일의 명 독일어
- **government** [gʌ́vərnmənt] 명 정부, 국가
- **happen** [hǽpən] 동 일어나다
- **healthy** [hélθi] 형 건강한
- **hidden** [hídn] 형 숨겨진
- **hide** [haid] 동 숨다, 숨기다
- **however** [hauévər] 부 그러나
- **improve** [imprúːv] 동 개선하다, 향상시키다
- **insect** [ínsèkt] 명 곤충, 벌레

- **lower** [lóuər] 동 낮추다
- **material** [mətíəriəl] 명 물질, 재료
- **nutrient** [njúːtriənt] 명 영양소, 영양분
- **pilot** [páilət] 명 비행사, 조종사
- **place** [pleis] 동 두다, 놓다
- **planet** [plǽnit] 명 행성, 혹성
- **poisonous** [pɔ́izənəs] 형 유독한, 독성의
- **prove** [pruːv] 동 증명하다
- **publish** [pʌ́bliʃ] 동 출판하다
- **radar** [réidɑːr] 명 레이더, 전파 탐지기
- **researcher** [risɔ́ːrtʃər] 명 연구원, 조사원
- **Scottish** [skátiʃ] 형 스코틀랜드의
- **secret** [síːkrit] 명 비밀
- **sensor** [sénsər] 명 감지기, 센서
- **snowboard** [snóubɔ̀ːrd] 명 스노보드
- **soak** [souk] 동 담그다, 적시다
- **soil** [sɔil] 명 흙, 토양
- **solve** [sɑlv] 동 해결하다
- **spinach** [spínitʃ] 명 시금치
- **statue** [stǽtʃuː] 명 조각상, 동상
- **stomachache** [stʌ́məkèik] 명 복통
- **system** [sístəm] 명 시스템, 체계, 장치
- **surprising** [sərpráiziŋ] 형 놀라운
- **technology** [teknálədʒi] 명 기술
- **trace** [treis] 명 흔적 동 추적하다
- **truth** [truːθ] 명 사실, 진실
- **vision** [víʒən] 명 시력
- **vitamin** [váitəmin] 명 비타민
- **world-famous** [wɔ́ːrldfèiməs] 형 세계적으로 유명한

Key Expressions

- **be afraid of** ~을 두려워하다
- **be good for** ~에 유익하다
- **be scared of** ~을 무서워하다
- **by -ing** ~함으로써
- **get some fresh air** 신선한 공기를 마시다
- **give it a try** 시도해 보다
- **have a fever** 몸에 열이 있다
- **in addition** 게다가
- **keep a secret** 비밀을 지키다

- **keep ~ away from ...** ~을 …로부터 멀리하다
- **Royal Air Force** 영국 공군
- **lose weight** 살을 빼다
- **no longer** 더 이상 ~가 아닌
- **soak up** 흡수하다, 빨아들이다
- **sore throat** 인후염
- **stay full** 포만감을 가지다
- **take medicine** 약을 먹다
- **turn A into B** A를 B로 바꾸다

Word Power

※ 서로 비슷한 뜻을 가진 어휘

- □ **absorb** 흡수하다 : **soak up** 빨아들이다, 적시다
- □ **cartoon** 만화 : **comic strip** 만화
- □ **consider** 여기다 : **regard** 간주하다

- □ **improve** 개선하다 : **upgrade** 개선하다
- □ **contain** 포함하다 : **involve** 포함하다
- □ **improve** 개선하다 : **get better** 좋아지다

※ 서로 반대되는 뜻을 가진 어휘

- □ **hide** 숨기다 ↔ **uncover** 밝혀내다

- □ **defeat** 물리치다 ↔ **yield** 굴복하다

※ 동사 - 동사+er/or = 명사(사람)

- □ **act** 행동하다 - **actor** 배우
- □ **fight** 싸우다 - **fighter** 전사, 전투기
- □ **invent** 발명하다 - **inventor** 발명가
- □ **research** 조사하다 - **researcher** 조사원

- □ **direct** 감독하다, 지휘하다 - **director** 감독
- □ **interview** 인터뷰하다 - **interviewer** 면접관
- □ **paint** 그리다 - **painter** 화가
- □ **visit** 방문하다 - **visitor** 방문자

※ 명사 - 명사+ist = 명사(사람)

- □ **art** 예술 - **artist** 예술가
- □ **science** 과학 - **scientist** 과학자

- □ **cartoon** 만화 - **cartoonist** 만화가
- □ **tour** 여행 - **tourist** 여행자

※ keep을 포함한 표현

- □ **keep ~ a secret** ~을 비밀로 하다
- □ **keep away** 멀리하다
- □ **keep in touch** 연락하다

- □ **keep a diary** 일기를 쓰다
- □ **keep ~ in mind** ~을 명심하다
- □ **keep track of** ~을 기록하다

English Dictionary

- □ **battleship** 전함
  → the largest type of ship used in war, with very big guns and heavy armour
  중무장을 하고 대형 대포를 가진 전쟁에 사용되는 가장 큰 형태의 선박

- □ **carrot** 당근
  → a long pointed orange vegetable that grows under the ground
  땅 밑에서 자라는 길고 뾰족한 오렌지색 채소

- □ **cartoon** 만화
  → a funny drawing in a newspaper or magazine
  신문이나 잡지에 실린 우스운 그림

- □ **character** 등장인물
  → a person in a book, play, film etc.
  책, 연극, 영화 등에 등장하는 사람

- □ **hide** 숨기다
  → to cover something so that it cannot be seen clearly
  명확하게 보이지 않도록 감추다

- □ **insect** 곤충
  → a small creature such as a fly or ant, that has six legs
  여섯 개의 다리를 가진 파리나 개미 같은 작은 생물

- □ **nutrient** 영양분
  → a chemical or food that provides what is needed for plants or animals to live and grow
  식물이나 동물이 살고 성장하기 위하여 필요한 것을 제공해 주는 화학 물질이나 음식

- □ **secret** 비밀
  → a fact that is known by only a small number of people, and is not told to anyone else
  소수의 사람들에 의해서만 알려진 사실이며 다른 누구에게도 말해지지 않는 어떤 것

- □ **statue** 동상
  → an image of a person or animal that is made in solid material such as stone or metal
  돌이나 금속 같은 단단한 재료로 만들어진 사람이나 동물의 이미지

01 다음 중 주어진 단어의 관계와 같은 것은?

> lower – raise

① similar – alike
② necessary – essential
③ truth – falsehood
④ unusual – uncommon
⑤ advantage – benefit

02 다음 영영풀이에 해당하는 단어로 가장 적절한 것은?

> a fact that is known by only a small number of people, and is not told to anyone else

① diary
② newspaper
③ secret
④ politician
⑤ news

03 〈중요〉 다음 중 밑줄 친 단어의 쓰임이 바르지 <u>않은</u> 것은?

① Jamie is a <u>dancer</u>. He dances very well.
② Polly is a <u>diver</u>. She can dive deep in the sea.
③ Chris is a <u>swimmer</u>. He swims like a fish.
④ Dave is an <u>actor</u>. He acts in a movie.
⑤ Jill is a <u>composor</u>. She composes beautiful music.

04 〈서답형〉 다음 우리말에 맞게 빈칸에 알맞은 말을 쓰시오. (3 단어)

> 그 곰을 두려워하지 마.
> ➡ Don't _____ the bear.

➡ _____

05 다음은 각 영영풀이에 알맞은 단어를 빈칸으로 표시한 것이다. 모형 '★' 안에 들어갈 알파벳을 순서대로 배열한 것은?

> • ___ ___ ___ ___ ★ : a person who is trained to fly an aircraft
> • ___ ★ ___ ___ : to put something into a liquid and leave it there
> • ___ ___ ___ ★ ___ ___ : to press something very hard to break it into pieces
> • ___ ___ ___ ___ ★ : someone whose job is acting in plays or films

① hide
② tone
③ town
④ hold
⑤ tour

06 〈서답형〉 다음 문장의 빈칸에 들어갈 말을 〈보기〉에서 골라 쓰시오.

> ┤ 보기 ├
> material   statue   bloom   character

(1) Flowers _____ every April.
(2) The white _____ of Kim Koo looks good.
(3) The _____ can be divided into two parts, iron and plastic.
(4) The main _____ in this book is very famous all around the world.

07 〈중요〉 다음 빈칸에 공통으로 들어갈 말로 가장 적절한 것은? (대 · 소문자 무시)

> • Do you see the house _____ the river?
> • He used to travel _____ train.
> • _____ doing this, I can help her.

① on
② in
③ at
④ about
⑤ by

01 주어진 단어의 관계와 같도록 빈칸에 알맞은 말을 쓰시오.

> fight – fighter : invent – _____

02 다음 영영풀이에 해당하는 단어를 〈보기〉에서 찾아 쓰시오.

> ┤ 보기 ├
>
> statue   insect   expect

(1) _____ : to believe that something will happen

(2) _____ : an image of a person or animal that is made in solid material such as stone or metal

(3) _____ : a small creature such as a fly or ant, that has six legs

03 우리말 의미에 맞게 주어진 단어를 바르게 나열하시오. (필요하다면 어형을 바꾸시오.)

(1) 졸업 후에, 나는 조사원으로서 NASA에 직장을 얻었다.

(research / graduation / with NASA / got / after / a job / I / as / a)

➡ _____

_____

(2) 그 면접관은 내게 나의 미래 계획에 관해 물었다.

(plans / asked / about / the / future / me / my / interview)

➡ _____

(3) 나는 만화가인 것이 자랑스러워.

(cartoon / I / proud / being / a / am / of)

➡ _____

_____

04 (A)~(C)에 각각 공통으로 들어가는 말을 순서대로 쓰시오.

(A) I think I _____ a fever.
    They _____ difficulty in reading books.
(B) I want you to _____ it a secret.
    Dave used to _____ a diary.
(C) I will _____ the medicine tonight.
    Shall we _____ a walk?

➡ (A) _____ (B) _____ (C) _____

05 주어진 우리말에 맞게 빈칸에 알맞은 말을 쓰시오.

(1) 운동은 우리의 몸과 마음에 유익하다.
    ➡ Exercise _____ _____ _____ our body and mind.
(2) 그 법은 더 이상 효력이 없습니다.
    ➡ The law is _____ _____ effective.
(3) 게다가, 나는 너무 어려요.
    ➡ _____ _____, I am too young.
(4) 여러분은 매일 계획을 세움으로써 이것을 할 수 있습니다.
    ➡ You can do this _____ _____ plans every day.
(5) 그것은 독성이 강한 물질로 만들어졌어요.
    ➡ It was made with a _____ _____.

06 다음 빈칸에 알맞은 말을 쓰시오.

> A: What do you want to be in the future?
> B: I want to be an _____. I like inventing things. Edison is my role model.

Conversation

① 안부 묻고 답하기

> **A** Is something wrong? 무슨 문제 있어?
> **B** I have a bad fever. 열이 심하게 나요.

- 상대방의 안부를 묻는 표현에는 우리가 잘 알고 있는 'How are you?'(잘 지내니?) 이외에도 'How have you been?'(어떻게 지냈니?) 또는 'What's up?', 'What's going on?'(무슨 일 있니?) 등의 다양한 표현들이 있다.

- 안부를 물을 때 상대방이 좋지 않아 보여서 걱정이 되는 상황일 때는 '무슨 문제가 있니?'라는 의미로 'Is something wrong?'(무슨 일 있니?), 'Is there anything wrong with you?' 또는 'What's wrong (with you)?' 등으로 물어본다.

- 상대방의 안부를 물을 때 대답은 본인의 상황에 따라서 'Great, very well. Thank you.', 'Fine, thanks.', 'Not bad.', 'I hurt ~.' 등으로 하면 되고, 'How about you?'로 되물을 수도 있다. 'How have you been?'(어떻게 지냈니?)에 대하여 응답할 때는 'I've been'은 생략하고 '(I've been) Good.', 'Fine.', 'Great.' 등을 쓸 수 있다.

안부 묻기

- Is something wrong? 무슨 문제 있어?
- What's wrong with you? 무슨 일 있니?
- How are you doing? 어떻게 지내니?
- What's the matter? 무슨 일 있어?
- How have you been? 그동안 어떻게 지냈어?
- How's it going? 어떻게 지내니?

핵심 Check

1. 다음 대화의 빈칸에 들어가기에 적절하지 <u>않은</u> 것은?

> **B:** Bomi, do you have some medicine?
> **G:** Why? _____
> **B:** I have a stomachache. I think I ate too much for lunch.
> **G:** Why don't you go for a walk?
> **B:** O.K. I'll give it a try.

① What's the matter?
② Is something wrong?
③ What's wrong?
④ Where have you been?
⑤ Is there anything wrong with you?

② 조언 구하기

> • **What do you think I should do?** 내가 뭘 해야 한다고 생각해?

- 어려운 일이나 안 좋은 일이 있어서 상대에게 조언을 구해야 할 때는 '무엇을 해야 할까요?'의 의미로 'What do you think I should do?'(제가 무엇을 해야 한다고 생각하세요?) 또는 'How can I ~?'(어떻게 ~할까요?) 등으로 물어본다.

- 조언을 구할 때 방법을 물어보는 의미로 'How can I ~?', 'What can I ~?'라고 할 수 있고, 'What can I do to ~?', 'What should I do to ~?'라고 하거나 'What's your advice?', 'What do you suggest?' 등으로 물어볼 수도 있다.

- 상대방에게 조언을 할 때는 '(I think) You should ~.', 'Make sure you ~.', 'I suggest (that) you ~.', 'You need to ~.', 'You have to ~.' 등으로 대답할 수 있으며, 'Why don't you ~?' 또는 'How/What about ~?' 등의 제안하는 표현을 이용하여 조언을 할 수도 있다.

조언 구하기

- What do you think I should do? 내가 뭘 해야 한다고 생각해요?
- What should I do to ~? ~하려면 뭘 해야 할까요?
- What do you suggest? 제안하는 게 뭔가요?
- What do you advise me to do? 무엇을 할지 조언해 주시겠습니까?
- If you were me, what would you do? 만약 제 입장이면 어떻게 하실 겁니까?

조언하기

- (I think) You should ~. ~해야 한다고 생각해.
- I suggest you ~. ~하라고 하고 싶어.
- Why don't you ~? ~하는 것이 어떠니?
- Make sure you ~. 반드시 ~해라.
- You need to ~. / You have to ~. 너는 ~해야 해.
- How about ~? / What about ~? ~하면 어때?

핵심 Check

2. 다음 대화의 내용에 어울리도록 빈칸에 주어진 단어를 적절하게 배열하시오.

B: It's so hard to lose weight. (you, I, what, do, do, think, should)?

G: Well, why don't you walk your dog every day?

B: My dog would love it, but would it help me lose weight?

G: Sure. When you walk your dog, you're actually exercising, too.

B: O.K. I'll think about it.

➡ _____

Listen and Speak 1 A-1

B: Bomi, do you have ❶some medicine?

G: Why? ❷Is something wrong?

B: I ❸have a stomachache. I think I ate too much for lunch.

G: ❹Why don't you go for a walk?

B: O.K. I'll ❺give it a try.

B: 보미야, 약 좀 있니?
G: 왜? 무슨 문제 있어?
B: 배가 아파. 점심을 너무 많이 먹었나 봐.
G: 산책을 좀 하는 게 어때?
B: 알겠어. 한번 해 볼게.

❶ some은 셀 수 있는 명사와 없는 명사를 모두 수식할 수 있다.
❷ 주로 상대방이 좋지 않아 보여서 걱정이 되는 상황일 때 쓰는 말로 'What's the matter?', 'Is anything wrong with you?'와 같다.
❸ 병이 있다고 말할 때는 주로 동사 have를 사용하여 말한다.
❹ 조언하는 말로 'How about ~?', '(I think) You should ~.' 등으로 대체하여 쓸 수 있다.
❺ give it a try: 시도하다, 한번 해 보다

Check(√) True or False

(1) Bomi ate too much for lunch. T ☐ F ☐

(2) The boy will try going for a walk. T ☐ F ☐

 Listen and Speak 2 A-1

B: It's so hard to lose weight. ❶What do you think I should do?

G: Well, ❷why don't you walk your dog every day?

B: My dog would love it, but would it help me ❸lose weight?

G: Sure. When you walk your dog, you're actually exercising, ❹too.

B: O.K. I'll think about it.

B: 몸무게를 줄이는 건 너무 어려워 내가 뭘 해야 한다고 생각해?
G: 글쎄, 매일 너의 개를 산책시키는 건 어때?
B: 우리 개는 좋아하겠지만, 그게 살을 빼는 데 도움이 될까?
G: 물론이지. 네가 개를 산책시키면, 사실은 너도 운동하는 거잖아.
B: 좋아. 생각해 볼게.

❶ 조언을 구하는 말로 'What should I do to ~?', 'What do you advise me to do?' 등으로 대체하여 쓸 수 있다.
❷ 조언하는 말로 'How about ~?', '(I think) You should ~.' 등으로 대체하여 쓸 수 있다.
❸ help는 목적격보어로 to부정사나 동사원형을 취하는 동사이다. lose weight: 체중을 줄이다
❹ 긍정에 대한 동의는 too를 쓴다.

Check(√) True or False

(3) The boy wants the girl to lose some weight. T ☐ F ☐

(4) The girl suggests an idea that will help the boy lose weight. T ☐ F ☐

(5) The boy will walk his dog in order to lose his weight. T ☐ F ☐

Listen and Speak 1 A-2

B: ❶Is something wrong? You don't look so good.

G: ❷I have a sore throat. I think it's because of the fine dust these days.

B: ❸Put some plants in your room. They take bad air in and produce fresh air.

G: Really? I'll get ❹a few plants right away.

❶ 주로 상대방이 좋지 않아 보여서 걱정이 되는 상황일 때 쓰는 말로 'What's the matter?', 'Is anything wrong with you?'와 같다.
❷ 병이 있다고 말할 때는 주로 동사 have를 사용하여 말한다.
❸ 명령문을 사용하여 조언하는 말을 할 수 있다.
❹ 셀 수 있는 명사를 수식하는 수량형용사이다.

 Listen and Speak 2 A-2

B: ❶How are your tomatoes doing? Are they growing well?

G: No. I've gotten only a few tomatoes ❷so far. ❸What do you think I should do?

B: Where do you have the pot?

G: In the kitchen.

B: Well, tomato plants need about 7 hours of sunlight a day.

G: Oh, ❹I see. I'll move the pot over to the window.

❶ 'How is[are] ~ doing?'은 안부를 묻는 말이다.
❷ 현재완료와 함께 쓰여 '지금까지'라는 의미로 사용된다.
❸ 조언을 구하는 말로 'What should I do to ~?', 'What do you advise me to do?' 등으로 대체하여 쓸 수 있다.
❹ I see는 I understand라는 의미로 사용된다.

 Communicate A

Anna: Suho, ❶is something wrong? You're very quiet today.

Suho: I'm just a bit tired. I slept very little last night.

Anna: Did you do something late last night?

Suho: Yes, I watched a movie on my phone until 2 a.m. That's what I often do these days.

Anna: Oh, ❷that's why you have red eyes. You should go to bed before midnight for your health.

Suho: I think my eyes are getting worse. What do you think I should do?

Anna: ❸Try eating lots of carrots and tomatoes. They're rich in vitamin A, so they'll keep your eyes healthy.

Suho: I see. Thank you, Anna.

❶ 'Is anything wrong with you?'라고 말해도 좋다.
❷ 'That's why ~.'는 결과를 이끄는 말이다.
❸ 'What about eating lots of carrots and tomatoes?'라고 말해도 좋다.

 Progress Check 1

B: ❶Is something wrong?

G: I'm just a little tired. I've watched a movie on my phone ❷for two hours.

B: ❸That's why you have red eyes. Try putting a warm towel over your eyes.

G: O.K. Thanks.

❶ 'What's the matter?'라고 물을 수 있다.
❷ '~ 동안'이라는 의미로 쓰인다.
❸ 'That is the reason why ~.'로 풀어 쓸 수 있다.

 Progress Check 2

G: What's wrong? You look worried.

B: Well, I broke my mom's favorite plate. ❶What do you think I should do?

G: ❷Tell her the truth. She will understand.

B: I hope you're right.

❶ 'What should I do?'라고 말해도 좋다.
❷ 'Why don't you tell her the truth?'라고 말할 수 있다.

Conversation **129**

● 다음 우리말과 일치하도록 빈칸에 알맞은 말을 쓰시오.

Listen & Speak 1 A-1

B: Bomi, do you have _____ _____?

G: Why? Is _____ _____?

B: I have _____ _____. I think I ate _____ _____ for lunch.

G: Why don't you _____ _____ _____ _____?

B: O.K. I'll give _____ _____ _____.

Listen & Speak 1 A-2

B: Is _____ _____? You don't look _____ _____.

G: I have _____ _____ _____. I think it's _____ _____ the fine dust these days.

B: _____ some plants in your room. They _____ bad air _____ and _____ fresh air.

G: Really? I'll _____ right away.

Listen & Speak 2 A-1

B: It's _____ _____ _____ _____ weight. What _____ _____ _____ I should do?

G: Well, why don't you _____ _____ _____ every day?

B: My dog would love _____, but would _____ _____ me _____ _____?

G: Sure. When you walk your dog, you're _____, _____.

B: O.K. I'll _____ _____ _____.

Listen & Talk 2 A-2

B: _____ _____ your tomatoes _____? Are they _____ well?

G: No. I've _____ only _____ _____ tomatoes _____ _____. What do you think _____ _____?

B: _____ do you have the pot?

G: _____ the kitchen.

B: Well, tomato plants _____ _____ 7 hours of sunlight _____ _____.

G: Oh, I see. I'll _____ the pot _____ to the window.

해석

B: 보미야, 약 좀 있니?
G: 왜? 무슨 문제 있어?
B: 배가 아파. 점심을 너무 많이 먹었나 봐.
G: 산책을 좀 하는 게 어때?
B: 알겠어. 한번 해 볼게.

B: 어디 안 좋아? 안색이 나빠 보이는데.
G: 목이 아파. 최근의 미세먼지 때문인 것 같아.
B: 방에 식물을 좀 놓아 봐. 나쁜 공기를 흡수하고 신선한 공기를 만들어 내.
G: 정말? 당장 식물을 몇 그루 가져와야겠어.

B: 몸무게를 줄이는 건 너무 어려워. 내가 뭘 해야 한다고 생각해?
G: 글쎄, 매일 너의 개를 산책시키는 건 어때?
B: 우리 개는 좋아하겠지만, 그게 살을 빼는 데 도움이 될까?
G: 물론이지. 네가 개를 산책시키면, 사실은 너도 운동하는 거잖아.
B: 좋아. 생각해 볼게.

B: 네 토마토들 어떠니? 잘 자라고 있어?
G: 아니. 지금까지 토마토 몇 개밖에 못 얻었어. 내가 뭘 해야 한다고 생각하니?
B: 화분을 어디에 두는데?
G: 부엌에.
B: 음, 토마토는 하루에 7시간 정도 햇빛을 받아야 해.
G: 오, 그렇구나. 화분을 창문 쪽으로 옮겨야겠다.

Communicate A

Anna: Suho, _____ _____ _____? You're very _____ today.

Suho: I'm just _____ _____ _____. I slept very _____ last night.

Anna: Did you do _____ _____ last night?

Suho: Yes, I watched a movie _____ my phone _____ 2 a.m. That's _____ _____ _____ _____ these days.

Anna: Oh, _____ _____ you have red eyes. You should go to bed _____ midnight for your health.

Suho: I think my eyes are _____ _____. What do you think _____ _____ _____?

Anna: Try _____ _____ _____ _____ and tomatoes. They're _____ _____ _____ A, so they'll _____ your eyes _____.

Suho: I _____. Thank you, Anna.

해석

Anna: 수호야, 무슨 일 있어? 오늘 굉장히 조용하네.

수호: 조금 피곤한 것뿐이야. 어젯밤에 정말 조금 잤거든.

Anna: 어젯밤 늦게까지 뭔가 했니?

수호: 응, 새벽 2시까지 휴대폰으로 영화를 봤어. 요즘 종종 하는 일이야.

Anna: 오, 그래서 눈이 충혈됐구나. 건강을 위해 자정 전에는 잠자리에 들어야 해.

수호: 눈이 점점 나빠지는 것 같아. 내가 뭘 해야 한다고 생각해?

Anna: 당근이랑 토마토를 많이 먹어 봐. 그것들은 비타민 A가 많아서, 네 눈을 건강하게 유지해 줄 거야.

수호: 알겠어. 고마워, Anna.

Progress Check 1

B: _____ something _____?

G: I'm just _____ _____ tired. I've _____ a movie on my phone _____ two hours.

B: That's _____ you have _____ _____. Try _____ a warm towel _____ your eyes.

G: O.K. Thanks.

B: 무슨 문제 있어?

G: 조금 피곤한 것뿐이야. 휴대전화로 영화를 두 시간 동안 봤거든.

B: 그래서 눈이 충혈됐구나. 따뜻한 수건으로 눈을 덮어 봐.

G: 알겠어. 고마워.

Progress Check 2

G: What's _____? You look _____.

B: Well, I _____ my mom's favorite _____. What _____ _____ _____ I should do?

G: _____ her the truth. She will _____.

B: I _____ you're _____.

G: 무슨 문제 있어? 걱정이 있는 것 같은데.

B: 그게, 어머니께서 가장 아끼시는 접시를 깨뜨렸어. 내가 뭘 해야 한다고 생각하니?

G: 솔직히 말씀 드려. 이해하실 거야.

B: 네 말이 맞길 바라.

01 다음 대화의 빈칸에 알맞은 것은?

> B: _____ You don't look so good.
>
> G: I have a sore throat.

① How do you care your neck?

② Is there something interesting?

③ What are you doing?

④ What is the matter?

⑤ How long have you been here?

02 다음 대화의 밑줄 친 부분과 바꾸어 쓸 수 있는 것은?

> B: I lost my wallet that my father gave me. <u>What do you think I should do?</u>
>
> G: I think you should tell him the truth. He will understand you.

① What should I find?　　② What did I do?

③ What do you suggest?　　④ How can you help me?

⑤ What can you say to him?

[03~04] 다음 대화를 읽고 물음에 답하시오.

> B: Is something wrong?
>
> G: I'm just a little ___(A)___ . I've watched a movie on my phone for two hours.
>
> B: That's why you have red eyes. Try putting a warm towel over your eyes.
>
> G: O.K. Thanks.

03 빈칸 (A)에 들어갈 말로 가장 적절한 것은?

① boring　　② upset　　③ tired

④ excited　　⑤ sleepy

04 How long has the girl watched a movie on her phone?

➡ _____

01 다음 대화의 밑줄 친 부분의 목적으로 가장 적절한 것은?

> A: I have a cold. <u>What do you think I should do?</u>
>
> B: Why don't you drink some hot honey tea?

① 안부 묻기　　　② 길 묻기
③ 조언 구하기　　④ 제안에 응하기
⑤ 승낙하기

02 다음 짝지어진 대화 중 <u>어색한</u> 것은?

① A: I lied to my mom. What should I do?
　 B: I think you should tell her the truth.
② A: Is something wrong?
　 B: I forgot to bring my umbrella.
③ A: How have you been?
　 B: Great. I have a sore throat.
④ A: What's wrong? You look upset.
　 B: I can't find my bicycle.
⑤ A: How are you doing?
　 B: Not bad. How are you?

[03~04] 다음 대화를 읽고 물음에 답하시오.

> B: Bomi, do you have some medicine?
> G: Why? Is something wrong?
> B: I have a stomachache. I think I ate too much for lunch.
> G: Why don't you go for a walk?
> B: O.K. (A)<u>I'll give it a try.</u>

03 다음 중 밑줄 친 (A)의 의미로 가장 적절한 것은?

① I will take the medicine.
② I will eat less next time.
③ I will try to exercise more often.
④ I will try walking.
⑤ I will go see a doctor.

서답형
04 Write the reason why the boy wants some medicine. Use the phrase below.

> It's because

➡ _____

[05~07] 다음 대화를 읽고 물음에 답하시오.

> B: It's so ①<u>hard</u> to lose weight. (A)<u>What do you think I should do?</u>
> G: Well, why don't you ②<u>walk</u> your dog every day?
> B: My dog would love it, but would it help me ③<u>losing</u> weight?
> G: Sure. When you walk your dog, you're actually ④<u>exercising</u>, ⑤<u>too</u>.
> B: O.K. I'll think about it.

05 다음 중 밑줄 친 (A)를 대신하여 쓸 수 있는 것은?

① What do you think I am doing?
② What can I do for you?
③ How come I should lose weight?
④ What do you advise me to do?
⑤ What do you think I am doing?

06 ①~⑤ 중 어법상 바르지 <u>않은</u> 것은?

①　　　②　　　③　　　④　　　⑤

07 위 대화를 읽고 답할 수 있는 것은?

① How does the girl think about the boy?
② What is the girl's suggestion for the boy's problem?
③ How long have they known each other?
④ Why does the boy want to lose weight?
⑤ How old is the boy's dog?

08 자연스러운 대화가 되도록 (A)~(D)를 바르게 나열하시오.

> (A) Well, I broke my mom's favorite plate. What do you think I should do?
> (B) I hope you're right.
> (C) What's wrong? You look worried.
> (D) Tell her the truth. She will understand.

➡ _____

09 다음 상황을 읽고 빈칸에 들어갈 말을 조건에 맞게 쓰시오.

> You fought with one of your friend, Mina, today. On your way home, you thought you were sorry to have blamed her. So you wanted some advice from your best friend, Mike. In this situation, what would you say to Mike?
> You: "Mike, _____ "
> (should / say sorry)

➡ _____

[10~11] 다음 대화를 읽고 물음에 답하시오.

> B: How are your tomatoes doing? Are they growing well?
> G: No. I've gotten only a few tomatoes so far. What do you think I should do?
> B: Where do you have the pot?
> G: In the kitchen.
> B: Well, tomato plants need about 7 hours of sunlight a day.
> G: Oh, I see. I'll move the pot over to the window.

10 Where does the girl have the tomato pot? Answer in English with a full sentence.

➡ _____

11 위 대화의 내용과 일치하는 것은?

① The boy doesn't know if the girl is growing tomatoes.
② The girl has gotten lots of tomatoes.
③ The boy wants some tomatoes.
④ The boy gives the girl a tip about growing tomatoes.
⑤ The girl will put the pot in the kitchen.

[12~13] 다음 대화를 읽고 물음에 답하시오.

> Anna: Suho, is something wrong? You're very ①quiet today.
> Suho: I'm just a bit tired. I slept very ②little last night.
> Anna: Did you do something ③late last night?
> Suho: Yes, I watched a movie on my phone until 2 a.m. That's what I often do these days.
> Anna: Oh, that's why you have red eyes. You should go to bed ④before midnight for your health.
> Suho: I think my eyes are getting worse. What do you think I should do?
> Anna: Try eating lots of carrots and tomatoes. They're rich in vitamin A, so they'll keep your eyes ⑤unhealthy.
> Suho: I see. Thank you, Anna.

12 ①~⑤ 중 대화의 흐름상 어색한 것은?

①   ②   ③   ④   ⑤

13 What does Suho often do these days? Answer in English with a full sentence.

➡ _____

01 주어진 단어를 활용하여 다음 우리말을 영어로 쓰시오.

A: I'm tired because of my neighbor. She keeps playing the piano at night. 내가 무엇을 해야 한다고 생각해?
(what / you / think / should)
B: Why don't you ask her to stop playing the piano at night?

➡ _____

[02~04] 다음 대화를 읽고 물음에 답하시오.

B: Is something wrong, Jane? You don't look so good.
G: I ___(A)___ a sore throat. I think it's because of the fine dust these days.
B: Put some plants in your room. They ___(B)___ bad air in and produce fresh air.
G: Really? I'll ___(C)___ a few plants right away.

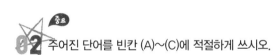

02 주어진 단어를 빈칸 (A)~(C)에 적절하게 쓰시오.

take / have / get

➡ (A) _____ (B) _____ (C) _____

03 대화의 내용에 맞게 빈칸에 알맞은 말을 쓰시오.

Jane thinks that _____ _____
_____ makes her throat _____ .

04 What is Jane likely to do after the conversation? Answer in English.

➡ _____

[05~06] 다음 대화를 읽고 물음에 답하시오.

B: (A)Is something wrong?
G: I'm just a little tired. I've watched a movie on my phone for two hours.
B: That's why you have red eyes. Try putting a warm towel over your eyes.
G: O.K. Thanks.

05 주어진 단어를 활용하여 밑줄 친 (A)와 같은 의미의 말을 4단어로 쓰시오.

(what / wrong)

➡ _____

06 Write the reason why the girl is tired. Use the phrase 'It's because.'

➡ _____

_____

07 자연스러운 대화가 되도록 (A)~(E)를 바르게 나열하시오.

(A) I have a stomachache. I think I ate too much for lunch.
(B) O.K. I'll give it a try.
(C) Bomi, do you have some medicine?
(D) Why don't you go for a walk?
(E) Why? Is something wrong?

➡ _____

08 다음 상황을 읽고 빈칸에 알맞은 말을 쓰시오. 한 칸에 하나의 단어만 쓰시오.

You meet your friend, Yumi, and find that she looks a little sad. You want to ask her if she is okay. In this situation, what do you say to her?
You: Yumi, _____ _____ _____ ?
You look sad.

Grammar
교과서

① 분사

> • Peter is a boy **throwing** a big ball. Peter는 큰 공을 던지는 소년이다.
> • I know the dog **barking** at Joseph. 나는 Joseph을 향해 짖는 개를 안다.

■ 현재분사는 '동사원형+-ing' 형태로 형용사처럼 명사를 앞 또는 뒤에서 꾸며준다. 일반적으로는 명사 앞에서, 다른 어구와 함께 구(phrase)를 이룰 때는 명사를 뒤에서 꾸민다.
 • **The crying baby** stopped kicking. 울고 있는 아기가 발차기를 멈췄다.
 • Did you see **the baby crying for the toy**? 장난감을 달라고 울고 있는 아기를 봤니?

■ 현재분사(-ing)는 능동/진행의 의미, 과거분사(p.p.)는 수동/완료의 의미를 갖는다.
 • The researchers are **searching** for the cause of storms. 연구진들은 폭풍우의 원인을 찾고 있는 중이다.
 • John saw the girl **dancing** on the stage. John은 무대에서 춤추고 있는 소녀를 봤다.
 • Watch out the **broken** pieces of glasses! 깨진 유리잔 조각들을 조심하세요!
 • The actors **invited** to the film festival showed up. 영화제에 초대된 배우들이 등장했다.

■ 명사를 뒤에서 꾸미는 분사구는 '주격 관계대명사+be동사'가 생략된 것으로 볼 수 있다.
 • The girl (**who was**) **wearing** Hanbok was Sophia. 한복을 입고 있는 그 소녀는 Sophia였다.
 • The students wanted to read the books (**which were**) **written** by O. Henry. 학생들은 O. Henry에 의해 쓰인 책들을 읽고 싶어했다.

■ 분사는 명사를 꾸며주는 한정 용법 외에, 주어나 목적어의 보충 설명을 하는 서술 용법이 있다. 이 경우, 분사가 주격 보어 또는 목적격 보어가 된다.
 • A gentleman stood **looking** at the picture. 한 신사가 그림을 보며 서 있었다.
 • The injured sheep lay **surrounded** by the wolves. 다친 양이 늑대들에게 둘러싸인 채로 누워 있었다.
 • He was sorry to keep me **waiting**. 그가 나를 기다리게 해서 미안해했다.
 • He heard his name **called**. 그는 그의 이름이 불리는 것을 들었다.
 • Susan had her dream house **built** in her hometown. Susan은 그녀의 고향에 자신의 꿈의 집이 건축되도록 했다.

핵심 Check

1. 다음 괄호 안에서 알맞은 단어를 고르시오.
  (1) A man (named / naming) Robert wanted to prove that tomatoes were safe to eat.
  (2) James had his arms (breaking / broken) while playing soccer.

❷ 동사 강조

> • I **do love** swimming in the lake. 나는 호수에서 수영하는 것을 정말 좋아한다.
> • James **does prefer** to eat spinach. James는 시금치 먹기를 정말 선호한다.

■ 문장에서 동사의 앞에 do를 써서 동사의 의미를 강조할 수 있다. 주어의 인칭과 시제에 맞춰 do/does/ did 등을 활용하며, really(정말)의 의미로 해석한다.
  • Popeye **did get** his superpower by eating spinach. Popeye는 시금치를 먹음으로써 그의 막강한 힘을 정말 얻었다.
  • Sam doesn't like horror movies, but he **does like** comedies. Sam은 공포영화를 좋아하지 않지만, 코미디 는 정말 좋아한다.

■ Be로 시작하는 명령문도, Be 앞에 Do를 써서 강조할 수 있다.
  • Be nice to others! = **Do** be nice to others! 다른 사람들에게 정말 착하게 대하라!

■ do는 동사를 강조하는데 반해, 재귀대명사는 (대)명사를 강조한다.
  • Emma **did play** the piano. Emma가 피아노를 정말 연주했다.
  • Emma played the piano **herself**. = Emma **herself** played the piano. Emma가 직접 피아노를 연주했다.

■ It ~ that 강조구문에서는 명사 또는 부사(구/절)를 강조한다. 강조하려는 대상에 따라 that을 관계대명 사 who(사람), which(사물)로, 또는 관계부사 when(시간), where(장소) 등으로 대체할 수 있다.
  • Clara broke the toy car at her cousin's house yesterday. Clara가 어제 사촌네 집에서 그 장난감 차를 부쉈다.
  → **It was** Clara **that**[**who**] broke the toy car at her cousin's house yesterday. 어제 사촌네 집에서 그 장 난감 차를 부순 것은 바로 Clara였다.
  → **It was** the toy car **that**[**which**] Clara broke at her cousin's house yesterday. Clara가 어제 사촌네 집 에서 부순 것은 바로 그 장난감 차였다.
  → **It was** yesterday **that**[**when**] Clara broke the toy car at her cousin's house. Clara가 사촌네 집에서 그 장난감 차를 부순 것은 바로 어제였다.
  → **It was** at her cousin's house **that**[**where**] Clara broke the toy car yesterday. 어제 Clara가 그 장난감 차를 부순 것은 바로 사촌네 집에서였다.

핵심 Check

2. 다음 괄호 안에서 알맞은 단어를 고르시오.
  (1) I (was / did) feel bad when I was passing by the smoking guys.
  (2) Carrots (does / do) contain a lot of vitamin A.

01 다음 문장에서 어법상 어색한 부분을 바르게 고쳐 쓰시오.

(1) In the future, carrots may actually be using in wars.

_____ ➡ _____

(2) I did called you the day before yesterday.

_____ ➡ _____

(3) Hannah is the one eats tomatoes right now.

_____ ➡ _____

(4) The manager received a letter writing in Latin.

_____ ➡ _____

02 다음 중 어법상 바르지 않은 것은?

① The villagers did build the castle about 100 years ago.
② Potatoes does help you in many ways.
③ Oliver does love what she cooks.
④ Patrick did come back home.
⑤ All of his family do like Anna's novel.

03 다음 대화의 밑줄 친 부분 중에서 어법상 잘못된 곳을 고르시오.

A: ①Aren't you ②tiring ③of eating spinach every day?
B: No, I'm not. I ④do ⑤feel healthy.

04 다음 우리말에 맞게 주어진 단어를 알맞게 배열하시오.

(1) 대부분의 미국인들은 토마토가 독성이 있다고 정말 생각했다. (did, were, poisonous, that, Americans, tomatoes, most, think)

➡ _____

(2) Lily가 찍은 사진들은 인상적이었다. (were, by, the, Lily, pictures, taken, impressive)

➡ _____

01 다음 괄호 안의 단어가 올바른 형태로 순서대로 짝지어진 것은?

> • The boy (pick) up the flower is my son.
> • The money (spend) for her tour in Europe was too much.
> • Some insects are (scare) of tomatoes.

① picking – spending – scaring
② picking – spent – scaring
③ picking – spent – scared
④ picked – spending – scared
⑤ picked – spent – scaring

02 다음 빈칸에 공통으로 들어갈 말로 알맞은 것은?

> • Kate _____ like her doll.
> • Sophie always _____ the laundry right after she comes home.

① does   ② has   ③ do
④ have   ⑤ don't

서답형

03 다음 예시와 같이 두 문장을 한 문장으로 연결할 때, 빈칸에 알맞은 말을 넣으시오.

> • British pilots improved their night vision.
> • They ate carrots.
> → British pilots eating carrots improved their night vision.

(1) • There were many people.
   • They were watching the pet contest.
   → There _____ _____ _____ the pet contest.

(2) • The swimming pool is very large.
   • It was built by my grandfather.
   → The swimming pool _____ _____ _____ _____ very large.

중요

04 밑줄 친 부분이 어법상 올바른 것은?

① The researcher did warned the people.
② Do be polite to the elderly!
③ The boy did changed his choice.
④ She does believed it is a dream.
⑤ My uncle does looks happy.

서답형

05 다음 문장에서 어법상 틀린 부분을 찾아 바르게 고쳐 쓰시오.

> He bought a shirt making in Vietnam.

_____ ➡ _____

06 다음 중 두 문장의 뜻이 같지 않은 것은?

① I do spend much time playing chess.
   → I really spend much time playing chess.
② Jenny did show me what she drew.
   → Jenny really showed me the picture that was drawn by her.
③ It was Ann that cooked me pizza.
   → It was Ann who cooked me pizza.
④ Sarah did break her leg.
   → Sarah really broke her leg.
⑤ He did find the missing kid in the amusement park.
   → He was able to find the missing kid in the amusement park.

중요

07 밑줄 친 부분의 쓰임이 다른 하나는?

① My dad hearing the news got disappointed.
② The kids tried locking the safe.
③ I want to raise a talking parrot.
④ The girl passing by them is Joan.
⑤ The barking wolf seemed like a puppy.

08 다음 우리말에 맞게 괄호 안에 주어진 단어를 알맞게 배열하시오.

> 꿀이 섞인 감자 주스가 당신의 피부를 부드럽게 만들어 준다.
> (honey, juice, potato, skin, with, soft, mixed, your, makes)

➡ _____

_____

09 다음 빈칸에 알맞은 말이 순서대로 바르게 짝지어진 것은?

> • Emily _____ love eating vegetables.
> • Peter and Mary _____ hope to be famous when they first made the group.

① did – does　　② do – did
③ does – did　　④ did – do
⑤ does – do

10 다음 밑줄 친 ⓐ, ⓑ를 어법상 알맞게 고친 것이 차례대로 짝지어진 것은?

> • She warned the little kid not to touch the ⓐburn fire.
> • The students ⓑsing by the tree were our school choir members.

① burning – sang　　② burning – singing
③ burnt – are singing　④ burnt – being sung
⑤ burning – be singing

11 다음 빈칸에 들어갈 말로 어색한 것은?

> A: Scott, you don't eat spinach any longer, do you?
> B: No, but I _____ when I was watching Popeye on TV.

① used to eat it a lot　　② ate it a lot
③ did ate it a lot　　　　④ used to do
⑤ did eat it a lot

12 다음 중 어법상 어색한 것을 모두 고르면?

① The little girl eats tomatoes on the chair is Sally.
② Spinach is actually considered one of the ten healthiest foods on the planet.
③ The researcher developing new material from carrots was Jenny.
④ Olivia was lied to all of us.
⑤ The people her family meeting in New York were so kind and gentle.

13 다음 밑줄 친 부분 중 어법상 어색한 것은?

① She did hide the book under the desk.
② All the jury do think she is innocent.
③ The poor do need the public support.
④ She does learn design 11 years ago.
⑤ Tom did repair his car this morning.

14 다음 중 어법상 옳은 것은?

① He sat surrounding by his friends.
② The old woman sat next to Mr. Brown was the mayor of the city.
③ Spinach can be using in a surprising way in the near future.
④ There was no pizza leaving for Mary.
⑤ The road leading to the city hall was full of traffic.

15 다음 문장의 밑줄 친 부분을 강조하는 문장으로 가장 알맞은 것은?

> Robert ate a basket of tomatoes.

① Robert ate so a basket of tomatoes.
② Robert did ate a basket of tomatoes.
③ Robert ate only a basket of tomatoes.
④ Robert did eat a basket of tomatoes.
⑤ Robert eating a basket of tomatoes.

서답형

16 다음 각 문장에서 어법상 어색한 부분을 하나씩 찾아서 알맞게 고치시오.

(1) Bill bought a book writing in Greek.

_____ ➡ _____

(2) Kate likes the potato juice mixing with honey.

_____ ➡ _____

(3) The volunteers took care of the cry babies in the orphanage.

_____ ➡ _____

17 다음 중 각 밑줄 친 부분의 쓰임이 주어진 문장의 밑줄 친 did와 같은 것은?

> The Americans **did** believe that something poisonous was in tomatoes.

① Everyone admitted Tom **did** his best.

② I **did** not have much information.

③ He **did** his role as a photographer.

④ I don't like it, but he **does** like it.

⑤ Monica has lots of things to **do**.

18 다음 중 밑줄 친 부분의 쓰임이 어색한 것을 모두 고르면?

① The students thought the story had lots of <u>touched</u> scenes.

② The dancing class may be the most <u>interesting</u> one here.

③ It was the most <u>excited</u> day of his life.

④ They were so curious that they tried to open the <u>locked</u> safe.

⑤ The clock is something <u>shown</u> you the time of the day.

19 다음 중 어법상 옳은 문장은?

① Spinach do keep our eyes healthy.

② Tim finally did made a sandwich cookie.

③ Liz does love seeing her pets.

④ Michael does plays the violin.

⑤ Barbara did called you yesterday.

서답형

20 다음 〈보기〉에 주어진 동사를 한 번씩만 사용하여 어법에 맞게 분사 형태로 빈칸을 완성하시오.

> ┤ 보기 ├
>
> know, cover, mean, name, use, make

> I'd like to introduce you to the snowboard (A)_____ from carrots. Carrots are well (B)_____ for having a lot of vitamin A. The Scottish researchers made a light and strong material (C)_____ carrots. The snowboard is so strong and light that it is (D)_____ Crosscarros, (E)_____ that carrots cross the steep mountain (F)_____ with snow.

21 Which of the following has the same usage as the underlined part below?

> The twins don't enjoy most vegetables, but they <u>do</u> like potatoes.

① Mary folds her arms and so <u>do</u> I.

② I'm sure that she <u>did</u> do her work.

③ Matt teaches math, <u>doesn't</u> he?

④ The students are <u>doing</u> some research on exercise.

⑤ What she <u>did</u> was to fix the roof.

서답형

22 다음 괄호 안의 어휘들을 배열하여, 우리말을 영작할 때 5번째와 10번째 단어를 쓰시오.

> 이것은 해바라기의 특성을 이용한다는 아이디어로부터 발명된 배터리이다.
>
> (using / a battery / of / the idea / sunflowers / this / the characteristic / invented from / of / is).

➡ _____, _____

01 다음 각 문장을 밑줄 친 부분을 강조하는 문장으로 바꿔 쓰시오.

(1) Sofia <u>found</u> her missing cat.

　➡ _____

(2) Gordon <u>knows</u> many K-pop songs.

　➡ _____

(3) Grace <u>wrote</u> these essays last week.

　➡ _____

02 다음 괄호 안의 단어들을 바르게 배열하여 문장을 완성하시오. (단, 동사를 어법상 알맞은 형태로 변형할 것.)

(1) The _____ is waiting for her boy friend. (stand / girl / the street / across)

(2) Do you know the music _____ _____? (by / on / play / the band / the stage)

(3) Luna is the one _____. (a / wear / shirt / red)

03 다음 대화의 빈칸을 채우되, 동사를 강조하는 'do'를 활용하시오.

(1) A: It's amazing. I can't believe David really built the huge tower.

　B: Yeah, but he _____ _____ it.

(2) A: Don't you think she should stop running?

　B: I _____ _____ so. I've been worried about her.

(3) A: Can you believe Evelyn wrote the classical music only at the age of 3?

　B: She _____ _____ the music at the age of 3.

04 다음 문장에서 어법상 어색한 부분을 찾아 바르게 고쳐 다시 쓰시오.

(1) This is the thing placing on the wall.

　➡ _____

(2) Sarah is the one wore glasses.

　➡ _____

(3) Mary is erasing the scores writing on the board.

　➡ _____

(4) I do love Susan, the girl drunk water.

　➡ _____

(5) The news was really shocked.

　➡ _____

05 다음 두 문장을 '분사'를 활용하여 한 문장으로 만들 때, 분사에 대한 조건에 맞게 빈칸에 석설한 단어를 넣으시오.

(1) Lily tried to play with the baby. The baby was crying. (명사 앞에서 수식)

　→ Lily tried to play _____ _____ _____ _____.

(2) They watched the birds. The birds were flying southwards. (명사 뒤에서 수식)

　→ They watched _____ _____ _____ _____.

(3) There is a taxi. It is illegally parked. (명사 앞에서 수식)

　→ There is _____ _____ _____ _____.

06 다음 우리말에 맞게 빈칸을 채우되, 괄호 안의 어휘를 이용하시오.

> Unlike Sarah (A)_____(sit) on a chair, the other members of the band played their instruments (B)_____(stand) on the stage, with Joy's eyes (C)_____ (close).
>
> (의자에 앉아 있는 Sarah와 달리, 다른 멤버들은 무대 위에 서서 그들의 악기를 연주했는데, Joy는 눈을 감고 있었다.)

07 다음 문장을 각각의 주어진 조건에 맞게 강조하는 문장으로 바꿔 쓰시오.

> Alex called you yesterday.

(1) Alex 강조. 재귀대명사 사용.

➡ _____

(2) you 강조. It ~ that 구문 사용.

➡ _____

(3) called 강조.

➡ _____

(4) yesterday 강조.

➡ _____

08 다음 괄호 안의 어휘를 배열하여 우리말에 맞게 빈칸을 채우시오.

> _____,
> (Ethan이 정말로 두통을 느꼈기 때문에), he went to the clinic for treatment. (feel, did, as, a, headache, Ethan)

09 다음 우리말에 맞게 영작할 때, 빈칸에 알맞은 단어를 〈보기〉에서 찾아, 어법에 맞게 활용하여 쓰시오.

> ┤ 보기 ├
> kill   call   hide   do

(1) Stella는 재즈 음악을 정말 좋아한다.

→ Stella _____ like Jazz music.

(2) 어떤 과학자들은 시금치의 특성을 이용해서 땅 속에 숨겨진 폭탄을 찾았다.

→ Some scientists used the characteristic of spinach to find bombs _____ in the ground.

(3) 그 곰이 개를 정말 죽였다.

→ The bear did _____ the dog.

(4) 코끼리 귀라고 불리는 식물은 독성이 있는 식물들 중 하나이다.

→ A plant _____ elephant ear is one of the poisonous plants.

10 다음 그림을 보고, 괄호 안의 어휘를 배열하여 우리말에 맞게 빈칸을 채우시오.

> If you want to keep insects away from your room, _____ in a corner of your room.
> 당신이 만약 당신의 방에서 벌레들을 쫓아내고 싶다면, 으깬 토마토 한 컵을 당신의 방 구석에 놓아두시오.
> (crushed / tomatoes / a cup / place / of)

➡ _____

Hidden Stories about Plants

Popeye and the Great Spinach

Popeye is a world-famous cartoon character. He gets his super power

by eating spinach. When Popeye became popular in the 1930s in the
by+동명사: '～함으로써'   '～할 때'(접속사)

United States, a lot of children began to eat spinach. Crystal City in
begin은 목적어로 to부정사와 동명사를 모두 사용할 수 있다.

Texas, which is called the spinach capital of the world, even built
관계대명사의 계속적 용법: 관계대명사 앞에 콤마가 있는 경우. that(×). is called: 수동태 구문

a statue of Popeye. Although eating spinach will not give us super
= Though

powers, spinach does have a lot of nutrients. It is actually considered
조동사 does가 일반동사인 have를 강조   └ '～라고 여겨진다' ┘

one of the ten healthiest foods on the planet.
one+of+the+최상급+복수 명사: '가장 ～한 … 중 하나'

Spinach can be used in a surprising way. When it absorbs water,
조동사가 있는 수동태: 조동사+be동사+p.p.

spinach also absorbs many other things from the soil. Some scientists

have used this characteristic of spinach to find bombs hidden in the
to부정사의 부사적 용법(목적)   bombs를 수식하는 과거분사로 앞에
'관계대명사+be동사'가 생략된 형태

ground. They make special spinach plants with sensors on their leaves.
～이 있는

When these plants soak up traces from bombs, the sensors light up.

---

hide 숨기다 (hide–hid–hidden)

spinach 시금치

cartoon 만화

capital 수도

statue 조각상, 동상

although ～임에도 불구하고, 비록 ～이지만

nutrient 영양소

consider 고려하다, 여기다

planet 행성, 세상

absorb 흡수하다, 빨아들이다

characteristic 특성, 특징

soak up 흡수하다, 빨아들이다

trace 흔적, 자취

 확인문제

● 다음 문장이 본문의 내용과 일치하면 T, 일치하지 <u>않으면</u> F를 쓰시오.

1 Popeye gets his super power by eating spinach. ☐

2 Crystal City in Texas, which is called the spinach center of the world, even built a statue of Popeye. ☐

3 Spinach is actually considered one of the ten healthiest foods on the planet. ☐

4 When it absorbs water, spinach also absorbs many other things from the air. ☐

5 Some scientists make special spinach plants with sensors on their leaves. ☐

6 When these special spinach plants soak up water from soils, the sensors light up. ☐

Carrots in World War II

In 1940, the Royal Air Force defeated German fighters during World War II by using a radar system. The British government wanted to keep this technology a secret, so it published an article in the newspaper. It said that British pilots improved their night vision because they ate a lot of carrots. Everybody believed the story and began to eat a lot more carrots than before. Can we really improve night vision by eating lots of carrots? Not really, but carrots contain a lot of vitamin A, which does keep our eyes healthy.

In the future, carrots may actually be used in wars. Scottish researchers have discovered a way to turn carrots into a very strong and light material. It can even be used to make battleships. This new material has already been used to make snowboards and bicycles.

Tomatoes, the Scariest Vegetables

We all know that tomatoes are good for our health. Up until the 1800s, however, most Americans thought that tomatoes were poisonous. In 1820, a man named Robert Johnson wanted to prove that tomatoes were safe to eat. So, he ate a basket of tomatoes in front of many people watching him. They all expected him to die, but nothing happened to him. Ever since then, Americans have enjoyed eating tomatoes.

We are no longer afraid of tomatoes, but some insects are still scared of them. If you want to keep insects away from your room, place a bowl of crushed tomatoes in a corner of your room. Insects will not come near the tomatoes.

---

defeat 물리치다, 패배시키다
radar 레이더, 전파 탐지기
system 시스템, 체계, 장치
government 정부, 국가
keep a secret 비밀을 지키다
article 기사
pilot 비행사, 조종사
improve 개선하다, 향상시키다
vision 시력
contain 함유하다, 들어 있다
researcher 연구원, 조사원
snowboard 스노보드
poisonous 유독한, 독성의
insect 곤충, 벌레
crush 으스러뜨리다

확인문제

● 다음 문장이 본문의 내용과 일치하면 T, 일치하지 않으면 F를 쓰시오.

1 In 1940, the Royal Air Force won against German fighters during World War II by using a radar system. ☐

2 British pilots improved their night vision because they ate a lot of carrots. ☐

3 Up until the 1800s, most Americans thought that tomatoes were safe. ☐

4 Some insects are still scared of tomatoes. ☐

5 If you place a bowl of crushed tomatoes in a corner of your room, insects will come near the tomatoes. ☐

● 우리말을 참고하여 빈칸에 알맞은 말을 쓰시오.

1 _____ Stories about Plants

2 Popeye and the Great _____

3 Popeye is a world-famous _____ _____.

4 He gets his super power _____ _____ _____.

5 When Popeye _____ _____ in the 1930s in the United States, a lot of children began to eat spinach.

6 Crystal City in Texas, which is called _____ _____ _____ of the world, even built _____ _____ of Popeye.

7 _____ eating spinach will not give us super powers, spinach _____ _____ a lot of nutrients.

8 It is actually considered _____ _____ _____ _____ _____ _____ on the planet.

9 Spinach can be used _____ _____ _____ _____.

10 When it absorbs water, spinach _____ _____ many other things _____ the soil.

11 Some scientists have used this characteristic of spinach to find bombs _____ _____ _____ _____.

12 They make special spinach plants _____ _____ _____ _____.

13 When these plants _____ _____ traces from bombs, the sensors _____ _____.

14 Carrots in _____ _____ _____

15 In 1940, the Royal Air Force _____ German fighters _____ World War II _____ _____ a radar system.

16 The British government wanted to _____ this technology a _____, so it published _____ _____ in the newspaper.

17 It said that British pilots _____ _____ _____ _____ _____ because they ate a lot of carrots.

1	식물에 대한 숨겨진 이야기
2	Popeye와 위대한 시금치
3	Popeye는 세계적으로 유명한 만화 캐릭터다.
4	그는 시금치를 먹음으로써 초인적인 힘을 얻는다.
5	Popeye가 1930년대 미국에서 인기를 얻었을 때, 많은 어린이들이 시금치를 먹기 시작했다.
6	텍사스의 크리스털 시티는 세계의 시금치 수도라고 불리는데, 이곳에서는 Popeye의 동상을 세우기까지 했다.
7	비록 시금치를 먹는 것이 우리에게 초인적인 힘을 주지는 않지만, 시금치는 정말로 많은 영양분을 가지고 있다.
8	이것은 실제로 지구상에서 가장 건강한 식품 10개 중 하나로 여겨진다.
9	시금치는 놀라운 용도로 사용될 수 있다.
10	그것이 물을 흡수할 때, 시금치는 흙으로부터 다른 많은 것들도 흡수한다.
11	몇몇 과학자들은 시금치의 이 특성을 땅에 숨겨진 폭탄을 찾는 데 사용했다.
12	그들은 잎에 감지기가 있는 특별한 시금치를 만든다.
13	이 식물들이 폭탄의 흔적을 흡수하면, 감지기가 빛난다.
14	제2차 세계대전에서의 당근
15	1940년, 영국 공군은 제2차 세계 대전에서 레이더 시스템을 사용해 독일군을 패배시켰다.
16	영국 정부는 이 기술을 비밀로 하기를 원했기 때문에, 신문에 기사를 하나 냈다.
17	그것은 영국 비행사들이 당근을 많이 먹어 야간 시력이 좋아졌다는 내용이었다.

18 Everybody believed the story and began to eat a lot more carrots _____ _____.

19 Can we really improve night vision _____ _____ lots of carrots?

20 Not really, but carrots contain a lot of vitamin A, _____ _____ _____ our eyes healthy.

21 In the future, carrots _____ _____ _____ _____ in wars.

22 Scottish researchers have discovered a way to _____ carrots _____ a very strong and light material.

23 It _____ _____ _____ _____ to make battleships.

24 This new material _____ _____ _____ _____ to make snowboards and bicycles.

25 Tomatoes, the _____ Vegetables

26 We all know that tomatoes _____ _____ _____ our health.

27 _____ _____ the 1800s, however, most Americans thought that tomatoes were _____.

28 In 1820, a man _____ Robert Johnson wanted to prove that tomatoes were _____ _____ _____.

29 So, he ate _____ _____ _____ tomatoes in front of many people _____ him.

30 They all expected him to die, but nothing _____ _____ him.

31 Ever since then, Americans _____ _____ _____ tomatoes.

32 We are _____ _____ afraid of tomatoes, but some insects are still _____ _____ them.

33 If you want to _____ insects _____ _____ your room, _____ a bowl of _____ tomatoes in a corner of your room.

34 Insects will not _____ _____ the tomatoes.

18 모두가 그 이야기를 믿었고 전보다 훨씬 많은 당근을 먹기 시작했다.

19 우리는 정말 당근을 많이 먹어서 야간 시력을 높일 수 있을까?

20 실제로 그렇지는 않지만, 당근은 많은 비타민 A를 함유하는데, 그것은 정말로 우리 눈을 건강하게 유지해 준다.

21 미래에는, 당근이 실제로 전쟁에 이용될지도 모른다.

22 스코틀랜드의 연구원들은 당근을 매우 강하고 가벼운 물질로 바꾸는 방법을 발견했다.

23 그것은 심지어 전함을 만드는 데 사용될 수도 있다.

24 이 새로운 소재는 이미 스노보드와 자전거를 만드는 데 사용되었다.

25 토마토, 가장 무서운 채소

26 우리는 모두 토마토가 건강에 좋다는 것을 안다.

27 그러나, 1800년대까지 대부분의 미국인들은 토마토에 독성이 있다고 생각했다.

28 1820년에, Robert Johnson이라는 이름의 남자가 토마토가 먹기에 안전하다는 것을 증명하기를 원했다.

29 그래서, 그는 그를 지켜보는 많은 사람들 앞에서 한 바구니의 토마토를 먹었다.

30 그들은 모두 그가 죽을 것이라고 예상했으나 그에게는 아무일도 일어나지 않았다.

31 그 이후로, 미국인들은 토마토를 먹는 것을 즐겼다.

32 우리는 더 이상 토마토를 두려워하지 않지만, 몇몇 곤충들은 여전히 그것을 무서워한다.

33 만약 곤충들이 방에 들어오지 않게 하고 싶다면, 으깬 토마토 한 그릇을 방구석에 놓아 두어라.

34 곤충들은 토마토 가까이 오지 않을 것이다.

● 우리말을 참고하여 본문을 영작하시오.

1 식물에 대한 숨겨진 이야기
➡ _____

2 Popeye와 위대한 시금치
➡ _____

3 Popeye는 세계적으로 유명한 만화 캐릭터다.
➡ _____

4 그는 시금치를 먹음으로써 초인적인 힘을 얻는다.
➡ _____

5 Popeye가 1930년대 미국에서 인기를 얻었을 때, 많은 어린이들이 시금치를 먹기 시작했다.
➡ _____

6 텍사스의 크리스털 시티는 세계의 시금치 수도라고 불리는데, 이곳에서는 Popeye의 동상을 세우기까지 했다.
➡ _____

7 비록 시금치를 먹는 것이 우리에게 초인적인 힘을 주지는 않지만, 시금치는 정말로 많은 영양분을 가지고 있다.
➡ _____

8 이것은 실제로 지구상에서 가장 건강한 식품 10개 중 하나로 여겨진다.
➡ _____

9 시금치는 놀라운 용도로 사용될 수 있다.
➡ _____

10 그것이 물을 흡수할 때, 시금치는 흙으로부터 다른 많은 것들도 흡수한다.
➡ _____

11 몇몇 과학자들은 시금치의 이 특성을 땅에 숨겨진 폭탄을 찾는 데 사용했다.
➡ _____

12 그들은 잎에 감지기가 있는 특별한 시금치를 만든다.
➡ _____

13 이 식물들이 폭탄의 흔적을 흡수하면, 감지기가 빛난다.
➡ _____

14 제2차 세계대전에서의 당근
➡ _____

15 1940년, 영국 공군은 제2차 세계 대전에서 레이더 시스템을 사용해 독일군을 패배시켰다.
➡ _____

16 영국 정부는 이 기술을 비밀로 하기를 원했기 때문에, 신문에 기사를 하나 냈다.
➡ _____

17 그것은 영국 비행사들이 당근을 많이 먹어 야간 시력이 좋아졌다는 내용이었다.

➡ _____

18 모두가 그 이야기를 믿었고 전보다 훨씬 많은 당근을 먹기 시작했다.

➡ _____

19 우리는 정말 당근을 많이 먹어서 야간 시력을 높일 수 있을까?

➡ _____

20 실제로 그렇지는 않지만, 당근은 많은 비타민 A를 함유하는데, 그것은 정말로 우리 눈을
건강하게 유지해 준다.

➡ _____

21 미래에는, 당근이 실제로 전쟁에 이용될지도 모른다.

➡ _____

22 스코틀랜드의 연구원들은 당근을 매우 강하고 가벼운 물질로 바꾸는 방법을 발견했다.

➡ _____

23 그것은 심지어 전함을 만드는 데 사용될 수도 있다.

➡ _____

24 이 새로운 소재는 이미 스노보드와 자전거를 만드는 데 사용되었다.

➡ _____

25 토마토, 가장 무서운 채소

➡ _____

26 우리는 모두 토마토가 건강에 좋다는 것을 안다.

➡ _____

27 그러나, 1800년대까지 대부분의 미국인들은 토마토에 독성이 있다고 생각했다.

➡ _____

28 1820년에, Robert Johnson이라는 이름의 남자가 토마토가 먹기에 안전하다는 것을 증명하기를 원했다.

➡ _____

29 그래서, 그는 그를 지켜보는 많은 사람들 앞에서 한 바구니의 토마토를 먹었다.

➡ _____

30 그들은 모두 그가 죽을 것이라고 예상했으나 그에게는 아무 일도 일어나지 않았다.

➡ _____

31 그 이후로, 미국인들은 토마토를 먹는 것을 즐겼다.

➡ _____

32 우리는 더 이상 토마토를 두려워하지 않지만, 몇몇 곤충들은 여전히 그것을 무서워한다.

➡ _____

33 만약 곤충들이 방에 들어오지 않게 하고 싶다면, 으깬 토마토 한 그릇을 방구석에 놓아 두어라.

➡ _____

_____

34 곤충들은 토마토 가까이 오지 않을 것이다.

➡ _____

[01~03] 다음 글을 읽고 물음에 답하시오.

Popeye is a world-famous cartoon ⓐ character. (①) He gets his super power by eating spinach. (②) When Popeye became popular in the 1930s in the United States, a lot of children began to eat spinach. (③) Crystal City in Texas, which is called the spinach capital of the world, even built a statue of Popeye. (④) It is actually considered one of the ten healthiest foods on the planet. (⑤)

중요

01 위 글의 흐름으로 보아, 주어진 문장이 들어가기에 가장 적절한 곳은?

> Although eating spinach will not give us super powers, spinach does have a lot of nutrients.

①   ②   ③   ④   ⑤

02 위 글의 밑줄 친 ⓐcharacter와 같은 의미로 쓰인 것을 고르시오.

① She is my sister, but we have very different character.
② He was a minor character in the book, but everyone loved him.
③ This Chinese character means good luck.
④ The climate of this city plays a big role in the city's character.
⑤ He is a man of fine character.

중요

03 According to the passage, which is NOT true?

① Popeye gets his super power by eating spinach.

② Many children began to eat spinach when Popeye became popular in the 1930s in the United States.
③ People call Crystal City in Texas the spinach capital of the world.
④ In fact, eating spinach will give us super powers.
⑤ Spinach is actually considered one of the ten healthiest foods on the earth.

[04~06] 다음 글을 읽고 물음에 답하시오.

Spinach can be used in a surprising way. When it absorbs water, spinach also absorbs many other things ____ⓐ____ the soil. Some scientists have used (A)this characteristic of spinach to find bombs hidden in the ground. They make special spinach plants ____ⓑ____ sensors on their leaves. (B)When these plants soak up traces from bombs, the sensors go out.

04 위 글의 빈칸 ⓐ와 ⓑ에 들어갈 전치사가 바르게 짝지어진 것은?

	ⓐ	ⓑ		ⓐ	ⓑ
①	from	with	②	on	to
③	on	from	④	from	at
⑤	to	with			

서답형

05 위 글의 밑줄 친 (A)this characteristic이 가리키는 것을 우리말로 쓰시오.

➡ _____

_____

서답형

06 위 글의 밑줄 친 (B)에서 흐름상 어색한 부분을 찾아 고치시오.

_____ ➡ _____

[07~09] 다음 글을 읽고 물음에 답하시오.

In 1940, the Royal Air Force defeated German fighters during World War II by using a radar system. The British government wanted to keep this technology a secret, so (A)it published an article in the newspaper. It said that British pilots improved their night ____ⓐ____ because they ate a lot of carrots. Everybody believed the story and began to eat a lot more carrots than before. Can we really improve night ____ⓑ____ by eating lots of carrots? Not really, but carrots contain a lot of vitamin A, which does keep our eyes healthy.

07 위 글의 빈칸 ⓐ와 ⓑ에 공통으로 들어갈 알맞은 말을 고르시오.

① version
② sense of touch
③ hearing
④ vision
⑤ sense of smell

서답형

08 위 글의 밑줄 친 (A)it이 가리키는 것을 본문에서 찾아 쓰시오.

➡ _____

09 위 글의 제목으로 알맞은 것을 고르시오.

① Hidden Stories about Nature
② Carrots in World War II
③ How to Eat a Lot More Carrots
④ A Radar System of the Royal Air Force
⑤ Carrots, Good for the Night Vision

[10~12] 다음 글을 읽고 물음에 답하시오.

In the future, ⓐ당근이 실제로 전쟁에 이용될지도 모른다. Scottish researchers have discovered a way to turn carrots into a very strong and light material. It can even be used to make battleships. This new material ⓑhas already been used to make snowboards and bicycles.

서답형

10 위 글의 밑줄 친 ⓐ의 우리말에 맞게 주어진 어휘를 이용하여 7 단어로 영작하시오.

actually, used

➡ _____

11 위 글의 밑줄 친 ⓑ의 현재완료 용법과 같은 용법으로 쓰인 것을 모두 고르시오.

① How long has he been ill in bed?
② I have just finished my homework.
③ They have never seen such a horrible movie.
④ Has she met him yet?
⑤ I have lost my pen.

12 Which question CANNOT be answered after reading the passage?

① In the future, is it possible for carrots to be used in wars?
② What have Scottish researchers discovered?
③ How do Scottish researchers turn carrots into a very strong and light material?
④ Can the very strong and light material made from carrots be used to make battleships?
⑤ Has the very strong and light material made from carrots been used yet?

[13~15] 다음 글을 읽고 물음에 답하시오.

We all know that tomatoes are good for our health. Up until the 1800s, ___@___, most Americans thought that tomatoes were poisonous. In 1820, a man named Robert Johnson wanted to prove that tomatoes were safe to eat. So, he ate a basket of tomatoes in front of many people watching him. They all expected him to die, but nothing happened to him. Ever since then, Americans have enjoyed eating tomatoes.

We are no longer afraid of tomatoes, but some insects are still scared of them. If you want to keep insects away from your room, place a bowl of crushed tomatoes in a corner of your room. Insects will not come near the tomatoes.

13 위 글의 빈칸 @에 들어갈 알맞은 말을 고르시오.

① as a result　　② furthermore
③ that is　　④ for example
⑤ however

14 위 글의 주제로 **알맞은** 것을 고르시오.

① eating tomatoes to be healthy
② the spread of tomatoes in America
③ the myth and truth about tomatoes
④ the danger of eating poisonous tomatoes
⑤ how to keep insects away from the room

서답형

15 본문의 내용과 일치하도록 다음 빈칸 (A)와 (B)에 알맞은 단어를 쓰시오.

If you place a bowl of (A)_____
_____ in a corner of your room,

you can keep insects away from your room. It's because some insects are still (B)_____ of tomatoes, they will not come near the tomatoes.

[16~18] 다음 글을 읽고 물음에 답하시오.

@Spinach can be used in a surprising way. When it absorbs water, spinach also absorbs many other things from the soil. Some scientists have used this characteristic of spinach ⓑto find bombs hidden in the ground. They make special spinach plants with sensors on their leaves. When these plants ⓒsoak up traces from bombs, the sensors light up.

서답형

16 위 글의 밑줄 친 문장 @의 구체적인 용도에 해당하는 문장을 본문에서 찾아, 첫 단어와 마지막 단어를 쓰시오

➡ 첫 단어: _____, 마지막 단어: _____

17 위 글의 밑줄 친 ⓑto find와 to부정사의 용법이 **다른** 것을 **모두** 고르시오.

① I've worked hard to find bombs.
② But I don't know how to find bombs.
③ Is it easy to find bombs hidden in the ground?
④ Who is the best person to find bombs?
⑤ Let's start to find bombs together.

서답형

18 위 글의 밑줄 친 ⓒsoak up을 본문에 나오는 어휘를 사용하여 한 단어로 바꿔 쓰시오.

➡ _____

[19~21] 다음 글을 읽고 물음에 답하시오.

Popeye is a world-famous cartoon character. He gets his super power by eating spinach. When Popeye became popular in the 1930s in the United States, a lot of children began to eat spinach. Crystal City in Texas, which is (A)[calling / called] the spinach (B)[capital / capitol] of the world, even built a statue of Popeye. Although ⓐeating spinach will not give us super powers, spinach (C)[did / does] have a lot of nutrients. It is actually considered one of the ten healthiest foods on the planet.

서답형

19 위 글의 괄호 (A)~(C)에서 문맥이나 어법상 알맞은 낱말을 골라 쓰시오.

➡ (A) _____ (B) _____ (C) _____

20 아래 〈보기〉에서 위 글의 밑줄 친 ⓐeating과 문법적 쓰임이 같은 것의 개수를 고르시오.

┌─── 보기 ├───
① Eating spinach will keep you healthy.
② I saw her eating spinach.
③ He is fond of eating spinach.
④ Is eating spinach really good for your health?
⑤ When I met her, she was eating spinach.
└───────────

① 1개   ② 2개   ③ 3개   ④ 4개   ⑤ 5개

서답형

21 How does Popeye get his super power? Answer in English in a full sentence. (6 words)

➡ _____

[22~24] 다음 글을 읽고 물음에 답하시오.

We all know that tomatoes are good for our health. Up until the 1800s, however, most Americans thought that tomatoes were poisonous. In 1820, a man named Robert Johnson wanted to prove that tomatoes were safe to eat. So, he ate a basket of tomatoes in front of many people watching him. They all expected him to die, but nothing happened to him. Ever since then, Americans have enjoyed eating tomatoes.

We are no longer afraid of tomatoes, but some insects are still scared of ⓐthem. If you want to keep insects away from your room, place a bowl of crushed tomatoes in a corner of your room. Insects will not come near the tomatoes.

서답형

22 위 글의 밑줄 친 ⓐthem이 가리키는 것을 본문에서 찾아 쓰시오.

서답형 ➡ _____

23 다음 문장에서 위 글의 내용과 <u>다른</u> 부분을 찾아서 고치시오.

┌─────────────────────────┐
│ In 1820, a man named Robert Johnson │
│ ate a basket of tomatoes in front of many │
│ people watching him and died against │
│ their expectations. │
└─────────────────────────┘

중요
_____ ➡ _____

24 위 글을 읽고 알 수 <u>없는</u> 것을 고르시오.

① Up until the 1800s, what did most Americans think about tomatoes?
② What did Robert Johnson want to prove?
③ Since when, have Americans enjoyed eating tomatoes?
④ What insects are scared of tomatoes?
⑤ If you place a bowl of crushed tomatoes in a corner of your room, what will happen?

[01~03] 다음 글을 읽고 물음에 답하시오.

Popeye is a world-famous cartoon character. He gets his super power by eating spinach. When Popeye became popular in the 1930s in the United States, a lot of children began to eat spinach. Crystal City in Texas, which is called the spinach capital of the world, even built a statue of Popeye. ⓐAs eating spinach will not give us super powers, spinach does have a lot of nutrients. ⓑIt actually considers one of the ten healthiest foods on the planet.

중요
01 위 글의 밑줄 친 ⓐ에서 흐름상 어색한 부분을 찾아 고치시오.

➡ _____ ➡ _____

02 위 글의 밑줄 친 ⓑ에서 어법상 틀린 부분을 찾아 고치시오.

➡ _____ ➡ _____

고난이도
03 본문의 내용과 일치하도록 다음 빈칸 (A)와 (B)에 알맞은 단어를 쓰시오.

Popeye, who gets his super power by eating spinach, is a world-famous (A)_____ _____. Thanks to Popeye, a lot of children in the United States began (B)_____ _____ in the 1930s.

[04~06] 다음 글을 읽고 물음에 답하시오.

Spinach can ___ⓐ___ in a surprising way. When it absorbs water, spinach also absorbs many other things from the soil. Some scientists have used this characteristic of spinach to find bombs ___ⓑ___ in the ground. ⓒThey make special spinach plants with sensors on ⓓtheir leaves. When these plants soak up traces from bombs, the sensors light up.

04 위 글의 빈칸 ⓐ에 use를, ⓑ에 hide를 각각 알맞은 형태로 쓰시오.

➡ ⓐ _____ ⓑ _____

중요
05 위 글의 밑줄 친 ⓒThey와 ⓓtheir가 가리키는 것을 본문에서 찾아 쓰시오.

➡ ⓒ _____ ⓓ _____

06 다음 빈칸 (A)와 (B)에 알맞은 단어를 넣어 땅에 숨겨진 폭탄을 찾는 데 시금치를 사용하는 방법을 완성하시오.

Spinach absorbs many other things in addition to water from the soil. When the special spinach plants with (A)_____ on their leaves soak up traces from bombs, the sensors light up and help people find (B)_____ under the ground.

[07~10] 다음 글을 읽고 물음에 답하시오.

In 1940, the Royal Air Force (A)[defeated / was defeated] German fighters (B)[during / while] ⓐWorld War II by using a radar system. The British government wanted to keep this technology a secret, so it published an article in the newspaper. ⓑIt said that British pilots improved their night vision because they ate a lot of carrots. Everybody believed the story and began to eat a lot more carrots than before. Can we really improve night vision by eating lots of carrots? Not really, but carrots contain a lot of vitamin A, which does keep our eyes (C)[healthy / healthily].

07 위 글의 괄호 (A)~(C)에서 문맥이나 어법상 알맞은 낱말을 골라 쓰시오.

➡ (A) _____ (B) _____ (C) _____

08 위 글의 밑줄 친 ⓐWorld War II를 읽는 법을 영어로 쓰시오.

➡ _____

09 위 글의 밑줄 친 ⓑIt이 가리키는 것을 본문에서 찾아 쓰시오.

➡ _____

10 위 글을 읽고, (1) 영국 정부가 신문기사로 당근의 효능에 관해 발표한 것과 (2) 당근의 실제 효능을 우리말로 쓰시오.

➡ (1) _____

_____

(2) _____

[11~14] 다음 글을 읽고 물음에 답하시오.

We all know that tomatoes are good for our health. Up until the 1800s, however, most Americans thought that tomatoes were poisonous. In 1820, a man named Robert Johnson wanted to prove that tomatoes were safe to eat. So, he ate a basket of tomatoes in front of many people watching him. They all expected him to die, but nothing happened to him. ⓐ그 이후로, 미국인들은 토마토를 먹는 것을 즐겼다.

ⓑWe are no longer afraid of tomatoes, but some insects are still scared of them. ⓒIf you want to keep insects away from your room, place a bowl of crushing tomatoes in a corner of your room. Insects will not come near the tomatoes.

11 위 글의 밑줄 친 ⓐ의 우리말에 맞게 주어진 어휘를 이용하여 8 단어로 영작하시오.

Ever, then, have enjoyed

➡ _____

12 위 글의 밑줄 친 ⓑ를 다음과 같이 바꿔 쓸 때 빈칸에 들어갈 알맞은 말을 두 단어로 쓰시오.

➡ We are not afraid of tomatoes _____

_____ ,

13 위 글의 밑줄 친 ⓒ에서 어법상 틀린 부분을 찾아 고치시오.

_____ ➡ _____

14 Why did Robert Johnson eat a basket of tomatoes in front of many people watching him? Answer in English beginning with "Because". (11 words)

➡ _____

_____

Inventions from Plants

The Sunflower Battery is a good way to produce energy. It is a battery
_{to부정사의 형용사적 용법}
invented from the idea of using the characteristic of sunflowers. Like
battery를 수식하는 과거분사(수동)   소유를 나타내는 of   전치사로 사용
sunflowers, it faces the sun during the day, so it produces more electricity than
= the Sunflower Battery   결과를 이끄는 접속사
other batteries.
other+복수 명사

구문해설 • way: 방법 • characteristic: 특성, 특징 • face: ~을 향하다
• produce: 만들다, 생산하다

해바라기 배터리는 에너지를 만드는 좋은 방법입니다. 그것은 해바라기의 특징을 이용한다는 생각에서 만들어진 배터리입니다. 해바라기처럼, 그것은 낮 동안에 태양을 향해서, 다른 배터리보다 더 많은 전기를 만들어 냅니다.

After You Read A Read and Match

1. **Spinach**

  • the secret of Popeye's super power

  • one of the ten healthiest foods on the planet
    one of the+복수 명사: ~ 중의 하나
  • used with sensors to find bombs hidden in the ground
    to부정사의 부사적 용법(목적)   과거분사(수동)

2. **Carrots**

  • used to make snowboards and bicycles
    to부정사의 부사적 용법(목적)
  • made into a very strong and light material
    ~으로(변화)
  • containing a lot of vitamin A, which keeps our eyes healthy
    = and it(계속적 용법의 관계대명사)   keep+목적어+목적격보어(형용사) healthily(×)

3. **Tomatoes**

  • good for keeping insects away
    keep ~ away: ~을 가까이 오지 못하게 하다
  • considered poisonous until the 1800s

구문해설 • spinach: 시금치 • snowboard: 스노보드 • contain: 함유하다, 들어 있다
• insect: 곤충, 벌레 • consider: 고려하다, 여기다

1. 시금치
• Popeye의 초인적인 힘의 비밀
• 지구상에서 가장 건강한 식품 10개 중 하나
• 땅에 숨겨진 폭탄을 찾기 위해 감지기와 함께 사용된다.

2. 당근
• 스노보드와 자전거를 만드는 데 사용된다.
• 매우 강하고 가벼운 물질이 된다.
• 많은 비타민 A를 함유하는데, 그것은 정말로 우리 눈을 건강하게 유지해 준다.

3. 토마토
• 곤충들이 가까이 오지 못하게 하는 데 좋다.
• 1800년대까지 독성이 있다고 여겨졌다.

Write

Potatoes are good for your health. They keep your heart healthy because they
5형식 V +목적어+목적보어   종속접속사(이유)
lower blood pressure. They also solve your skin problems. Potato juice mixed
과거분사
with honey makes your skin soft and clear. In addition, they help you lose
단수 동사에 유의   목적보어1 목적보어2 (병렬구조)   to lose도 가능(help: 준사역동사)
weight. If you eat potatoes, you will stay full for a long time. Potatoes help
2형식 V+형용사(주격보어)
you stay healthy in many ways.

구문해설 • be good for: ~에 좋다 • keep+A+형용사: A를 ~한 상태로 유지시켜 주다 • lower: 낮추다
• blood pressure: 혈압 • in addition: 게다가 • stay full: 배부른 상태를 유지하다

감자는 당신의 건강에 좋다. 감자는 혈압을 낮춰주기 때문에 당신의 심장을 건강하게 지켜준다. 감자는 또한 당신의 피부 문제를 해결해 준다. 꿀을 넣은 감자 주스는 당신의 피부를 부드럽고 깨끗하게 만들어 준다. 게다가, 감자는 당신이 살을 빼도록 도와준다. 당신이 감자를 먹으면, 오랜 시간 배부른 상태를 유지할 것이다. 감자는 여러 가지 면에서 당신을 건강하게 지내도록 도와준다.

01 다음 중 단어의 관계가 다른 하나는?

① improve – get better
② absorb – soak up
③ contain – involve
④ consider – regard
⑤ defeat – yield

02 다음 중 주어진 단어를 풀이하는 말로 가장 적절한 것은?

> nutrient

① someone who is asking questions at an interview
② an occasion when people sit down and eat, usually at a regular time
③ a chemical or food that provides what is needed for plants for animals to live and grow
④ all the different foods you use when you are cooking a particular dish
⑤ taste of a food or drink

03 주어진 단어를 활용하여 다음 우리말을 영어로 쓰시오.

(1) 그 마법사는 모자를 토끼로 바꾸었다.
   (magician / turn)
   ➡ _____

(2) 내가 무엇을 하도록 조언하시겠어요?
   (advise)
   ➡ _____

(3) 신선한 공기를 마시는 건 어때?
   (why / you / some)
   ➡ _____

04 다음 빈칸에 공통으로 들어갈 말로 가장 적절한 것은?

> • Yesterday the ship disappeared without _____.
> • They could finally _____ him to an address in New York.

① happen   ② email   ③ trace
④ rule   ⑤ notice

05 다음 중 주어진 단어의 밑줄 친 부분과 같은 의미로 쓰인 것은?

> Crystal City in Texas is called the spinach <u>capital</u> of the world.

① English is written with a <u>capital</u> 'E'.
② A large amount of <u>capital</u> is invested in the company.
③ Paris is the fashion <u>capital</u> of the world.
④ The firm is having difficulty raising <u>capital</u>.
⑤ The cause of business failure is a lack of <u>capital</u>.

06 다음 우리말에 맞게 빈칸에 알맞은 말을 쓰시오.

(1) 그 감독과 배우 둘 다 정말 놀라운 사람들이야.
   ➡ Both _____ _____ and _____
      _____ are really _____ people.

(2) 몇몇 방문객들은 그 개를 두려워했습니다.
   ➡ Some _____ _____ _____
      _____ the dog.

Conversation

07 다음 대화의 빈칸에 들어갈 말로 적절하지 <u>않은</u> 것은?

> **A:** I forgot my promise with Sumi. I think she is really upset. _____
>
> **B:** Why don't you just say sorry to her? She will accept your apology.

① What do you think I should do?
② What do you suggest?
③ How I should keep the promise?
④ What's your advice?
⑤ What do you advise me to do?

[08~09] 다음 대화를 읽고 물음에 답하시오.

> **B:** Is ①something wrong? You don't look so ②good.
>
> **G:** I have a sore throat. I think ③it's because of the fine dust these days.
>
> **B:** Put ④some plants in your room. They take bad air in and produce fresh air.
>
> **G:** Really? I'll get ⑤a little plants right away.

08 ①~⑤ 중 어법상 바르지 <u>않은</u> 것을 찾아 바르게 고쳐 쓰시오.

_____ ➡ _____

09 다음 중 대화의 내용과 일치하는 것은?

① The boy doesn't care if something is wrong with the girl.
② The girl feels great because of the fresh air.
③ The boy thinks that the fine dust made the girl's throat sore.
④ The girl is going to get some plants after a long time.
⑤ The boy advises the girl to get some plants in her room.

[10~11] 다음 대화를 읽고 물음에 답하시오.

> **B:** How are your tomatoes doing? Are they growing well? (①)
>
> **G:** No. I've gotten only a few tomatoes so far. (②)
>
> **B:** Where do you have the pot? (③)
>
> **G:** In the kitchen.
>
> **B:** Well, tomato plants need about 7 hours of sunlight a day. (④)
>
> **G:** Oh, I see. I'll move the pot over to the window. (⑤)

10 ①~⑤ 중 주어진 문장이 들어가기에 가장 적절한 곳은?

> What do you think I should do?

①   ②   ③   ④   ⑤

11 대화의 내용에 맞게 빈칸에 알맞은 말을 여섯 단어로 쓰시오.

> For the pot to get enough sunlight, the girl will _____.

➡ _____

12 다음 대화의 밑줄 친 부분을 내신하여 쓸 수 있는 것은?

> **B:** Is something wrong?
>
> **G:** I'm just a little tired. I've watched a movie on my phone for two hours.
>
> **B:** That's why you have red eyes. Try putting a warm towel over your eyes.
>
> **G:** <u>O.K. Thanks.</u>

① Alright. Never mind.
② Okay, but I'm sorry.
③ I'll give it a try.
④ You should keep that in mind.
⑤ O.K. You're welcome.

Grammar

13 다음 중 어법상 올바른 문장은?

① A man naming Popeye is so strong.
② The teacher recommended vegetables growing by the farmers.
③ This is the material made out of carrots.
④ I love eating carrots contained a lot of vitamin A.
⑤ Those inviting to the party didn't show up.

14 다음 중 어법상 올바른 문장은?

① Vegetables does make you healthy.
② He does says she's crazy.
③ Jason is looks handsome on the stage.
④ Shelly did make a decision.
⑤ The Smiths do met them last year.

15 다음 빈칸에 알맞은 말이 바르게 짝지어진 것은?

• In the future, carrots may actually be _____ in wars.
• Some kinds of insects are still _____ of tomatoes.

① used – scared ② using – scaring
③ using – scared ④ used – scary
⑤ use – scaring

16 다음 우리말을 괄호 안의 단어를 활용하여 영작하고, 주어진 조건에 맞는 문장으로 바꾸시오.

Robert가 자신을 지켜보는 많은 사람들 앞에서 한 바구니의 토마토를 먹었다.

(1) 영작
= Robert _____
_____ .
(tomatoes / many people / watch / eat / a basket of / him / in front of)
(2) '먹었다'를 강조, '관계대명사+be동사' 추가
- Robert _____
_____ .

17 다음 밑줄 친 부분의 쓰임이 나머지와 다른 것은?

① Potatoes do help you in many ways.
② They do eat tomatoes every morning.
③ Angela does work for the company.
④ Maybe you can do some laundry once in a while.
⑤ Ron did play the superhero character.

18 다음 밑줄 친 부분의 쓰임이 나머지 셋과 다른 것은? (2개)

① Carrots containing a lot of vitamin A help keep you healthy.
② The researchers were busy developing the new material from carrots.
③ Many people watching 'Popeye' on TV liked to eat spinach.
④ People reading the article believed that carrots improved night vision.
⑤ Popeye gets his super power by eating spinach.

19 다음 그림을 보고 괄호 안의 단어를 활용해서 빈칸에 알맞게 채우시오.

(1)

➡ When I finished reading *The Little Prince*, it _____ (do) make me impressed.

(2)

➡ The most famous Egyptian pyramids are those _____ (find) at Giza, Egypt.

20 다음 문장들에서 우리말을 영어로 옮긴 것 중 어법상 어색한 것을 고르시오.

① 선생님은 팔짱을 낀 채로 학생들에게 얘기를 시작했다.
 → The teacher began talking to the students with his arms folded.
② 그는 창문을 열어 놓은 채로 잠이 들었다.
 → He fell asleep with the window open.
③ Scarlet은 다리를 꼰 채로 경찰관을 쳐다보았다.
 → Scarlet looked at the police officer with her legs crossing.
④ 나는 셔츠가 완전히 젖은 채로 집에 왔다.
 → I came home with my shirt all wet.
⑤ Elsa는 눈을 감은 채로 노래를 불렀다.
 → Elsa sang with her eyes closed.

21 다음 중 각각의 (A)와 (B)에서 밑줄 친 부분의 쓰임이 서로 같은 것을 고르시오.

① (A) Frank <u>did</u> keep his promise.
 (B) They <u>did</u> something to correct it.
② (A) What should he <u>do</u> now?
 (B) Emma <u>does</u> believe what he says.
③ (A) Peter <u>does</u> eat a lot of spinach.
 (B) Susan knows that I <u>do</u> believe her.
④ (A) Everyone wonders how he <u>did</u> it.
 (B) <u>Do</u> be nice to others.
⑤ (A) <u>Do</u> you know when she will come?
 (B) People don't trust him even if he <u>does</u> good things.

22 다음 중 어법상 <u>어색한</u> 것을 <u>모두</u> 고르시오.

① The room does feel too cold.
② His uncle do likes playing with him.
③ Sandy did believe what you said.
④ Do be careful when you drive.
⑤ Mom did forced me to eat tomatoes.

23 다음 두 문장을 현재분사를 이용하여, 한 문장으로 만드시오.

• The man was Robert Johnson.
• He wanted to prove that tomatoes were safe to eat.

➡ The man _____
_____.

Reading

[24~26] 다음 글을 읽고 물음에 답하시오.

Popeye is a world-famous cartoon character. He gets his super power by eating spinach. When Popeye became popular in the 1930s in the United States, a lot of children began to eat spinach. Crystal City in Texas, which is called the spinach ⓐcapital of the world, even built a statue of Popeye. Although eating spinach will not give us super powers, spinach does have a lot of nutrients. ⓑ이것은 실제로 지구상에서 가장 건강한 식품 10개 중 하나로 여겨진다.

24 위 글의 밑줄 친 ⓐcapital과 같은 의미로 쓰인 것을 고르시오.

① We need capital investment.
② Please write in capital letters.
③ Cairo is the capital of Egypt.
④ He set up a business with a starting capital of £100,000.
⑤ He was sentenced to a capital punishment.

25 위 글의 밑줄 친 ⓑ의 우리말에 맞게 주어진 어휘를 이용하여 13 단어로 영작하시오.

actually, consider, healthiest, planet

➡ _____

_____

26 본문의 내용과 일치하도록 다음 빈칸 (A)~C)에 알맞은 단어를 쓰시오.

We won't get super powers by eating (A)_____, but it really has lots of (B)_____. In fact, people consider it one of the ten (C)_____ foods on the planet.

[27~29] 다음 글을 읽고 물음에 답하시오.

In 1940, the Royal Air Force defeated German fighters during World War II by using a radar system. (①) The British government wanted to keep ⓐthis technology a secret, so it published an article in the newspaper. (②) Everybody believed the story and began to eat a lot more carrots than before. (③) Can we really improve night vision by eating lots of carrots? (④) Not really, but carrots contain a lot of vitamin A, which does keep our eyes healthy. (⑤)

27 위 글의 흐름으로 보아, 주어진 문장이 들어가기에 가장 적절한 곳은?

It said that British pilots improved their night vision because they ate a lot of carrots.

①　　　②　　　③　　　④　　　⑤

28 위 글의 밑줄 친 ⓐthis technology가 가리키는 것을 본문에서 찾아 쓰시오.

➡ _____

29 According to the passage, which is NOT true?

① In 1940, German fighters were defeated by the Royal Air Force during World War II.
② The British government published an article in the newspaper, which said that British pilots improved their night vision by eating a lot of carrots.
③ Everybody believed the article and began to eat a lot more carrots than before.
④ We can really improve night vision by eating lots of carrots.
⑤ Vitamin A contained a lot in carrots does keep our eyes healthy.

01 다음 중 단어의 관계가 나머지 넷과 <u>다른</u> 하나는? 출제율 95%

① edit – editor
② teach – teacher
③ cook – cooker
④ sail – sailor
⑤ visit – visitor

02 다음 중 밑줄 친 단어의 우리말 의미가 바르지 <u>않은</u> 것은? 출제율 100%

① I am <u>afraid of</u> darkness. (~을 두려워하다)
② Why don't you <u>get some fresh air</u>? (신선한 공기를 마시다)
③ I think I <u>have a fever</u>. (열이 나다)
④ <u>In addition</u>, you should try harder. (게다가)
⑤ You should <u>keep away from</u> it. (~에 가까워지다)

03 다음과 같이 풀이되는 단어로 가장 적절한 것은? 출제율 90%

a person in a book, play, film etc.

① actor   ② director
③ character   ④ founder
⑤ writer

04 주어진 단어를 활용하여 다음 우리말을 아홉 단어로 이루어진 한 문장의 영어로 쓰시오 출제율 95%

너는 여전히 너의 친구들과 연락하고 지내니?
(keep / still)

➡ _____

05 자연스러운 대화가 되도록 (A)~(D)를 바르게 나열하시오. 출제율 100%

(A) I have a sore throat. I think it's because of the fine dust these days.
(B) Really? I'll get a few plants right away.
(C) Put some plants in your room. They take bad air in and produce fresh air.
(D) Is something wrong? You don't look so good.

➡ _____

[06~08] 다음 대화를 읽고 물음에 답하시오.

G: What's wrong? You look worried.
B: Well, I broke my mom's favorite plate.
                    (A)
G: (B)Tell her the truth. She will understand.
B: I hope you're right.

06 다음 중 빈칸 (A)에 들어갈 말로 적절하지 <u>않은</u> 것은? 출제율 95%

① What do you think I should do?
② What do you suggest?
③ What do you advise me to do?
④ What is your advise?
⑤ What can you do for me?

07 주어진 단어를 활용하여 밑줄 친 (B)와 같은 의미의 문장을 쓰시오. 출제율 90%

what about

➡ _____

08 Write the reason why the boy looks worried. Use the phrase 'It's because.' 출제율 95%

➡ _____

09 다음 대화의 내용과 일치하는 것은?

> B: Bomi, do you have some medicine?
> G: Why? Is something wrong?
> B: I have a stomachache. I think I ate too much for lunch.
> G: Why don't you go for a walk?
> B: O.K. I'll give it a try.

① Bomi is suffering from a stomachache.
② There is a matter with Bomi.
③ Bomi will go for a walk.
④ Bomi wants to know why the boy needs some medicine.
⑤ Bomi doesn't give any advice to the boy.

10 다음 중 빈칸에 들어갈 말로 적절하지 <u>않은</u> 것은?

> A: I've found some money on the street. What do you think I should do?
> B: _____

① You should take it to the police station.
② How about taking it to the police station?
③ I suggest you should take it to the police station.
④ If I were you, I would take it to the police station.
⑤ Make sure taking it to the police station.

11 다음 중 밑줄 친 단어의 바로 앞에 '주격 관계대명사+be동사'가 생략되어 있다고 볼 수 <u>없는</u> 것을 <u>모두</u> 고르면?

① Spinach is the vegetable <u>considered</u> one of the 10 healthiest foods.
② What is the language <u>spoken</u> in Mali?
③ I'm <u>interested</u> in Mexican artworks.
④ Don't touch the baby bears <u>sleeping</u> with their mother.

⑤ Is there anyone who saw the <u>sleeping</u> beauty in the woods?
⑥ There are many school buses <u>parked</u> at the parking lot.
⑦ Jason's presentation was not impressive at all and even <u>boring</u>.
⑧ The cameras <u>made</u> in Taiwan are quite inexpensive and good in quality.

12 다음 중 어법상 어색한 문장을 <u>모두</u> 고르시오.

① You are make me happy.
② Carrots do contains vitamin A.
③ Sean did take good care of his dogs.
④ Munch did paint *The Scream*.
⑤ The kid did believe what the magician showed.
⑥ The citizens did understood what the mayor announced.
⑦ It were the books that he bought there.

13 다음 중 밑줄 친 부분의 용법이 나머지 넷과 <u>다른</u> 것은?

① She liked collecting the leaves <u>fallen</u> on the road.
② Some students went to see the works of Picasso <u>displayed</u> in the art museum.
③ Kelly was so proud of <u>being</u> the fan of BTS that she couldn't help crying.
④ My dad came home with a huge box <u>filled</u> with toys.
⑤ Do you know that pretty girl <u>smiling</u> at a lady?

14 다음 중 괄호 안의 단어를 분사로 바꾸어 빈칸에 넣을 때, 분사의 종류가 나머지 셋과 <u>다른</u> 두 개를 고르시오.

① Cathy likes to help _____ dogs. (abandon)

② The boys saw grey smoke _____ out of the chimney. (come)

③ Brandon must make himself _____ in Japanese. (understand)

④ She kept him _____ while she took some pictures. (wait)

⑤ Sofia didn't see the boy _____ at her at the meeting. (smile)

15 다음 두 문장을 접속사 Although로 시작하는 한 문장으로 고쳐 쓰되, 밑줄 친 부분을 강조하여 쓰시오.

> • Eating spinach won't give us super powers.
> • But spinach <u>has</u> a lot of nutrients.

➡ Although _____
_____ .

[16~18] 다음 글을 읽고 물음에 답하시오.

Popeye is a world-famous cartoon character. He gets his super power by eating spinach. When Popeye became popular in the 1930s in the United States, a lot of children began to eat spinach. Crystal City in Texas, which is called the spinach capital of the world, even built a statue of Popeye. ⓐAlthough eating spinach will not give us super powers, spinach ⓑdoes have a lot of nutrients. It is actually considered one of the ten healthiest foods on the planet.

16 위 글의 밑줄 친 ⓐ를 3형식 문장으로 고치시오.

➡ _____
_____

17 위 글의 밑줄 친 ⓑdoes와 문법적 쓰임이 같은 것을 고르시오.

① She does not like fish.

② Not only does she speak Spanish, she's also good with computers.

③ Mom does the dishes.

④ What does he do in his free time?

⑤ He does look tired.

18 위 글을 읽고, (1) Popeye가 준 시금치의 이미지와 (2) 시금치에 관한 실제 사실을 우리말로 쓰시오.

➡ (1) Popeye가 준 시금치의 이미지: _____
_____

(2) 시금치에 관한 실제 사실: _____
_____
_____

[19~21] 다음 글을 읽고 물음에 답하시오.

In the future, carrots may actually be used in wars. Scottish researchers have discovered a way to turn carrots into a very strong and light material. ⓐIt can even be used to making battleships. ⓑThis new material has already been used to make snowboards and bicycles.

19 위 글의 밑줄 친 ⓐ에서 어법상 틀린 부분을 찾아 고치시오.

_____ ➡ _____

20 다음 빈칸 (A)와 (B)에 알맞은 단어를 넣어 위 글의 밑줄 친 ⓑ에 대한 소개를 완성하시오.

출제율 90%

> It is a very (A)_____ _____ _____ material made from (B)_____ by Scottish researchers.

21 위 글의 주제로 알맞은 것을 고르시오.

출제율 100%

① the way to turn carrots into a very strong and light material
② the advantage of a very strong and light material
③ the uses of carrots in wars in the future
④ the products made from the same raw material
⑤ the material used to make snowboards and bicycles

[22~24] 다음 글을 읽고 물음에 답하시오.

We all know that tomatoes are good for our health. (①) Up until the 1800s, however, most Americans thought that tomatoes were poisonous. (②) In 1820, ⓐRobert Johnson이라는 이름의 남자가 토마토가 먹기에 안전하다는 것을 증명하기를 원했다. (③) So, he ate a basket of tomatoes in front of many people watching him. (④) Ever since then, Americans have enjoyed eating tomatoes. (⑤)

We are no longer afraid of tomatoes, but some insects are still scared of them. If you want to keep insects away from your room, place a bowl of crushed tomatoes in a corner of your room. Insects will not come near the tomatoes.

22 위 글의 흐름으로 보아, 주어진 문장이 들어가기에 가장 적절한 곳은?

출제율 95%

> They all expected him to die, but nothing happened to him.

①   ②   ③   ④   ⑤

23 위 글의 밑줄 친 ⓐ의 우리말에 맞게 주어진 어휘를 알맞게 배열하시오.

출제율 90%

> that / to eat / Robert Johnson / safe / tomatoes / a man / were / wanted / named / to prove

➡ _____

24 According to the passage, which is NOT true?

출제율 100%

① All of us know that tomatoes are healthy food.
② Up until the 1800s, most Americans thought that it was safe to eat tomatoes.
③ Robert Johnson ate a basket of tomatoes while many people were watching him.
④ We are not afraid of tomatoes any more.
⑤ You can keep insects away from your room by placing a bowl of crushed tomatoes in a corner of your room.

[25~26] 다음 글을 읽고 물음에 답하시오.

Potatoes are good for your health. They keep your heart healthy because they lower blood pressure. They also solve your skin problems. Potato juice mixed with honey makes your skin soft and clear. ____ⓐ____, they help you lose weight. If you eat potatoes, you will stay full for a long time. ⓑPotatoes help you stay healthy in many ways.

25 위 글의 빈칸 ⓐ에 들어갈 알맞은 말을 고르시오.

출제율 95%

① In addition   ② Therefore   ③ However
④ By contrast   ⑤ For example

26 위 글의 밑줄 친 ⓑ의 내용을 본문에서 찾아 우리말로 쓰시오. (세 가지)

출제율 90%

➡ (1) _____
(2) _____
(3) _____

[01~02] 다음 대화를 읽고 물음에 답하시오.

> B: (A)몸무게를 줄이는 건 너무 어려워. What do you think I should do?
>
> G: Well, why don't you walk your dog every day?
>
> B: My dog would love it, but would it help me lose weight?
>
> G: Sure. When you walk your dog, you're actually exercising, too.
>
> B: O.K. I'll think about it.

01 주어진 단어를 활용하여 밑줄 친 우리말 (A)를 영어로 쓰시오.

> (it / so / hard)

➡ _____

02 대화의 내용에 맞게 빈칸에 알맞은 말을 쓰시오.

> The girl suggests that the boy walk his dog every day because she thinks it will help him _____ _____.

03 다음 상황을 읽고 빈칸에 알맞은 말을 쓰시오. 한 칸에 하나의 단어만 쓰시오.

> You come home from school and find that your mom is sitting on a chair. She looks like she is sick. You want to ask her if she is all right. What do you say to her?
>
> **You:** Mom, _____ _____ _____?

04 다음 중 밑줄 친 부분을 어법에 맞게 고치고, 고친 단어의 종류가 다른 두 개를 찾아, 그 이유를 설명하시오.

> ⓐ Spinach can be used in a surprise way.
> ⓑ They are waiting for the train leave at 7:00.
> ⓒ Popeye gets his power by eat spinach.
> ⓓ We saw a beautiful wall of a building cover with ivy.
> ⓔ She memorized a poem write by Ralph Waldo Emerson.
> ⓕ Since Robert's experiment, Americans have enjoyed eat tomatoes.

➡ ⓐ _____ ⓑ _____ ⓒ _____
　ⓓ _____ ⓔ _____ ⓕ _____

이유: _____

05 다음 주어진 문장을 밑줄 친 부분을 강조하는 문장으로 바꾸어 쓰시오.

(1) British pilots ate a lot of carrots.
　➡ _____

(2) Place a bowl of crushed tomatoes in a corner of your room.
　➡ _____
　_____

(3) People in Hong Kong love freedom.
　➡ _____

06 다음 그림을 보고 괄호 안의 단어를 알맞게 배열하여 빈칸에 넣으시오. (동사는 어법에 맞게 변형 가능)

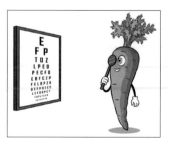

➡ Can we really improve night vision by eating lots of carrots? Not really, but carrots contain a lot of vitamin A, _____ .

(keep, eyes, which, our, healthy, do)

09 위 글을 읽고, (1) 1800년대까지 대부분의 미국인들의 토마토에 대한 생각과 (2) 1820년 이후의 미국인들의 토마토에 대한 태도를 우리말로 쓰시오.

➡ (1) 1800년대까지 대부분의 미국인들의 토마토에 대한 생각: _____

(2) 1820년 이후의 미국인들의 토마토에 대한 태도: _____

[07~09] 다음 글을 읽고 물음에 답하시오.

We all know that tomatoes are good for our health. Up until the 1800s, however, most Americans thought that tomatoes were poisonous. In 1820, a man (A)[naming / named] Robert Johnson wanted to prove that tomatoes were safe to eat. So, he ate a basket of tomatoes in front of many people (B) [watching / watched] him. They all expected him ⓐ___ , but nothing (C)[happened / was happened] to him. Ever since then, Americans have enjoyed eating tomatoes.

We are no longer afraid of tomatoes, but some insects are still scared of them. If you want to keep insects away from your room, place a bowl of crushed tomatoes in a corner of your room. Insects will not come near the tomatoes.

[10~11] 다음 글을 읽고 물음에 답하시오.

In 1940, the Royal Air Force defeated German fighters during World War II by using a radar system. ⓐ영국 정부는 이 기술을 비밀로 하기를 원했기 때문에, 신문에 기사를 하나 냈다. It said that British pilots improved their night vision because they ate a lot of carrots. Everybody believed ⓑthe story and began to eat a lot more carrots than before. Can we really improve night vision by eating lots of carrots? Not really, but carrots contain a lot of vitamin A, which does keep our eyes healthy.

10 위 글의 밑줄 친 ⓐ의 우리말에 맞게 주어진 어휘를 알맞게 배열하시오.

a secret / published / to keep / so / wanted / the British government / it / in the newspaper / this technology / an article / ,

➡ _____

_____

07 위 글의 빈칸 ⓐ에 die를 알맞은 형태로 쓰시오.

➡ _____

11 위 글의 밑줄 친 ⓑthe story가 가리키는 것을 본문에서 찾아 쓰시오.

➡ _____

_____

08 위 글의 괄호 (A)~(C)에서 어법상 알맞은 낱말을 골라 쓰시오.

➡ (A) _____ (B) _____ (C) _____

01 다음 대화를 참고하여 빈칸에 알맞은 말을 쓰시오.

> Brian: How are your tomatoes doing? Are they growing well?
>
> Grace: No. I've gotten only a few tomatoes so far. What do you think I should do?
>
> Brian: Where do you have the pot?
>
> Grace: In the kitchen.
>
> Brian: Well, tomato plants need about 7 hours of sunlight a day.
>
> Grace: Oh, I see. I'll move the pot over to the window.

> Brain wonders if Grace's tomatoes are _____. However, Grace says
> _____ so far. Grace wants Brain to give _____, so he asks
> her _____. Grace answers she has it _____. Brian tells her that
> _____, so Grace says that _____
> _____.

02 다음 그림들을 보고, 괄호 안에 주어진 어휘들을 필요한 만큼 활용하여, 분사가 들어가는 문장을 영작하시오. (두 문장 모두 Unlike 로 시작하고 인칭과 시제 등에 유의하여 활용할 것.)

(boss, sleep, man, present the plan)   (I, my sister, read a book, sofa, clean, table, on)

(1) _____.

(2) _____.

03 다음 내용을 바탕으로 감자의 이로운 점을 설명하는 글을 쓰시오.

> **Main Idea**   • lower blood pressure
> Potatoes are good for your health.   **Supporting Detail 2**
> **Supporting Detail 1**   solve your skin problems
> keep your heart healthy   • make your skin soft and clear

> Potatoes are good for (A)_____. They keep your heart healthy because they
> (B)_____. They also solve your (C)_____. Potato juice mixed with
> honey makes your skin (D)_____.

단원별 모의고사

01 다음 중 빈칸에 들어갈 말이 <u>다른</u> 하나는?

① I can't promise I can _____ it a secret.

② Kate, _____ away from the edge of the cliff.

③ After our summer class ends, let's _____ in touch!

④ We can _____ better use of our resources.

⑤ I told the driver to _____ the change.

02 다음 중 주어진 단어와 같은 관계가 <u>아닌</u> 것은?

> library – librarian

① call – caller

② play – player

③ science – scientist

④ economic – economist

⑤ visit – visitor

03 다음 중 단어의 영영풀이가 바르지 <u>않은</u> 것은?

① hide: to cover something so that you cannot be seen clearly

② cartoon: funny drawing in a newspaper or magazine

③ carrot: a long pointed orange vegetable that grows under the ground

④ defeat: not to succeed in winning the battle

⑤ discover: to become aware of something that you didn't know about before

04 자연스러운 대화가 되도록 (A)~(E)를 바르게 나열하시오.

> (A) Well, why don't you walk your dog every day?
>
> (B) O.K. I'll think about it.
>
> (C) It's so hard to lose weight. What do you think I should do?
>
> (D) Sure. When you walk your dog, you're actually exercising, too.
>
> (E) My dog would love it, but would it help me lose weight?

➡ _____

[05~06] 다음 대화를 읽고 물음에 답하시오.

B: _____ (A) _____ You don't look so good.

G: I have a sore throat. I think it's because of the fine dust these days.

B: Put some plants in your room. They take bad air in and produce fresh air.

G: Really? I'll get a few plants right away.

05 다음 중 빈칸 (A)에 들어갈 말로 적절하지 <u>않은</u> 것은?

① Is something wrong?

② Did anything go wrong?

③ What's the matter with you?

④ What did you do wrong?

⑤ Did something happen?

06 대화의 내용에 맞게 빈칸에 알맞은 말을 쓰시오.

> The girl thinks that because there is _____ _____ these days, she has a sore throat. So the boy advises her to _____ _____ _____ in her room.

07 다음 대화 중 자연스럽지 <u>않은</u> 것은?

① A: What's wrong?
   B: I made a few mistakes in the math test.
② A: I have a headache. What do you think I should do?
   B: Why don't you go see a doctor?
③ A: Is something wrong?
   B: I can't sleep well these days. What should I do?
④ A: I lied to my friend, Sumi. Please give me advice.
   B: I think you should apologize to her.
⑤ A: I can't save any money. What do you suggest?
   B: How about buying more clothes?

08 다음 대화의 빈칸에 들어갈 말로 적절하지 <u>않은</u> 것은?

> A: Is something wrong?
> B: This problem is too hard to solve. What do you think I should do?
> A: _____

① Why don't you ask the teacher for help?
② How about asking the teacher for help?
③ Make sure the teacher asks you for help.
④ I suggest you should ask the teacher for help.
⑤ You should ask the teacher for help.

09 다음 대화의 밑줄 친 우리말을 일곱 단어로 이루어진 한 문장의 영어로 쓰시오.

> A: Is something wrong?
> B: I am so nervous about tomorrow's contest. 내가 뭘 해야 한다고 생각해?
> A: Why don't you relax and practice more?

➡ _____

[10~12] 다음 대화를 읽고 물음에 답하시오.

> Anna: Suho, is something ①<u>wrong</u>? You're very quiet today.
> Suho: I'm just a bit tired. I slept very little last night.
> Anna: Did you do something ②<u>late</u> last night?
> Suho: Yes, I watched a movie on my phone until 2 a.m. That's what I often do these days.
> Anna: Oh, ③<u>that's because</u> you have red eyes. You should go to bed before midnight for your health.
> Suho: I think my eyes are getting ④<u>worse</u>. What do you think I should do?
> Anna: Try eating lots of carrots and tomatoes. They're rich in vitamin A, so they'll keep your eyes healthy.
> Suho: ⑤<u>I see.</u> Thank you, Anna.

10 ①~⑤ 중 글의 흐름상 어색한 것은?

①   ②   ③   ④   ⑤

11 Write the reason why Anna advises Suho to try eating lots of carrots and tomatoes. Use the phrase 'It's because.'

➡ _____
_____

12 위 대화를 읽고 답할 수 <u>없는</u> 것은?

① Why is Suho very quiet today?
② Why did Suho sleep very little last night?
③ What does Suho often do these days?
④ What does Anna advise Suho to do for his health?
⑤ How long does Suho watch a movie on his phone?

13 다음 밑줄 친 부분 중 어법상 어색한 것을 고르시오.

① The new material <u>using</u> carrots can even be used to make battleships.
② Kevin felt <u>interested</u> in the healthy effects of spinach.
③ She likes the sound of <u>falling</u> rain.
④ Clocks are something <u>showing</u> you the time.
⑤ Olivia bought some vegetables <u>included</u> spinach, carrots, and tomatoes.

14 다음 중 주어진 문장의 밑줄 친 부분과 쓰임이 같은 것을 모두 고르시오.

When it takes in water, spinach also <u>does</u> absorb many other things.

① <u>Do</u> we really improve night vision by eating a lot of carrots?
② She <u>doesn't</u> have any food to eat.
③ They <u>do</u> think it's even healthier to eat tomatoes every day.
④ <u>Do</u> not expect the man to help us.
⑤ Susan <u>did</u> the dishes by herself.
⑥ We all <u>do</u> know that tomatoes are good for our health.
⑦ I wonder how he <u>did</u> the trick.

15 괄호 안의 단어를 사용하여 어법에 맞게 주어진 문장의 빈칸을 쓸 때, 빈칸에 들어갈 말과 쓰임이 같지 않은 것을 고르시오.

Scottish scientists turned carrots into a very strong and light material, which is already _____ (use) to make snowboards and bicycles.

① My father has invented a box _____ (design) to keep tomatoes fresh.

② She can't attend the meeting _____ (schedule) on Thursday.
③ Many people eat carrots _____ (contain) a lot of vitamin A.
④ Don't touch the tomato _____ (crush) to make insect repellent.
⑤ Sue gathered the dishes _____ (break) by her mistake.

16 우리말과 일치하도록 괄호 안의 어구를 바르게 배열하시오.

(1) 이 새로운 물질이 벌써 자전거를 만들기 위해 사용되어져 왔다.
(bicycles, material, been, has, to, new, this, used, make, already).

➡ _____

_____

(2) 어떤 과학자들은 땅 속에 숨겨진 폭탄을 찾기 위해 시금치의 이러한 특성을 이용해 왔다.
(this characteristic, bombs, to find, used, of, some scientists, have, spinach, in the ground, hidden).

➡ _____

_____

17 다음 중 밑줄 친 단어의 쓰임이 나머지 넷과 <u>다른</u> 것은?

① Crystal City in Texas <u>called</u> the spinach capital of the world is a small town.
② Vitamin A <u>contained</u> in carrots does keep our eyes healthy.
③ Some insects <u>scared</u> of tomatoes don't come near tomato crush.
④ Chinese do love eating <u>boiled</u> vegetables.
⑤ The female pop singer, IU, has <u>composed</u> a lot of good songs.

[18~19] 다음 글을 읽고 물음에 답하시오.

Popeye is a world-famous cartoon character. He gets his super power by eating spinach. When Popeye became popular in the 1930s in the United States, a lot of children began to eat spinach. Crystal City in Texas, which is called the spinach capital of the world, even built a statue of Popeye. Although eating spinach will not give us super powers, spinach does have a lot of nutrients. ⓐIt is actually considered one of the ten healthiest foods on the planet.

18 다음 문장에서 위 글의 내용과 다른 부분을 찾아서 고치시오.

Popeye is a real person.

_____ ➡ _____

19 위 글의 밑줄 친 ⓐIt이 가리키는 것을 본문에서 찾아 쓰시오.

➡ _____

[20~22] 다음 글을 읽고 물음에 답하시오.

In 1940, the Royal Air Force defeated German fighters during World War II by using a radar system. The British government wanted to keep this technology a secret, so it published an (A)article in the newspaper. It said that British pilots improved their night vision because they ate a lot of carrots. Everybody believed the story and began to eat a lot more carrots than before. Can we really improve night vision by eating lots of carrots? Not really, but carrots contain a lot of vitamin A, (B)which ⓐ_____ our eyes healthy.

20 위 글의 빈칸 ⓐ에 keeps를 강조하는 형태로 바꿔 쓰시오.

➡ _____

21 위 글의 밑줄 친 (A)article과 같은 의미로 쓰인 것을 고르시오.

① We need an article of clothing.
② Have you seen that article about young fashion designers?
③ She didn't pay for the article she had bought.
④ According to the article 3, it is against the law.
⑤ This shampoo is a first class article.

22 위 글의 밑줄 친 (B)를 접속사를 사용하여 고치시오.

➡ _____

[23~25] 다음 글을 읽고 물음에 답하시오.

We all know that tomatoes are good for our health. Up until the ⓐ1800s, however, most Americans thought that tomatoes were poisonous. In ⓑ1820, a man named Robert Johnson wanted to prove that tomatoes were safe ⓒto eat. So, he ate a basket of tomatoes in front of many people watching him. They all expected him to die, but nothing happened to him. Ever since then, Americans have enjoyed eating tomatoes.

We are no longer afraid of tomatoes, but some insects are still scared of them. If you want to keep insects away from your room, place a bowl of crushed tomatoes in a corner of your room. Insects will not come near the tomatoes.

23 위 글의 밑줄 친 ⓐ1800s와 ⓑ1820을 읽는 법을 영어로 쓰시오.

➡ ⓐ _____ ⓑ _____

24 위 글의 밑줄 친 ⓒto eat과 to부정사의 용법이 다른 것을 모두 고르시오.

① It was safe to eat tomatoes.
② What is the best way to eat tomatoes?
③ I'm too young to eat tomatoes well.
④ Who chose to eat tomatoes?
⑤ Robert Johnson was brave enough to eat tomatoes.

25 위 글의 제목으로 알맞은 것을 고르시오.

① Tomatoes, Good for Our Health
② The Reason Americans Were Afraid of Tomatoes
③ Robert Johnson Liked Tomatoes Very Much
④ Tomatoes, the Scariest Vegetables
⑤ The Kind of Insects Which Are Scared of Tomatoes

[26~27] 다음 글을 읽고 물음에 답하시오.

We all know that tomatoes are good for our health. Up until the 1800s, however, most Americans thought that tomatoes were ____ⓐ____ . In 1820, a man named Robert Johnson wanted to prove that tomatoes were ____ⓑ____ to eat. So, he ate a basket of tomatoes in front of many people watching him. They all expected him to die, but nothing happened to him. Ever since then, Americans ⓒhave enjoyed eating tomatoes.

26 위 글의 빈칸 ⓐ와 ⓑ에 들어갈 알맞은 말을 고르시오.

① safe – harmless
② poisonous – safe
③ precious – harmful
④ harmless – precious
⑤ evil – poisonous

27 위 글의 밑줄 친 ⓒhave enjoyed와 현재완료의 용법이 다른 것을 모두 고르시오.

① I have studied English since the second grade of elementary school.
② They have lived in this house for 10 years.
③ She has never visited the National Museum of Korea.
④ His father has been dead for ten years.
⑤ I have watched the movie twice.

[28~29] 다음 글을 읽고 물음에 답하시오.

Garlic is good for your health. It keeps your heart healthy because it lowers blood pressure. It also helps you get over a cold. ⓐGarlic tea mixed with honey makes you get better faster. In addition, it helps you prevent future sickness. Eating garlic helps your body fight against bad viruses. Garlic helps you stay healthy in many ways.

28 How can garlic keep your heart healthy? Answer in English beginning with "By". (4 words)

➡ _____

29 위 글의 밑줄 친 문장 ⓐ에 생략된 단어들을 넣어 문장을 다시 쓰시오.

➡ _____
_____

MEMO

INSIGHT
on the textbook

교과서 파헤치기

Lesson **1** **Young Enough to Change the World**

Lesson **2** **Timeless Tales of Gods and Heroes**

Lesson **3** **Plants That Feed Us**

※ 다음 영어를 우리말로 쓰시오.

01 marine

02 adopt

03 endangered

04 fix

05 generation

06 child-care center

07 deliver

08 actually

09 educate

10 throat

11 various

12 expression

13 book review

14 rubber

15 neighborhood

16 translate

17 collect

18 raise

19 although

20 probably

21 reduce

22 spill

23 donate

24 charity

25 rescue

26 specialist

27 supply

28 teenager

29 non-profit organization

30 occur

31 waste

32 volunteer

33 gulf

34 signature

35 die from

36 run into

37 be able to 동사원형

38 throw up

39 in addition to

40 break down

41 be covered with

42 read A to B

43 ask for help

※ 다음 우리말을 영어로 쓰시오.

01	자선단체, 자선		22	멸종 위기의
02	전문가		23	구조, 구출
03	다양한, 여러 가지의		24	입양하다
04	일어나다, 발생하다		25	표현
05	쓰레기		26	가르치다, 교육하다
06	해양의		27	서명
07	모으다, 수집하다		28	만
08	아마도		29	고무
09	기부하다, 기증하다		30	탁아소, 보육원
10	공급		31	마요네즈
11	줄이다		32	십 대, 청소년
12	목구멍, 목		33	자원봉사자; 자원하다
13	전달하다, 배달하다		34	주차 공간
14	번역하다		35	~으로 죽다
15	유출		36	더 이상, 이제는
16	이웃, 근처		37	A를 B에게 읽어주다
17	비록 ~이지만		38	토하다
18	고치다		39	~으로 뒤덮여 있다
19	세대		40	고장나다
20	실제로		41	(곤경, 어려움 등을) 만나다[겪다]
21	기르다		42	~ 이외에, ~에 더하여
			43	A를 B와 나누다, 공유하다

※ 다음 영영풀이에 알맞은 단어를 <보기>에서 골라 쓴 후, 우리말 뜻을 쓰시오.

1 _____ : to happen: _____

2 _____ : in danger of extinction: _____

3 _____ : a large area of sea partly enclosed by land: _____

4 _____ : to repair something that is broken or not working properly: _____

5 _____ : to save somebody/something from a dangerous or harmful situation: _____

6 _____ : to teach a child at a school, college, or university: _____

7 _____ : relating to the sea and the creatures that live there: _____

8 _____ : to care for a child or young animal until it is able to take care of itself: _____

9 _____ : something you say, write, or do that shows what you think or feel: _____

10 _____ : to change written or spoken words into another language: _____

11 _____ : to make something smaller or less in size, amount, or price: _____

12 _____ : to take goods, letters, packages etc. to a particular place or person: _____

13 _____ : your name written in the way you usually write it, for example at the end of a letter, or on a cheque etc, to show that you have written it: _____

14 _____ : someone who knows a lot about a particular subject, or is very skilled at it: _____

15 _____ : to give something, especially money, to a person or an organization in order to help them: _____

16 _____ : an organization which raises money in order to help people who are sick or very poor, or who have a disability: _____

보기			
donate	marine	reduce	fix
signature	rescue	specialist	gulf
charity	raise	deliver	occur
expression	educate	translate	endangered

※ 다음 우리말과 일치하도록 빈칸에 알맞은 말을 쓰시오.

Listen and Speak 1 A

1. **G:** What are you _____ _____ _____?
   B: I'm _____ _____ _____ some _____ _____ at the child-care center.
   G: _____ would you do there?
   B: I would _____ _____ some books _____ the children.
   G: That _____ interesting. Can I _____ you?
   B: Of _____.

2. **B:** What _____ _____ going _____ _____ for the book _____ _____?
   G: I'm _____ of reading a book about _____ _____.
   B: Good idea. I _____ the _____ _____ for you.
   G: Oh, could you _____ it to me?
   B: Sure. I'll _____ it tomorrow.

Listen and Speak 1 B

1. **A:** _____ your plan for _____ _____?
   B: I'm _____ of watching a movie _____ _____.

2. **A:** _____ your _____ for this year?
   B: I'm _____ learning _____ _____ play baduk.

3. **A:** _____ your _____ _____ this year?
   B: I'm _____ _____ _____ swimming _____.

Listen and Speak 2 A

1. **G:** Dad, I'm _____ bit hungry. Is _____ anything _____ eat?
   M: Do you _____ _____ _____ cook tteokbokki for you?
   G: That'd be great. I love tteokbokki.
   M: O.K. Give me _____ _____ _____.

2. **B:** Sujin, can you help us?
   G: Sure. _____ _____ _____ for you?
   B: We're going to _____ the school _____ _____ _____ a _____ _____ for bicycles.
   G: That's a great idea. Do you _____ _____ _____ you _____ _____ from students?
   B: That would help us _____ _____. Thanks!

1. G: 이번 주말에 뭐 하니?
   B: 나는 보육원에서 봉사 활동을 좀 하려고 해.
   G: 거기서 뭘 할 것 같아?
   B: 아마 아이들에게 책을 좀 읽어 줄 것 같아.
   G: 그거 흥미로워 보인다. 나도 함께 가도 될까?
   B: 물론이지.

2. B: 너는 독후감 숙제로 뭘 읽을 거니?
   G: 나는 젊은 지도자들에 관한 책을 읽을까 해.
   B: 좋은 생각이야. 나한테 너에게 딱 맞는 책이 있어.
   G: 오, 내게 빌려줄 수 있어?
   B: 그럼. 내일 그걸 가져올게.

1. A: 올해 너의 계획이 뭐니?
   B: 나는 주말마다 영화를 볼까 해.

2. A: 올해 너의 계획이 뭐니?
   B: 나는 바둑 두는 걸 배울까 해.

3. A: 올해 너의 계획이 뭐니?
   B: 나는 수영 강습을 받을까 해.

1. G: 아빠, 저 배가 좀 고파요. 먹을 게 좀 있나요?
   M: 네게 떡볶이를 만들어 줄까?
   G: 그거 정말 좋겠어요. 전 떡볶이를 매우 좋아해요.
   M: 알겠다. 잠시만 시간을 줌.

2. B: 수진아, 우리를 좀 도와줄 수 있니?
   G: 물론이야. 무엇을 해 줄까?
   B: 우리는 학교에 자전거 주차 공간을 만들어 달라고 요청하려 해.
   G: 그거 멋진 생각이다. 학생들에게 사인을 받는 것을 도와줄까?
   B: 그건 우리에게 큰 도움이 될 거야. 고마워!

Listen and Speak 2 B

1. **A:** My bike _____ _____.

   B: Do you _____ _____ _____ _____ it?

   A: Yes, please.

2. **A:** I didn't _____ an umbrella.

   B: Do you want me to _____ my _____ _____ you?

   A: Yes, please.

3. **A:** _____ box is _____ _____.

   B: Do you _____ _____ _____ _____ you _____ it?

   A: Yes, please.

4. **A:** My _____ is too short.

   B: Do you _____ _____ _____ _____ a picture of you?

   A: Yes, please.

Communicate A

Suho: Anna, do you have any children's books _____ _____ read _____ _____?

Anna: Sure. Why?

Suho: _____ _____ _____ _____ some books to children in Africa. My aunt _____ _____ _____ they need books _____ _____.

Anna: Good idea, Suho! Wait, _____ your books in Korean?

Suho: Oh, that's a problem.

Anna: Well, how _____ _____ them _____ English?

Suho: _____? That's a great idea, Anna.

Anna: _____ _____ _____ _____ _____ _____ _____?

Suho: Sure. If we _____ _____ any _____ _____, let's ask our English teacher _____ _____.

Anna: O.K. It's really great _____ _____ can _____ the children in Africa.

1. **A:** 내 자전거가 고장 났어.
   B: 내가 그것을 고쳐 줄까?
   A: 응, 부탁해.

2. **A:** 나 우산을 안 가져왔어.
   B: 내가 우산을 너와 함께 쓸까?
   A: 응, 부탁해.

3. **A:** 이 상자는 너무 무거워.
   B: 내가 그것을 나르는 걸 도와줄까?
   A: 응, 부탁해.

4. **A:** 내 팔이 너무 짧아.
   B: 내가 네 사진을 찍어줄까?
   A: 응, 부탁해.

수호: Anna, 너는 더 이상 읽지 않는 아동용 도서들을 가지고 있니?
Anna: 물론이지. 왜?
수호: 나는 아프리카의 아이들에게 책을 좀 보낼 생각을 하고 있어. 우리 이모가 내게 그 아이들이 읽을 책이 필요하다고 말씀하셨어.
Anna: 좋은 생각이야, 수호야! 잠깐만, 네 책들은 한글로 되어 있지 않니?
수호: 오, 그게 문제구나.
Anna: 음. 그것들을 영어로 번역하는 건 어때?
수호: 번역? 그거 좋은 생각이다, Anna.
Anna: 너는 내가 너를 도와주기를 원하니?
수호: 물론이지. 만약 어려운 표현들이 나오면, 영어 선생님께 도움을 요청하자.
Anna: 알겠어. 우리가 아프리카의 아이들을 도울 수 있어서 정말 좋다.

Communicate B

A: (춤추는 동작을 한다.)

B: Arc you _____ _____ _____ taekwondo?

A: No.

C: _____ _____ _____ _____ learning _____ _____?

A: Yes. _____ _____ _____ _____ K-pop dancing.

C: Do you _____ _____ _____ _____ you?

A: Sure. That'd be great.

A: (춤추는 동작을 한다.)
B: 너 태권도 배우려고 하니?
A: 아니야.
C: 춤추는 걸 배우려고 하니?
A: 그래. K-pop 춤을 배우려고 해.
C: 내가 가르쳐 줄까?
A: 그래. 그거 좋겠다.

Progress Check 1

B: _____ _____ you _____ this weekend?

G: _____ _____ _____ going for a _____ _____.

B: Sounds good. _____ I _____ you?

G: Sure. _____ meet _____ _____ _____ the park at ten.

B: O.K.

B: 이번 주말에 뭐 하니?
G: 자전거를 타러 가려고 해.
B: 좋겠구나. 나도 함께 해도 되니?
G: 물론이야. 공원 앞에서 10시에 보자.
B: 그래.

Progress Check 2

M: _____ _____ have pancakes _____ breakfast?

W: Sure. Oh, we _____ have any eggs.

M: Do you _____ _____ _____ _____ to the store and _____ some?

W: Thanks, Mike. Can you get _____ _____, _____?

M: Sure.

M: 아침으로 팬케이크를 먹을까요?
W: 좋아요. 오, 달걀이 없네요.
M: 가게에 가서 좀 사올까요?
W: 고마워요, Mike. 블루베리 시럽도 사와 줄래요?
M: 물론이죠.

※ 다음 우리말에 맞도록 대화를 영어로 쓰시오.

해석

Listen and Speak 1 A

1. G: _____
   B: _____
   G: _____
   B: _____
   G: _____
   B: _____

2. B: _____
   G: _____
   B: _____
   G: _____
   B: _____

1. G: 이번 주말에 뭐 하니?
   B: 나는 보육원에서 봉사 활동을 좀 하려고 해.
   G: 거기서 뭘 할 것 같아?
   B: 아마 아이들에게 책을 좀 읽어 줄 것 같아.
   G: 그거 흥미로워 보인다. 나도 함께 가도 될까?
   B: 물론이지.

2. B: 너는 독후감 숙제로 뭘 읽을 거니?
   G: 나는 젊은 지도자들에 관한 책을 읽을까 해.
   B: 좋은 생각이야. 나한테 너에게 딱 맞는 책이 있어.
   G: 오, 내게 빌려줄 수 있어?
   B: 그럼. 내일 그걸 가져올게.

Listen and Speak 1 B

1. A: _____
   B: _____

2. A: _____
   B: _____

3. A: _____
   B: _____

1. A: 올해 너의 계획이 뭐니?
   B: 나는 주말마다 영화를 볼까 해.

2. A: 올해 너의 계획이 뭐니?
   B: 나는 바둑 두는 걸 배울까 해.

3. A: 올해 너의 계획이 뭐니?
   B: 나는 수영 강습을 받을까 해.

Listen and Speak 2 A

1. G: _____
   M: _____
   G: _____
   M: _____

2. B: _____
   G: _____
   B: _____
   G: _____
   B: _____

1. G: 아빠, 저 배가 좀 고파요. 먹을 게 좀 있나요?
   M: 네게 떡볶이를 만들어 줄까?
   G: 그거 정말 좋겠어요. 전 떡볶이를 매우 좋아해요.
   M: 알겠다. 잠시만 시간을 주렴.

2. B: 수진아, 우리를 좀 도와줄 수 있니?
   G: 물론이야. 무엇을 해 줄까?
   B: 우리는 학교에 자전거 주차 공간을 만들어 달라고 요청하려 해.
   G: 그거 멋진 생각이다. 학생들에게 사인을 받는 것을 도와줄까?
   B: 그건 우리에게 큰 도움이 될 거야. 고마워!

Listen and Speak 2 B

1. A: _____

    B: _____

    A: _____

2. A: _____

    B: _____

    A: _____

3. A: _____

    B: _____

    A: _____

4. A: _____

    B: _____

    A: _____

1. A: 내 자전거가 고장 났어.
    B: 내가 그것을 고쳐 줄까?
    A: 응, 부탁해.

2. A: 나 우산을 안 가져왔어.
    B: 내가 우산을 너와 함께 쓸까?
    A: 응, 부탁해.

3. A: 이 상자는 너무 무거워.
    B: 내가 그것을 나르는 걸 도와줄까?
    A: 응, 부탁해.

4. A: 내 팔이 너무 짧아.
    B: 내가 네 사진을 찍어줄까?
    A: 응, 부탁해.

Communicate A

Suho: _____

Anna: _____

Suho: _____

_____

Anna: _____

Suho: _____

Anna: _____

Suho: _____

Anna: _____

Suho: _____

_____

Anna: _____

수호: Anna, 너는 더 이상 읽지 않는 아동용 도서들을 가지고 있니?
Anna: 물론이지. 왜?
수호: 나는 아프리카의 아이들에게 책을 좀 보낼 생각을 하고 있어. 우리 이모가 내게 그 아이들이 읽을 책이 필요하다고 말씀하셨어.
Anna: 좋은 생각이야, 수호야! 잠깐만, 네 책들은 한글로 되어 있지 않니?
수호: 오, 그게 문제구나.
Anna: 음. 그것들을 영어로 번역하는 건 어때?
수호: 번역? 그거 좋은 생각이다, Anna.
Anna: 너는 내가 너를 도와주기를 원하니?
수호: 물론이지. 만약 어려운 표현들이 나오면, 영어 선생님께 도움을 요청하자.
Anna: 알겠어. 우리가 아프리카의 아이들을 도울 수 있어서 정말 좋다.

Communicate B

A: (춤추는 동작을 한다.)

B: _____

A: _____

C: _____

A: _____

C: _____

A: _____

Progress Check 1

B: _____

G: _____

B: _____

G: _____

B: _____

Progress Check 2

M: _____

W: _____

M: _____

W: _____

M: _____

A: (춤추는 동작을 한다.)
B: 너 태권도 배우려고 하니?
A: 아니야.
C: 춤추는 걸 배우려고 하니?
A: 그래. K-pop 춤을 배우려고 해.
C: 내가 가르쳐 줄까?
A: 그래. 그거 좋겠다.

B: 이번 주말에 뭐 하니?
G: 자전거를 타러 가려고 해.
B: 좋겠구나. 나도 함께 해도 되니?
G: 물론이야. 공원 앞에서 10시에 보자.
B: 그래.

M: 아침으로 팬케이크를 먹을까요?
W: 좋아요. 오, 달걀이 없네요.
M: 가게에 가서 좀 사올까요?
W: 고마워요, Mike. 블루베리 시럽도
   사와 줄래요?
M: 물론이죠.

※ 다음 우리말과 일치하도록 빈칸에 알맞은 것을 골라 쓰시오.

1 _____ in _____
A. Action   B. Teens

2 Many young people are _____ the _____ a _____
_____ .
A. better   B. making   C. place   D. world

3 _____ _____, Carter and Olivia Ries have become leaders _____ _____ animals.
A. saving   B. example   C. in   D. for

4 _____ they are only teenagers, they _____ actually _____ a _____ in the world.
A. difference   B. although   C. made   D. have

5 _____ were they _____ _____ do that?
A. able   B. how   C. to

6 _____ _____ _____ Carter.
A. hear   B. let's   C. from

7 _____ I was five, my _____ sister Olivia and I _____ _____ a cheetah.
A. each   B. little   C. adopted   D. when

8 Did we _____ cheetahs _____ _____?
A. at   B. raise   C. home

9 No, we _____ a _____ that _____ wild cheetahs in South Africa.
A. protects   B. donated   C. charity   D. to

10 Our parents told us that if we did not _____ them, we _____ not be _____ to see cheetahs in the _____ future.
A. able   B. near   C. might   D. protect

11 We soon _____ _____ helping other _____ animals.
A. endangered   B. interested   C. in   D. became

12 A few years _____, with help from our parents, we _____ a _____ _____ to protect them.
A. created   B. later   C. organization   D. non-profit

13 We wanted the next _____ to be able to see these animals, _____ we _____ our _____ One More Generation.
A. generation   B. named   C. organization   D. so

14 We also _____ animals and _____ our _____ about them.
A. educated   B. studied   C. friends   D. endangered

15 Then one day, a _____ _____ _____ _____ in the Gulf of Mexico.
A. spill   B. terrible   C. occurred   D. oil

1 활약하는 십 대들

2 많은 젊은 사람들이 세상을 더 좋은 곳으로 만들고 있다.

3 예를 들어, Carter Ries와 Olivia Ries는 동물을 구하는 일에 리더가 되어 왔다.

4 비록 그들은 십 대일 뿐이지만, 실제로 세상에 변화를 일으켜 왔다.

5 그들은 어떻게 그것을 할 수 있었을까?

6 Carter의 이야기를 들어보자.

7 내가 다섯 살이었을 때, 나의 여동생 Olivia와 나는 각자 치타를 입양했다.

8 우리가 치타를 집에서 길렀을까?

9 아니, 우리는 남아프리카 공화국에 있는 야생 치타를 보호하는 자선단체에 기부했다.

10 부모님께서는 우리에게 우리가 그들을 보호하지 않으면, 가까운 미래에 치타를 볼 수 없을지도 모른다고 말씀하셨다.

11 우리는 곧 다른 멸종 위기의 동물들을 도와주는 것에 관심을 갖게 되었다.

12 몇 년 후에, 부모님의 도움으로, 우리는 그들을 보호하기 위해 비영리 단체를 만들었다.

13 우리는 다음 세대가 이러한 동물들을 볼 수 있기를 원했기에, 우리 단체를 One More Generation이라고 이름 붙였다.

14 우리는 또한 멸종 위기의 동물들을 연구했고 친구들에게 그들에 대해 가르쳐 주었다.

15 그러던 어느 날, 끔찍한 석유 유출 사건이 멕시코만에서 발생했다.

16 A lot of sea animals were _____ _____ _____ oil, and they were _____.
    A. covered   B. dying   C. with   D. completely

17 We _____ _____ _____ something.
    A. to   B. had   C. do

18 We started collecting animal _____ _____ such _____ pet carrying cages and rubber gloves from everyone in our _____.
    A. supplies   B. neighborhood   C. as   D. rescue

19 Four months later, our family drove to the Gulf of Mexico to _____ _____ we _____ and helped to _____ the animals.
    A. collected   B. deliver   C. save   D. what

20 _____ we were _____ there, we learned _____ very _____.
    A. something   B. working   C. useful   D. while

21 When we put mayonnaise _____ a turtle's _____, the turtle _____ _____.
    A. throat   B. up   C. into   D. threw

22 That _____, we were able to _____ oil _____ _____ _____ turtles.
    A. out   B. get   C. of   D. way

23 I never knew mayonnaise could _____ _____ _____ _____ animals!
    A. save   B. be   C. to   D. used

24 On our _____ day, we met a _____ _____ _____.
    A. life   B. last   C. specialist   D. marine

25 She told us that plastic _____ is more _____ to sea animals _____ oil _____ are.
    A. dangerous   B. spills   C. waste   D. than

26 A lot of sea animals and sea birds _____ _____ _____ _____ plastic _____.
    A. from   B. eating   C. die   D. waste

27 After we came home, we _____ an _____ project about _____ to _____ plastic waste.
    A. reduce   B. educational   C. how   D. created

28 In _____ to this, our organization _____ to do _____ projects to _____ animals.
    A. various   B. addition   C. save   D. continues

29 _____ we started small, we are _____ a _____ _____.
    A. big   B. although   C. difference   D. making

30 _____ you do today can _____ the world, so _____ that first _____!
    A. take   B. change   C. step   D. what

---

16 많은 해양 동물들이 완전히 기름을 뒤집어썼고, 죽어가고 있었다.

17 우리는 무엇인가를 해야만 했다.

18 우리는 애완동물 수송용 우리와 고무장갑과 같은 동물 구조 물품들을 동네의 모든 사람으로부터 모으기 시작했다.

19 4개월 후에, 우리 가족은 우리가 모았던 것들을 전달하기 위해서 멕시코만으로 운전해 갔으며 동물들을 구하는 일을 도왔다.

20 거기서 일하는 동안에, 우리는 매우 유용한 것을 배웠다.

21 마요네즈를 거북이의 목구멍에 집어넣으면, 거북이가 토했다.

22 그런 식으로, 우리는 거북이들에게서 기름을 빼낼 수 있었다.

23 나는 마요네즈가 동물을 구하는 데 사용될 수 있다는 것을 전혀 알지 못했다!

24 마지막 날에, 우리는 해양 생물 전문가를 만났다.

25 그녀는 우리에게 석유 유출보다 플라스틱 쓰레기가 해양 동물에게 더 위험하다고 말했다.

26 많은 해양 동물과 바다 새들이 플라스틱 쓰레기를 먹어서 죽는다.

27 집으로 돌아온 후, 우리는 플라스틱 쓰레기를 줄일 수 있는 방법에 관한 교육 프로젝트를 만들었다.

28 이것 외에도, 우리 단체는 동물들을 구하기 위한 다양한 프로젝트들을 계속하고 있다.

29 비록 우리는 작은 것부터 시작했지만, 큰 변화를 만들어 내고 있는 중이다.

30 당신이 오늘 하는 일이 세상을 바꿀 수 있기에, 첫발을 내디뎌라!

※ 다음 우리말과 일치하도록 빈칸에 알맞은 말을 쓰시오.

1 Teens _____ _____

2 _____ young people are making the world _____ _____ _____.

3 _____ _____, Carter and Olivia Ries have become leaders _____ _____ _____.

4 _____ they are only _____, they _____ _____ _____ _____ _____ in the world.

5 _____ were they _____ _____ do that?

6 _____ _____ _____ Carter.

7 When I was five, my _____ _____ Olivia and I _____ _____ a cheetah.

8 Did we _____ cheetahs _____ _____ _____?

9 No, we _____ _____ _____ _____ that _____ wild cheetahs in _____ _____.

10 Our parents told us that if we did not protect them, we _____ _____ _____ _____ _____ _____ in the near future.

11 We soon _____ _____ helping _____ _____.

12 _____ _____ later, with help from our parents, we _____ _____ _____ to protect them.

13 We wanted _____ _____ _____ to _____ _____ _____ see these animals, so we named our organization One More Generation.

14 We also studied _____ _____ and _____ _____ about them.

15 Then one day, _____ _____ _____ _____ _____ in the Gulf of Mexico.

16 A lot of sea animals _____ _____ _____ _____
_____, and they _____ _____.

17 We _____ _____ _____ something.

18 We started _____ _____ _____ _____ such as pet
carrying cages and rubber gloves from everyone _____ _____
_____.

19 Four months _____, our family drove to the Gulf of Mexico
to deliver _____ _____ _____ and helped _____
_____ _____ _____.

20 _____ we were _____ there, we learned _____ _____
_____.

21 When we _____ mayonnaise _____ a turtle's throat, the
turtle _____ _____.

22 That way, we were able to _____ oil _____ turtles.

23 I never knew mayonnaise _____ _____ _____ _____ _____
_____ animals!

24 On our last day, we met a _____ _____ _____.

25 She told us that plastic waste is _____ _____ to sea animals
_____ _____ _____ are.

26 A lot of sea animals and sea birds _____ _____ _____
_____.

27 After we came home, we _____ _____ _____
about _____ _____ _____ _____ plastic waste.

28 _____ _____ _____ this, our organization continues to do
various _____ _____ _____ animals.

29 _____ we started small, we are _____ _____
_____.

30 _____ you do today can change the world, so _____
_____ _____ _____ _____!

---

16 많은 해양 동물들이 완전히 기름을 뒤집어썼고, 죽어가고 있었다.

17 우리는 무엇인가를 해야만 했다.

18 우리는 애완동물 수송용 우리와 고무장갑과 같은 동물 구조 물품들을 동네의 모든 사람으로부터 모으기 시작했다.

19 4개월 후에, 우리 가족은 우리가 모았던 것들을 전달하기 위해서 멕시코만으로 운전해 갔으며 동물들을 구하는 일을 도왔다.

20 거기서 일하는 동안에, 우리는 매우 유용한 것을 배웠다.

21 마요네즈를 거북이의 목구멍에 집어넣으면, 거북이가 토했다.

22 그런 식으로, 우리는 거북이들에게서 기름을 빼낼 수 있었다.

23 나는 마요네즈가 동물을 구하는 데 사용될 수 있다는 것을 전혀 알지 못했다!

24 마지막 날에, 우리는 해양 생물 전문가를 만났다.

25 그녀는 우리에게 석유 유출보다 플라스틱 쓰레기가 해양 동물에게 더 위험하다고 말했다.

26 많은 해양 동물과 바다 새들이 플라스틱 쓰레기를 먹어서 죽는다.

27 집으로 돌아온 후, 우리는 플라스틱 쓰레기를 줄일 수 있는 방법에 관한 교육 프로젝트를 만들었다.

28 이것 외에도, 우리 단체는 동물들을 구하기 위한 다양한 프로젝트들을 계속하고 있다.

29 비록 우리는 작은 것부터 시작했지만, 큰 변화를 만들어 내고 있는 중이다.

30 당신이 오늘 하는 일이 세상을 바꿀 수 있기에, 첫발을 내디뎌라!

※ 다음 문장을 우리말로 쓰시오.

1 Teens in Action

➡ _____

2 Many young people are making the world a better place.

➡ _____

3 For example, Carter and Olivia Ries have become leaders in saving animals.

➡ _____

4 Although they are only teenagers, they have actually made a difference in the world.

➡ _____

5 How were they able to do that?

➡ _____

6 Let's hear from Carter.

➡ _____

7 When I was five, my little sister Olivia and I each adopted a cheetah.

➡ _____

8 Did we raise cheetahs at home?

➡ _____

9 No, we donated to a charity that protects wild cheetahs in South Africa.

➡ _____

10 Our parents told us that if we did not protect them, we might not be able to see cheetahs in the near future.

➡ _____

11 We soon became interested in helping other endangered animals.

➡ _____

12 A few years later, with help from our parents, we created a non-profit organization to protect them.

➡ _____

13 We wanted the next generation to be able to see these animals, so we named our organization One More Generation.

➡ _____

_____

14 We also studied endangered animals and educated our friends about them.

➡ _____

15 Then one day, a terrible oil spill occurred in the Gulf of Mexico.

➡ _____

16 A lot of sea animals were completely covered with oil, and they were dying.

➡ _____

17 We had to do something.

➡ _____

18 We started collecting animal rescue supplies such as pet carrying cages and rubber gloves from everyone in our neighborhood.

➡ _____

19 Four months later, our family drove to the Gulf of Mexico to deliver what we collected and helped to save the animals.

➡ _____

_____

20 While we were working there, we learned something very useful.

➡ _____

21 When we put mayonnaise into a turtle's throat, the turtle threw up.

➡ _____

22 That way, we were able to get oil out of turtles.

➡ _____

23 I never knew mayonnaise could be used to save animals!

➡ _____

24 On our last day, we met a marine life specialist.

➡ _____

25 She told us that plastic waste is more dangerous to sea animals than oil spills are.

➡ _____

26 A lot of sea animals and sea birds die from eating plastic waste.

➡ _____

27 After we came home, we created an educational project about how to reduce plastic waste.

➡ _____

28 In addition to this, our organization continues to do various projects to save animals.

➡ _____

29 Although we started small, we are making a big difference.

➡ _____

30 What you do today can change the world, so take that first step!

➡ _____

※ 다음 괄호 안의 단어들을 우리말에 맞도록 바르게 배열하시오.

1 (in / Teens / Action)
➡ _____

2 (young / many / are / people / making / world / the / better / a / place.)
➡ _____

3 (example, / for / Olivia / and / Ries / Carter / become / have / leaders / in / animals. / saving)
➡ _____

4 (they / although / are / teenagers, / only / have / they / made / actually / difference / a / the / world. / in)
➡ _____
_____

5 (were / how / able / they / do / that? / to)
➡ _____

6 (hear / let's / Carter. / from)
➡ _____

7 (I / when / five, / was / little / my / Olivia / sister / I / and / adopted / each / cheetah. / a)
➡ _____

8 (wc / did / chcctahs / raisc / home? / at)
➡ _____

9 (we / no, / donated / a / to / charity / protects / that / cheetahs / wild / South / in / Africa.)
➡ _____

10 (parents / our / us / told / if / that / did / we / protect / not / them, / might / we / be / not / to / able / cheetahs / see / the / in / future. / near)
➡ _____

11 (soon / we / interested / became / helping / in / endangered / other / animals.)
➡ _____

12 (few / a / later, / years / help / with / our / from / parents, / created / we / non-profit / a / organization / protect / to / them.)
➡ _____

13 (wanted / we / next / the / to / generation / be / to / able / these / see / so / animals, / we / our / named / organization / More / One / Generation.)
➡ _____

14 (also / we / endangered / studied / and / animals / our / educated / friends / them. / about)
➡ _____
_____

15 (one / then / day, / terrible / a / spill / oil / in / occurred / the / of / Mexico. / Gulf)
➡ _____

1 활약하는 십 대들

2 많은 젊은 사람들이 세상을 더 좋은 곳으로 만들고 있다.

3 예를 들어, Carter Ries와 Olivia Ries는 동물을 구하는 일에 리더가 되어 왔다.

4 비록 그들은 십 대일 뿐이지만, 실제로 세상에 변화를 일으켜 왔다.

5 그들은 어떻게 그것을 할 수 있었을까?

6 Carter의 이야기를 들어보자.

7 내가 다섯 살이었을 때, 나의 여동생 Olivia와 나는 각자 치타를 입양했다.

8 우리가 치타를 집에서 길렀을까?

9 아니, 우리는 남아프리카 공화국에 있는 야생 치타를 보호하는 자선단체에 기부했다.

10 부모님께서는 우리에게 우리가 그들을 보호하지 않으면, 가까운 미래에 치타를 볼 수 없을지도 모른다고 말씀하셨다.

11 우리는 곧 다른 멸종 위기의 동물들을 도와주는 것에 관심을 갖게 되었다.

12 몇 년 후에, 부모님의 도움으로, 우리는 그들을 보호하기 위해 비영리 단체를 만들었다.

13 우리는 다음 세대가 이러한 동물들을 볼 수 있기를 원했기에, 우리 단체를 One More Generation이라고 이름 붙였다.

14 우리는 또한 멸종 위기의 동물들을 연구했고 친구들에게 그들에 대해 가르쳐 주었다.

15 그러던 어느 날, 끔찍한 석유 유출 사건이 멕시코만에서 발생했다.

16 (lot / a / sea / of / animals / completely / were / with / covered / oil, / they / and / dying. / were)
➡ _____

17 (had / we / do / to / something.)
➡ _____

18 (started / we / animal / collecting / supplies / rescue / as / such / carrying / pet / cages / and / gloves / rubber / from / in / everyone / neighborhood. / our)
➡ _____

19 (months / four / laters, / family / our / to / drove / the / of / Gulf / to / Mexico / deliver / we / what / and / collected / to / helped / save / animals. / the)
➡ _____

20 (we / while / working / were / there, / learned / we / very / useful. / something)
➡ _____

21 (we / when / mayonnaise / put / a / into / throat, / turtle's / the / threw / turtle / up.)
➡ _____

22 (way, / that / were / we / to / able / get / out / oil / turtles. / of)
➡ _____

23 (never / I / mayonnaise / knew / be / could / to / used / save / animals!)
➡ _____

24 (our / on / day, / last / met / we / marine / a / specialist. / life)
➡ _____

25 (told / she / that / us / waste / plastic / is / dangerous / more / sea / to / than / animals / oil / are. / spills)
➡ _____

26 (lot / a / sca / of / animals / sca / and / birds / cating / from / die / waste. / plastic)
➡ _____

27 (we / after / home, / came / created / we / educational / an / about / project / how / reduce / to / waste. / plastic)
➡ _____

28 (addition / in / this, / to / organization / our / to / continues / various / do / projects / save / to / animals.)
➡ _____

29 (we / although / started / small, / are / we / a / making / difference. / big)
➡ _____

30 (you / what / today / do / change / can / world, / the / take / so / first / step! / that)
➡ _____

---

16 많은 해양 동물들이 완전히 기름을 뒤집어썼고, 죽어가고 있었다.

17 우리는 무엇인가를 해야만 했다.

18 우리는 애완동물 수송용 우리와 고무장갑과 같은 동물 구조 물품들을 동네의 모든 사람으로부터 모으기 시작했다.

19 4개월 후에, 우리 가족은 우리가 모았던 것들을 전달하기 위해서 멕시코만으로 운전해 갔으며 동물들을 구하는 일을 도왔다.

20 거기서 일하는 동안에, 우리는 매우 유용한 것을 배웠다.

21 마요네즈를 거북이의 목구멍에 집어넣으면, 거북이가 토했다.

22 그런 식으로, 우리는 거북이들에게서 기름을 빼낼 수 있었다.

23 나는 마요네즈가 동물을 구하는 데 사용될 수 있다는 것을 전혀 알지 못했다!

24 마지막 날에, 우리는 해양 생물 전문가를 만났다.

25 그녀는 우리에게 석유 유출보다 플라스틱 쓰레기가 해양 동물에게 더 위험하다고 말했다.

26 많은 해양 동물과 바다 새들이 플라스틱 쓰레기를 먹어서 죽는다.

27 집으로 돌아온 후, 우리는 플라스틱 쓰레기를 줄일 수 있는 방법에 관한 교육 프로젝트를 만들었다.

28 이것 외에도, 우리 단체는 동물들을 구하기 위한 다양한 프로젝트들을 계속하고 있다.

29 비록 우리는 작은 것부터 시작했지만, 큰 변화를 만들어 내고 있는 중이다.

30 당신이 오늘 하는 일이 세상을 바꿀 수 있기에, 첫발을 내디뎌라!

※ 다음 우리말을 영어로 쓰시오.

1 활약하는 십 대들

➡ _____

2 많은 젊은 사람들이 세상을 더 좋은 곳으로 만들고 있다.

➡ _____

3 예를 들어, Carter Ries와 Olivia Ries는 동물을 구하는 일에 리더가 되어 왔다.

➡ _____

4 비록 그들은 십 대일 뿐이지만, 실제로 세상에 변화를 일으켜 왔다.

➡ _____

5 그들은 어떻게 그것을 할 수 있었을까?

➡ _____

6 Carter의 이야기를 들어보자.

➡ _____

7 내가 다섯 살이었을 때, 나의 여동생 Olivia와 나는 각자 치타를 입양했다.

➡ _____

8 우리가 치타를 집에서 길렀을까?

➡ _____

9 아니, 우리는 남아프리카 공화국에 있는 야생 치타를 보호하는 자선단체에 기부했다.

➡ _____

10 부모님께서는 우리에게 우리가 그들을 보호하지 않으면, 가까운 미래에 치타를 볼 수 없을지도 모른다고 말씀하셨다.

➡ _____

_____

11 우리는 곧 다른 멸종 위기의 동물들을 도와주는 것에 관심을 갖게 되었다.

➡ _____

12 몇 년 후에, 부모님의 도움으로, 우리는 그들을 보호하기 위해 비영리 단체를 만들었다.

➡ _____

13 우리는 다음 세대가 이러한 동물들을 볼 수 있기를 원했기에, 우리 단체를 One More Generation 이라고 이름 붙였다.

➡ _____

_____

14 우리는 또한 멸종 위기의 동물들을 연구했고 친구들에게 그들에 대해 가르쳐 주었다.

➡ _____

15 그러던 어느 날, 끔찍한 석유 유출 사건이 멕시코만에서 발생했다.

➡ _____

16 많은 해양 동물들이 완전히 기름을 뒤집어썼고, 죽어가고 있었다.

➡ _____

17 우리는 무엇인가를 해야만 했다.

➡ _____

18 우리는 애완동물 수송용 우리와 고무장갑과 같은 동물 구조 물품들을 동네의 모든 사람으로부터 모으기 시작했다.

➡ _____

_____

19 4개월 후에, 우리 가족은 우리가 모았던 것들을 전달하기 위해서 멕시코만으로 운전해 갔으며 동물들을 구하는 일을 도왔다.

➡ _____

_____

20 거기서 일하는 동안에, 우리는 매우 유용한 것을 배웠다.

➡ _____

21 마요네즈를 거북이의 목구멍에 집어넣으면, 거북이가 토했다.

➡ _____

22 그런 식으로, 우리는 거북이들에서 기름을 빼낼 수 있었다.

➡ _____

23 나는 마요네즈가 동물을 구하는 데 사용될 수 있다는 것을 전혀 알지 못했다!

➡ _____

24 마지막 날에, 우리는 해양 생물 전문가를 만났다.

➡ _____

25 그녀는 우리에게 석유 유출보다 플라스틱 쓰레기가 해양 동물에게 더 위험하다고 말했다

➡ _____

26 많은 해양 동물과 바다 새들이 플라스틱 쓰레기를 먹어서 죽는다.

➡ _____

27 집으로 돌아온 후, 우리는 플라스틱 쓰레기를 줄일 수 있는 방법에 관한 교육 프로젝트를 만들었다.

➡ _____

28 이것 외에도, 우리 단체는 동물들을 구하기 위한 다양한 프로젝트들을 계속하고 있다.

➡ _____

29 비록 우리는 작은 것부터 시작했지만, 큰 변화를 만들어 내고 있는 중이다.

➡ _____

30 당신이 오늘 하는 일이 세상을 바꿀 수 있기에, 첫발을 내디뎌라!

➡ _____

※ 다음 우리말과 일치하도록 빈칸에 알맞은 말을 쓰시오.

After You Read B

1. A: _____ _____ _____ _____ One More Generation?

2. B: _____ is _____?

3. A: It is a _____ _____ that _____ _____ animals.

4. B: What _____ One More Generation _____?

5. A: The organization wants the next _____ _____ _____ _____ _____ _____ those animals.

6. B: That's a great _____. I'll _____ it.

Link Science – Share

1. Asian black bears have a _____ _____ _____ _____ _____.

2. They _____ _____ _____ _____ _____ in Asia.

3. They've _____ _____ _____ people _____ them for their _____ _____ and _____ _____.

4. We'll tell you _____ _____ _____ _____ for them.

5. First, _____ _____ paper _____ _____ _____.

6. Second, you _____ _____ any Asian _____ _____ _____.

Write

1. Air pollution is _____ of the _____ _____ these days.

2. _____ cars _____ our lives _____, they produce _____ _____ _____ that _____ the air.

3. That is a _____ _____.

4. Here is _____ _____ _____ _____ _____.

5. We can _____ _____ _____ or _____ more.

6. We can also _____ _____ _____ because they _____ _____ _____ very far.

7. _____ _____ _____ _____ these can help.

1. A: One More Generation에 가입하는 것이 어때?
2. B: 그게 무엇이니?
3. A: 그것은 멸종 위기의 동물들을 보호하는 비영리 단체야.
4. B: One More Generation이 무슨 뜻이니?
5. A: 그 단체는 다음 세대가 그러한 동물들을 볼 수 있기를 원해.
6. B: 그것은 멋진 단체구나. 나는 거기에 가입할게.

1. 아시아흑곰은 가슴에 흰색의 V 모양을 갖고 있습니다.
2. 그들은 주로 아시아의 숲에서 삽니다.
3. 그들은 사람들이 그들의 신체 부분을 얻으려고 사냥을 하고 숲을 파괴하기 때문에 멸종 위기에 처했습니다.
4. 우리는 그들을 위해 여러분이 무엇을 할 수 있는지 말하고자 합니다.
5. 첫째, 숲을 보호하기 위해서 종이를 덜 사용하세요.
6. 둘째, 어떤 아시아의 흑곰 제품도 사지 말아야 합니다.

1. 공해는 요즘 가장 심각한 환경 문제들 중의 하나이다.
2. 비록 자동차가 우리의 생활을 편리하게 하지만, 자동차는 공기를 오염시키는 매연을 많이 만들어낸다.
3. 그것은 커다란 문제이다.
4. 우리가 할 수 있는 일이 있다.
5. 우리는 버스나 지하철을 더 많이 이용할 수 있다.
6. 우리는 또한 현지에서 생산된 상품은 멀리까지 배송될 필요가 없기 때문에 지역의 제품들을 구매할 수 있다.
7. 이런 일들과 같은 간단한 행동들조차 환경에는 도움이 될 수 있다.

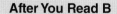

※ 다음 우리말을 영어로 쓰시오.

After You Read B

1. A: One More Generation에 가입하는 것이 어때?
   ➡ _____

2. B: 그게 무엇이니?
   ➡ _____

3. A: 그것은 멸종 위기의 동물들을 보호하는 비영리 단체야.
   ➡ _____

4. B: One More Generation이 무슨 뜻이니?
   ➡ _____

5. A: 그 단체는 다음 세대가 그러한 동물들을 볼 수 있기를 원해.
   ➡ _____

6. B: 그것은 멋진 단체구나. 나는 거기에 가입할게.
   ➡ _____

Link Science – Share

1. 아시아흑곰은 가슴에 흰색의 V 모양을 갖고 있습니다.
   ➡ _____

2. 그들은 주로 아시아의 숲에서 삽니다.
   ➡ _____

3. 그들은 사람들이 그들의 신체 부분을 얻으려고 사냥을 하고 숲을 파괴하기 때문에 멸종 위기에 처했습니다.
   ➡ _____

4. 우리는 그들을 위해 여러분이 무엇을 할 수 있는지 말하고자 합니다.
   ➡ _____

5. 첫째, 숲을 보호하기 위해서 종이를 덜 사용하세요.
   ➡ _____

6. 둘째, 어떤 아시아의 흑곰 제품도 사지 말아야 합니다.
   ➡ _____

Write

1. 공해는 요즘 가장 심각한 환경 문제들 중의 하나이다.
   ➡ _____

2. 비록 자동차가 우리의 생활을 편리하게 하지만, 자동차는 공기를 오염시키는 매연을 많이 만들어낸다.
   ➡ _____

3. 그것은 커다란 문제이다.
   ➡ _____

4. 우리가 할 수 있는 일이 있다.
   ➡ _____

5. 우리는 버스나 지하철을 더 많이 이용할 수 있다.
   ➡ _____

6. 우리는 또한 현지에서 생산된 상품은 멀리까지 배송될 필요가 없기 때문에 지역의 제품들을 구매할 수 있다.
   ➡ _____

7. 이런 일들과 같은 간단한 행동들조차 환경에는 도움이 될 수 있다.
   ➡ _____

※ 다음 영어를 우리말로 쓰시오.

01 accept _____

02 treasure _____

03 bloom _____

04 produce _____

05 borrow _____

06 mysterious _____

07 adventure _____

08 myth _____

09 dwarf _____

10 bet _____

11 golden _____

12 giant _____

13 harvest _____

14 smith _____

15 undo _____

16 kingdom _____

17 moreover _____

18 poem _____

19 carriage _____

20 challenge _____

21 choose _____

22 precious _____

23 enemy _____

24 prove _____

25 magical _____

26 seafood _____

27 wisdom _____

28 immediately _____

29 decision _____

30 protect _____

31 spear _____

32 order _____

33 control _____

34 trick _____

35 be into _____

36 give up _____

37 turn into ~ _____

38 come up with ~ _____

39 had better ~ _____

40 in that case _____

41 be famous for ~ _____

42 fall asleep _____

43 come along _____

※ 다음 우리말을 영어로 쓰시오.

01 모험

02 지혜, 슬기, 현명함

03 마차, 객차

04 도전, 결투 신청

05 수확, 추수

06 받아들이다, 수락하다

07 창

08 선택하다

09 시

10 놓치다

11 강력한

12 게다가

13 조절하다

14 결정, 판결

15 난쟁이

16 꽃이 피다

17 결정하다

18 만들어 내다, 제조하다

19 보물

20 마법 같은

21 언짢아하다, 상관하다

22 지키다, 보호하다

23 적, 적군

24 망치

25 즉시, 곧

26 왕국, 왕조

27 거인

28 신비로운

29 신화

30 귀중한, 값어치 있는

31 장난, 묘기

32 원상태로 돌리다

33 증명하다

34 해산물

35 잠들다

36 ～하는 편이 더 낫다

37 ～을 생각해 내다

38 ～ 자신의

39 뿌리를 내리다

40 ～로 유명하다

41 포기하다

42 그렇다면, 그런 경우에는

43 ～로 되다

※ 다음 영영풀이에 알맞은 단어를 <보기>에서 골라 쓴 후, 우리말 뜻을 쓰시오.

1 _____ : to produce flowers: _____

2 _____ : to request food or drinks from a restaurant: _____

3 _____ : a group of valuable things such as gold, silver, jewels, etc.: _____

4 _____ : a creature like a small person with pointed ears, who has magic powers: _____

5 _____ : someone who makes and repairs things made of iron: _____

6 _____ : fish and shellfish that live in the ocean and are used for food: _____

7 _____ : a vehicle with wheels that is pulled by a horse: _____

8 _____ : someone who hates you and wants to harm you: _____

9 _____ : a pole with a sharp pointed blade at one end, used as a weapon in the past: _____

10 _____ : something you do to surprise someone and to make other people laugh: _____

11 _____ : to decide which thing or person you want out of the ones that are available: _____

12 _____ : to risk money on the result of a race, game, competition, or other future event: _____

13 _____ : something new and difficult which requires great effort and determination: _____

14 _____ : a tool with a heavy metal part on a long handle, used for hitting nails into wood: _____

15 _____ : to send something from your hand through the air by moving your hand or arm quickly: _____

16 _____ : the ability to use your experience and knowledge in order to make sensible decisions or judgments: _____

보기			
throw	bet	choose	elf
hammer	trick	smith	order
enemy	spear	seafood	treasure
bloom	carriage	wisdom	challenge

대화문 Test

※ 다음 우리말과 일치하도록 빈칸에 알맞은 말을 쓰시오.

 해석

Listen & Speak 1 A-1

W: Is _____ your first time _____ _____ Korea, Mike?

M: Yes, it _____. I've _____ _____ _____ _____ _____ _____ Seoul.

W: _____ _____ you come here?

M: I'm really _____ Korean TV shows. I'm _____ _____ _____ _____ the places _____ _____ on TV.

W: _____ fun!

W: 한국엔 처음 방문하는 거야, Mike?
M: 응. 나는 언제나 서울에 오고 싶었어.
W: 이곳에 온 이유가 뭐니?
M: 나는 한국의 TV 프로그램들을 정말 좋아해. TV에서 봤던 장소들에 갈 거야.
W: 재미있게 지내!

Listen & Speak 1 A-2

B: April is _____ _____ _____ _____ the year.

G: _____ _____ you _____ so?

B: Flowers are _____ , but I _____ _____ _____ _____ to study for my exams.

G: Oh, I know _____ _____ _____ .

B: 4월은 1년 중 최악의 달이야.
G: 왜 그렇게 생각해?
B: 꽃은 피는데, 나는 시험 공부를 하느라 집에 있어야 해.
G: 오, 무슨 소린지 알겠어.

Listen & Speak 2 A-1

G: Dad, do you mind _____ _____ _____ the channel?

M: No, _____ _____ _____ .

G: Thank you. I _____ _____ a program _____ Norway.

M: Norway? _____ ?

G: Well, we're _____ _____ Norway _____ _____ .

M: Oh, I _____ .

G: 아빠, 제가 채널을 돌려도 될까요?
M: 물론이지.
G: 고마워요. 노르웨이에 대한 프로그램을 봐야 해서요.
M: 노르웨이? 왜?
G: 그게, 수업 시간에 노르웨이에 대해 배우고 있거든요.
M: 오, 그렇구나.

Listen & Speak 2 A-2

M: Jane, do you _____ _____ _____ _____ the window?

W: Sorry, but I _____ _____ _____ , and it's _____ _____ today.

M: O.K. No _____ . _____ _____ some hot tea? It'd be _____ _____ your cold.

W: That _____ _____ great. Thanks.

M: Jane, 내가 창문을 열어도 되겠니?
W: 미안, 내가 감기에 걸려서, 그리고 오늘 바람이 꽤 많이 불거든.
M: 그래. 괜찮아. 따뜻한 차 좀 줄까? 감기에 도움이 될 거야.
W: 그거 좋겠다. 고마워.

Communicate A

Jaden: Hi, Yuri, What're you _____?

Yuri: Hi, Jaden. I'm _____ a book _____ Norse myths. I'm really _____ _____ _____ _____.

Jaden: _____ makes you _____ _____ so much?

Yuri: The stories are very _____, and there are _____ _____ movies about Norse myths.

Jaden: Are they _____ _____?

Yuri: Yes. There's actually a new movie _____ Thor, a _____ _____ in Norse myths.

Jaden: Oh, I know him. He's my _____ online game _____.

Yuri: _____ _____ _____, we should _____ _____ the movie _____.

Jaden: Do you mind _____ _____ _____ your book when you're _____? I want to read _____ _____ we see the movie.

Yuri: No, not _____ _____. I'm sure you'll _____ _____ _____, _____.

Jaden: 안녕, 유리야. 뭐 하고 있니?
유리: 안녕, Jaden. 난 북유럽 신화들에 관한 책을 읽고 있어. 요즘 이 신화들에 정말 푹 빠졌어.
Jaden: 네가 그것들을 그렇게 좋아하게 만드는 게 뭐니?
유리: 이야기들이 정말 흥미롭고, 북유럽 신화에 대한 영화들도 많이 있거든.
Jaden: 영화들이 좀 괜찮니?
유리: 응. 사실 북유럽 신화에서 유명한 신인 Thor에 관한 새 영화가 나왔어.
Jaden: 오, 그를 알아. 그는 내가 제일 좋아하는 온라인 게임 캐릭터야.
유리: 그렇다면, 우린 같이 그 영화를 보러 가야겠다.
Jaden: 네가 네 책을 다 읽으면 내가 빌려도 될까? 우리가 그 영화를 보기 전에 그걸 읽고 싶어.
유리: 그럼, 당연하지. 너도 이 책을 좋아할 것이라고 확신해.

Progress Check 1

B: April is the best month _____ _____ _____.

G: What _____ you _____ so?

B: The weather is not _____, and _____ _____ _____.

G: I love April _____ my birthday is _____ _____.

B: Really? We should _____ you _____ _____.

B: 4월은 1년 중 최고의 달이야.
G: 왜 그렇게 생각해?
B: 날씨도 춥지 않고, 꽃도 피어나잖아.
G: 나는 내 생일이 4월에 있어서 4월을 아주 좋아해.
B: 정말? 우리 너를 위해 파티를 열어야겠다.

Progress Check 2

M: Excuse me, do you _____ _____ _____ _____ this chair? We need one _____.

W: I'm sorry, but I'm _____ _____ my friend. She'll be here _____.

M: Oh, I see. _____ _____.

W: You can _____ the waiter _____ _____ more chairs.

M: 실례합니다, 제가 이 의자를 가져가도 괜찮을까요? 하나가 더 필요해서요.
W: 죄송합니다만, 제 친구를 기다리고 있어서요. 곧 올 거예요.
M: 오, 그렇군요. 신경 쓰지 마세요.
W: 웨이터에게 의자를 더 가져다 달라고 부탁해 보세요.

※ 다음 우리말에 맞도록 대화를 영어로 쓰시오.

Listen & Speak 1 A-1

W: _____

M: _____

W: _____

M: _____

W: _____

W: 한국엔 처음 방문하는 거야, Mike?
M: 응. 나는 언제나 서울에 오고 싶었어.
W: 이곳에 온 이유가 뭐니?
M: 나는 한국의 TV 프로그램들을 정말 좋아해. TV에서 봤던 장소들에 갈 거야.
W: 재미있게 지내!

Listen & Speak 1 A-2

B: _____

G: _____

B: _____

G: _____

B: 4월은 1년 중 최악의 달이야.
G: 왜 그렇게 생각해?
B: 꽃은 피는데, 나는 시험 공부를 하느라 집에 있어야 해.
G: 오, 무슨 소린지 알겠어.

Listen & Speak 2 A-1

G: _____

M: _____

G: _____

M: _____

G: _____

M: _____

G: 아빠, 제가 채널을 돌려도 될까요?
M: 물론이지.
G: 고마워요. 노르웨이에 대한 프로그램을 봐야 해서요.
M: 노르웨이? 왜?
G: 그게, 수업 시간에 노르웨이에 대해 배우고 있거든요.
M: 오, 그렇구나.

Listen & Speak 2 A-2

M: _____

W: _____

M: _____

W: _____

M: Jane, 내가 창문을 열어도 되겠니?
W: 미안, 내가 감기에 걸려서, 그리고 오늘 바람이 꽤 많이 불거든.
M: 그래. 괜찮아. 따뜻한 차 좀 줄까? 감기에 도움이 될 거야.
W: 그거 좋겠다. 고마워.

Communicate A

Jaden: _____

Yuri: _____

Jaden: _____

Yuri: _____

_____

Jaden: _____

Yuri: _____

Jaden: _____

Yuri: _____

Jaden: _____

_____

Yuri: _____

Jaden: 안녕, 유리야. 뭐 하고 있니?

유리: 안녕, Jaden. 난 북유럽 신화들에 관한 책을 읽고 있어. 요즘 이 신화들에 정말 푹 빠졌어.

Jaden: 네가 그것들을 그렇게 좋아하게 만드는 게 뭐니?

유리: 이야기들이 정말 흥미롭고, 북유럽 신화에 대한 영화들도 많이 있거든.

Jaden: 영화들이 좀 괜찮니?

유리: 응. 사실 북유럽 신화에서 유명한 신인 Thor에 관한 새 영화가 나왔어.

Jaden: 오, 그를 알아. 그는 내가 제일 좋아하는 온라인 게임 캐릭터야.

유리: 그렇다면, 우린 같이 그 영화를 보러 가야겠다.

Jaden: 네가 네 책을 다 읽으면 내가 빌려도 될까? 우리가 그 영화를 보기 전에 그걸 읽고 싶어.

유리: 그럼, 당연하지. 너도 이 책을 좋아할 것이라고 확신해.

Progress Check 1

B: _____

G: _____

B: _____

G: _____

B: _____

B: 4월은 1년 중 최고의 달이야.

G: 왜 그렇게 생각해?

B: 날씨도 춥지 않고, 꽃도 피어나잖아.

G: 나는 내 생일이 4월에 있어서 4월을 아주 좋아해.

B: 정말? 우리 너를 위해 파티를 열어야겠다.

Progress Check 2

M: _____

W: _____

M: _____

W: _____

M: 실례합니다, 제가 이 의자를 가져가도 괜찮을까요? 하나가 더 필요해서요.

W: 죄송합니다만, 제 친구를 기다리고 있어서요. 곧 올 거예요.

M: 오, 그렇군요. 신경 쓰지 마세요.

W: 웨이터에게 의자를 더 가져다 달라고 부탁해 보세요.

※ 다음 우리말과 일치하도록 빈칸에 알맞은 것을 골라 쓰시오.

1 _____ for _____ _____
   A. Gods   B. Three   C. Treasures

2 _____ _____ **Gods**
   A. Norse   B. Important

3 Odin, who is the _____ god, _____ _____ his eye for
   _____.
   A. wisdom   B. gave   C. highest   D. up

4 Thor is Odin's son and _____ _____ _____ of all.
   A. strongest   B. the   C. god

5 Frey, who is the _____ of the _____, _____ the _____.
   A. controls   B. harvest   C. weather   D. god

6 Loki is a god who _____ _____ _____ _____.
   A. tricks   B. on   C. others   D. plays

7 Thor _____ and knew immediately _____ was _____.
   A. something   B. wrong   C. woke

8 His _____ beautiful golden hair _____ _____.
   A. gone   B. was   C. wife's

9 He knew only Loki could do _____ _____ _____ _____.
   A. a   B. thing   C. such   D. terrible

10 Thor soon _____ Loki, _____ _____ _____ at home.
   A. was   B. found   C. drinking   D. who

11 "You'd _____ _____ _____ you did, or you'll be sorry,"
   Thor said _____ to Loki.
   A. undo   B. angrily   C. better   D. what

12 Loki _____ _____.
   A. scared   B. was

13 He _____ that he _____ _____ golden hair for Thor's
   _____.
   A. get   B. promised   C. wife   D. would

14 Loki knew _____ the _____ of Ivaldi could make _____
   _____ hair.
   A. fine   B. only   C. sons   D. golden

15 He went to them and said, "I _____ Brokk and his brother are
   the _____ _____. Is that _____?"
   A. smiths   B. heard   C. finest   D. true

16 "No, _____ _____ we _____ are the finest smiths," the
   sons of Ivaldi _____.
   A. who   B. replied   C. is   D. it

1 세 명의 신을 위한 보물

2 북유럽 신화의 주요 신들

3 Odin은 가장 높은 신이며, 지혜를 위해 한쪽 눈을 포기했다.

4 Thor는 Odin의 아들이며 모든 신들 중에서 가장 강한 신이다.

5 Frey는 수확의 신으로 날씨를 다스린다.

6 Loki는 다른 신들에게 농간을 부리는 신이다.

7 Thor는 잠에서 깨어 즉시 무엇인가가 잘못되었다는 것을 알았다.

8 그의 아내의 아름다운 금발머리가 사라졌다.

9 그는 오직 Loki만이 이런 끔찍한 일을 할 수 있다는 것을 알고 있었다.

10 Thor는 곧 Loki를 찾았는데, 그는 집에서 술을 마시고 있었다.

11 "네가 한 짓을 되돌려 놓는 것이 좋을 거야. 그렇지 않으면 후회하게 될 거다." Thor는 노하여 Loki에게 말했다.

12 Loki는 겁이 났다.

13 그는 Thor의 아내를 위해 금발머리를 얻어 오겠다고 약속했다.

14 Loki는 Ivaldi의 아들들만이 훌륭한 금발머리를 만들 수 있다는 것을 알고 있었다.

15 그는 그들에게 가서 "내가 듣기로 Brokk와 그의 남동생이 가장 훌륭한 대장장이라고 하던데. 그것이 사실인가?"라고 말했다.

16 "아니요, 가장 훌륭한 대장장이는 바로 우리들이요." Ivaldi의 아들들이 대답했다.

17 "They're _____ _____ _____ for Odin, Thor, and Frey," said Loki.

A. treasures   B. making   C. three

18 "Do you think you can _____ _____ _____ _____ theirs?"

A. treasures   B. than   C. make   D. better

19 "_____ _____ we can," they _____.

A. answered   B. course   C. of

20 "O.K., then you _____ also _____ three _____ them," said Loki.

A. for   B. make   C. should   D. treasures

21 "The gods will _____ _____ the best _____."

A. treasure   B. on   C. decide

22 Loki also told them that _____ of the treasures _____ _____ _____ golden hair.

A. be   B. one   C. to   D. had

23 They went _____ _____ _____.

A. immediately   B. to   C. work

24 Loki then _____ _____ _____ Brokk and his brother.

A. to   B. went   C. see

25 "Ivaldi's sons _____ _____ three treasures _____ Odin, Thor, and Frey," _____ Loki.

A. for   B. making   C. said   D. are

26 "I _____ that you can never make treasures _____ _____ theirs."

A. as   B. bet   C. fine   D. as

27 Brokk _____ angry and _____ the _____.

A. accepted   B. became   C. challenge

28 He and his brother _____ three treasures _____ _____.

A. of   B. produced   C. own   D. their

29 Loki went to see the three gods _____ _____ _____ _____.

A. all   B. treasures   C. the   D. with

30 Brokk _____ _____.

A. along   B. came

31 Loki _____ them the _____ _____ Ivaldi's _____.

A. from   B. treasures   C. showed   D. sons

32 The first treasure was _____ Odin, who had _____ _____.

A. one   B. for   C. eye   D. only

33 It was a _____ that never _____ its _____.

A. missed   B. spear   C. target

17 "그들은 Odin과 Thor와 Frey 를 위해서 보물을 만들고 있네." Loki는 말했다.

18 "너희들이 그들의 보물보다 더 나은 보물을 만들 수 있다고 생각하는가?"

19 "물론 할 수 있소." 그들이 대답했다.

20 "좋아, 그러면 너희도 그들을 위해 세 개의 보물을 만들어야 한다." Loki가 말했다.

21 "그 신들이 가장 훌륭한 보물을 결정할 것이다."

22 Loki는 또한 그들에게 보물 중하나는 금발머리이어야 한다고 말했다.

23 그들은 즉시 일에 착수했다.

24 Loki는 그 다음에 Brokk와 그의 남동생을 보러 갔다.

25 "Ivaldi의 아들들이 Odin과 Thor, 그리고 Frey를 위해 세 개의 보물을 만들고 있어." Loki 가 말했다.

26 "너희들은 절대 그들의 보물만 큼 훌륭한 보물을 만들 수 없다 는 것을 내 장담하지."

27 Brokk는 화가 나서 그 도전을 받아들였다.

28 그와 그의 남동생은 그들만의 세 가지 보물을 만들었다.

29 Loki는 모든 보물을 가지고 세 신을 만나러 갔다.

30 Brokk가 같이 갔다.

31 Loki는 그들에게 Ivaldi의 아들들 이 만든 보물들을 보여 주었다.

32 첫 번째 보물은 Odin을 위한 것으로, 그는 눈이 한쪽밖에 없었다.

33 그것은 목표물을 절대로 빗나가 지 않는 창이었다.

34 The second treasure was a big ship that could _____ _____ a
_____ of _____.

    A. into   B. cloth   C. piece   D. turn

35 It _____ _____ Frey.

    A. for   B. was

36 The _____ _____ was _____ Thor.

    A. treasure   B. for   C. third

37 Loki _____ Thor the _____ _____ _____ for his wife.

    A. golden   B. showed   C. hair   D. flowing

38 Thor _____ the hair _____ his wife's head, and it _____
_____ and became real hair.

    A. root   B. on   C. put   D. took

39 It was now Brokk's _____ to _____ the gods his _____.

    A. show   B. turn   C. gifts

40 He gave Odin a gold arm ring that produced _____ _____
gold rings _____ _____ night.

    A. more   B. ninth   C. eight   D. every

41 Brokk then _____ _____ a _____.

    A. pig   B. gave   C. Frey

42 It could _____ his _____ than _____ horse.

    A. carriage   B. pull   C. any   D. faster

43 "_____ _____ _____ is for you, Thor," said Brokk.

    A. treasure   B. third   C. my

44 "This is the _____ Mjolnir, _____ you'll _____.

    A. love   B. hammer   C. which

45 If you _____ it, it'll always _____ _____ to you.

    A. back   B. throw   C. come

46 _____, _____ can ever _____ it."

    A. break   B. nothing   C. moreover

47 It was an easy _____ to _____ the _____ _____.

    A. choose   B. decision   C. treasure   D. greatest

48 _____ was Mjolnir that the three _____ _____ _____.

    A. most   B. gods   C. it   D. liked

49 They _____ the hammer would _____ the gods _____
their _____.

    A. protect   B. enemies   C. from   D. thought

50 "Brokk and his brother," said Odin, "are _____ _____
_____."

    A. smiths   B. better   C. the

51 Brokk _____ that Loki was _____, and the three gods now
had _____ _____.

    A. wrong   B. treasures   C. proved   D. precious

34 두 번째 보물은 천 조각으로 변할 수 있는 큰 배였다.

35 그것은 Frey를 위한 것이었다.

36 세 번째 보물은 Thor를 위한 것이었다.

37 Loki는 Thor에게 그의 아내를 위한 매끈하게 늘어진 금발머리를 보여 주었다.

38 Thor가 그 머리카락을 그의 아내의 머리에 얹었더니 그것이 뿌리를 내려서 진짜 머리카락이 되었다.

39 이제 Brokk가 신들에게 그의 선물들을 보여 줄 차례였다.

40 그는 Odin에게 아홉 번째 밤이 될 때마다 8개의 금팔찌를 더 만들어 내는 금팔찌를 주었다.

41 그러고 나서 Brokk는 Frey에게 돼지를 한 마리 주었다.

42 그것은 어떤 말보다도 그의 마차를 더 빨리 끌 수 있었다.

43 "나의 세 번째 보물은 당신을 위한 것입니다. Thor." Brokk가 말했다.

44 "이것은 몰니르라는 망치인데 당신은 마음에 드실 겁니다.

45 그것을 던지면, 그것은 항상 당신에게 되돌아 올 것입니다.

46 게다가, 그 무엇도 이것을 부술 수 없지요."

47 가장 훌륭한 보물을 선택하는 것은 쉬운 결정이었다.

48 세 명의 신들이 가장 마음에 든 것은 몰니르였다.

49 그들은 그 망치가 신들을 그들의 적들로부터 보호해 줄 것이라고 생각했다.

50 "Brokk와 그의 남동생이 더 훌륭한 대장장이다." Odin이 말했다.

51 Brokk는 Loki가 틀렸다는 것을 증명해 냈고, 세 신들은 이제 소중한 보물을 가지게 되었다.

※ 다음 우리말과 일치하도록 빈칸에 알맞은 말을 쓰시오.

1 _____ for Three _____

2 _____ _____ **Gods**

3 Odin, who is the _____ god, _____ _____ his eye for wisdom.

4 Thor is Odin's son and _____ _____ _____ _____ all.

5 Frey, who is the god of the _____, _____ _____ _____ _____.

6 Loki is a god who _____ _____ _____ others.

7 Thor woke and knew immediately _____ _____ _____.

8 His wife's beautiful _____ hair _____ _____.

9 He knew only Loki could do _____ _____ _____ _____.

10 Thor soon _____ Loki, _____ _____ _____ at home.

11 " _____ _____ _____ what you did, or you'll be sorry," Thor said _____ to Loki.

12 Loki was _____.

13 He _____ that he _____ _____ golden hair for Thor's wife.

14 Loki knew only the sons of Ivaldi could make _____ _____ _____.

15 He went to them and said, "I heard Brokk and his brother are _____ _____ _____. Is that _____?"

16 "No, _____ _____ we _____ are the finest smiths," the sons of Ivaldi _____.

1 세 명의 신을 위한 보물

2 북유럽 신화의 주요 신들

3 Odin은 가장 높은 신이며, 지혜를 위해 한쪽 눈을 포기했다.

4 Thor는 Odin의 아들이며 모든 신들 중에서 가장 강한 신이다.

5 Frey는 수확의 신으로 날씨를 다스린다.

6 Loki는 다른 신들에게 농간을 부리는 신이다.

7 Thor는 잠에서 깨어 즉시 무엇인가가 잘못되었다는 것을 알았다.

8 그의 아내의 아름다운 금발머리가 사라졌다.

9 그는 오직 Loki만이 이런 끔찍한 일을 할 수 있다는 것을 알고 있었다.

10 Thor는 곧 Loki를 찾았는데, 그는 집에서 술을 마시고 있었다.

11 "네가 한 짓을 되돌려 놓는 것이 좋을 거야. 그렇지 않으면 후회하게 될 거다." Thor는 노하여 Loki에게 말했다.

12 Loki는 겁이 났다.

13 그는 Thor의 아내를 위해 금발머리를 얻어 오겠다고 약속했다.

14 Loki는 Ivaldi의 아들들만이 훌륭한 금발머리를 만들 수 있다는 것을 알고 있었다.

15 그는 그들에게 가서 "내가 듣기로 Brokk와 그의 남동생이 가장 훌륭한 대장장이라고 하던데. 그것이 사실인가?"라고 말했다.

16 "아니요, 가장 훌륭한 대장장이는 바로 우리들이요." Ivaldi의 아들들이 대답했다.

17 "They're making _____ _____ for Odin, Thor, and Frey," said Loki.

18 "Do you think you can make _____ _____ _____ _____ _____?"

19 "_____ _____ we can," they _____.

20 "O.K., then you should also _____ three treasures _____ _____," said Loki.

21 "The gods will _____ _____ the _____ _____."

22 Loki also told them that _____ _____ the treasures _____ _____ _____ golden hair.

23 They went _____ _____ _____.

24 Loki then _____ _____ _____ Brokk and his brother.

25 "Ivaldi's sons _____ _____ three treasures _____ Odin, Thor, and Frey," said Loki.

26 "_____ _____ that you can never make treasures _____ _____ _____ _____."

27 Brokk became _____ and _____ _____ _____.

28 He and his brother produced three treasures _____ _____ _____.

29 Loki went to see the three gods _____ _____ _____ _____.

30 Brokk _____ _____.

31 Loki _____ them the treasures _____ Ivaldi's sons.

32 The first treasure was _____ Odin, who had _____ _____ _____.

33 _____ _____ a spear _____ never _____ its target.

17 "그들은 Odin과 Thor와 Frey를 위해서 보물을 만들고 있네." Loki는 말했다.

18 "너희들이 그들의 보물보다 더 나은 보물을 만들 수 있다고 생각하는가?"

19 "물론 할 수 있소." 그들이 대답했다.

20 "좋아. 그러면 너희도 그들을 위해 세 개의 보물을 만들어야 한다." Loki가 말했다.

21 "그 신들이 가장 훌륭한 보물을 결정할 것이다."

22 Loki는 또한 그들에게 보물 중 하나는 금발머리이어야 한다고 말했다.

23 그들은 즉시 일에 착수헸다.

24 Loki는 그 다음에 Brokk와 그의 남동생을 보러 갔다.

25 "Ivaldi의 아들들이 Odin과 Thor, 그리고 Frey를 위해 세 개의 보물을 만들고 있어." Loki가 말했다.

26 "너희들은 절대 그들의 보물만큼 훌륭한 보물을 만들 수 없다는 것을 내 장담하지."

27 Brokk는 화가 나서 그 도전을 받아들였다.

28 그와 그의 남동생은 그들만의 세 가지 보물을 만들었다.

29 Loki는 모든 보물을 가지고 세 신을 만나러 갔다.

30 Brokk가 같이 갔다.

31 Loki는 그들에게 Ivaldi의 아들들이 만든 보물들을 보여 주었다.

32 첫 번째 보물은 Odin을 위한 것으로, 그는 눈이 한쪽밖에 없었다.

33 그것은 목표물을 절대로 빗나가지 않는 창이었다.

34 The second treasure was a big ship that could _____ _____ a
_____ _____ _____.

35 It was _____ Frey.

36 _____ _____ _____ was for Thor.

37 Loki showed Thor the _____ _____ _____ for his wife.

38 Thor _____ the hair _____ his wife's head, and it _____
_____ and _____ _____ _____.

39 It was now _____ _____ to show the gods his _____.

40 He gave Odin a gold arm ring that produced _____ _____
gold rings _____ _____ _____.

41 Brokk then gave _____ _____ _____.

42 It could pull his carriage _____ _____ _____ _____.

43 "_____ _____ _____ is for you, Thor," said Brokk.

44 "This is the _____ Mjolnir, _____ you'll love.

45 If you throw it, it'll always _____ _____ you.

46 _____, nothing can ever _____ _____."

47 It was an easy decision to choose _____ _____ _____.

48 It was Mjolnir that _____ _____ _____ _____.

49 They thought the hammer would _____ the gods _____ their
_____.

50 "Brokk and his brother," said Odin, "are _____ _____
_____."

51 Brokk _____ that Loki was _____, and the three gods now
had _____ _____.

---

34 두 번째 보물은 천 조각으로 변할 수 있는 큰 배였다.

35 그것은 Frey를 위한 것이었다.

36 세 번째 보물은 Thor를 위한 것이었다.

37 Loki는 Thor에게 그의 아내를 위한 매끈하게 늘어진 금발머리를 보여 주었다.

38 Thor가 그 머리카락을 그의 아내의 머리에 얹었더니 그것이 뿌리를 내려서 진짜 머리카락이 되었다.

39 이제 Brokk가 신들에게 그의 선물들을 보여 줄 차례였다.

40 그는 Odin에게 아홉 번째 밤이 될 때마다 8개의 금팔찌를 더 만들어 내는 금팔찌를 주었다.

41 그러고 나서 Brokk는 Frey에게 돼지를 한 마리 주었다.

42 그것은 어떤 말보다도 그의 마차를 더 빨리 끌 수 있었다.

43 "나의 세 번째 보물은 당신을 위한 것입니다, Thor." Brokk가 말했다.

44 "이것은 뮬니르라는 망치인데 당신은 마음에 드실 겁니다.

45 그것을 던지면, 그것은 항상 당신에게 되돌아 올 것입니다.

46 게다가, 그 무엇도 이것을 부술 수 없지요."

47 가장 훌륭한 보물을 선택하는 것은 쉬운 결정이었다.

48 세 명의 신들이 가장 마음에 든 것은 뮬니르였다.

49 그들은 그 망치가 신들을 그들의 적들로부터 보호해 줄 것이라고 생각했다.

50 "Brokk와 그의 남동생이 더 훌륭한 대장장이다." Odin이 말했다.

51 Brokk는 Loki가 틀렸다는 것을 증명해 냈고, 세 신들은 이제 소중한 보물을 가지게 되었다.

※ 다음 문장을 우리말로 쓰시오.

1 Treasures for Three Gods

➡ _____

2 Important Norse Gods

➡ _____

3 Odin, who is the highest god, gave up his eye for wisdom.

➡ _____

4 Thor is Odin's son and the strongest god of all.

➡ _____

5 Frey, who is the god of the harvest, controls the weather.

➡ _____

6 Loki is a god who plays tricks on others.

➡ _____

7 Thor woke and knew immediately something was wrong.

➡ _____

8 His wife's beautiful golden hair was gone.

➡ _____

9 He knew only Loki could do such a terrible thing.

➡ _____

10 Thor soon found Loki, who was drinking at home.

➡ _____

11 "You'd better undo what you did, or you'll be sorry," Thor said angrily to Loki.

➡ _____

12 Loki was scared.

➡ _____

13 He promised that he would get golden hair for Thor's wife.

➡ _____

14 Loki knew only the sons of Ivaldi could make fine golden hair.

➡ _____

15 He went to them and said, "I heard Brokk and his brother are the finest smiths. Is that true?"

➡ _____
_____

16 "No, it is we who are the finest smiths," the sons of Ivaldi replied.

➡ _____

17 "They're making three treasures for Odin, Thor, and Frey," said Loki.

➡ _____

18 "Do you think you can make treasures better than theirs?"

➡ _____

19 "Of course we can," they answered.

➡ _____

20 "O.K., then you should also make three treasures for them," said Loki.

➡ _____

21 "The gods will decide on the best treasure."

➡ _____

22 Loki also told them that one of the treasures had to be golden hair.

➡ _____

23 They went to work immediately.

➡ _____

24 Loki then went to see Brokk and his brother.

➡ _____

25 "Ivaldi's sons are making three treasures for Odin, Thor, and Frey," said Loki.

➡ _____

26 "I bet that you can never make treasures as fine as theirs."

➡ _____

27 Brokk became angry and accepted the challenge.

➡ _____

28 He and his brother produced three treasures of their own.

➡ _____

29 Loki went to see the three gods with all the treasures.

➡ _____

30 Brokk came along.

➡ _____

31 Loki showed them the treasures from Ivaldi's sons.

➡ _____

32 The first treasure was for Odin, who had only one eye.

➡ _____

33 It was a spear that never missed its target.

➡ _____

34 The second treasure was a big ship that could turn into a piece of cloth.

➡ _____

35 It was for Frey.

➡ _____

36 The third treasure was for Thor.

➡ _____

37 Loki showed Thor the flowing golden hair for his wife.

➡ _____

38 Thor put the hair on his wife's head, and it took root and became real hair.

➡ _____

39 It was now Brokk's turn to show the gods his gifts.

➡ _____

40 He gave Odin a gold arm ring that produced eight more gold rings every ninth night.

➡ _____

41 Brokk then gave Frey a pig.

➡ _____

42 It could pull his carriage faster than any horse.

➡ _____

43 "My third treasure is for you, Thor," said Brokk.

➡ _____

44 "This is the hammer Mjolnir, which you'll love.

➡ _____

45 If you throw it, it'll always come back to you.

➡ _____

46 Moreover, nothing can ever break it."

➡ _____

47 It was an easy decision to choose the greatest treasure.

➡ _____

48 It was Mjolnir that the three gods liked most.

➡ _____

49 They thought the hammer would protect the gods from their enemies.

➡ _____

50 "Brokk and his brother," said Odin, "are the better smiths."

➡ _____

51 Brokk proved that Loki was wrong, and the three gods now had precious treasures.

➡ _____

※ **다음 괄호 안의 단어들을 우리말에 맞도록 바르게 배열하시오.**

1 (for / Treasures / Gods / Three)
➡ _____

2 (Norse / Important / Gods)
➡ _____

3 (who / Odin, / the / is / god, / highest / up / gave / for / eye / his / wisdom.)
➡ _____

4 (is / Thor / son / Odin's / the / and / god / strongest / all. / of)
➡ _____

5 (who / Frey, / the / is / of / god / harvest, / the / the / weather. / controls)
➡ _____

6 (is / Loki / god / a / plays / who / on / others. / tricks)
➡ _____

7 (woke / Thor / knew / and / something / immediately / wrong. / was)
➡ _____

8 (wife's / his / golden / beautiful / hair / gone. / was)
➡ _____

9 (knew / he / Loki / only / do / could / a / such / thing. / terrible)
➡ _____

10 (soon / Thor / Loki, / found / was / who / at / drinking / home.)
➡ _____

11 (better / "you'd / what / undo / did, / you / or / be / you'll / sorry," / said / Thor / to / angrily / Loki.)
➡ _____

12 (was / Loki / scared.)
➡ _____

13 (promised / he / that / would / he / golden / get / for / hair / wife. / Thor's)
➡ _____

14 (knew / Loki / the / only / of / sons / Ivaldi / make / could / golden / hair. / fine)
➡ _____

15 (went / he / them / to / said, / and / heard / "I / and / Brokk / brother / his / the / are / smiths. / finest // that / true? / is)
➡ _____

16 ("no, / is / it / who / we / the / are / smiths," / finest / the / of / sons / repiled. / Ivaldi)
➡ _____

1 세 명의 신을 위한 보물

2 북유럽 신화의 주요 신들

3 Odin은 가장 높은 신이며, 지혜를 위해 한쪽 눈을 포기했다.

4 Thor는 Odin의 아들이며 모든 신들 중에서 가장 강한 신이다.

5 Frey는 수확의 신으로 날씨를 다스린다.

6 Loki는 다른 신들에게 농간을 부리는 신이다.

7 Thor는 잠에서 깨어 즉시 무엇인가가 잘못되었다는 것을 알았다.

8 그의 아내의 아름다운 금발머리가 사라졌다.

9 그는 오직 Loki만이 이런 끔찍한 일을 할 수 있다는 것을 알고 있었다.

10 Thor는 곧 Loki를 찾았는데, 그는 집에서 술을 마시고 있었다.

11 "네가 한 짓을 되돌려 놓는 것이 좋을 거야, 그렇지 않으면 후회하게 될 거다." Thor는 노하여 Loki에게 말했다.

12 Loki는 겁이 났다.

13 그는 Thor의 아내를 위해 금발머리를 얻어 오겠다고 약속했다.

14 Loki는 Ivaldi의 아들들만이 훌륭한 금발머리를 만들 수 있다는 것을 알고 있었다.

15 그는 그들에게 가서 "내가 듣기로 Brokk와 그의 남동생이 가장 훌륭한 대장장이라고 하던데. 그것이 사실인가?"라고 말했다.

16 "아니요, 가장 훌륭한 대장장이는 바로 우리들이요." Ivaldi의 아들들이 대답했다.

17 (making / "they're / treasures / three / Odin, / for / and / Thor, / Frey," / Loki. / said)

➡ _____

18 (you / "do / you / think / make / can / better / treasures / than / theirs?")

➡ _____

19 (course / "of / can," / we / answered. / they)

➡ _____

20 ("O.K., / you / then / also / should / three / make / them," / for / treasures / Loki. / said)

➡ _____

21 ("the / will / gods / on / decide / best / the / treasure.")

➡ _____

22 (also / Loki / them / told / one / that / the / of / had / treasures / be / to / hair. / golden)

➡ _____

23 (went / they / work / to / immediately.)

➡ _____

24 (then / Loki / to / went / Brokk / see / his / and / brother.)

➡ _____

25 (sons / "Ivaldi's / are / three / making / for / treasures / Odin, / and / Thor, / Frey," / Loki. / said)

➡ _____

26 (bet / "I / you / that / never / can / treasures / make / fine / as / theirs." / as)

➡ _____

27 (became / Brokk / and / accepted / angry / challenge. / the)

➡ _____

28 (his / and / he / brother / three / produced / of / treasures / own. / their)

➡ _____

29 (went / Loki / see / to / the / gods / three / all / with / treasures. / the)

➡ _____

30 (came / Brokk / along.)

➡ _____

31 (showed / Loki / the / them / treasures / Ivaldi's / from / sons.)

➡ _____

32 (first / the / was / treasure / Odin, / for / had / who / one / eye. / only)

➡ _____

33 (was / it / spear / a / never / that / its / missed / target.)

➡ _____

---

17 "그들은 Odin과 Thor와 Frey를 위해서 보물을 만들고 있네." Loki는 말했다.

18 "너희들이 그들의 보물보다 더 나은 보물을 만들 수 있다고 생각하는가?"

19 "물론 할 수 있소." 그들이 대답했다.

20 "좋아, 그러면 너희도 그들을 위해 세 개의 보물을 만들어야 한다." Loki가 말했다.

21 "그 신들이 가장 훌륭한 보물을 결정할 것이다."

22 Loki는 또한 그들에게 보물 중 하나는 금발머리이어야 한다고 말했다.

23 그들은 즉시 일에 착수했다.

24 Loki는 그 다음에 Brokk와 그의 남동생을 보러 갔다.

25 "Ivaldi의 아들들이 Odin과 Thor, 그리고 Frey를 위해 세 개의 보물을 만들고 있어." Loki가 말했다.

26 "너희들은 절대 그들의 보물만큼 훌륭한 보물을 만들 수 없다는 것을 내 장담하지."

27 Brokk는 화가 나서 그 도전을 받아들였다.

28 그와 그의 남동생은 그들만의 세 가지 보물을 만들었다.

29 Loki는 모든 보물을 가지고 세 신을 만나러 갔다.

30 Brokk가 같이 갔다.

31 Loki는 그들에게 Ivaldi의 아들들이 만든 보물들을 보여 주었다.

32 첫 번째 보물은 Odin을 위한 것으로, 그는 눈이 한쪽밖에 없었다.

33 그것은 목표물을 절대로 빗나가지 않는 창이었다.

34 (second / the / was / treasure / a / ship / big / could / that / into / turn / piece / a / cloth. / of)
➡ _____

35 (was / it / Frey. / for)
➡ _____

36 (third / the / was / treasure / Thor. / for)
➡ _____

37 (showed / Loki / the / Thor / golden / flowing / for / hair / wife. / his)
➡ _____

38 (put / Thor / hair / the / his / on / head, / wife's / and / took / it / and / root / real / became / hair.)
➡ _____

39 (was / it / Brokk's / now / to / turn / show / gods / the / gifts. / his)
➡ _____

40 (gave / he / a / Odin / gold / ring / arm / produced / that / eight / gold / more / every / rings / night. / ninth)
➡ _____

41 (then / Brokk / Frey / gave / pig. / a)
➡ _____

42 (could / it / his / pull / faster / carriage / than / horse. / any)
➡ _____

43 (third / "my / is / treasure / for / you, / said / Brokk. / Thor,")
➡ _____

44 (is / "this / hammer / the / which / Mjolnir, / love. / you'll)
➡ _____

45 (you / if / it, / throw / always / it'll / back / come / you. / to)
➡ _____

46 (nothing / moreover, / ever / can / it." / break)
➡ _____

47 (was / it / easy / to / an / decision / choose / greatest / the / treasure.)
➡ _____

48 (was / it / that / Mjolnir / three / the / gods / most. / liked)
➡ _____

49 (thought / they / hammer / the / protect / would / gods / the / their / from / enemies.)
➡ _____

50 (and / "Brokk / brother," / his / Odin, / said / the / "are / smiths." / better)
➡ _____

51 (proved / Brokk / Loki / that / wrong, / was / the / and / gods / three / had / now / treasures. / precious)
➡ _____

34 두 번째 보물은 천 조각으로 변할 수 있는 큰 배였다.
35 그것은 Frey를 위한 것이었다.
36 세 번째 보물은 Thor를 위한 것이었다.
37 Loki는 Thor에게 그의 아내를 위한 매끈하게 늘어진 금발머리를 보여 주었다.
38 Thor가 그 머리카락을 그의 아내의 머리에 얹었더니 그것이 뿌리를 내려서 진짜 머리카락이 되었다.
39 이제 Brokk가 신들에게 그의 선물들을 보여 줄 차례였다.
40 그는 Odin에게 아홉 번째 밤이 될 때마다 8개의 금팔찌를 더 만들어 내는 금팔찌를 주었다.
41 그리고 나서 Brokk는 Frey에게 돼지를 한 마리 주었다.
42 그것은 어떤 말보다도 그의 마차를 더 빨리 끌 수 있었다.
43 "나의 세 번째 보물은 당신을 위한 것입니다. Thor." Brokk가 말했다.
44 "이것은 몰니르라는 망치인데 당신은 마음에 드실 겁니다.
45 그것을 던지면, 그것은 항상 당신에게 되돌아 올 것입니다.
46 게다가, 그 무엇도 이것을 부술 수 없지요."
47 가장 훌륭한 보물을 선택하는 것은 쉬운 결정이었다.
48 세 명의 신들이 가장 마음에 든 것은 몰니르였다.
49 그들은 그 망치가 신들을 그들의 적들로부터 보호해 줄 것이라고 생각했다.
50 "Brokk와 그의 남동생이 더 훌륭한 대장장이다." Odin이 말했다.
51 Brokk는 Loki가 틀렸다는 것을 증명해 냈고, 세 신들은 이제 소중한 보물을 가지게 되었다.

※ 다음 우리말을 영어로 쓰시오.

1 세 명의 신을 위한 보물

➡ _____

2 북유럽 신화의 주요 신들

➡ _____

3 Odin은 가장 높은 신이며, 지혜를 위해 한쪽 눈을 포기했다.

➡ _____

4 Thor는 Odin의 아들이며 모든 신들 중에서 가장 강한 신이다.

➡ _____

5 Frey는 수확의 신으로 날씨를 다스린다.

➡ _____

6 Loki는 다른 신들에게 농간을 부리는 신이다.

➡ _____

7 Thor는 잠에서 깨어 즉시 무엇인가가 잘못되었다는 것을 알았다.

➡ _____

8 그의 아내의 아름다운 금발머리가 사라졌다.

➡ _____

9 그는 오직 Loki만이 이런 끔찍한 일을 할 수 있다는 것을 알고 있었다.

➡ _____

10 Thor는 곧 Loki를 찾았는데, 그는 집에서 술을 마시고 있었다.

➡ _____

11 "네가 한 짓을 되돌려 놓는 것이 좋을 거야, 그렇지 않으면 후회하게 될 거다." Thor는 노하여 Loki에게 말했다.

➡ _____

12 Loki는 겁이 났다.

➡ _____

13 그는 Thor의 아내를 위해 금발머리를 얻어 오겠다고 약속했다.

➡ _____

14 Loki는 Ivaldi의 아들들만이 훌륭한 금발머리를 만들 수 있다는 것을 알고 있었다.

➡ _____

15 그는 그들에게 가서 "내가 듣기로 Brokk와 그의 남동생이 가장 훌륭한 대장장이라고 하던데, 그것이 사실인가?"라고 말했다.

➡ _____

16 "아니요, 가장 훌륭한 대장장이는 바로 우리들이요." Ivaldi의 아들들이 대답했다.

➡ _____

17 "그들은 Odin과 Thor와 Frey를 위해서 보물을 만들고 있네." Loki는 말했다.

➡ _____

18 "너희들이 그들의 보물보다 더 나은 보물을 만들 수 있다고 생각하는가?"

➡ _____

19 "물론 할 수 있소." 그들이 대답했다.

➡ _____

20 "좋아, 그러면 너희도 그들을 위해 세 개의 보물을 만들어야 한다." Loki가 말했다.

➡ _____

21 "그 신들이 가장 훌륭한 보물을 결정할 것이다."

➡ _____

22 Loki는 또한 그들에게 보물 중 하나는 금발머리이어야 한다고 말했다.

➡ _____

23 그들은 즉시 일에 착수했다.

➡ _____

24 Loki는 그 다음에 Brokk와 그의 남동생을 보러 갔다.

➡ _____

25 "Ivaldi의 아들들이 Odin과 Thor, 그리고 Frey를 위해 세 개의 보물을 만들고 있어." Loki가 말했다.

➡ _____

26 "너희들은 절대 그들의 보물만큼 훌륭한 보물을 만들 수 없다는 것을 내 장담하지."

➡ _____

27 Brokk는 화가 나서 그 도전을 받아들였다.

➡ _____

28 그와 그의 남동생은 그들만의 세 가지 보물을 만들었다.

➡ _____

29 Loki는 모든 보물을 가지고 세 신을 만나러 갔다.

➡ _____

30 Brokk가 같이 갔다.

➡ _____

31 Loki는 그들에게 Ivaldi의 아들들이 만든 보물들을 보여 주었다.

➡ _____

32 첫 번째 보물은 Odin을 위한 것으로, 그는 눈이 한쪽밖에 없었다.

➡ _____

33 그것은 목표물을 절대로 빗나가지 않는 창이었다.

➡ _____

34 두 번째 보물은 천 조각으로 변할 수 있는 큰 배였다.

➡ _____

35 그것은 Frey를 위한 것이었다.

➡ _____

36 세 번째 보물은 Thor를 위한 것이었다.

➡ _____

37 Loki는 Thor에게 그의 아내를 위한 매끈하게 늘어진 금발머리를 보여 주었다.

➡ _____

38 Thor가 그 머리카락을 그의 아내의 머리에 얹었더니 그것이 뿌리를 내려서 진짜 머리카락이 되었다.

➡ _____

39 이제 Brokk가 신들에게 그의 선물들을 보여 줄 차례였다.

➡ _____

40 그는 Odin에게 아홉 번째 밤이 될 때마다 8개의 금팔찌를 더 만들어 내는 금팔찌를 주었다.

➡ _____

41 그러고 나서 Brokk는 Frey에게 돼지를 한 마리 주었다.

➡ _____

42 그것은 어떤 말보다도 그의 마차를 더 빨리 끌 수 있었다.

➡ _____

43 "나의 세 번째 보물은 당신을 위한 것입니다, Thor." Brokk가 말했다.

➡ _____

44 "이것은 묠니르라는 망치인데 당신은 마음에 드실 겁니다.

➡ _____

45 그것을 던지면, 그것은 항상 당신에게 되돌아 올 것입니다.

➡ _____

46 게다가, 그 무엇도 이것을 부술 수 없어요."

➡ _____

47 가장 훌륭한 보물을 선택하는 것은 쉬운 결정이었다.

➡ _____

48 세 명의 신들이 가장 마음에 든 것은 묠니르였다.

➡ _____

49 그들은 그 망치가 신들을 그들의 적들로부터 보호해 줄 것이라고 생각했다.

➡ _____

50 "Brokk와 그의 남동생이 더 훌륭한 대장장이야." Odin이 말했다.

➡ _____

51 Brokk는 Loki가 틀렸다는 것을 증명해 냈고, 세 신들은 이제 소중한 보물을 가지게 되었다.

➡ _____

※ 다음 우리말과 일치하도록 빈칸에 알맞은 말을 쓰시오.

After You Read A

1. (1) Loki _____ the beautiful _____ _____ of Thor's wife, _____ Thor _____ _____ _____ him.

2. Loki _____ _____ _____ _____ _____ for Thor's wife.

3. (2) Loki _____ the sons of Ivaldi _____ _____ _____ _____ Odin, Thor, and Frey.

4. He also _____ Brokk and his brother _____ _____ _____ _____.

5. Loki _____ that Ivaldi's sons _____ _____ _____ _____ _____.

6. (3) Loki _____ the _____ the _____ Ivaldi's sons.

7. They were a _____, a _____ _____, and _____ _____.

8. _____ _____ _____ Brokk and his brother _____ a _____ _____ _____, a pig, _____ _____ _____.

9. (4) The gods _____ _____ _____ _____.

10. They each had _____ _____ _____ _____.

Link Create

1. I _____ always _____ friends with Sif, _____ is the wife of _____ _____ _____.

2. A _____ _____ ago, I cut her golden hair _____ _____ _____, and her husband _____ _____ _____ me.

3. I _____ _____ _____ a good idea _____ _____ her hair _____.

4. I asked the sons of Ivaldi _____ _____ _____ _____.

Culture Project

1. The _____ _____ _____ _____ in the World

2. Hercules, _____ was the son of Zeus, _____ _____ _____ _____ _____.

3. _____ _____ _____ Hercules killed the Nemean lion and the _____ _____ _____ _____ _____.

4. He _____ _____ the _____ Hydra.

5. I think _____ is Hercules _____ is _____ _____ _____ in the world.

1. (1) Loki가 Thor의 아내의 아름다운 금발머리를 가져가서, Thor는 그에게 화가 났다.
2. Loki는 Thor의 아내를 위해 금발머리를 얻어 오겠다고 약속했다.
3. (2) Loki는 Ivaldi의 아들들에게 Odin과 Thor와 Frey를 위해서 보물을 만들어 달라고 부탁했다.
4. 그는 또한 Brokk와 그의 남동생에게 신들을 위한 세 개의 보물을 만들게 시켰다.
5. Loki는 Ivaldi의 아들들이 더 훌륭한 보물을 만들 것이라고 장담했다.
6. (3) Loki는 세 명의 신들에게 Ivaldi의 아들들이 만든 보물들을 보여 주었다.
7. 그것들은 창과 큰 배와 금발머리였다.
8. Brokk와 그의 남동생이 만든 보물들은 금팔찌와 돼지 한 마리와 망치였다.
9. (4) 신들이 가장 마음에 든 것은 망치였다.
10. 그들은 각자 그들의 소중한 보물을 가지게 되었다.

1. 나는 가장 강한 신의 아내인 Sif와 항상 친구로 지내왔다.
2. 며칠 전에 나는 그녀의 금발을 단지 재미로 잘랐고 그녀의 남편은 나에게 화가 났다.
3. 나는 그녀의 머리를 되돌릴 좋은 생각이 났다.
4. 나는 Ivaldi의 아들들에게 훌륭한 금발 머리를 만들어 달라고 부탁했다.

1. 세상에서 가장 강한 신들과 영웅들
2. 제우스의 아들인 헤라클레스는 그의 많은 모험들로 유명하다.
3. 용감하고 강한 헤라클레스는 네메아의 사자를 죽이고, 그 가죽을 외투로 입었다.
4. 그는 또한 머리가 여러 개 달린 히드라와 싸웠다.
5. 나는 헤라클레스가 세상에서 가장 강한 영웅이라고 생각한다.

※ 다음 우리말을 영어로 쓰시오.

After You Read A

1. (1) Loki가 Thor의 아내의 아름다운 금발머리를 가져가서, Thor는 그에게 화가 났다.
➡ _____

2. Loki는 Thor의 아내를 위해 금발머리를 얻어 오겠다고 약속했다.
➡ _____

3. (2) Loki는 Ivaldi의 아들들에게 Odin과 Thor와 Frey를 위해서 보물을 만들어 달라고 부탁했다.
➡ _____

4. 그는 또한 Brokk와 그의 남동생에게 신들을 위한 세 개의 보물을 만들게 시켰다.
➡ _____

5. Loki는 Ivaldi의 아들들이 더 훌륭한 보물을 만들 것이라고 장담했다.
➡ _____

6. (3) Loki는 세 명의 신들에게 Ivaldi의 아들들이 만든 보물들을 보여 주었다.
➡ _____

7. 그것들은 창과 큰 배와 금발머리였다.
➡ _____

8. Brokk와 그의 남동생이 만든 보물들은 금팔찌와 돼지 한 마리와 망치였다.
➡ _____

9. (4) 신들이 가장 마음에 든 것은 망치였다.
➡ _____

10. 그들은 각자 그들의 소중한 보물을 가지게 되었다.
➡ _____

Link Create

1. 나는 가장 강한 신의 아내인 Sif와 항상 친구로 지내왔다.
➡ _____

2. 며칠 전에 나는 그녀의 금발을 단지 재미로 잘랐고 그녀의 남편은 나에게 화가 났다.
➡ _____

3. 나는 그녀의 머리를 되돌릴 좋은 생각이 났다.
➡ _____

4. 나는 Ivaldi의 아들들에게 훌륭한 금발머리를 만들어 달라고 부탁했다.
➡ _____

Culture Project

1. 세상에서 가장 강한 신들과 영웅들
➡ _____

2. 제우스의 아들인 헤라클레스는 그의 많은 모험들로 유명하다.
➡ _____

3. 용감하고 강한 헤라클레스는 네메아의 사자를 죽이고, 그 가죽을 외투로 입었다.
➡ _____

4. 그는 또한 머리가 여러 개 달린 히드라와 싸웠다.
➡ _____

5. 나는 헤라클레스가 세상에서 가장 강한 영웅이라고 생각한다.
➡ _____

※ 다음 영어를 우리말로 쓰시오.

01	prove	
02	absorb	
03	publish	
04	bloom	
05	capital	
06	secret	
07	actually	
08	solve	
09	discover	
10	soak	
11	erase	
12	expect	
13	spinach	
14	face	
15	defeat	
16	character	
17	statue	
18	article	
19	battleship	
20	government	
21	bean	

22	hidden	
23	consider	
24	happen	
25	hide	
26	characteristic	
27	improve	
28	lower	
29	contain	
30	nutrient	
31	world-famous	
32	crush	
33	trace	
34	poisonous	
35	lose weight	
36	soak up	
37	keep ~ away from …	
38	turn A into B	
39	no longer	
40	be scared of	
41	give it a try	
42	keep a secret	
43	in addition	

※ 다음 우리말을 영어로 쓰시오.

01 흡수하다 _____

02 기사, 논문 _____

03 전함 _____

04 꽃을 피우다 _____

05 수도 _____

06 등장인물 _____

07 기대하다 _____

08 고려하다, 여기다 _____

09 물리치다, 패배시키다 _____

10 특성, 특장; 특징적인 _____

11 으스러뜨리다 _____

12 유독한, 독성의 _____

13 포함하다, 담고 있다 _____

14 숨다, 숨기다 _____

15 출판하다 _____

16 조각상, 동상 _____

17 개선하다, 향상시키다 _____

18 낮추다 _____

19 사실, 진실 _____

20 흔적; 추적하다 _____

21 시금치 _____

22 물질, 재료 _____

23 숨겨진 _____

24 영양소, 영양분 _____

25 증명하다 _____

26 세계적으로 유명한 _____

27 담그다, 적시다 _____

28 행성 _____

29 시력 _____

30 비밀 _____

31 해결하다 _____

32 만화 _____

33 연구원, 조사원 _____

34 정부, 국가 _____

35 포만감을 가지다 _____

36 게다가 _____

37 ～에 유익하다 _____

38 살을 빼다 _____

39 비밀을 지키다 _____

40 더 이상 ～가 아닌 _____

41 흡수하다, 빨아들이다 _____

42 시도해 보다 _____

43 약을 먹다 _____

※ 다음 영영풀이에 알맞은 단어를 <보기>에서 골라 쓴 후, 우리말 뜻을 쓰시오.

1 _____ : a person in a book, play, film, etc.: _____

2 _____ : a funny drawing in a newspaper or magazine: _____

3 _____ : to cover something so that it cannot be seen clearly: _____

4 _____ : to use facts, evidence, etc. to show that something is true: _____

5 _____ : a small creature such as a fly or ant, that has six legs: _____

6 _____ : to prepare and produce a book, magazine, etc. for sale: _____

7 _____ : to put something in a liquid for a period of time: _____

8 _____ : a long pointed orange vegetable that grows under the ground: _____

9 _____ : a plant with dark green leaves that are eaten as a vegetable: _____

10 _____ : the largest type of ship used in war, with very big guns and heavy armour: _____

11 _____ : a fact that is known by only a small number of people, and is not told to anyone else: _____

12 _____ : a chemical or food that provides what is needed for plants or animals to live and grow: _____

13 _____ : an image of a person or animal that is made in solid material such as stone or metal: _____

14 _____ : a seed that is eaten as a vegetable and that comes from any one of many different kinds of climbing plants: _____

15 _____ : something such as a mark or an object which shows that someone or something was in a particular place: _____

16 _____ : a board like a wide ski that is used for sliding down hills of snow while standing: _____

보기

snowboard	secret	battleship	hide
statue	bean	insect	character
trace	nutrient	prove	carrot
publish	spinach	soak	cartoon

※ 다음 우리말과 일치하도록 빈칸에 알맞은 말을 쓰시오.

Listen & Speak 1 A-1

B: Bomi, do you have _____ _____?

G: Why? Is _____ _____?

B: I have _____ _____. I think I ate _____ _____ for lunch.

G: _____ _____ you _____ _____ _____ _____?

B: O.K. I'll give _____ _____ _____.

B: 보미야, 약 좀 있니?
G: 왜? 무슨 문제 있어?
B: 배가 아파. 점심을 너무 많이 먹었나 봐.
G: 산책을 좀 하는 게 어때?
B: 알겠어. 한번 해 볼게.

Listen & Speak 1 A-2

B: Is _____ _____? You don't _____ _____ _____.

G: I have _____ _____ _____. I think it's _____ _____ the fine dust _____ _____.

B: _____ some plants in your room. They _____ bad air _____ and _____ _____ _____.

G: Really? I'll _____ _____ _____ _____ right away.

B: 어디 안 좋아? 안색이 나빠 보이는데.
G: 목이 아파. 최근의 미세먼지 때문인 것 같아.
B: 방에 식물을 좀 놓아 봐. 나쁜 공기를 흡수하고 신선한 공기를 만들어 내.
G: 정말? 당장 식물을 몇 그루 가져와야 겠어.

Listen & Speak 2 A-1

B: It's _____ _____ _____ _____ _____. What _____ _____ _____ I should do?

G: Well, why don't you _____ _____ _____ every day?

B: My dog would love _____, but would _____ _____ me _____ _____?

G: Sure. _____ you _____ your dog, you're _____ _____, _____.

B: O.K. I'll _____ _____ _____.

B: 몸무게를 줄이는 건 너무 어려워. 내가 뭘 해야 한다고 생각해?
G: 글쎄, 매일 너의 개를 산책시키는 건 어때?
B: 우리 개는 좋아하겠지만, 그게 살을 빼는 데 도움이 될까?
G: 물론이지. 네가 개를 산책시키면, 사실은 너도 운동하는 거잖아.
B: 좋아. 생각해 볼게.

Listen & Speak 2 A-2

B: _____ _____ your tomatoes _____? Are they _____ well?

G: No. I've _____ only _____ _____ tomatoes _____ _____. What do you think _____ _____ _____?

B: _____ do you have the pot?

G: _____ the kitchen.

B: Well, tomato plants _____ _____ 7 hours of sunlight _____ _____.

G: Oh, I see. I'll _____ the pot _____ to the window.

B: 네 토마토들 어떠니? 잘 자라고 있어?
G: 아니. 지금까지 토마토 몇 개밖에 못 얻었어. 내가 뭘 해야 한다고 생각하니?
B: 화분을 어디에 두는데?
G: 부엌에.
B: 음, 토마토는 하루에 7시간 정도 햇빛을 받아야 해.
G: 오, 그렇구나. 화분을 창문 쪽으로 옮겨야겠다.

Communicate A

Anna: Suho, _____ _____ _____? You're very _____ today.

Suho: I'm just _____ _____ _____. I slept very _____ last night.

Anna: Did you do _____ _____ last night?

Suho: Yes, I watched a movie _____ my phone _____ 2 a.m. That's _____ _____ _____ _____ _____ _____.

Anna: Oh, _____ _____ you have red eyes. You should go to bed _____ _____ for your health.

Suho: I think my eyes are _____ _____. What do you think _____ _____ _____?

Anna: Try _____ _____ _____ _____ and tomatoes. They're _____ _____ _____ A, so they'll _____ your eyes _____.

Suho: I _____. Thank you, Anna.

Anna: 수호야, 무슨 일 있어? 오늘 굉장히 조용하네.

수호: 조금 피곤한 것뿐이야. 어젯밤에 정말 조금 잤거든.

Anna: 어젯밤 늦게까지 뭔가 했니?

수호: 응, 새벽 2시까지 휴대폰으로 영화를 봤어. 요즘 종종 하는 일이야.

Anna: 오, 그래서 눈이 충혈됐구나. 건강을 위해 자정 전에는 잠자리에 들어야 해.

수호: 눈이 점점 나빠지는 것 같아. 내가 뭘 해야 한다고 생각해?

Anna: 당근이랑 토마토를 많이 먹어 봐. 그것들은 비타민 A가 많아서, 네 눈을 건강하게 유지해 줄 거야.

수호: 알겠어. 고마워, Anna.

Progress Check 1

B: _____ something _____?

G: I'm just _____ _____ _____. I've _____ a movie on my phone _____ _____ _____.

B: That's _____ you have _____ _____. Try _____ a warm towel _____ your eyes.

G: O.K. Thanks.

B: 무슨 문제 있어?

G: 조금 피곤한 것뿐이야. 휴대전화로 영화를 두 시간 동안 봤거든.

B: 그래서 눈이 충혈됐구나. 따뜻한 수건으로 눈을 덮어 봐.

G: 알겠어. 고마워.

Progress Check 2

G: What's _____? You _____ _____.

B: Well, I _____ my mom's favorite _____. What _____ _____ _____ I should do?

G: _____ her the _____. She will _____.

B: I _____ you're _____.

G: 무슨 문제 있어? 걱정이 있는 것 같은데.

B: 그게, 어머니께서 가장 아끼시는 접시를 깨뜨렸어. 내가 뭘 해야 한다고 생각하니?

G: 솔직히 말씀 드려. 이해하실 거야.

B: 네 말이 맞길 바라.

※ 다음 우리말에 맞도록 대화를 영어로 쓰시오.

Listen & Speak 1 A-1

B: _____

G: _____

B: _____

G: _____

B: _____

B: 보미야, 약 좀 있니?
G: 왜? 무슨 문제 있어?
B: 배가 아파. 점심을 너무 많이 먹었나 봐.
G: 산책을 좀 하는 게 어때?
B: 알겠어. 한번 해 볼게.

Listen & Speak 1 A-2

B: _____

G: _____

B: _____

G: _____

B: 어디 안 좋아? 안색이 나빠 보이는데.
G: 목이 아파. 최근의 미세먼지 때문인 것 같아.
B: 방에 식물을 좀 놓아 봐. 나쁜 공기를 흡수하고 신선한 공기를 만들어 내.
G: 정말? 당장 식물을 몇 그루 가져와야 겠어.

Listen & Speak 2 A-1

B: _____

G: _____

B: _____

G: _____

B: _____

B: 몸무게를 줄이는 건 너무 어려워. 내가 뭘 해야 한다고 생각해?
G: 글쎄, 매일 너의 개를 산책시키는 건 어때?
B: 우리 개는 좋아하겠지만, 그게 살을 빼는 데 도움이 될까?
G: 물론이시. 네가 개를 산책시키면, 사실은 너도 운동하는 거잖아.
B: 좋아. 생각해 볼게.

Listen & Speak 2 A-2

B: _____

G: _____

B: _____

G: _____

B: _____

G: _____

B: 네 토마토들 어떠니? 잘 자라고 있어?
G: 아니. 지금까지 토마토 몇 개밖에 못 얻었어. 내가 뭘 해야 한다고 생각하니?
B: 화분을 어디에 두는데?
G: 부엌에.
B: 음, 토마토는 하루에 7시간 정도 햇빛을 받아야 해.
G: 오, 그렇구나. 화분을 창문 쪽으로 옮겨야겠다.

Communicate A

Anna: _____

Suho: _____

Anna: _____

Suho: _____

_____

Anna: _____

_____

Suho: _____

Anna: _____

_____

Suho: _____

Anna: 수호야, 무슨 일 있어? 오늘 굉장히 조용하네.

수호: 조금 피곤한 것뿐이야. 어젯밤에 정말 조금 잤거든.

Anna: 어젯밤 늦게까지 뭔가 했니?

수호: 응, 새벽 2시까지 휴대폰으로 영화를 봤어. 요즘 종종 하는 일이야.

Anna: 오, 그래서 눈이 충혈됐구나. 건강을 위해 자정 전에는 잠자리에 들어야 해.

수호: 눈이 점점 나빠지는 것 같아. 내가 뭘 해야 한다고 생각해?

Anna: 당근이랑 토마토를 많이 먹어 봐. 그것들은 비타민 A가 많아서. 네 눈을 건강하게 유지해 줄 거야.

수호: 알겠어. 고마워, Anna.

Progress Check 1

B: _____

G: _____

B: _____

G: _____

B: 무슨 문제 있어?

G: 조금 피곤한 것뿐이야. 휴대전화로 영화를 두 시간 동안 봤거든.

B: 그래서 눈이 충혈됐구나. 따뜻한 수건으로 눈을 덮어 봐.

G: 알겠어. 고마워.

Progress Check 2

G: _____

B: _____

G: _____

B: _____

G: 무슨 문제 있어? 걱정이 있는 것 같은데.

B: 그게, 어머니께서 가장 아끼시는 접시를 깨뜨렸어. 내가 뭘 해야 한다고 생각하니?

G: 솔직히 말씀 드려. 이해하실 거야.

B: 네 말이 맞길 바라.

※ 다음 우리말과 일치하도록 빈칸에 알맞은 것을 골라 쓰시오.

1 _____ Stories about _____
A. Plants   B. Hidden

2 Popeye and the _____ _____
A. Great   B. Spinach

3 Popeye is a _____ _____ _____.
A. character   B. cartoon   C. world-famous

4 He _____ his super power _____ _____ _____.
A. eating   B. by   C. gets   D. spinach

5 _____ Popeye _____ _____ in the 1930s in the United States, a _____ of children began to eat spinach.
A. popular   B. lot   C. became   D. when

6 Crystal City in Texas, which is _____ the spinach _____ of the world, even _____ a _____ of Popeye.
A. built   B. called   C. statue   D. capital

7 _____ eating spinach will not give us super _____, _____ does have a lot of _____.
A. spinach   B. although   C. nutrients   D. powers

8 It is actually _____ one of the ten _____ _____ on the _____.
A. healthiest   B. planet   C. considered   D. foods

9 Spinach can be _____ in a _____ _____.
A. surprising   B. used   C. way

10 _____ it absorbs water, spinach also _____ many _____ things from the _____.
A. absorbs   B. soil   C. other   D. when

11 Some scientists have used this _____ of spinach to find _____ _____ in the _____.
A. characteristic   B. ground   C. bombs   D. hidden

12 They make special spinach plants _____ _____ their _____.
A. ensors   B. leaves   C. on   D. with

13 When these plants _____ up traces from _____, the sensors _____ _____.
A. light   B. bombs   C. up   D. soak

14 Carrots in _____ _____ _____
A. War   B. World   C. II

15 In 1940, the Royal Air Force _____ German fighters _____ World War II _____ _____ a radar system.
A. by   B. defeated   C. using   D. during

16 The British government wanted to _____ this technology a _____, so it _____ an _____ in the newspaper.
A. secret   B. keep   C. published   D. article

17 It _____ that British pilots _____ their night _____ because they _____ a lot of carrots.
A. vision   B. said   C. ate   D. improved

1 식물에 대한 숨겨진 이야기

2 Popeye와 위대한 시금치

3 Popeye는 세계적으로 유명한 만화 캐릭터다.

4 그는 시금치를 먹음으로써 초인적인 힘을 얻는다.

5 Popeye가 1930년대 미국에서 인기를 얻었을 때, 많은 어린이들이 시금치를 먹기 시작했다.

6 텍사스의 크리스털 시티는 세계의 시금치 수도라고 불리는데, 이곳에서는 Popeye의 동상을 세우기까지 했다.

7 비록 시금치를 먹는 것이 우리에게 초인적인 힘을 주지는 않지만, 시금치는 정말로 많은 영양분을 가지고 있다.

8 이것은 실제로 지구상에서 가장 건강한 식품 10개 중 하나로 여겨진다.

9 시금치는 놀라운 용도로 사용될 수 있다.

10 그것이 물을 흡수할 때, 시금치는 흙으로부터 다른 많은 것들도 흡수한다.

11 몇몇 과학자들은 시금치의 이 특성을 땅에 숨겨진 폭탄을 찾는 데 사용했다.

12 그들은 잎에 감지기가 있는 특별한 시금치를 만든다.

13 이 식물들이 폭탄의 흔적을 흡수하면, 감지기가 빛난다.

14 제2차 세계대전에서의 당근

15 1940년, 영국 공군은 제2차 세계 대전에서 레이더 시스템을 사용해 독일군을 패배시켰다.

16 영국 정부는 이 기술을 비밀로 하기를 원했기 때문에, 신문에 기사를 하나 냈다.

17 그것은 영국 비행사들이 당근을 많이 먹어 야간 시력이 좋아졌다는 내용이었다.

18 Everybody _____ the story and began to eat a _____ more carrots _____ _____.

    A. than   B. lot   C. before   D. believed

19 Can we really _____ night vision _____ _____ lots of _____?

    A. improve   B. eating   C. by   D. carrots

20 Not really, but carrots _____ a lot of _____ A, which does _____ our eyes _____.

    A. vitamin   B. healthy   C. contain   D. keep

21 In the _____, carrots _____ actually be _____ in _____.

    A. used   B. future   C. wars   D. may

22 Scottish researchers have _____ a way to _____ carrots _____ a very strong and _____ material.

    A. turn   B. discovered   C. light   D. into

23 It can _____ _____ to make _____.

    A. be   B. battleships   C. used   D. even

24 This new material _____ _____ _____ _____ to make snowboards and bicycles.

    A. been   B. has   C. used   D. already

25 **Tomatoes, the _____ _____**

    A. Vegetables   B. Scariest

26 We all know that tomatoes _____ _____ _____ our _____.

    A. good   B. health   C. are   D. for

27 _____ _____ the 1800s, _____, most Americans thought that tomatoes were _____.

    A. until   B. poisonous   C. up   D. however

28 In 1820, a man _____ Robert Johnson wanted to _____ that tomatoes were _____ to _____.

    A. prove   B. eat   C. named   D. safe

29 So, he _____ a _____ of tomatoes in _____ of many people _____ him.

    A. front   B. basket   C. watching   D. ate

30 They all _____ him to die, but _____ _____ him.

    A. nothing   B. expected   C. to   D. happened

31 Ever _____ then, Americans _____ _____ _____ tomatoes.

    A. enjoyed   B. since   C. eating   D. have

32 We are _____ _____ afraid of tomatoes, but some insects are still _____ _____ them.

    A. scared   B. no   C. of   D. longer

33 If you want to _____ insects _____ from your room, _____ a bowl of _____ tomatoes in a corner of your room.

    A. away   B. crushed   C. keep   D. place

34 _____ will not _____ _____ the tomatoes.

    A. come   B. insects   C. near

---

18 모두가 그 이야기를 믿었고 전보다 훨씬 많은 당근을 먹기 시작했다.

19 우리는 정말 당근을 많이 먹어서 야간 시력을 높일 수 있을까?

20 실제로 그렇지는 않지만, 당근은 많은 비타민 A를 함유하는데, 그것은 정말로 우리 눈을 건강하게 유지해 준다.

21 미래에는, 당근이 실제로 전쟁에 이용될지도 모른다.

22 스코틀랜드의 연구원들은 당근을 매우 강하고 가벼운 물질로 바꾸는 방법을 발견했다.

23 그것은 심지어 전함을 만드는 데 사용될 수도 있다.

24 이 새로운 소재는 이미 스노보드와 자전거를 만드는 데 사용되었다.

25 토마토, 가장 무서운 채소

26 우리는 모두 토마토가 건강에 좋다는 것을 안다.

27 그러나, 1800년대까지 대부분의 미국인들은 토마토에 독성이 있다고 생각했다.

28 1820년에, Robert Johnson이라는 이름의 남자가 토마토가 먹기에 안전하다는 것을 증명하기를 원했다.

29 그래서, 그는 그를 지켜보는 많은 사람들 앞에서 한 바구니의 토마토를 먹었다.

30 그들은 모두 그가 죽을 것이라고 예상했으나 그에게는 아무 일도 일어나지 않았다.

31 그 이후로, 미국인들은 토마토를 먹는 것을 즐겼다.

32 우리는 더 이상 토마토를 두려워하지 않지만, 몇몇 곤충들은 여전히 그것을 무서워한다.

33 만약 곤충들이 방에 들어오지 않게 하고 싶다면, 으깬 토마토 한 그릇을 방구석에 놓아 두어라.

34 곤충들은 토마토 가까이 오지 않을 것이다.

※ 다음 우리말과 일치하도록 빈칸에 알맞은 것을 골라 쓰시오.

1 _____ Stories about _____

2 **Popeye and the Great** _____

3 Popeye is a _____ _____ _____ .

4 He gets his super power _____ _____ _____ .

5 When Popeye _____ _____ in the 1930s in the United States, _____ _____ _____ children began to eat spinach.

6 Crystal City in Texas, _____ is called _____ _____ _____ of the world, even built _____ _____ of Popeye.

7 _____ _____ spinach will not give us super powers, spinach _____ _____ a lot of _____ .

8 It is actually considered _____ _____ _____ _____ _____ _____ on the planet.

9 Spinach can be used _____ _____ _____ _____ .

10 _____ it _____ water, spinach _____ _____ many other things _____ the soil.

11 Some scientists have used this characteristic of spinach _____ _____ bombs _____ _____ _____ _____ .

12 They make special spinach plants _____ _____ _____ _____ _____ .

13 When these plants _____ _____ _____ from bombs, the sensors _____ _____ .

14 **Carrots in** _____ _____ _____ _____

15 In 1940, the Royal Air Force _____ German fighters _____ World War II _____ _____ a radar system.

16 The British government wanted to _____ this technology a _____ , so it _____ _____ _____ in the newspaper.

17 It said that British pilots _____ _____ _____ _____ _____ they ate a lot of carrots.

1 식물에 대한 숨겨진 이야기
2 Popeye와 위대한 시금치
3 Popeye는 세계적으로 유명한 만화 캐릭터다.
4 그는 시금치를 먹음으로써 초인적인 힘을 얻는다.
5 Popeye가 1930년대 미국에서 인기를 얻었을 때, 많은 어린이들이 시금치를 먹기 시작했다.
6 텍사스의 크리스털 시티는 세계의 시금치 수도라고 불리는데, 이곳에서는 Popeye의 동상을 세우기까지 했다.
7 비록 시금치를 먹는 것이 우리에게 초인적인 힘을 주지는 않지만, 시금치는 정말로 많은 영양분을 가지고 있다.
8 이것은 실제로 지구상에서 가장 건강한 식품 10개 중 하나로 여겨진다.
9 시금치는 놀라운 용도로 사용될 수 있다.
10 그것이 물을 흡수할 때, 시금치는 흙으로부터 다른 많은 것들도 흡수한다.
11 몇몇 과학자들은 시금치의 이 특성을 땅에 숨겨진 폭탄을 찾는 데 사용했다.
12 그들은 잎에 감지기가 있는 특별한 시금치를 만든다.
13 이 식물들이 폭탄의 흔적을 흡수하면, 감지기가 빛난다.
14 제2차 세계대전에서의 당근
15 1940년, 영국 공군은 제2차 세계 대전에서 레이더 시스템을 사용해 독일군을 패배시켰다.
16 영국 정부는 이 기술을 비밀로 하기를 원했기 때문에, 신문에 기사를 하나 냈다.
17 그것은 영국 비행사들이 당근을 많이 먹어 야간 시력이 좋아졌다는 내용이었다.

18 Everybody believed the story and began to eat _____ _____ more carrots _____ _____.

19 Can we really _____ night vision _____ _____ lots of carrots?

20 Not really, but carrots contain a lot of vitamin A, _____ _____ _____ our eyes _____.

21 In the future, carrots _____ _____ _____ _____ in wars.

22 Scottish researchers have discovered a way to _____ carrots _____ a very strong and _____ _____.

23 It _____ _____ _____ _____ to make battleships.

24 This new material _____ _____ _____ _____ to make snowboards and bicycles.

25 **Tomatoes, the _____ Vegetables**

26 We all know that tomatoes _____ _____ _____ our health.

27 _____ _____ the 1800s, _____, most Americans thought that tomatoes were _____.

28 In 1820, a man _____ Robert Johnson wanted _____ that tomatoes were _____ _____ _____.

29 So, he ate _____ _____ _____ tomatoes _____ _____ _____ many people _____ him.

30 They all expected him to die, but nothing _____ _____ him.

31 Ever _____ then, Americans _____ _____ tomatoes.

32 We are _____ _____ afraid of tomatoes, but some insects are still _____ _____ them.

33 If you want to _____ insects _____ _____ your room, _____ a bowl of _____ tomatoes in a corner of your room.

34 Insects will not _____ _____ the tomatoes.

18 모두가 그 이야기를 믿었고 전보다 훨씬 많은 당근을 먹기 시작했다.

19 우리는 정말 당근을 많이 먹어서 야간 시력을 높일 수 있을까?

20 실제로 그렇지는 않지만, 당근은 많은 비타민 A를 함유하는데, 그것은 정말로 우리 눈을 건강하게 유지해 준다.

21 미래에는, 당근이 실제로 전쟁에 이용될지도 모른다.

22 스코틀랜드의 연구원들은 당근을 매우 강하고 가벼운 물질로 바꾸는 방법을 발견했다.

23 그것은 심지어 전함을 만드는 데 사용될 수도 있다.

24 이 새로운 소재는 이미 스노보드와 자전거를 만드는 데 사용되었다.

25 토마토, 가장 무서운 채소

26 우리는 모두 토마토가 건강에 좋다는 것을 안다.

27 그러나, 1800년대까지 대부분의 미국인들은 토마토에 독성이 있다고 생각했다.

28 1820년에, Robert Johnson이라는 이름의 남자가 토마토가 먹기에 안전하다는 것을 증명하기를 원했다.

29 그래서, 그는 그를 지켜보는 많은 사람들 앞에서 한 바구니의 토마토를 먹었다.

30 그들은 모두 그가 죽을 것이라고 예상했으나 그에게는 아무 일도 일어나지 않았다.

31 그 이후로, 미국인들은 토마토를 먹는 것을 즐겼다.

32 우리는 더 이상 토마토를 두려워하지 않지만, 몇몇 곤충들은 여전히 그것을 무서워한다.

33 만약 곤충들이 방에 들어오지 않게 하고 싶다면, 으깬 토마토 한 그릇을 방구석에 놓아 두어라.

34 곤충들은 토마토 가까이 오지 않을 것이다.

※ 다음 문장을 우리말로 쓰시오.

1   Hidden Stories about Plants

➡ _____

2   Popeye and the Great Spinach

➡ _____

3   Popeye is a world-famous cartoon character.

➡ _____

4   He gets his super power by eating spinach.

➡ _____

5   When Popeye became popular in the 1930s in the United States, a lot of children began to eat spinach.

➡ _____

6   Crystal City in Texas, which is called the spinach capital of the world, even built a statue of Popeye.

➡ _____

7   Although eating spinach will not give us super powers, spinach does have a lot of nutrients.

➡ _____

8   It is actually considered one of the ten healthiest foods on the planet.

➡ _____

9   Spinach can be used in a surprising way.

➡ _____

10   When it absorbs water, spinach also absorbs many other things from the soil.

➡ _____

11   Some scientists have used this characteristic of spinach to find bombs hidden in the ground.

➡ _____

12   They make special spinach plants with sensors on their leaves.

➡ _____

13   When these plants soak up traces from bombs, the sensors light up.

➡ _____

14   Carrots in World War II

➡ _____

15   In 1940, the Royal Air Force defeated German fighters during World War II by using a radar system.

➡ _____

16   The British government wanted to keep this technology a secret, so it published an article in the newspaper.

➡ _____

17 It said that British pilots improved their night vision because they ate a lot of carrots.

➡ _____

18 Everybody believed the story and began to eat a lot more carrots than before.

➡ _____

19 Can we really improve night vision by eating lots of carrots?

➡ _____

20 Not really, but carrots contain a lot of vitamin A, which does keep our eyes healthy.

➡ _____

21 In the future, carrots may actually be used in wars.

➡ _____

22 Scottish researchers have discovered a way to turn carrots into a very strong and light material.

➡ _____

23 It can even be used to make battleships.

➡ _____

24 This new material has already been used to make snowboards and bicycles.

➡ _____

25 Tomatoes, the Scariest Vegetables

➡ _____

26 We all know that tomatoes are good for our health.

➡ _____

27 Up until the 1800s, however, most Americans thought that tomatoes were poisonous.

➡ _____

28 In 1820, a man named Robert Johnson wanted to prove that tomatoes were safe to eat.

➡ _____

29 So, he ate a basket of tomatoes in front of many people watching him.

➡ _____

30 They all expected him to die, but nothing happened to him.

➡ _____

31 Ever since then, Americans have enjoyed eating tomatoes.

➡ _____

32 We are no longer afraid of tomatoes, but some insects are still scared of them.

➡ _____

33 If you want to keep insects away from your room, place a bowl of crushed tomatoes in a corner of your room.

➡ _____

34 Insects will not come near the tomatoes.

➡ _____

※ 다음 괄호 안의 단어들을 우리말에 맞도록 바르게 배열하시오.

1 (Stories / Hidden / Plants / about)
➡ _____

2 (and / Popeye / the / Spinach / Great)
➡ _____

3 (is / Popeye / a / cartoon / world-famous / character.)
➡ _____

4 (gets / he / his / power / super / eating / by / spinach.)
➡ _____

5 (Popeye / when / popular / became / the / in / 1930s / the / in / States, / United / lot / a / of / began / children / eat / to / spinach.)
➡ _____

6 (City / Crystal / Texas, / in / is / which / the / called / spinach / of / capital / world, / the / bulit / even / statue / a / Popeye. / of)
➡ _____
_____

7 (eating / although / will / spinach / give / not / super / us / powers, / does / spinach / have / lot / a / of / nutrients.)
➡ _____
_____

8 (is / it / considered / actually / of / one / the / healthiest / ten / on / foods / planet. / the)
➡ _____

9 (can / spinach / be / used / a / in / way. / surprising)
➡ _____

10 (it / when / water, / absorbs / also / spinach / many / absorbs / things / other / the / from / soil.)
➡ _____
_____

11 (scientists / some / used / have / characteristic / this / spinach / of / find / to / hidden / bombs / the / in / ground.)
➡ _____
_____

12 (make / they / spinach / special / with / plants / on / sensors / leaves. / their)
➡ _____

13 (these / when / soak / plants / traces / up / bombs, / from / sensors / the / up. / light)
➡ _____

14 (in / Carrots / War / World / II)
➡ _____

15 (1940, / in / Royal / the / Force / Air / German / defeated / during / fighters / War / World / by / II / using / radar / system. / a)
➡ _____

16 (British / the / wanted / government / keep / to / this / a / technology / secret, / it / so / an / published / article / the / in / newspaper.)
➡ _____

17 (said / it / British / that / improved / pilots / night / their / because / vision / ate / they / lot / a / carrots. / of)
➡ _____

1 식물에 대한 숨겨진 이야기
2 Popeye와 위대한 시금치
3 Popeye는 세계적으로 유명한 만화 캐릭터다.
4 그는 시금치를 먹음으로써 초인 적인 힘을 얻는다.
5 Popeye가 1930년대 미국에서 인기를 얻었을 때, 많은 어린이 들이 시금치를 먹기 시작했다.
6 텍사스의 크리스털 시티는 세계 의 시금치 수도라고 불리는데, 이곳에서는 Popeye의 동상을 세우기까지 했다.
7 비록 시금치를 먹는 것이 우리 에게 초인적인 힘을 주지는 않 지만, 시금치는 정말로 많은 영 양분을 가지고 있다.
8 이것은 실제로 시구상에서 가상 건강한 식품 10개 중 하나로 여 겨진다.
9 시금치는 놀라운 용도로 사용될 수 있다.
10 그것이 물을 흡수할 때, 시금치 는 흙으로부터 다른 많은 것들 도 흡수한다.
11 몇몇 과학자들은 시금치의 이 특성을 땅에 숨겨진 폭탄을 찾 는 데 사용했다.
12 그들은 잎에 감지기가 있는 특 별한 시금치를 만든다.
13 이 식물들이 폭탄의 흔적을 흡 수하면, 감지기가 빛난다.
14 제2차 세계대전에서의 당근
15 1940년, 영국 공군은 제2차 세 계 대전에서 레이더 시스템을 사용해 독일군을 패배시켰다.
16 영국 정부는 이 기술을 비밀로 하기를 원했기 때문에, 신문에 기사를 하나 냈다.
17 그것은 영국 비행사들이 당근을 많이 먹어 야간 시력이 좋아졌 다는 내용이었다.

18 (believed / everybody / story / the / and / to / began / eat / lot / a / carrots / more / before. / than)

➡ _____

19 (we / can / improve / really / vision / night / eating / by / of / carrots? / lots)

➡ _____

20 (really, / not / carrots / but / a / contain / of / lot / A, / vitamin / does / which / our / keep / healthy. / eyes)

➡ _____

21 (the / in / future, / may / carrots / be / actually / used / be / wars. / in)

➡ _____

22 (researchers / Scottish / discovered / have / way / a / turn / to / into / carrots / very / a / strong / and / material. / light)

➡ _____

23 (can / it / be / even / to / used / battleships. / make)

➡ _____

24 (new / this / has / material / been / already / to / used / make / and / snowboards / bycycles.)

➡ _____

25 (the / Tomatoes, / Vegetables / Scariest)

➡ _____

26 (all / we / that / know / are / tomatoes / good / our / for / health.)

➡ _____

27 (until / up / 1800s, / the / most / however, / thought / Americans / that / were / tomatoes / poisonous.)

➡ _____

28 (1820, / in / man / a / named / Johnson / Robert / to / wanted / that / prove / tomatoes / safe / were / eat. / to)

➡ _____

29 (he / so, / ate / of / basket / a / tomatoes / front / in / many / of / watching / people / him.)

➡ _____

30 (all / they / him / expected / die, / to / nothing / but / to / happened / him.)

➡ _____

31 (since / ever / then, / have / Americans / eating / enjoyed / tomatoes.)

➡ _____

32 (are / we / longer / no / of / afraid / tomatoes, / some / but / are / insects / still / of / scared / them.)

➡ _____

33 (you / if / to / want / insects / keep / from / away / room, / your / a / place / of / bowl / tomatoes / crushed / a / in / of / corner / room. / your)

➡ _____

34 (will / insects / come / not / the / near / tomatoes.)

➡ _____

18 모두가 그 이야기를 믿었고 전보다 훨씬 많은 당근을 먹기 시작했다.

19 우리는 정말 당근을 많이 먹어서 야간 시력을 높일 수 있을까?

20 실제로 그렇지는 않지만, 당근은 많은 비타민 A를 함유하는데, 그것은 정말로 우리 눈을 건강하게 유지해 준다.

21 미래에는, 당근이 실제로 전쟁에 이용될지도 모른다.

22 스코틀랜드의 연구원들은 당근을 매우 강하고 가벼운 물질로 바꾸는 방법을 발견했다.

23 그것은 심지어 전함을 만드는데 사용될 수도 있다.

24 이 새로운 소재는 이미 스노보드와 자전거를 만드는 데 사용되었다.

25 토마토, 가장 무서운 채소

26 우리는 모두 토마토가 건강에 좋다는 것을 안다.

27 그러나, 1800년대까지 대부분의 미국인들은 토마토에 독성이 있다고 생각했다.

28 1820년에, Robert Johnson이라는 이름의 남자가 토마토가 먹기에 안전하다는 것을 증명하기를 원했다.

29 그래서, 그는 그를 지켜보는 많은 사람들 앞에서 한 바구니의 토마토를 먹었다.

30 그들은 모두 그가 죽을 것이라고 예상했으나 그에게는 아무 일도 일어나지 않았다.

31 그 이후로, 미국인들은 토마토를 먹는 것을 즐겼다.

32 우리는 더 이상 토마토를 두려워하지 않지만, 몇몇 곤충들은 여전히 그것을 무서워한다.

33 만약 곤충들이 방에 들어오지 않게 하고 싶다면, 으깬 토마토 한 그릇을 방구석에 놓아 두어라.

34 곤충들은 토마토 가까이 오지 않을 것이다.

※ 다음 우리말을 영어로 쓰시오.

1 식물에 대한 숨겨진 이야기
➡ _____

2 Popeye와 위대한 시금치
➡ _____

3 Popeye는 세계적으로 유명한 만화 캐릭터다.
➡ _____

4 그는 시금치를 먹음으로써 초인적인 힘을 얻는다.
➡ _____

5 Popeye가 1930년대 미국에서 인기를 얻었을 때, 많은 어린이들이 시금치를 먹기 시작했다.
➡ _____

6 텍사스의 크리스털 시티는 세계의 시금치 수도라고 불리는데, 이곳에서는 Popeye의 동상을 세우기까지 했다.
➡ _____
_____

7 비록 시금치를 먹는 것이 우리에게 초인적인 힘을 주지는 않지만, 시금치는 정말로 많은 영양분을 가지고 있다.
➡ _____

8 이것은 실제로 지구상에서 가장 건강한 식품 10개 중 하나로 여겨진다.
➡ _____

9 시금치는 놀라운 용도로 사용될 수 있다.
➡ _____

10 그것이 물을 흡수할 때, 시금치는 흙으로부터 다른 많은 것들도 흡수한다.
➡ _____

11 넻넣 과학사들은 시금지의 이 특성블 땅에 숨겨진 폭탄을 찾는 데 사용했다.
➡ _____

12 그들은 잎에 감지기가 있는 특별한 시금치를 만든다.
➡ _____

13 이 식물들이 폭탄의 흔적을 흡수하면, 감지기가 빛난다.
➡ _____

14 제2차 세계대전에서의 당근
➡ _____

15 1940년, 영국 공군은 제2차 세계 대전에서 레이더 시스템을 사용해 독일군을 패배시켰다.
➡ _____

16 영국 정부는 이 기술을 비밀로 하기를 원했기 때문에, 신문에 기사를 하나 냈다.
➡ _____

17 그것은 영국 비행사들이 당근을 많이 먹어 야간 시력이 좋아졌다는 내용이었다.

➡ _____

18 모두가 그 이야기를 믿었고 전보다 훨씬 많은 당근을 먹기 시작했다.

➡ _____

19 우리는 정말 당근을 많이 먹어서 야간 시력을 높일 수 있을까?

➡ _____

20 실제로 그렇지는 않지만, 당근은 많은 비타민 A를 함유하는데, 그것은 정말로 우리 눈을
건강하게 유지해 준다.

➡ _____

21 미래에는, 당근이 실제로 전쟁에 이용될지도 모른다.

➡ _____

22 스코틀랜드의 연구원들은 당근을 매우 강하고 가벼운 물질로 바꾸는 방법을 발견했다.

➡ _____

23 그것은 심지어 전함을 만드는 데 사용될 수도 있다.

➡ _____

24 이 새로운 소재는 이미 스노보드와 자전거를 만드는 데 사용되었다.

➡ _____

25 토마토, 가장 무서운 채소

➡ _____

26 우리는 모두 토마토가 건강에 좋다는 것을 안다.

➡ _____

27 그러나, 1800년대까지 대부분의 미국인들은 토마토에 독성이 있다고 생각했다.

➡ _____

28 1820년에, Robert Johnson이라는 이름의 남자가 토마토가 먹기에 안전하다는 것을 증명하기를 원했다.

➡ _____

29 그래서, 그는 그를 지켜보는 많은 사람들 앞에서 한 바구니의 토마토를 먹었다.

➡ _____

30 그들은 모두 그가 죽을 것이라고 예상했으나 그에게는 아무 일도 일어나지 않았다.

➡ _____

31 그 이후로, 미국인들은 토마토를 먹는 것을 즐겼다.

➡ _____

32 우리는 더 이상 토마토를 두려워하지 않지만, 몇몇 곤충들은 여전히 그것을 무서워한다.

➡ _____

33 만약 곤충들이 방에 들어오지 않게 하고 싶다면, 으깬 토마토 한 그릇을 방구석에 놓아 두어라.

➡ _____

34 곤충들은 토마토 가까이 오지 않을 것이다.

➡ _____

※ 다음 우리말과 일치하도록 빈칸에 알맞은 말을 쓰시오.

Inventions from Plants

1. The Sunflower Battery is a _____ _____ _____ _____ energy.

2. It is a _____ _____ _____ the idea _____ _____ the _____ _____ _____.

3. _____ sunflowers, it _____ the sun _____ _____ _____, so it produces _____ _____ _____ _____ _____.

1. 해바라기 배터리는 에너지를 만드는 좋은 방법입니다.
2. 그것은 해바라기의 특징을 이용한다는 생각에서 만들어진 배터리입니다.
3. 해바라기처럼, 그것은 낮 동안에 태양을 향해서, 다른 배터리보다 더 많은 전기를 만들어 냅니다.

After You Read A Read and Match

1. 1. _____
2. • the _____ of Popeye's _____ _____
3. • _____ _____ _____ _____ _____ _____ on the planet
4. • used _____ sensors _____ _____ _____ _____ _____ in the ground
5. 2. _____
6. • used _____ _____ _____ and bicycles
7. • made _____ a very strong and _____ _____
8. • containing a lot of vitamin A, _____ _____ _____ _____ _____
9. 3. _____
10. • good for _____ _____ _____ _____
11. • considered _____ _____ the 1800s

1. 1. 시금치
2. • Popeye의 초인적인 힘의 비밀
3. • 지구상에서 가장 건강한 식품 10개 중 하나
4. • 땅에 숨겨진 폭탄을 찾기 위해 감지기와 함께 사용된다.
5. 2. 당근
6. • 스노보드와 자전거를 만드는 데에 사용된다.
7. • 매우 강하고 가벼운 물질이 된다.
8. • 많은 비타민 A를 함유하는데, 그것은 정말로 우리 눈을 건강하게 유지해 준다.
9. 3. 토마토
10. • 곤충들이 가까이 오지 못하게 하는데 좋다.
11. • 1800년대까지 독성이 있다고 여겨졌다.

Write

1. Potatoes _____ _____ _____ your health.
2. They _____ _____ _____ _____ because they _____ _____ _____.
3. They also _____ _____ _____ _____ _____.
4. Potato juice _____ _____ honey _____ your skin _____ and _____.
5. _____ _____, they _____ you _____.
6. If you eat potatoes, you will _____ _____ _____ _____ _____ _____.
7. Potatoes _____ you _____ _____ in many ways.

1. 감자는 당신의 건강에 좋다.
2. 감자는 혈압을 낮춰주기 때문에 당신의 심장을 건강하게 지켜준다.
3. 감자는 또한 당신의 피부 문제를 해결해 준다.
4. 꿀을 넣은 감자 주스는 당신의 피부를 부드럽고 깨끗하게 만들어 준다.
5. 게다가, 감자는 당신이 살을 빼도록 도와준다.
6. 당신이 감자를 먹으면, 오랜 시간 배부른 상태를 유지할 것이다.
7. 감자는 여러 가지 면에서 당신을 건강하게 지내도록 도와준다.

※ 다음 우리말을 영어로 쓰시오.

Inventions from Plants

1. 해바라기 배터리는 에너지를 만드는 좋은 방법입니다.
➡ _____

2. 그것은 해바라기의 특징을 이용한다는 생각에서 만들어진 배터리입니다.
➡ _____

3. 해바라기처럼, 그것은 낮 동안에 태양을 향해서, 다른 배터리보다 더 많은 전기를 만들어 냅니다.
➡ _____

After You Read A Read and Match

1. 1. 시금치
➡ _____

2. • Popeye의 초인적인 힘의 비밀
➡ _____

3. • 지구상에서 가장 건강한 식품 10개 중 하나
➡ _____

4. • 땅에 숨겨진 폭탄을 찾기 위해 감지기와 함께 사용된다.
➡ _____

5. 2. 당근
➡ _____

6. • 스노보드와 자전거를 만드는 데에 사용된다.
➡ _____

2. • 매우 강하고 가벼운 물질이 된다.
➡ _____

3. • 많은 비타민 A를 함유하는데, 그것은 정말로 우리 눈을 건강하게 유지해 준다.
➡ _____

4. 3. 토마토
➡ _____

5. • 곤충들이 가까이 오지 못하게 하는데 좋다.
➡ _____

6. • 1800년대까지 독성이 있다고 여겨졌다.
➡ _____

Write

1. 감자는 당신의 건강에 좋다.
➡ _____

2. 감자는 혈압을 낮춰주기 때문에 당신의 심장을 건강하게 지켜준다.
➡ _____

3. 감자는 또한 당신의 피부 문제를 해결해 준다.
➡ _____

4. 꿀을 넣은 감자 주스는 당신의 피부를 부드럽고 깨끗하게 만들어 준다.
➡ _____

5. 게다가, 감자는 당신이 살을 빼도록 도와준다.
➡ _____

6. 당신이 감자를 먹으면, 오랜 시간 배부른 상태를 유지할 것이다.
➡ _____

7. 감자는 여러 가지 면에서 당신을 건강하게 지내도록 도와준다.
➡ _____

MEMO

영어 기출 문제집

적중100

1학기

정답 및 해설

미래 | 최연희

중 3

적중100

영어 기출 문제집

적중100

1학기

정답 및 해설

미래엔 | 최연희

중 3

Young Enough to Change the World

시험대비 실력평가   p.08

01 ①   02 ④   03 ①
04 (e)ducate   05 ②   06 ④
07 (1) waste   (2) marine

01 ① 이외의 보기들은 -ion이나 -tion을 이용해 명사형으로 만든다. ② imagine: 상상하다 imagination: 상상 ③ educate: 교육하다, 가르치다 education: 교육 ④ act: 행동하다 action: 행동 ⑤ collect: 모으다, 수집하다 collection: 수집 ① succeed: 성공하다 success: 성공

02 a bit: 조금, 약간 a little: 약간 / 나는 약간 피곤하다.

03 (A) lend 사물 to 사람: …에게 ~을 빌려주다 / 은행은 우리에게 돈을 빌려주는 것을 거절했다. (B) ask for help: 도움을 청하다 / 도움을 청하는 것을 어려워하지 마세요. (C) be covered with: ~으로 덮여 있다, ~으로 뒤집어쓰다 / 책상은 서류들로 덮여 있었다.

04 educate: 가르치다, 교육하다 / 학교 또는 대학에서 아이들을 가르치다

05 ① occurred, occur: 일어나다, 발생하다 / 오후 4시 30분쯤 사고가 발생했다고 경찰이 말했다. ② donate, donate: 기부하다, 기증하다 / 콘서트 주최자는 그들이 모든 수익을 자선단체에 기부할 것이라고 말한다. ③ educated, educate: 가르치다, 교육하다 / 그는 Bristol 대학에서 교육받았다. ④ fix, fix: 고치다 / Ellis는 문제를 빠르게 발견하고 고칠 수 있다. ⑤ bring, bring: ~을 데려오다 / 나의 부모님은 항상 우리에게 친구들을 집에 데려오도록 격려하셨다.

06 decrease: 줄이다 reduce: 줄이다 / 우리는 비용을 줄이고 더 효과적인 것들에 투자를 하는 중이다.

07 (1) waste: 쓰레기 (2) marine: 해양의

서술형 시험대비   p.09

01 (1) invitation (2) endangered
02 (Al)though / (al)though / (Al)though
03 various
04 (1) Do you want me to close the window?
  (2) She decided to name her dog Mary.
  (3) The mountain is covered with snow.

(4) Many people die from drinking dirty water.
(5) I plan to do volunteer work during the vacation.
(6) The man was asked to quit smoking.
05 (1) translated (2) collecting (3) raised (4) deliver

01 (1) invite: 초대하다 invitation: 초대 (2) danger: 위험 endangered: 멸종 위기의

02 although: ~임에도 불구하고, 비록 ~이지만 / 날씨가 너무 추웠지만 아이들은 놀기 위해 나갔다. 그녀는 너무 배고팠지만 아무것도 먹지 않았다. 모두가 잘 싸웠지만 우리는 그 경기에서 졌다.

03 various: 다양한, 여러 가지의 / 이제 환경 친화적인 다양한 자동차들이 있다.

04 (1) want+목적어+to부정사: ~가 …하는 것을 원하다 (2) name+목적어+목적격보어(명사): ~를 …라고 이름 짓다 (3) be covered with: ~으로 뒤덮여 있다, ~을 뒤집어쓰다 (4) die from: ~으로 죽다 (5) do volunteer work: 자원봉사를 하다

05 (1) translate: 번역하다 / 그 책은 27개의 언어로 번역되었다. (2) collect: 모으다, 수집하다 / Tony의 취미 중 하나는 희귀한 동전을 모으는 것이다. (3) raise: 기르다 / 나는 거북 두 마리를 1년 동안 키워 왔다. (4) deliver: 전달하다, 배달하다 / 우리는 당신의 주문을 정오에서 오후 1시 사이에 배달할 것입니다.

교과서

Conversation

핵심 Check   p.10~11

1 I'm, of ordering
2 I'm thinking of buying a scarf.
3 I'm considering buying a car.
4 (B) → (C) → (A)
5 Do you want me to help you with your homework?
6 you want me to wake you up

교과서 대화문 익히기

Listen & Speak 1 A

1. doing this / thinking of, volunteer / What / read, to / sounds, join

2. are you, to read / thinking, young / have / lend / bring

Listen & Speak 1 B

1. What's / thinking

2. What's, plan / thinking of

3. What's, plan for / thinking of taking

Listen & Speak 2 A

1. a, there, to / want me to / few

2. What can I do / ask, to make / want me to help, collect / a lot

Listen & Speak 2 B

1. broke / want me to

2. bring / share, umbrella with

3. This, too / want me to help, carry

4. arm / want me to take

Communicate A

you don't, any longer / I'm thinking of sending, told me that, to / aren't / about translating, into / Translating / Do you want me to help you / run into, expressions / that we, help

Communicate B

thinking of learning / Are you thinking, to dance / I'm thinking, learning / want me to

Progress Check 1

What, doing / I'm thinking of / Let's

Progress Check 2

Can we, for / don't / want me to go, get

01 ④   02 ④   03 ②

01 'I'm thinking of ~.'는 '나는 ~할까 생각 중이다'라는 뜻으로 of 뒤에 동명사를 취해 의도나 계획을 나타낼 때 쓰는 표현이며, 같은 의미로 'I'm considering 동명사 ~.', 'I intend to 동사원형 ~.', 'I'm planning to 동사원형 ~.'등을 사용할 수 있다.

02 여자아이가 책을 다시 읽어야 하는지는 알 수 없다.

03 수진에게 도움을 부탁하는 말을 하고, (B) 수진은 좋다고 대답하며 무엇을 도와줘야 하는지 물어보고, (C) 자전거를 주차해 놓을 장소를 만들자고 학교에 요청할 예정이라고 대답한다. (A) 주차 공간을 요청할 목적으로 서명을 받는 것을 도와주기를 원하는지 질문하자, (D) 그러는 것이 도움이 되겠다고 하면서, 감사를 표현한다.

01 ④   02 ②   03 ①, ④   04 ③

05 ⑤   06 ⑤   07 ①   08 ①

09 ②

10 I'm thinking of learning how to play baduk.

01 'Do you want me to+동사원형 ~?(당신은 내가 ~해 주기를 원하십니까?)'으로 상대방에게 도움을 제안하는 말을 하고, 제안하는 말에 대한 대답으로 'That'd be great.(그게 좋겠다.)' 라고 대답하는 것이 적절하다.

02 Do you want me to+동사원형 ~?: 당신은 내가 ~해 주기를 원하십니까? 여기서 want는 5형식으로 사용되어 목적어(me) 와 목적격보어(to cook tteokbokki)를 취하고 있다.

03 ① 여자아이가 떡볶이를 좋아한다. ④ 'Give me a few minutes.'에서 떡볶이 만드는 데 시간이 많이 걸리지 않는다는 것을 알 수 있다.

04 현장학습에 무엇을 가져갈지 묻는 질문에 현장학습이 기다려진다는 대답은 어색하다.

05 식탁 차리는 것을 도와주기를 원하느냐고 묻는 말에 긍정의 대답을 하고 자신이 한다고 말하는 것은 어색하다.

06 아침식사로 팬케이크를 먹을 수 있는지 질문하자, (C) 물론이라고 대답하며 달걀이 없다고 말한다. (D) 가게에 가서 달걀을 사오는 것을 원하는지 도움을 제안하는 질문을 하자 (B) 고맙다고 대답하며 블루베리 시럽도 사오라고 부탁하자 (A) 알았다고 대답한다.

07 우산을 안 가져왔다는 말에 같이 우산을 쓰는 것을 원하는지 묻는 것이 어울린다.

08 'I'm thinking of ~.'는 '나는 ~할까 생각 중이다'라는 뜻으로 의향을 말할 때 사용한다. ① 'I'd like to+동사원형'을 이용해 바람이나 소원을 말하는 표현이다. ⑤ 'I'm concerned about[for] ~.'는 '~에 대해 걱정하다.'의 의미로 걱정이나 두려움을 말할 때 사용하는 표현이다.

09 ① 보육원 ② 여자아이는 흥미롭다고 생각했지만 남자아이의 생각은 언급되어 있지 않았다. ③ 네 ④ 보육원에 가서 아이들에게 책을 읽어줄 것이다. ⑤ 아이들에게 책을 읽어줄 것이다.

10 I'm thinking of ~: 나는 ~할까 생각 중이다 how to 동사원형: ~하는 방법

01 to make

02 Do you want me to help you (to) collect signatures from students?

03 into

04 do you have any children's books you don't read any longer?

05 I'm thinking of sending some books to children in
Africa.

06 Do you want me to cook tteokbokki for you?

01 ask+목적어+to 동사원형: …가 ~할 것을 요청하다

02 'Do you want me to 동사원형 ~?'은 '당신은 내가 ~해 주기
를 원하십니까?'라는 뜻으로 상대방에게 도움이 필요한지 묻는
표현이다. collect: 모으다, 수집하다 signature: 서명

03 translate ~ into 언어: …를 ~로 번역하다 run into: (곤경,
어려움 등을) 만나다[겪다]

04 not ~ any longer: 더 이상 ~ 않다 books와 you 사이에 목적
격 관계대명사가 that[which]이 생략되어 있다.

05 I'm thinking of ~: 나는 ~할까 생각 중이다 send A to B: A를
B에게 보내다

06 'Do you want me to+동사원형 ~?'은 '당신은 내가 ~해 주기
를 원하십니까?'라는 뜻으로 상대방에게 도움이 필요한지 묻는
표현이다.

교과서
Grammar

핵심 Check
p.22~23

1 (1) What are made in the shop are cookies.
(2) Sandra told me what she knew.
2 (1) Despite (2) although

시험대비 기본평가
p.24

01 (1) which → what (2) despite → though[although]
(3) did → didn't (4) what → that
02 ③   03 ④   04 what

01 (1) 전치사 by의 목적어와 held의 목적어 두 개의 명사가 필요
한 자리에 관계대명사 what을 쓴다. (2) 전치사 despite는 뒤
에 명사 또는 명사구가 오는 반면에, 접속사는 '주어+동사'가 온
다. 어색한 한 단어만 찾아 고치는 문제이므로, she had hit이
라는 문장을 고려하여, despite를 though[although]로 바꾸
는 것이 적절하다. (3) Even though가 이끄는 종속절과 주절
의 내용은 서로 상반되어야 하므로, did를 didn't로 쓰는 것이
적절하다. (4) 선행사 all 뒤에는 관계대명사 that을 쓴다. All
을 삭제하는 것도 어법상 적절하다.

02 접속사 although가 이끄는 종속절과 주절의 내용은 상반되어야
한다. Mary가 약속을 깼음에도 Tom이 화를 내지 않았다거나,
Mary가 약속을 깼기 때문에 Tom이 화났다가 자연스럽다.

03 전치사가 필요한 자리이므로, ①, ②, ⑤는 부적절하며, ③의
전치사 within은 기간 또는 범위 등이 '~ 이내'라는 뜻이므로 문
맥상 맞지 않다. 의미와 어법상 전치사 despite가 적절하다.

04 선행사인 the things와 관계대명사 that을 한 단어로 바꾸려면,
선행사를 포함하는 관계대명사 what을 쓰는 것이 적절하다.

시험대비 실력평가
p.25~27

01 ④   02 ③   03 ⓐ, ⓑ, ⓒ, ⓔ, ⓖ
04 ④   05 that → what
06 Even though   07 ④   08 ④
09 ③   10 ⑤   11 ③   12 ④, ⑤
13 ③   14 ①   15 ⑤   16 네 번째
17 ④   18 ④   19 ⑤
20 what, was   21 ⑤

01 두 문장이 하나가 되었으므로, 앞 문장에서의 보어와 뒤 문장에
서의 buy의 목적어로 명사 두 개가 필요한데, 이 조건을 충족시
키는 것은 관계대명사 what이다.

02 커피는 마시지만 볶은 커피콩의 향은 좋아하지 않는다는 상반되
는 내용을 이끄는 접속사들 중 하나와, 선행사와 관계대명사를
포함하여 명사절을 이끄는 what이 적절하다.

03 ⓐ which → what ⓑ what → which[that] ⓒ The thing
→ The thing that[which] 또는 What ⓔ that → what ⓖ
That → What

04 '비록 Jessy가 읽기 장애가 있지만, 많은 언어를 알고 있다.'라
는 문장들이다. ④의 so를 but으로 고치면 다른 문장들과 같은
의미가 된다.

05 what was worse는 '설상가상으로'라는 뜻이다.

06 두 개의 빈칸에 맞는 '양보' 접속사가 적절하다.

07 빈칸 뒤의 '주어+동사' 구조로 보아 접속사가 필요한 자리이므
로 ①, ②는 부적절하다. ③의 등위접속사 for와 ⑤ 접속사로
서의 since는 이유 또는 원인을 나타내는데 문맥상 적절하지 않
다. '양보' 의미의 though를 써야 한다.

08 관계대명사 what과 의문대명사 what의 문장 구조는 동일할 때
가 있다. 구분의 기준은 해석으로서 관계대명사는 '~하는 것'으
로, 의문대명사는 '무엇(이을) ~하는지'로 한다. ④ 그녀는 나
에게 내가 무엇을 할 것인지 물어보았다.

09 접속사 although가 이끄는 '양보'의 부사절은 주절의 내용과 상
반된다. 피곤한 것과 전날 밤을 샌 것은 상반되는 내용이 아니
다.

10 돈을 많이 가진 것과, 비싼 물건을 사는 것은 상반되는 내용이
아니다.

11 '숙제가 끝나지 않았는데도 불구하고'라는 양보절 뒤에, '나는 바
로 숙제를 해야 한다'는 호응 관계가 어색하다.

12 ④ what → which[that] ⑤ Which → What

13 '양보' 접속사 although와, 주절과 종속절이 상반되는 문장을 찾는다. ① In spite that과 ⑤ despite of는 부적절한 표현이다. ② Even though 또는 but 중 하나 삭제

14 ① 정답을 평서문으로 바꿔 쓰면 what이 옳게 쓰였다는 사실이 쉽게 이해된다. This cat is what she is looking for. ② a new car와 his daughter의 자리를 바꿔야 한다. ③ what → that ④ what → which[that] ⑤ said him → said to him(또는 told him)

15 접속사 뒤에는 '주어+동사'를, 전치사 뒤에는 명사를 쓰는 것이 기본이다. ①, ③, ④는 전치사 despite 또는 in spite of를 알맞게 써야 하고, ②는 접속사 though[although]가 적절하다.

16 Pay attention to what the boss is saying.

17 관계대명사 what과 의문대명사 what을 구분하는 문제이다. 명백하게 '무엇이(을) ~하는지'로 해석되면 의문사이다. ④ 나는 그녀가 내게 무엇을 줄 것인지 궁금했다.

18 선행사를 포함하는 관계대명사 what은 선행사 the game 뒤에 쓸 수 없다. which[that]로 고치는 것이 적절하다.

19 ① In spite → Though ② Although → Despite ③ get → got ④ though worked → though he worked

20 과거의 그: what he was, 과거의 재산: what he had 현재의 그: what he is, 현재의 재산: what he has

21 ① what → which[that] ② which → why[that] ③ which → that[in which], 또는 which 생략 ④ what → where

서술형 시험대비 p.28~29

01 (1) fall asleep, books, read
   (2) it is, playing soccer
   (3) their colors, love each other

02 (1) I don't believe what Eva said to me.
   (2) Show me what you put in your pocket.
   (3) Despite her fear of his attitude, she looked him right in the eye.
   (4) That Josh asked me to help her was not natural.

03 (1) What Sam bought were mystery books.
   (2) Harold couldn't believe what the reporters referred to.
   (3) What was discussed was surprising.

04 Although Jackie was not hungry, she ate what the cook had made for her.

05 (1) Mongol maintains an old tradition although it is a small country.
   (2) Kelly was so easygoing although she was late for the wedding.

   (3) Walter caused a serious car accident although he was a careful driver.
   (4) Michael regularly buys many books although he doesn't read them at all.

06 (1) What Mary found in the cave surprised the villagers.
   (2) Despite the policy of the museum, the kids were not quiet.
   (3) What Candy bought at the market were all inexpensive.

07 (1) Sue finally accepted what Tom gave.
   (2) Despite his wealth, he was lonely.
   (3) That is far different from what Sunny has been waiting for.
   (4) That I met her yesterday is true.
   (5) What people believed in the past is called superstition.

08 Although Audrey Hepburn passed away 25 years ago, her beautiful spirit will remain with us

02 (1) believe의 목적어와 said의 목적어 두 개 역할의 what이 적절하다. (2) 나에게 '당신이 주머니에 넣은 것'을 보여 달라는 문장이므로 접속사 that을 관계대명사 what으로 바꾼다. (3) Though는 접속사이므로 명사구가 올 수 없다. 어법상 또는 내용상 despite나 in spite of가 적절하다. (4) What 뒤에는 불완전한 문장 구조가 와야 한다. 주어 역할을 하는 명사절을 이끄는 접속사 That이 적절하다.

03 관계대명사 what은 문맥에 따라 단/복수 취급에 유의해야 한다. (1) Sam이 산 것들은 미스터리 책들이었다. (2) Harold는 기자들이 언급한 것을 믿을 수 없었다. (3) 논의된 것은 놀라웠다.

04 '양보'의 접속사 although와 관계대명사 what을 적절히 활용한다.

05 although를 후반부에 배치하여, 상반되는 두 문장을 하나로 묶는 문제이다. 대명사에 유의하여 영작한다. easygoing: 태평한, 느긋한

06 (1) 관계대명사 what을 활용한다. (2) 전치사 despite를 활용한다. (3) be동사를 were로 사용하는 것에 주의한다. what은 문맥에 따라 복수 취급이 가능하다.

07 (1) 'Tom이 준 것'이므로 what이 적절하다. (2) 한 단어만 틀렸으므로, 접속사 though를 전치사 despite로 바꿔야 한다. (3) 'Sunny가 기다려왔던 것'이므로 what이 적절하다. (4) What 뒤에 완전한 절이 올 수 없다. 내용상 '내가 어제 그녀를 만난 것'이라는 명사절로서 접속사 That이 적절하다. (5) '사람들이 과거에 믿었던 것'이므로 What이 적절하다.

08 forever가 마지막에 오려면, 접속사 although가 문두에 와야 한다. 내용에 알맞게 주어진 단어들을 배열하도록 한다.

5

1 T   2 F   3 T   4 F   5 T   6 F

1 T   2 F   3 T   4 F   5 T   6 F

교과서 확인학습 A   p.32~33

01 in Action   02 a better place

03 in saving animals

04 Although, have actually made a difference

05 How, able to   06 hear from

07 each adopted   08 raise, at home

09 donated to a charity

10 might not be able to see cheetahs

11 became interested in, endangered animals

12 created a non-profit organization

13 the next generation   14 educated our friends

15 a terrible oil spill

16 were completely covered with oil

17 had to do

18 animal rescue supplies, in our neighborhood

19 what we collected, to save the animals

20 something very useful   21 threw up

22 get, out of   23 could be used

24 marine life specialist

25 more dangerous, than   26 die from eating

27 created an educational project

28 In addition to

29 making a big difference

30 What, take that first step

교과서 확인학습 B   p.34~35

1 Teens in Action

2 Many young people are making the world a better place.

3 For example, Carter and Olivia Ries have become leaders in saving animals.

4 Although they are only teenagers, they have actually made a difference in the world.

5 How were they able to do that?

6 Let's hear from Carter.

7 When I was five, my little sister Olivia and I each adopted a cheetah.

8 Did we raise cheetahs at home?

9 No, we donated to a charity that protects wild cheetahs in South Africa.

10 Our parents told us that if we did not protect them, we might not be able to see cheetahs in the near future.

11 We soon became interested in helping other endangered animals..

12 A few years later, with help from our parents, we created a non-profit organization to protect them.

13 We wanted the next generation to be able to see these animals, so we named our organization One More Generation.

14 We also studied endangered animals and educated our friends about them.

15 Then one day, a terrible oil spill occurred in the Gulf of Mexico.

16 A lot of sea animals were completely covered with oil, and they were dying.

17 We had to do something.

18 We started collecting animal rescue supplies such as pet carrying cages and rubber gloves from everyone in our neighborhood.

19 Four months later, our family drove to the Gulf of Mexico to deliver what we collected and helped to save the animals.

20 While we were working there, we learned something very useful.

21 When we put mayonnaise into a turtle's throat, the turtle threw up.

22 That way, we were able to get oil out of turtles.

23 I never knew mayonnaise could be used to save animals!

24 On our last day, we met a marine life specialist.

25 She told us that plastic waste is more dangerous to sea animals than oil spills are.

26 A lot of sea animals and sea birds die from eating plastic waste.

27 After we came home, we created an educational project about how to reduce plastic waste.

28 In addition to this, our organization continues to do various projects to save animals.

29 Although we started small, we are making a big difference.

30 What you do today can change the world, so take that first step!

01 ④	02 ①, ③	03 possible	04 ③
05 ①	06 ①	07 ①, ④ / ②, ③, ⑤	
08 ③	09 ②	10 ①, ④	

11 A lot of sea animals and sea birds die from eating plastic waste.

12 Since → Although(Though)		13 ③
14 difference	15 ⑤	16 ③	17 ⑤
18 adopted	19 ③	20 ④	21 ④
22 vomited		23 ④

01 많은 젊은 사람들이 세상을 더 좋은 곳으로 만들고 있는 예로 Carter와 Olivia Ries를 들고 있으므로, For example이 적절하다. ① 그 결과, ② 게다가, 더욱이, ⑤ 게다가, 더욱이 ④ 예를 들면

02 ⓑ와 ①, ③: actually = in fact = really = in reality = in effect = in practice: 실제로, ② 특히, ④ 극도로, 극히, ⑤ 아마

03 사람+can(=be able to)+동사원형 = It is possible for 사람 to부정사

04 ⓐ donate to: (특히 자선단체에) 기부[기증]하다, ⓑ become interested in: ~에 관심을 갖게 되다

05 ①번은 'wild cheetahs'를 가리키고 나머지는 다 '멸종 위기의 동물들'을 가리킨다.

06 Carter와 Olivia는 야생 치타를 보호하는 자선단체에 치타를 기부했다.

07 ⓐ와 ①, ④: 명사적 용법, ⓑ와 ②, ③, ⑤: 부사적 용법

08 위 글은 '멕시코만에서 발생한 끔찍한 석유 유출 사건으로 죽어가고 있는 많은 해양 동물들을 구조하기 위해 벌인 활동'에 관한 글이므로, 주제로는 ③번 '석유 유출 사건으로 죽어가고 있는 동물들을 구조하기 위한 활동'이 적절하다.

09 전반부의 'A lot of sea animals were completely covered with oil, and they were dying. We had to do something.'을 통해 'sympathetic'을, 하반부의 'I never knew mayonnaise could be used to save animals!'를 통해 'surprised'를 찾을 수 있다. ① delighted: 아주 기뻐[즐거워]하는, puzzled: 어리둥절해하는, ② sympathetic: 동정적인, 동정어린, ③ depressed: 우울한, nervous: 초조한, ④ regretful: 유감스러워[애석해] 하는, confused: 혼란스러워하는, ⑤ relieved: 안도하는, 다행으로 여기는, astonished: 깜짝[크게] 놀란

10 앞에 나오는 내용에 추가하는 내용이 뒤에 이어지므로 Besides(게다가, 뿐만 아니라) 혹은 In addition to(~에 더하여, ~일 뿐 아니라)가 가장 적절하다. ②~와 대조를 이루어, ③ ~ 대신에, ⑤ ~의 결과로

11 die from: ~으로 죽다

12 '비록' 우리는 작은 것부터 시작했지만, 큰 변화를 만들어 내고 있는 중이라고 해야 하므로, Since를 Although[Though]로 고치는 것이 적절하다.

13 ⓐ와 ③, ④: 동명사, ①, ②, ⑤: 현재분사

14 do that은 앞 문장의 make a difference in the world를 받는다.

15 본문 끝부분에서 '십 대일 뿐이지만, 실제로 세상에 변화를 일으켜 온 사람들이 어떻게 그것을 할 수 있었을까?'라면서 'Carter의 이야기를 들어보자.'라고 했으므로, 다음에 올 내용으로는 '세상에 변화를 일으켜 온 Carter의 이야기'가 적절하다.

16 ⓐ와 ③: 쓰레기, ① 낭비[허비](되는 상황), ② (기회 등을) 놓치다(동사), ④ 이용[활용]되고 있지 않은(형용사), waste talents: 빛을 못 보고 있는 재능, ⑤ (돈·시간·재능 등을) 낭비하다

17 '비록 우리는 작은 것부터 시작했지만, 큰 변화를 만들어 내고 있는 중이다. 당신이 오늘 하는 일이 세상을 바꿀 수 있기에, 첫 발을 내디뎌라!'라는 글의 마지막 내용으로 보아, 어울리는 속담으로는 ⑤번 '시작이 반이다.'가 적절하다. ① 잘 생각해 보고 행동하라[돌다리도 두드려 보고 건너라]. ② 안 좋은 일은 겹쳐서 일어나기 마련이다[불운은 한꺼번에 닥친다]. ③ 급할수록 돌아가라. ④ 손 안에 든 새 한 마리는 풀숲에 있는 두 마리 새의 가치가 있다.

18 adopt: 입양하다, 자신의 가족으로 받아들이다

19 ③번 다음 문장의 our organization에 주목한다. 주어진 문장의 a non-profit organization을 받고 있으므로 ③번이 적절하다.

20 위 글은 'Carter와 Olivia가 치타를 입양한 후에 다른 멸종 위기의 동물들을 도와주는 것에도 관심을 갖게 되어 One More Generation을 만들게 되는 과정'에 관한 글이므로, 제목으로는 ④번 'One More Generation의 탄생 배경'이 적절하다.

21 선행사를 포함하는 관계대명사 what을 쓰는 것이 적절하다.

22 throw up = vomit: 토하다.

23 Carter의 가족은 멕시코만으로 비행기를 타고 간 것이 아니라 '운전해 갔다.'

01 endangered

02 with help from our parents, we created a non-profit organization to protect them 또는 we created a non-profit organization to protect them with help from our parents

03 They donated to a charity that protects wild cheetahs in South Africa.

04 was occurred → occurred

05 the things which[that]

06 (A) threw up　(B) mayonnaise

07 a cheetah → two cheetahs, it → them

08 Their parents　　　　　09 As

10 dangerous to sea animals

11 우리가 플라스틱 쓰레기를 줄일 수 있는 방법에 관한 교육 프로젝트를 만든 것.

12 reduce plastic waste

01 '가까운 미래에 치타를 볼 수 없을지도 모른다.'는 것은 치타가 '멸종 위기의' 동물이라는 뜻이다.

02 with help from ~: ~의 도움으로

03 그들은 남아프리카 공화국에 있는 야생 치타를 보호하는 자선단체에 기부했다.

04 occur는 수동태로 쓸 수 없는 동사이다.

05 관계대명사 what을 '선행사+관계대명사'로 바꿔 쓸 수 있다. 가족이 전달한 것들은 동네의 모든 사람으로부터 모은 동물 구조 물품들이기 때문에 복수 형태인 the things로 쓰는 것이 적절하다.

06 '마요네즈'를 거북이의 목구멍에 집어넣으면, 거북이가 '토한다'는 것을 배웠다..

07 Carter and Olivia가 각자 치타를 입양한 것이기 때문에, 치타 두 마리를 입양하여 자선단체에 기부한 것이다.

08 '그들의 부모님'이 도와주셨다.

09 so 대신 맨 앞에 이유를 나타내는 접속사 As[Because 등]를 쓰는 것이 적절하다.

10 석유 유출이 '해양 동물에게 위험한' 것보다 플라스틱 쓰레기가 해양 동물에게 더 위험하다.

11 In addition to having created an educational project about how to reduce plastic waste로 고칠 수 있다. in addition to ~ing: ~에 더하여, ~일 뿐 아니라

12 Carter의 가족은 석유 유출보다 플라스틱 쓰레기가 해양 동물에게 더 위험하다는 것을 알게 되어서, '플라스틱 쓰레기를 줄일 수 있는' 방법에 관한 교육 프로젝트를 만들었다.

영역별 핵심문제　　　　　　p.43~47

01 ③　　　　02 ②　　　　03 protection

04 made / made　　　05 ⑤　　　06 ⑤

07 ①　　　08 to fix　　　09 ③　　　10 ②

11 translate　　12 Do you want me to help you?

13 ②　　　　　　　　14 ①

15 (1) Even though　(2) what　　　16 ③

17 (1) This is not what Hermione has always wanted.

　(2) The neighbors know what happened two
　　　months ago.

18 (1) Though[Although] Helen's family was poor

　(2) Though[Although] figure skating was an

unpopular sport

19 It was so hot that I sweated a lot even though I fanned myself.

20 ②, ⑤ / ①, ③, ④　　　21 ⑤　　　22 ⑤

23 ③　　　　24 ①

25 ⓐ marine　ⓑ making a big difference

26 What you do today can change the world

27 ③　　　28 How[What] about　　29 ④

01 repair: 수리하다, 수선하다 fix: 고치다 / 너는 그들이 그 손상된 것을 수선할 수 있다고 생각하니?

02 ① in addition to: ~ 이외에, ~에 더하여 / 할인에 더하여 그들은 무료 선물을 제공한다. ② share A with B: A를 B와 나누다, 공유하다 / 나는 침실을 동생과 같이 쓴다. ③ read A to B: A를 B에게 읽어 주다 / 그가 우리에게 그 편지를 소리 내어 읽어 주었다. ④ send A to B: A를 B에게 보내다 / 그걸 제게 팩스로 보내 줄 수 있으세요? ⑤ lend 사물 to 사람: ~에게 ~을 빌려주다 / 내일까지 나에게 돈을 좀 빌려줄 수 있겠니?

03 주어진 단어는 동사와 명사의 관계이다. marry: 결혼하다 marriage: 결혼 protect: 보호하다 protection: 보호

04 make a difference: 차이를 낳다, 변화를 가져오다 / 저는 운동이 제 삶에 어떤 차이점을 만들어 줬는지 이루 말할 수가 없습니다. make a discovery: 발견하다 / 그들은 화성에서 물의 흔적을 찾는 엄청난 발견을 했다.

05 주어진 문장은 'Can I join you?(나도 함께 할 수 있어?)'의 질문에 긍정의 대답을 한 후 만나는 장소와 시간을 정하는 것이 어울리므로 ⑤가 적절하다.

06 현재진행형의 형태이지만 this weekend라는 미래를 나타내는 어구와 함께 쓰여 가까운 미래를 나타내 이번 주에 무엇을 할 예정인지 묻고 있으므로 ⑤가 적절하다.

07 break down: 고장나다

08 want+목적어+to부정사: ~가 …하는 것을 원하다 'Do you want me to+동사원형 ~?'은 '당신은 내가 ~하기를 원하십니까?'라는 뜻으로 상대방에게 도움이 필요한지 묻는 표현이다.

09 어려운 표현들이 나온다는 말과 영어 선생님께 도움을 요청하자는 말을 연결할 때 조건의 접속사 If를 사용해서 '만약 어려운 표현들이 나오면, 영어 선생님께 도움을 요청하자.'라고 두 문장을 연결하는 것이 적절하다.

10 to read는 명사 books를 꾸며주는 to부정사의 형용사적 용법으로 사용되고 있다. ②는 to부정사의 부사적 용법(~하기 위해서)으로 사용되어 있고 나머지 보기들은 형용사적 용법으로 사용되고 있다. ① 모든 학생은 올해 성취할 한 가지를 썼다. ② 가난한 사람들을 돕기 위해서 학교에서 벼룩시장을 열고 싶다. ③ 나는 밤에 입을 따뜻한 재킷이 필요하다. ④ 나는 비행기에서 읽을 책이 필요하다. ⑤ 나는 써야 할 편지가 많다.

11 translate: 번역하다 / 쓰여지거나 말해진 단어들을 다른 언어로 바꾸다

12 want+목적어+to부정사: ~가 …하는 것을 원하다 'Do you want me to+동사원형 ~?'은 '당신은 내가 ~해 주기를 원하십니까?'라는 뜻으로 상대방에게 도움이 필요한지 묻는 표현이다.

13 ⓐ In spite of → Though[Although] ⓑ Despite → Though[Although] ⓒ Though → Despite[In spite of] ⓓ even though → despite[in spite of] ⓔ Although → Despite[In spite of] ⓕ 고칠 곳 없음

14 첫 번째 문장에서는 '청와대 앞에서 찍힌 것들(사진들)'을 가리키는 말이므로 what이 적절하다. 두 번째 문장에서는 빈칸 앞뒤가 상반되는 내용이므로 접속사 though 또는 although가 적절하다.

15 (1) 책 '노인과 바다'를 3일 동안 읽어오고 있지만, 전혀 이해할 수 없다는 상반된 내용이 있으므로, '양보'의 접속사가 필요한데, 빈칸이 2개이므로 Even though가 적절하다. (2) showed와 believed의 목적어가 들어갈 자리이므로 what이 적절하다.

16 모든 문장이 '양보'의 접속사 Although로 시작하지만, 상반되는 내용을 가진 것은 ③번뿐이다. 각각 Although를 ① 접속사 Because(Since/As)로, ② 접속사 When으로, ④ 접속사 Because(Since/As)로, ⑤ 접속사 Whether로 바꿔야 한다. immunity: 면역(성), 면역질

17 관계대명사 what은 선행사를 포함하며, 문맥에 따라 단/복수 취급한다. (1) 이것은 Hermione가 항상 원해 왔던 것이 아니다. (2) 이웃들은 두 달 전에 생긴 일들을 알고 있다.

18 상반되는 내용을 접속사 but으로 연결하는 문장은 '양보' 접속사를 이용하여 바꾸면 같은 의미가 된다.

19 '날이 너무 더워서 부채질을 했는데도 땀이 너무 많이 났다'라는 내용으로, 양보의 접속사 even though를 활용한다.

20 ⓐ는 관계 대명사 ⓑ는 접속사

21 멸종 위기의 동물들을 연구했고 친구들에게 그들에 대해 가르쳐 주었다.

22 ⓐ '목구멍에' 집어넣은 것이므로 into가 적절하다. ⓑ 기름을 몸 '밖으로' 빼낸 것이므로 out of가 적절하다.

23 ③번 다음 문장의 what we collected에 주목한다. 주어진 문장의 'animal rescue supplies'를 받고 있으므로 ③번이 적절하다.

24 끔찍한 석유 유출 사건은 '글쓴이의 동네'에서 발생한 것이 아니라 '멕시코만'에서 발생했다.

25 ⓐ marine: 바다의, 해양의, ⓑ make a difference: 변화를 가져오다, 차이를 낳다, 중요하다, <영영풀이: 행동을 수행하고, 그 결과가 매우 의미심장한 변화를 이루다>

26 관계대명사 what을 보충하여 What you do today를 주어로 쓰는 것이 적절하다.

27 이 글은 '석유 유출보다 플라스틱 쓰레기가 해양 동물에게 더 위험하다는 이야기를 들은 뒤에, 비록 작은 것부터 시작했지만 동물들을 구하기 위한 다양한 프로젝트들을 계속하여 큰 변화를 만들어 내고 있는 중'이라는 내용의 글이므로, 주제로는 ③번 '동물들을 구하기 위한 다양한 프로젝트들을 행함으로써 큰 변화를 만들어 내기'가 적절하다.

28 Why don't you 동사원형 ~? = How[What] about ~ing?: ~하는 게 어때?

29 ④는 '다음 세대'를 가리키고, 나머지는 다 비영리 단체인 'One More Generation'을 가리킨다.

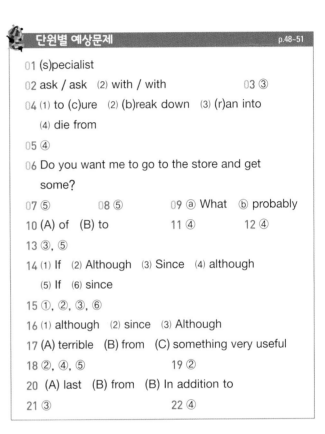

단원별 예상문제   p.48~51

01 (s)pecialist
02 ask / ask   (2) with / with   **03** ③
04 (1) to (c)ure   (2) (b)reak down   (3) (r)an into
     (4) die from
05 ④
06 Do you want me to go to the store and get
     some?
07 ⑤   **08** ⑤   **09** ⓐ What   ⓑ probably
10 (A) of   (B) to   **11** ④   **12** ④
13 ③, ⑤
14 (1) If   (2) Although   (3) Since   (4) although
     (5) If   (6) since
15 ①, ②, ③, ⑥
16 (1) although   (2) since   (3) Although
17 (A) terrible   (B) from   (C) something very useful
18 ②, ④, ⑤   **19** ②
20 (A) last   (B) from   (B) In addition to
21 ③   **22** ④

01 주어진 단어는 동의어 관계이다. occur: 일어나다, 발생하다 happen: 발생하다 expert: 전문가 specialist: 전문가

02 (1) ask for help: 도움을 청하다 / 자녀들이 숙제를 도와 달라고 요청하면 당신은 어떻게 할 건가요? ask+목적어+to 동사원형: …가 ~할 것을 요청하다 / 이 편지 타이핑을 부탁해도 괜찮겠습니까? (2) share A with B: A를 B와 나누다, 공유하다 / 여기 그들이 나와 함께 공유했던 몇 가지 조언들이 있다. be covered with: ~으로 뒤덮여 있다, ~을 뒤집어쓰다 / 그는 길을 걸어가다가 먼지를 뒤덮어 썼다.

03 (A) in addition to: ~ 이외에, ~에 더하여 / 사망자뿐 아니라, 부상자도 한 명 더 있었다. (B) although: ~임에도 불구하고, 비록 ~이지만 / 비록 그녀가 돈이 많을지라도 행복하지 않다. Despite와 In spite of는 전치사이므로 뒤에 명사나 동명사가 올 수 있다.

04 (1) be able to 동사원형: ~할 수 있다 (2) break down: 고장 나다 (3) run into: (곤경, 어려움 등을) 만나다[겪다] (4) die from: ~으로 죽다 starvation: 기아

9

05 달걀이 없는 상황에서 달걀을 사올 것을 원하는지 도움을 제안하는 말을 먼저하고 블루베리 시럽도 사올 수 있는지 묻는 것이 주어진 문장의 대답인 'Sure.(물론이지.)'와 어울리므로 ④가 적절하다.

06 'Do you want me to+동사원형 ~?'은 상대방에게 도움이 필요한지 묻는 표현이다.

07 자전거가 고장났다는 말에, 자전거를 고쳐주는 것을 원하는지에 대한 도움을 제안하는 말이 어울린다.

08 주어진 문장은 '나도 같이 해도 돼?'의 의미로 맥락상 남자아이가 보육원에서 책을 읽어 준다고 얘기하니, 이것에 대해서 여자아이가 흥미롭다며 같이 하고 싶다고 말하는 것이 자연스럽다.

09 ⓐ 이번 주에 무엇을 하는지 묻는 질문과 보육원에서 자원봉사를 할 생각이라는 대답이 어울린다. ⓑ 동사 read를 수식하므로 부사 probably가 어울린다. probably: 아마도

10 (A) 'I'm thinking of ~.'는 '나는 ~할까 생각 중이다'라는 뜻으로 of 뒤에 동명사를 취해 의도나 계획을 나타낼 때 사용한다. (B) read A to B: A를 B에게 읽어 주다

11 ⓐ to read ⓑ thinking ⓒ reading ⓓ lend ⓔ bring I'm thinking of ~: 나는 ~할까 생각 중이다 (= I'm considering 동명사 ~.) 전치사 of가 있으므로 thinking을 사용해야 한다.

12 ④번 다음 문장의 it이 주어진 문장의 the perfect book을 가리키므로 ④번이 적절하다.

13 what이 관계대명사인지 의문대명사인지 구분하는 것은 해석을 기준으로 한다. 때로, 구분이 모호한 경우도 많지만 일반적으로 의문사 what은 '무엇이[을] ~한지'로, 관계대명사 what은 '~하는 것'으로 해석한다. ① 의문대명사 ② 의문대명사 ③ 관계대명사 ④ 의문대명사 ⑤ 관계대명사 (과거에 도덕적인 것으로 여겨졌던 것이 오늘날 항상 그렇게 여겨지는 것은 아니다.)

14 <보기>의 if는 '조건', although는 '양보', since는 '이유, 원인'의 부사절을 이끈다. 각각 (1) 조건 (2) 양보 (3) 이유 (4) 양보 (5) 조건 (6) 이유의 부사절이다.

15 ① 선행사 the only person 뒤에는 which가 아니라 who 또는 that이 적절하다. ② 관계대명사 what이 이끄는 명사절이 있는데, 목적어 something valuable이 나왔다. 둘 중 하나는 삭제해야 한다. ③ 전치사 Despite 뒤에 절이 나왔다. 접속사 Though[Although]로 바꿔야 한다. ⑥ 'It ~ that 강조 구문'이다. what을 that으로 바꾸는 것이 적절하다. give ~ the cold shoulder: ~를 쌀쌀맞게 대하다

16 (1)과 (3)은 상반된 내용이므로 '양보'의 접속사 although를, (2)는 이유를 나타내는 내용이므로 접속사 since를 쓴다.

17 (A) '끔찍한' 석유 유출 사건이라고 해야 하므로 terrible이 적절하다. terrific: 아주 좋은, 멋진, 훌륭한, (B) 동네의 모든 '사람으로부터' 동물 구조 물품들을 모으기 시작했다고 해야 하므로 from이 적절하다. (C) '-thing'으로 끝나는 말은 형용사가 뒤에서 수식해야 하므로 something very useful이 적절하다.

18 ⓐ와 ②, ④, ⑤: 동명사(목적, 용도를 나타냄), pet carrying

cages: 애완동물 수송용 우리, ① 현재분사형 형용사, ③: 현재분사

19 애완동물 수송용 우리를 만든 것이 아니라, 동물 구조 물품들을 동네의 모든 사람으로부터 모으기 시작했다.

20 (A) '마지막' 날이라고 해야 하므로 last가 적절하다. latest: 최근의, (B) '플라스틱 쓰레기를 먹어서 죽는다'고 해야 하므로 from이 적절하다. die from: 상처, 부상으로 인한 사망(최근에는 die from 대신에 die of를 쓰는 일이 많음. die of: 주로 질병, 굶주림, 노령으로 인한 사망에 사용), die for: ~을 위해 죽다, ~하고 싶어 죽다[못 견디다], (C) '이것 외에도', 다양한 프로젝트들을 계속하고 있다고 해야 하므로 In addition to가 적절하다. in spite of: ~에도 불구하고

21 ③번 뒤 문장의 this에 주목한다. 주어진 문장의 내용을 받고 있으므로 ③번이 적절하다.

22 Carter의 가족은 '플라스틱 쓰레기'를 줄일 수 있는 방법에 관한 교육 프로젝트를 만들었다.

🦉 서술형 실전문제 · p.52~53

01 a little → a few

02 Do you want me to cook tteokbokki for you?

03 I'm considering doing some volunteer work at the child-care center.
I'm planning to do some volunteer work at the child-care center.
I intend to do some volunteer work at the child-care center.

04 (1) Although James made a few mistakes, he succeeded in the project.
(2) Although Mr. Park left for the station earlier than usual, he missed the train.
(3) Although Angela caught a bad cold, she exercised in the morning.
(4) Although Jinho prepared for the civil service exam for 4 years, he failed it.

05 (1) What you do is much more important than what you speak.
(2) Paula must make the most of what she has.

06 what   **07** less   **08** we should[could]

09 change the world   **10** to be

11 (A) adopted   (B) raise   (C) protects

12 (1) 몇 년 후에 부모님의 도움으로, 그들은 멸종 위기의 동물들을 보호하기 위해 비영리 단체를 만들고 One More Generation이라고 이름 붙였다
(2) 멸종 위기의 동물들을 연구했다.
(3) 친구들에게 멸종 위기의 동물들에 대해 가르쳐 주었다.

01 a little 다음에는 셀 수 없는 명사가 오므로 a few로 바꾸어야
한다. a few: 어느 정도, 조금

02 'Do you want me to+동사원형 ~?'은 '당신은 내가 ~해 주기
를 원하십니까?'라는 뜻으로 상대방에게 도움이 필요한지 묻는
표현이다. for: ~을 위해

03 'I'm thinking of ~.'는 '나는 ~할까 생각 중이다'라는 뜻으로
of 뒤에 동명사를 취해 의도나 계획을 나타낼 때 쓰는 표현이다.
'I'm thinking of ~.' 대신에 'I'm considering 동명사 ~.', 'I
intend to 동사원형 ~.', 'I'm planning to 동사원형 ~.' 등을
사용할 수 있다.

04 '양보'의 부사절 접속사 Although를 사용하여 문장을 바꾸면,
본래 문장의 but은 삭제해야 한다.

05 (1) 관계대명사 what을 활용해야 글자 수에 맞는 영작이 가능
하다. (2) make the most of: ~을 최대한 활용하다

06 the thing+that[which] = what.

07 석유 유출이 플라스틱 쓰레기보다 해양 동물에게 '덜' 위험하다

08 의문사+to부정사 = 의문사+주어+조동사 should[can]+동사
원형

09 우리가 오늘 하는 일이 '세상을 바꿀 수' 있기 때문이다.

10 'want+목적어+to부정사'로 써야 하므로 to be로 쓰는 것이 적
절하다.

11 (A) 치타를 '입양했다'고 해야 하므로 adopted가 적절하다.
adapt: (새로운 용도·상황에) 맞추다[조정하다], adopt: 입양
하다, (B) 치타를 집에서 '길렀을까?'라고 해야 하므로 raise가
적절하다. raise: 기르다, 올리다, rise: 오르다, 올라가다, (C)
야생 치타를 '보호하는' 자선단체라고 해야 하므로 protects가
적절하다. prevent: 막다[예방/방지하다]

12 두 번째 단락 'We soon became interested in helping
other endangered animals.' 다음의 내용을 쓰면 된다.

창의사고력 서술형 문제
p.54

|모범답안|

01 they are thinking of going swimming, She is
considering visiting an art museum, is planning
to read a book at home

02 We love each other although we are different. /
Although we are different, we love each other.

03 (A) plastic waste   (B) sea animals
(C) reuse and recycle   (D) bottle
(E) shopping bag

01 go swimming: 수영하러 가다 visit: 방문하다 art museum:
미술관 at home: 집에서 'I'm thinking of ~.'는 '나는 ~할
까 생각 중이다'라는 뜻으로 of 뒤에 동명사를 취해 의도나 계획
을 나타낼 때 쓰는 표현이다. 'I'm thinking of ~.' 대신에 'I'm
considering (동)명사 ~.', 'I intend to 동사원형 ~.', 'I'm
planning to 동사원형 ~.' 등을 사용할 수 있다.

단원별 모의고사
p.55~60

01 ①   02 ④   03 ①

04 (1) (e)ndangered
(2) Donate, non-profit organization
(3) (r)escue   (4) problem, (p)robably, (v)arious

05 ⑤   06 (p)lan

07 I'm thinking of watching a movie every weekend.

08 ③   09 translating

10 (A) longer   (B) that   (C) expressions

11 ①   12 ①, ③

13 (1) what Sullivan wrote in his note
(2) What Gale says

14 (1) Peter was absent from, but he got a perfect
score
(2) Although Peter was absent from, he got a
perfect score
(3) Despite his absence, Peter got a perfect score

15 (1) This is what Frank purchased from a
Japanese fisherman last Sunday.
(2) He went to work although he was very sick.
(3) Although John fixed the photocopier, it didn't
work the next day.

16 (1) Jason bought the magazine though he didn't
have to read it.
(2) This watch still works well though it is much
older than my grandfather.
(3) I don't know much about Ray though she has
been my classmate for 4 years.
(4) The strawberry had a nasty smell though it
looked fine on the surface.
(5) The paper desk didn't break though many
people climbed up on it.

17 ④

18 What made me who I am today is my mother's
love.

19 we donated to a charity that protects wild
cheetahs in South Africa

20 unless we protected them

21 다음 세대가 이러한 멸종 위기의 동물들을 볼 수 있기를
원했기 때문이다.

22 be used   23 (A) oil   (B) the Gulf of Mexico

24 be shipped   25 cars / local products

26 ⑤   27 to do

28 (A) paper   (B) forests   (C) body parts   29 ⑤

30 A lot of plastic waste goes into the ocean and
many sea animals eat it.

31 (A) to reuse   (B) to recycle   (C) bottle
(D) shopping bag

01 actually: 실제로 / 그것은 올림픽 종목이 되었지만 사실은 그렇게 새로운 것은 아닙니다. although: ~임에도 불구하고, 비록 ~이지만 / 그는 비록 어렸지만, 이 수학 문제를 풀 수 있다.

02 spill: 유출 / 기름 유출이 있었고 그 기름이 자연을 파괴했다.

03 donate: 기부하다, 기증하다 charity: 자선단체, 자선 / A: 얼마나 기부했나요? B: 나는 자선단체에 100달러를 보냈어요.

04 (1) endangered: 멸종 위기의 (2) donate: 기부하다, 기증하다 non-profit organization: 비영리 단체 (3) rescue: 구조, 구출 (4) problem: 문제 probably: 아마도 various: 다양한, 여러 가지의

05 (C) 아빠한테 배가 조금 고프다고 말하면서 먹을 것이 있는지 질문하자, (D) 떡볶이를 해주기를 원하느냐고 묻는다. (B) 좋다고 대답하며 떡볶이를 좋아한다고 말하자 (A) 알았다고 말하면서 (떡볶이를 만들) 시간을 조금 달라고 얘기한다.

06 plan: 계획 What's your plan for ~?: ~에 무엇을 할 계획이니? 바꿔 쓸 수 있는 표현으로 'What are you planning to do for ~?', 'What are you going to do for ~?'가 있다.

07 I'm thinking of ~: 나는 ~할까 생각 중이다 watch a movie: 영화를 보다

08 ⓐ too heavy ⓑ want ⓒ to help ⓓ carry ⓔ it / This box는 단수이므로 them이 아니라 it이 어울린다.

09 translate ... into ~: …를 ~로 번역하다

10 (A) any longer: 더 이상, 이제는 (B) told의 직접목적어로 that절이 적절하다. that 다음에 완전한 절이 나온다. (C) expression: 표현 experience: 경험

11 How? → Why?

12 ① Anna는 더 이상 읽지 않는 아동용 도서들을 가지고 있다. ③ 책을 모으기 위해서가 아니라 영어로 번역할 때 어려운 표현들이 나오면 선생님에게 도움을 청할 것이다.

13 (1)과 (2) 각각의 선행사와 관계대명사를 써보면, the strange letters which[that], the thing which[that]이다. 문맥상 what으로 바꾸는 데 무리가 없다.

14 (1) be absent from: 결석하다. (2), (3) 접속사와 '주어+be 동사'로 양보절을 구로 바꿀 때는 동명사 being을 활용한다. Although he was absent = Despite his being absent 최근 영문법에서는 his 대신 him을 쓰기도 한다. (3)의 종속절에 his가 있으므로, 주절에 Peter를 쓰는 것이 적절하다.

16 접속사 though를 문장 중간에 위치할 때, but을 사용했던 원문의 순서가 반대가 된다. 명사와 그 명사를 지칭하는 대명사를 바뀐 순서에 맞게 적절하게 배치한다.

17 ①, ②, ③, ⑤는 모두 what이 들어가면 된다. ④는 what은 쓸 수 없고, which 또는 that을 써야 한다.

18 기자는 '오늘밤의 수상에 대해 누구 또는 무엇에게 공로를 돌리고 싶은지'를 물었고, 수상자의 대답을 관계대명사 what을 활용하여, 단어를 적절히 배열한다.

19 주격 관계대명사 that이 선행사인 a charity를 수식하도록 배열

하는 것이 적절하다.

20 unless = if ~ not

21 Carter와 Olivia는 다음 세대가 이러한 동물들을 볼 수 있기를 원했기에, 그들의 단체를 One More Generation이라고 이름 붙였다.

22 마요네즈가 동물을 구하는 데 사용되는 것이므로 수동태로 쓰는 것이 적절하다.

23 그들은 '멕시코만'에서 발생한 끔찍한 석유 유출 사건으로 인해 완전히 '기름'을 뒤집어썼기 때문에 죽어가고 있었다.

24 멀리 '수송될' 필요가 없으므로 수동태로 쓰는 것이 적절하다.

25 (A)는 '자동차'를, (B)는 '지역 생산품들'을 가리킨다.

26 지역 생산품들은 그리 멀리 수송될 필요가 '없다.'

27 의문사+to부정사 = 의문사+주어+조동사 should[can]+동사원형

28 아시아흑곰들이 주로 아시아의 '숲'에 살기 때문에 숲을 보호하기 위해 '종이'를 덜 사용해야 하고, 사람들이 그들의 '몸 부위'를 얻기 위해 그들을 사냥하기 때문에 아시아 흑곰으로 만든 제품을 사지 말아야 한다.

29 아시아흑곰으로 무슨 제품을 만들 수 있는지는 알 수 없다. ① A white V-shape on their chests. ② In forests in Asia. ③ Because of hunting and forest destruction. ④ We should use less paper to protect forests. And we should not buy any Asian black bear products.

30 앞부분의 내용을 가리킨다.

31 플라스틱 제품을 '재사용', '재활용'하고 자신의 '병'과 '쇼핑백'을 가지고 오는 것이다.

Timeless Tales of Gods and Heroes

를 하라고 말하는 것은 '요청하다(ask)', (3) 손이나 팔을 빠르게 움직여 어떤 물체를 놓음으로써 그 물체가 공기 중으로 움직이게 하는 것은 '던지다(throw)'이다.

06 'with+명사'는 부사의 의미를 갖는다. 따라서 carefully로 쓰는 것이 적절하다.

시험대비 실력평가 p.64

01 ④ 02 ⑤ 03 ⑤ 04 undo
05 (p)riceless 06 protect
07 harvest 08 ②

01 말이 끄는 바퀴 달린 탈것은 '마차(carriage)'이다.

02 주어진 문장의 order는 '주문하다'라는 의미로 쓰였다. ① 명령하다 ② 정돈(된 상태) / 그녀가 생활을 정리해야 할 때였다. ③ 질서 ④ 명령, 지시 ⑤ 주문하다

03 turn into: ~이 되다

04 undo: 무효로 만들다, 원상태로 돌리다

05 reply와 respond는 유의어 관계이다. 따라서 precious와 유의어 관계에 있는 priceless를 쓰는 것이 적절하다.

06 어떤 사물이나 사람이 다치지 않도록 막아준다는 '보호하다(protect)'이다.

07 곡식을 모으는 것은 '추수, 수확(harvest)'이라고 한다.

08 주어진 단어는 '창'이다. 따라서 ②번이 적절하다. 각각 ① sow ③ promise ④ treasure ⑤ accept를 풀이한 말이다.

서술형 시험대비 p.65

01 (1) give (2) come (3) plays (4) like
02 (A) of (B) up (C) for
03 (1) Children will fall asleep in the room.
   (2) You had better go home early.
   (3) Moreover, he was scared.
04 turned into
05 (1) poem (2) ask (3) throw
06 carefully

01 give up: ~을 포기하다, come along: 함께 가다, play tricks on: ~에게 장난치다, How do you like ~?: ~가 마음에 드니?

02 of one's own: 자기 자신의, come up with: ~을 생각해 내다, be famous for: ~으로 유명하다

03 (1) fall asleep: 잠들다 (2) had better: ~하는 편이 낫다 (3) moreover: 더욱이, 게다가

04 '~로 되다'는 의미로 쓰이는 것은 'turn into'이다.

05 (1) 단어가 미적 요소와 소리에 따라 선택되고 조심스럽게 배열되는 글은 '시(poem)', (2) 누군가에게 당신이 원하는 무언가

교과서 **Conversation**

핵심 Check p.66~67

1 What makes you 2 ⑤

교과서 대화문 익히기

Check(√) True or False p.68

1 F 2 T 3 F 4 T 5 F 6 F

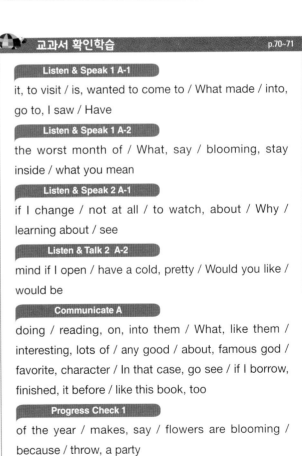

교과서 확인학습 p.70~71

Listen & Speak 1 A-1
it, to visit / is, wanted to come to / What made / into, go to, I saw / Have

Listen & Speak 1 A-2
the worst month of / What, say / blooming, stay inside / what you mean

Listen & Speak 2 A-1
if I change / not at all / to watch, about / Why / learning about / see

Listen & Talk 2 A-2
mind if I open / have a cold, pretty / Would you like / would be

Communicate A
doing / reading, on, into them / What, like them / interesting, lots of / any good / about, famous god / favorite, character / In that case, go see / if I borrow, finished, it before / like this book, too

Progress Check 1
of the year / makes, say / flowers are blooming / because / throw, a party

Progress Check 2
mind if I take, more / waiting for, soon / Never mind / ask, to bring

01 ④　　　02 ②　　　03 ③

04 She is learning about Norway in class.

01 왜 그렇게 생각하는지를 묻는 표현이 들어가는 것이 적절하다. 따라서 ④번이 적절하다.

02 허락을 구하는 표현이므로 ②번과 바꾸어 쓸 수 있다. 대화의 밑줄 친 부분은 내가 창문을 열겠다는 것이므로, 창문을 열어달라고 상대에게 요청하는 표현인 ③, ④번은 적절하지 않다.

03 'Do you mind if ~?'는 허락을 구하는 표현이다.

04 소녀는 수업 시간에 노르웨이에 관하여 배우고 있다고 하였다.

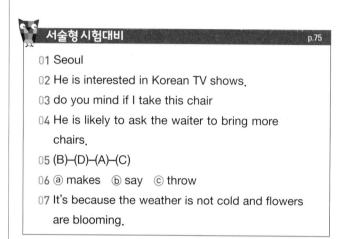

01 ③　　　02 ③　　　03 ②

04 It's because she needs to watch a program about Norway.

05 (C)–(A)–(D)–(B)　　　06 ③　　　07 ④

08 ⑤　　　09 it's pretty windy today　　　10 ③

11 ⑤번 → No, not at all.

12 He wants to read the book before he sees the movie.

13 ⑤

01 답변으로 미루어 보아 아이슬란드로 가고 싶어 하는 이유를 묻는 말이 들어가는 것이 적절하다.

02 'Do you mind if ~?'는 허락을 구하는 표현이다.

03 'Do you mind if ~?'에 대한 대답이 'No, not at all.'이면 승낙한다는 의미이므로 ②번은 글의 내용과 일치하지 않는다.

04 소녀가 채널을 돌려야 하는 이유는 노르웨이에 관한 프로그램을 보아야 하기 때문이다.

05 (C) 4월은 연중 최악의 달이라는 말에 (A) 그렇게 말하는 이유를 묻고 (D) 이유를 답하자 (B) 무슨 말인지 알겠다고 말하는 것이 가장 자연스럽다.

06 bloom은 '꽃이 피다'라는 의미로, opening으로 쓸 수 있다.

07 A의 다음 말로 보아 요청을 허락한 것임을 알 수 있다. 따라서 거절하는 표현인 ④번은 적절하지 않다.

08 @는 허락을 구하는 표현이므로 ⑤번으로 대신할 수 있다.

09 날씨를 표현할 때 쓰이는 주어는 비인칭 주어 It이다. pretty는 '예쁜'이라는 의미의 형용사 외에도 '꽤'라는 의미의 부사로도 쓰인다.

10 Jane에게 따뜻한 차를 권했고, Jane이 이에 응했으므로 ③번이 가장 적절하다.

11 이어지는 말로 보아 책을 빌려달라는 요청의 말에 승낙했음을 알 수 있다. 'Of course not.', 'Certainly not.', 'No, I don't.', 'No problem.', 'Sure. Go ahead.' 등으로 고쳐도 무방하다.

12 Jaden은 영화를 보러 가기 전에 유리가 읽고 있는 책을 빌려서 읽기를 원한다.

13 Jaden은 유리에게 그녀가 읽고 있는 책을 빌려달라고 하였으므로 ⑤번이 대화의 내용과 일치한다.

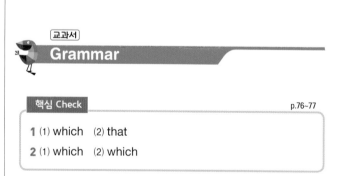

01 Seoul

02 He is interested in Korean TV shows.

03 do you mind if I take this chair

04 He is likely to ask the waiter to bring more chairs.

05 (B)–(D)–(A)–(C)

06 @ makes　ⓑ say　ⓒ throw

07 It's because the weather is not cold and flowers are blooming.

01 Mike는 항상 서울에 와 보고 싶었다고 하였으므로 here는 서울을 가리키는 말이다.

02 남자가 관심 있는 것은 한국 텔레비전 쇼라고 하였다.

03 대답으로 미루어 보아 의자를 사용해도 되는지 허락을 구하는 표현이 들어가는 것이 적절하다.

04 대화가 끝난 후 남자는 웨이터에게 의자를 더 가져다 달라고 요청할 것이다.

05 (B) 창문을 열어도 되느냐고 요청하는 말에, (D) 거절하며 그 이유로 감기에 걸렸다고 설명하자, (A) 따뜻한 차를 마시겠냐고 권하고, (C) 이에 응하는 것이 가장 자연스럽다.

06 이유를 묻는 표현은 'What makes you say so?'이다. throw a party: 파티를 열다

07 소녀가 1년 중 4월이 최고의 달이라고 말하는 이유는 날씨가 춥지 않고 꽃이 피기 때문이라고 하였다.

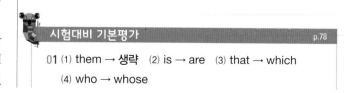

교과서
Grammar

1 (1) which　(2) that

2 (1) which　(2) which

01 (1) them → 생략　(2) is → are　(3) that → which
　(4) who → whose

02 ⑤   03 ④
04 It is those necklaces that[which] Veronika has always wanted to have.

01 (1) 선행사 the pictures를 받는 관계대명사가 있으므로 them은 생략한다. (2) 주어가 복수이므로 are가 적절하다. (3) Robert가 그녀의 문제를 언급한 내용 전체가 선행사가 되는 계속적 용법의 관계대명사 자리이다. that은 계속적 용법으로 쓸 수 없다. (4) 'Sue의 나이'를 가리키는 것이므로 소유격 관계대명사인 whose가 적절하다.

02 강조 구문에서 명사를 강조하면 that 뒤에 불완전한 절이 와야 한다. ⑤에서 the bus를 강조했는데 구조가 완전하다. 내용상 Sam이 그의 시계를 잃어버린 장소를 강조하는 문장이 되어야 하기 때문에 the bus를 in the bus로 바꾸는 것이 적절하다.

03 계속적 용법의 관계대명사로서, 선행사는 사람인 the girl이다. 콤마 뒤에 who가 적절하다.

04 목적어를 강조하는 것이므로, 'It ~ that' 강조구문을 사용한다. 강조되는 대상이 복수라 하더라도 be동사는 is/was만 가능하며, 주절의 문장이 현재완료 시제이므로, 강조구문의 시제도 is로 하는 것에 유의한다.

시험대비 실력평가   p.79~81

01 ⓑ where → which 또는 in 생략, ⓒ that → which, ⓓ run → runs 또는 ran, ⓔ which → that 또는 in which

02 ③   03 it was Tom that tore the newspaper

04 ③

05 (1) All villagers in town like the bridge, which was built 100 years ago.
(2) I learned Chinese from Lily, who made me speak freely in Beijing.
(3) There lived a hero named Hercules, who was the son of Zeus.
(4) They will go to Jagalchi market, where they will buy fresh seafood.

06 ③   07 ②   08 ④   09 ⑤

10 ④

11 My uncles know Sarah, who speaks Chinese like a native.

12 It is Jonathan who is responsible for taking care of the flower.

13 ⑤   14 ②   15 ②

16 ②, ③, ⑤

01 ⓑ 전치사 in이 있으므로, where를 which로 고치거나 in을 생략한다. ⓒ 계속적 용법에서 that 불가 ⓓ 선행사 a horse가

단수이므로 runs 또는 ran이 적절하다. ⓔ the way+that[in which]

02 ③의 that은 동격의 접속사로 쓰였다. 나머지는 모두 'It ~ that' 강조구문의 that이다.

03 과거시제 동사 tore 형태에 유의하여, 'It ~ that' 강조구문을 글자 수에 맞게 쓴다.

04 내용상 기술자에게 수리를 맡겼고, '그 기술자가 차를 수리한 것'이 선행사이므로, 관계대명사 which가 적절하다.

05 사람과 사물은 각각 who와 which로 받고, 문장에 나온 there는 장소의 부사이므로 where로 받는다.

06 ③번은 가주어 It과 진주어 명사절을 이끄는 접속사 that이 쓰였다. 나머지는 모두 'It ~ that' 강조구문이다.

07 ②번은 가주어 It과 진주어 명사절을 이끄는 접속사 that이 쓰였다. 나머지는 모두 'It ~ that' 강조구문이다.

08 내용상 '월드컵이 서울에서 개최된' 2002년을 선행사로 받는 관계대명사이므로, 관계대명사 앞에 in이 있어야 한다. Seoul 앞의 in과는 무관하다. which를 in which 또는 관계부사 when으로 바꿔야 한다.

09 빈칸은 모두 계속적 용법의 관계대명사가 들어가는 자리이다. 문장의 선행사는 각각 (A) a wheel, (B) Tiffany's aunt, (C) a couple이다.

10 ①번은 동사의 수의 일치가 부적절, ②, ③, ⑤번은 계속적 용법의 관계대명사 which가 적절하다. ① come → comes, ② of which → which, ③ that → which, ⑤ who → which

11 My uncles know Sarah and she speaks Chinese like a native.에서 and she를 계속적 용법의 관계대명사 who로 바꿔 영작한다.

12 내용상 엄마가 기르는 꽃에 대한 책임을 맡고 있는 사람을 강조하는 문장이므로 'It ~ who' 강조구문을 사용한다. 전치사 for 뒤의 동명사 taking의 형태에 주의한다.

13 ⑤번 문장의 that은 동격의 접속사로 쓰였다. 나머지는 모두 'It ~ that' 강조구문의 that이다.

14 옳은 문장은 ⓕ, ⓖ 2개이다. ⓐ and who → who 또는 and she, ⓑ were → was, ⓒ that → which, ⓓ who → which, ⓔ which → who 또는 that

15 ①, ③ 'It ~ that' 강조구문에서는 강조되는 명사의 성격에 따라 that을 who 또는 which로 대체할 수 있다. ②번은 진주어 명사절을 이끄는 접속사 that이며 다른 단어로 대체 불가하다. ④, ⑤ 선행사가 사물일 때 관계대명사 that은 which로 바꿔 쓸 수 있다.

16 ② 선행사가 단수이므로, which 뒤에 sells가 적절하다. ③ Mr. King's lecture가 선행사이므로 which가 적절하다. ⑤ 계속적 용법이므로 that은 불가능하다. which가 적절하다.

01 (A) It is Lucas that[who] is going to wear a mask at the party this weekend.

(B) It is a mask that[which] Lucas is going to wear at the party this weekend.

(C) It is at the party that Lucas is going to wear a mask this weekend.

02 (1) 답변 불가

(2) It was Ellen that[who] had Grace's car repaired.

(3) It was three weeks ago that Ellen had Grace's car repaired.

(4) 답변 불가

(5) It was at the shop that Grace's car was repaired three weeks ago.

03 (1) the auditorium → in the auditorium

(2) who → which[that]

(3) Anthony was chairman of the council.

(4) the evening → in the evening

(5) He rescued the injured carefully.

04 (1) All the people there were so selfish, which made the two parties even farther away.

(2) Thomas is widely known for dancing, which is not true.

(3) Emma fell in love with Alex, whom she met only once.

05 on January 20, 1993 that Audrey Hepburn was

06 (1) that → which   (2) who → which

(3) but which → but 삭제 또는 but it

(4) he made → made him

07 (1) The teacher blamed Susan, who didn't mean to be late.

(2) Jackson's father looked a lot younger than she thought, which Jackson was ashamed of.

(3) Almost everyone in the factory stops working at noon, when they go out for lunch.

(4) Isabella received a letter of apology from her boyfriend, which she hasn't opened yet.

(5) Bentley's family went to Mexico, where they saw some Mayan ruins.

08 Camila made over 15 pancakes with her dad, which was so fun.

01 It is ~ that 구문을 쓴다. 강조하는 대상이 사람일 때는 that 대신 who, 사물일 때는 that 대신 which를 쓸 수 있다.

02 (1) 5형식 문장의 사역동사 'have+목적어+p.p' 형태에서는 명시적 표현이 없으면 행위자 파악 불가. (4) 주어진 문장만으로는 수리 시점(3주 전)만을 알 수 있고, 수리 기간은 파악할 수 없음. (2), (3), (5)번은 'It ~ that' 강조구문에 맞춰 적절히 영작한다.

03 (1) '부사구'로 장소를 강조하는 것이므로 전치사를 써야 한다. (2) 강조 대상이 사람이 아니므로 who는 쓸 수 없다. which 또는 that이 적절하다. (3) '주격보어'는 'It ~ that' 강조구문의 강조 대상이 될 수 없다. (4) '부사구'로 시간을 강조하는 것이므로 전치사를 써야 한다. (5) 태도를 나타내는 '양태 부사'는 'It ~ that' 강조구문의 강조 대상이 될 수 없다.

04 (1), (2)의 선행사는 앞 문장 전체, (3)은 Alex이다.

05 '1993년 1월 20일이 Audrey Hepburn이 사망한 날'이라는 문장을 '부사구'를 강조하는 'It ~ that 강조구문'으로 표현한다. 전치사 on과 함께 쓰는 것에 유의하여 영작한다.

06 (1) 앞 문장 전체가 선행사이므로, 계속적 용법의 which, (2) 선행사가 발레 동작이므로 which가 적절하다. (3) 앞 문장 전체가 선행사이므로 접속사 but을 삭제하거나, 앞 문장 전체를 받는 대명사로 바꾸는 것이 적절하다. (4) 앞 문장 전체가 선행사이고, 목적어 him으로 바꿔 위치를 수정한다.

07 선행사에 따라 who, which, when, where에 유의하여 영작한다.

08 '계속적' 용법의 관계대명사 which를 사용하여, 앞 문장 전체 내용을 선행사로 하는 문장을 만든다.

교과서
Reading

확인문제   p.84

1 T   2 F   3 T   4 F   5 T   6 F

확인문제   p.85

1 T   2 F   3 T   4 F   5 T   6 F

확인문제   p.86

1 T   2 F   3 T   4 F   5 T   6 F

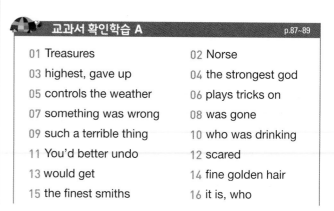

교과서 확인학습 A   p.87~89

01 Treasures   02 Norse

03 highest, gave up   04 the strongest god

05 controls the weather   06 plays tricks on

07 something was wrong   08 was gone

09 such a terrible thing   10 who was drinking

11 You'd better undo   12 scared

13 would get   14 fine golden hair

15 the finest smiths   16 it is, who

17 three treasures
18 better than theirs
19 Of course
20 make, for them
21 decide on
22 had to be
23 immediately
24 went to see
25 are making, for
26 I bet, as fine as theirs
27 accepted the challenge
28 of their own
29 with all the treasures
30 came along
31 showed, from
32 for, only one eye
33 It was, that
34 turn into
35 for
36 The third treasure
37 flowing golden hair
38 put, on, took root
39 Brokk's turn
40 eight more, every ninth night
41 Frey a pig
42 faster than any horse
43 My third treasure
44 which
45 come back to
46 break it
47 the greatest treasure
48 the three gods liked most
49 protect, from
50 the better smiths
51 proved, precious treasures

교과서 확인학습 B   p.90~92

1 Treasures for Three Gods

2 Important Norse Gods

3 Odin, who is the highest god, gave up his eye for wisdom.

4 Thor is Odin's son and the strongest god of all.

5 Frey, who is the god of the harvest, controls the weather.

6 Loki is a god who plays tricks on others.

7 Thor woke and knew immediately something was wrong.

8 His wife's beautiful golden hair was gone.

9 He knew only Loki could do such a terrible thing.

10 Thor soon found Loki, who was drinking at home.

11 "You'd better undo what you did, or you'll be sorry," Thor said angrily to Loki.

12 Loki was scared.

13 He promised that he would get golden hair for Thor's wife.

14 Loki knew only the sons of Ivaldi could make fine golden hair.

15 He went to them and said, "I heard Brokk and his brother are the finest smiths. Is that true?"

16 "No, it is we who are the finest smiths," the sons of Ivaldi replied.

17 "They're making three treasures for Odin, Thor, and Frey," said Loki.

18 "Do you think you can make treasures better than theirs?"

19 "Of course we can," they answered.

20 "O.K., then you should also make three treasures for them," said Loki.

21 "The gods will decide on the best treasure."

22 Loki also told them that one of the treasures had to be golden hair.

23 They went to work immediately.

24 Loki then went to see Brokk and his brother.

25 "Ivaldi's sons are making three treasures for Odin, Thor, and Frey," said Loki.

26 "I bet that you can never make treasures as fine as theirs."

27 Brokk became angry and accepted the challenge.

28 He and his brother produced three treasures of their own.

29 Loki went to see the three gods with all the treasures.

30 Brokk came along.

31 Loki showed them the treasures from Ivaldi's sons.

32 The first treasure was for Odin, who had only one eye.

33 It was a spear that never missed its target.

34 The second treasure was a big ship that could turn into a piece of cloth.

35 It was for Frey.

36 The third treasure was for Thor.

37 Loki showed Thor the flowing golden hair for his wife.

38 Thor put the hair on his wife's head, and it took root and became real hair.

39 It was now Brokk's turn to show the gods his gifts.

40 He gave Odin a gold arm ring that produced eight more gold rings every ninth night.

41 Brokk then gave Frey a pig.

42 It could pull his carriage faster than any horse.

43 "My third treasure is for you, Thor," said Brokk.

44 "This is the hammer Mjolnir, which you'll love.

45 If you throw it, it'll always come back to you.

46 Moreover, nothing can ever break it."

47 It was an easy decision to choose the greatest treasure.

17

48 It was Mjolnir that the three gods liked most.

49 They thought the hammer would protect the gods from their enemies.

50 "Brokk and his brother," said Odin, "are the better smiths."

51 Brokk proved that Loki was wrong, and the three gods now had precious treasures.

시험대비 실력평가
p.93~97

01 Norse	02 ③	03 ①	04 ⑤
05 ②	06 who is → who are		
07 one of the treasures had to be golden hair			
08 as		09 ③, ④	
10 making treasures as fine as Ivaldi's sons'			
11 which	12 ②	13 nine	14 ③
15 ③	16 ④	17 ⑤	18 ①
19 treasure → treasures		20 ③	21 ⑤
22 ②, ④	23 ③	24 ②	25 ③
24 ②			
24 (A) fine golden hair (B) the challenge			

01 Norse: 고대 스칸디나비아(사람[말])의, 노르웨이(사람[말])의, (특히 고대) 노르웨이[스칸디나비아]어, 영영풀이: 1. 중세 시대 스칸디나비아 국가에 속하는 또는 관련된, 2. 노르웨이의 또는 노르웨이와 관련된 또는 노르웨이 사람, 문화, 언어

02 ⓑ play tricks on: ~에게 농간을 부리다, ~에게 장난을 치다, ⓒ get: 사다, 구입하다(buy, purchase), 구하다, 얻다 (obtain)의 뜻으로, 3형식으로 고칠 때 전치사 for를 사용한다.

03 본문은 인물과 배경이 제시되고, 사건의 실마리를 제공하는 도입 단계에 해당하므로, ① '발단'이 적절하다.

04 'Loki'가 Thor의 아내를 위해 금발머리를 얻어 오겠다고 약속했다.

05 ②는 Brokk and his brother를 가리키고, 나머지는 다 the sons of Ivaldi를 가리킨다.

06 we are the finest smiths에서 주어인 we를 강조한 것이기 때문에 'who are'로 고치는 것이 적절하다..

07 told라는 과거시제에 맞추어 목적절인 that 이하의 시제도 has to(~해야 한다)의 과거인 had to로 쓰는 것이 적절하다.

08 as ... as ~: '~만큼 …한', 형용사 원급을 사용하여 두 대상을 비교하는 구문이다.

09 (A)와 ①, ②, ⑤: 틀림없이 ~하다, 내 의견으로는 틀림없이 ~할 것이다, ③ doubtful: 의심스러운, ④ unlikely: ~할[일] 것 같지 않은, 있음직하지[있을 것 같지] 않은

10 'Ivaldi의 아들들의 보물만큼 훌륭한 보물을 만드는 것'을 가리킨다.

11 선행사가 사물이고 계속적 용법이므로 which가 적절하다.

12 앞에 나오는 내용에 추가하는 내용이 뒤에 이어지므로 Moreover가 가장 적절하다. Moreover: 게다가, 더욱이, ③ 그러므로, ④ 다시 말해서

13 every+서수+단수명사 = every+기수+복수명사: ~마다, every ninth night: 아홉 번째 밤이 될 때마다

14 이 글은 '모든 보물을 세 명의 신에게 보여주고 그 중에서 가장 훌륭한 보물을 선택하는' 내용의 글이므로, 제목으로는 ③번 '무엇이 신들에게 보여진 가장 훌륭한 보물인가?'가 적절하다.

15 Loki가 겁을 내며 Thor의 아내를 위해 금발머리를 얻어 오겠다고 약속했다는 내용이 이어지고 있으므로, "네가 한 짓을 되돌려 놓는 것이 좋을 거야"라고 하는 것이 적절하다. undo 원상태로 돌리다

16 ④ gradually: 서서히, 나머지는 다 '즉시', ⑤ without delay: 지체 없이, 즉시

17 Loki가 왜 다른 신들에게 농간을 부리는지는 대답할 수 없다. ① Odin. ② Thor. ③ Frey. ④ The weather.

18 ⓐ와 ①: It is[was] ... that[who, whom, which, etc.]의 구문으로 문장의 주어·(동사 또는 전치사의) 목적어·부사 어구를 강조하여 쓰인 대명사, ② 그것(앞에 이미 언급되었거나 현재 이야기되고 있는 사물·동물을 가리킴), ③ 가주어, ④ [사정·상황을 막연히 기리기는] 비인칭 주어, ⑤ 가목적어

19 one+of+the+복수명사: ~ 중의 하나

20 Brokk와 그의 남동생이 'Odin과 Thor와 Frey'를 위해서 보물을 만들고 있다고 말했다. ⑤ on the spot: 즉각[즉석에서]

21 ⓐ와 ⑤: 빗나가다, ① 이해[파악]하지 못하다, ② (기회를) 놓치다, ③ (어디에 참석하지 않아서 그 일을) 놓치다, ④ 그리워[아쉬워]하다

22 ⓑ와 ①, ③, ⑤: 최상급의 뜻. '비교급+than any (other)+단수 명사'로 최상급을 나타낼 수 있는데, 비교 대상이 같은 그룹에 속해 있지 않은 경우에는 any other 대신 any만 쓴다. 부정주어+비교급+than = 부정주어+as(so)+원급+as도 최상급의 뜻을 나타낸다.

23 ③번 다음 문장의 They에 주목한다. 주어진 문장의 'the three gods'를 받고 있으므로 ③번이 적절하다.

24 Frey를 위한 보물은 '큰 배'와 '돼지 한 마리'였다.

25 ③은 'Ivaldi의 아들들'을 가리키고, 나머지는 다 'Brokk와 그의 남동생'을 가리킨다.

26 Ivaldi의 아들들과 Brokk와 그의 남동생에게 각각 거짓말로 경쟁을 하도록 부추기는 것으로 보아 '교활한' 성격이라고 하는 것이 적절하다. ① 성실한, ③ 거만한, ④ 관대한, ⑤ 인내심이 있는

27 Loki는 '훌륭한 금발머리'를 원했는데, Ivaldi의 아들들만이 그것을 만들 수 있었다. 그래서 그는 Ivaldi의 아들들이 경쟁심을 느끼고 '도전'을 받아들이도록 하기 위해서 Brokk와 그의 남동생을 언급했다.

01 (A) gone   (B) angrily   (C) scared

02 stronger than

03 Loki가 Thor의 아내의 아름다운 금발머리를 사라지게 한 것

04 on   05 Brokk and his brother's treasures

06 competitive

07 (A) a spear   (B) a big ship

    (C) the flowing golden hair

08 They liked Mjolnir most.

09 He thought 'Brokk and his brother' were the better smiths.

10 his eye   11 and he

12 he would get Thor's wife golden hair

---

01 (A) disappear는 수동태로 쓸 수 없으므로 gone이 적절하다. be gone = disappear: 사라지다, (B) 동사 said를 수식하는 것이므로, 부사인 angrily가 적절하다. (C) Loki가 '겁이 난' 것이므로 scared가 적절하다. scared: 무서워하는, 겁먹은, scaring: 놀라운, 위협적인

02 비교급+than+any other+단수명사: 최상급의 뜻을 나타낸다.

03 'Loki가 Thor의 아내의 아름다운 금발머리를 사라지게 한' 일을 가리킨다.

04 decide on: ~에 관해 결정을 하다

05 'Brokk와 그의 남동생의 보물'을 가리킨다.

06 Loki는 Ivaldi의 아들들이 훌륭한 금발머리를 만들도록 하기 위해 그들의 '경쟁심'을 촉발시켰다. competitive spirit: 경쟁심

07 Ivaldi의 아들들은 Odin을 위해 '창'을, Frey를 위해 '큰 배'를, Thor의 아내를 위해 '매끈하게 늘어진 금발머리'를 만들었다.

08 세 명의 신들이 가장 마음에 든 것은 '묠니르'였다.

09 'Brokk와 그의 남동생'이 더 훌륭한 대장장이라고 Odin은 생각했다.

10 '지혜를 위해 한쪽 눈을 포기했다'는 것은 '한쪽 눈을 희생하여(대가로 치루고) 지혜를 얻었다'는 뜻이다. at the expense[cost/price] of: ~을 희생하여

11 계속적 용법의 관계대명사는 '접속사+대명사'로 바꿔 쓸 수 있다.

12 get: 사다, 구입하다(buy, purchase), 구하다, 얻다(obtain)의 뜻으로, 3형식으로 고칠 때 전치사 for를 사용한 것을 '간접목적어+직접목적어' 순서로 쓰면 4형식이 된다.

---

01 ③   02 ④   03 ③

04 decide   05 ④

---

06 (1) was gone   (2) come along   (3) turned into

07 (1) How did you come up with the idea?

    (2) Don't play tricks on your little sister.

    (3) He is famous for a smith.

08 Do you mind if I play it?

09 ⑤   10 ②   11 ③

12 It's because she is waiting for her friend and she'll be here soon.

13 ③   14 ②   15 ③   16 ④

17 ③   18 ①   19 ④   20 ②

21 ⑤   22 smiths   23 ②   24 which

25 ②, ⑤ / ①, ③, ④

26 It was Mjolnir that the three gods liked most.

27 ④   28 ④   29 ⑤   30 ④

31 asking the sons of Ivaldi to make fine golden hair

---

01 take root: 뿌리를 내리다, take a walk: 산책하다, take a break: 쉬다

02 '형용사+ly'는 부사로 쓰이지만 '명사+ly'는 형용사로 쓰인다.

03 cloth는 '옷감'이라는 의미로 쓰인다. '옷'은 clothes이다.

04 다른 가능성에 대해 주의 깊게 생각한 후 무언가를 하기로 선택하다는 '결정하다(decide)'이다.

05 주어진 문장에서 miss는 '(기회를) 놓치다'는 의미로 쓰였다. 따라서 ④번이 가장 적절하다. ① 그리워하다 ② (식사를) 거르다 ③ 이해하지 못하다 ⑤ (있어야 할 것이) 없다는 것을 알다[눈치채다]

06 (1) be gone: 사라지다, 없어지다 (2) come along: 함께 가다 (3) turn into: ~으로 되다 (1) safe: 금고

07 come up with: ~을 생각해 내다, play tricks on: ~에게 장난을 치다 (3) be famous for: ~로 유명하다

08 허락을 구하는 표현은 'Do you mind if ~?'이다.

09 'Sure, go ahead.'라고 답하는 것이 적절하다. 'I do'라고 하였으므로 상대가 집으로 일찍 가는 것을 꺼린다는 말이 되므로 Sure와 의미상 맞지 않다.

10 (D) 4월이 가장 좋다고 말하자 (B) 그렇게 말한 이유를 묻고 (A) 이유를 답하고 (E) 자신이 4월을 좋아하는 이유는 생일이 있기 때문이라고 하자 (C) 파티를 열어주겠다고 말하는 것이 가장 자연스럽다.

11 허락을 요청하는 말이 들어가는 것이 적절하다. ③번은 권하는 말이다.

12 여자는 친구를 기다리고 있고 그 친구가 곧 도착할 것이기 때문에 의자를 줄 수 없다고 하였다.

13 Mike는 한국 텔레비전 쇼에 관심이 있다고 하였다. be into ~: ~에 흥미가 있다

14 ① which → who ② that → who ③ what → which ⑤ what → which 또는 that

15 'It ~ that' 강조구문에서 어떤 사건이 일어난 해를 가리키는 부사구 표현은 연도 앞에 in을 쓰는 것이 적절하다.

16 ④번은 가주어 It과 진주어 명사절 접속사 that이 쓰인 문장이다. 나머지는 모두 'It ~ that' 강조구문이 쓰였다.

17 <보기>의 which는 관계대명사로서 '계속적 용법'으로 사용되었다. ③번의 which는 의문형용사로서 '어느'라는 뜻이다. 나머지는 모두 관계대명사 which로 사용되었다. to no avail: 보람 없이, 헛되이

18 ① what → that[which]

19 'Stella는 친구 다섯 명이 있는데, Stella가 운동을 싫어한다는 것을 그들 모두가 알고 있다'는 내용으로 풀어볼 수 있다. ④번은 접속사 and와 관계대명사 whose friends가 같이 있어서 틀렸다. whose를 her로 바꾸거나 and를 삭제해야 한다.

20 ②번의 that은 so ~ that 부사절의 접속사로 쓰였다. 나머지는 모두 'It ~ that' 강조구문의 that이다. persuasion: 설득

21 which are → which is

22 smith: 대장장이, 금속 세공인, <영영풀이: 금속을 다루는 일을 하는 사람들, 특히 망치질로 금속의 형태를 만드는 사람들>

23 이 글은 'Loki가 Ivaldi의 아들들로 하여금 훌륭한 금발머리를 만들도록 하기 위해 그들의 경쟁심을 이용하는' 내용의 글이므로, 주제로는 ②번 '자신의 목적을 성취하기 위해 타인의 경쟁심을 활용하기'가 적절하다. ① craftsman: (숙련된) 장인

24 '접속사+대명사'를 계속적 용법의 관계대명사 which로 바꿔 쓰는 것이 적절하다. it은 the hair를 가리킨다.

25 ⓑ와 ②, ⑤: 형용사적 용법, to show는 turn을 꾸며 주어 '보여 줄 차례'라는 의미로 쓰임, ⓒ와 ①, ③, ④: 명사적 용법, ③번의 to show는 진주어로 쓰인 명사적 용법

26 that이나 which를 보충하면 된다. It was와 that[which]사이에 강조하고자 하는 말을 넣어 배열하는 것이 적절하다.

27 ④ Brokk와 그의 남동생이 Frey를 위해 만들어 준 것은 'a pig'였다.

28 본문 (3)번은 이야기에서 갈등과 긴장이 최고조에 도달하고 주제가 선명하게 부각되는 부분으로, 어떤 결말을 낼 것인가를 결정하는 계기를 제공하는 절정 단계에 해당하므로, ④ '절정'이 적절하다.

29 대장장이들이 각각 어떤 보상을 받았는지는 알 수 없다. ① Loki, Odin, Thor, and Frey. the sons of Ivaldi, Brokk and his brother ② Loki가 Thor의 아내의 아름다운 금발머리를 사라지게 했다. ③ Loki가 세 명의 신들에게 보물을 보여주었다. ④ 신들은 망치를 가장 마음에 들어 했고, 각자 소중한 보물을 가지게 되었다.

30 단지 재미로 남의 머리를 자르는 것으로 보아, 'I'는 Loki에 해당한다고 하는 것이 적절하다. play tricks (on): 농간을 부리다, 장난을 치다

31 'Ivaldi의 아들들에게 훌륭한 금발머리를 만들어 달라고 부탁하는 것'을 가리킨다.

단원별 예상문제 p.107~111

01 ④, ⑤	02 ③	03 ⑤	04 ④
05 ③	06 Why do you say so?		
07 ④	08 ⑤		

09 What makes you like them so much?

10 ⑤	11 ⑤

12 (1) ⓐ (2) ⓑ (3) ⓐ (4) ⓐ (5) ⓑ (6) ⓐ

13 ④	14 ⑤

15 ⓐ It was Tom that[who] bought a tablet at the mall 3 weeks ago.
   ⓑ It was a tablet that[which] Tom bought at the mall 3 weeks ago.
   ⓒ It was at the mall that Tom bought a tablet 3 weeks ago.
   ⓓ It was 3 weeks ago that Tom bought a tablet at the mall.

16 Our school introduced a new system, which would help improve the students' math grade that had always been under average.

17 Brokk and his brother are the finest smiths

18 it is we who are the finest smiths

19 fine golden hair	20 ⑤	
21 ④	22 ②	23 and you'll love it

24 a spear and a gold arm ring / a big ship and a pig / the flowing golden hair for his wife and the hammer Mjolnir

25 ①	26 a strange voice	27 ④

01 주어진 단어는 '명사-형용사'의 관계로 '금 – 금으로 만든, 금빛의'라는 의미이다. ④번은 '흙 – 흙으로 만든', ⑤번은 '나무 – 나무로 만든'이란 의미이다. 나머지는 모두 '형용사-동사'의 관계이다.

02 주어진 문장의 빈칸에는 take가 쓰인다. ① make a noise: 소음을 만들다 ② make a decision: 결정을 내리다 ③ take place: 발생하다 ④ get angry: 화내다 ⑤ get along with: ~와 사이좋게 지내다

03 주어진 단어는 '조각'이라는 의미이므로 ⑤번이 가장 적절하다. ① mysterious ② miss ③ reply ④ skin

04 답변으로 보아 왜 왔는지를 물어보는 말이 들어가는 것이 가장 적절하다.

05 한국을 처음으로 방문한 Mike는 자신이 TV 속에서 보았던 장소들을 둘러볼 것이라고 하였다.

06 밑줄 친 (A)는 왜 그렇게 말하는지를 묻는 말이다. 'Why do you think so?', 'Why is that?' 등으로 써도 무방하다.

07 대답으로 미루어 보아 빈칸에는 거절하는 말이 들어가는 것이 적절하다. ④번은 요청에 응하는 답변이다.

08 주어진 문장의 it은 책을 가리키는 말이며 책을 빌려달라고 말하는 이유를 설명하고 있으므로 ⑤번이 가장 적절하다.

정답 및 해설

09 이유를 묻는 표현으로 'What makes you ~?'를 쓴다. 이때 make는 사역동사이므로 목적격 보어로 동사원형을 쓰는 것에 유의한다.

10 두 사람은 새로 나온 토르 영화를 볼 예정이다.

11 관계대명사 '계속적' 용법의 문장들이다. ⑤번의 that을 which로 고쳐야 한다.

12 (2), (5)는 접속사 that이 이끄는 진주어 명사절이 쓰였다. 나머지는 모두 'It ~ that' 강조구문인데, 그 중 (4), (6)은 의문사를 강조하고 있다. genetic engineering: 유전 공학

13 ④번은 선행사가 sea water가 아니라 '앞 문장 전체'이다.

14 장소의 부사구가 강조될 때는 that을 쓴다.

15 강조하는 대상에 따라 that 외에 who, which도 사용한다.

16 본문에 나온 표현만으로 계속적 용법의 관계대명사와 제한적 용법의 관계대명사를 모두 사용해야 하기 때문에, 보충 설명이 필요한 두 번째 문장을 계속적 용법의 'which'로 연결하는 것이 적절하다.

17 'Brokk와 그의 남동생이 가장 훌륭한 대장장이'라는 것을 가리킨다.

18 It is와 that[who/which] 사이에 강조하고자 하는 말을 넣는다. 강조하고자 하는 말이 사람일 경우 that 대신 who를 사용할 수 있다.

19 Loki는 Ivaldi의 아들들만이 '훌륭한 금발머리'를 만들 수 있다는 것을 알고 있었기 때문이다.

20 Ivaldi의 아들들이 세 명의 신들을 위해 무슨 보물들을 만들었는지는 대답할 수 없다. ① Because he knew only they could make fine golden hair. ② He said, "I heard Brokk and his brother are the finest smiths. Is that true?" ③ They felt proud of it. craftsmanship: 손재주, (훌륭한) 솜씨, ④ Yes.

21 위 글은 '신화'이다. ① (신문·잡지의) 글, 기사, ② 수필, ③ 전기, ⑤ (책·연극·영화 등에 대한) 논평[비평], 감상문

22 이 글은 'Ivaldi의 아들들과 Brokk와 그의 남동생이 세 명의 신을 위해 만든 보물들을 소개하면서, 신들이 그 중에서 가장 훌륭한 보물을 선택하는 것'에 관한 내용의 글이므로, 주제로는 ②번 '세 신을 위한 보물과 그들 중 가장 훌륭한 보물을 선택하는 것'이 적절하다.

23 계속적 용법의 관계대명사는 '접속사+대명사'로 바꿔 쓸 수 있다.

24 Odin의 소중한 보물: '창'과 '금팔찌', Frey의 소중한 보물: '큰 배'와 '돼지 한 마리', Thor의 소중한 보물: '그의 아내를 위한 매끈하게 늘어진 금발머리'와 '묠니르라는 망치'

25 ①번은 '일반적인 왕'을 가리키고, 나머지는 다 '6 가야의 왕들'을 가리킨다.

26 '이상한 목소리'를 가리킨다.

27 여섯 개의 알이 어떻게 여섯 명의 소년들로 변했는지는 알 수 없다. ① In the southeastern part of Korea. ② It was a small hill. ③ From the sky. ⑤ King Kim Suro.

01 (1) angrily (2) easy (3) happily
02 What made you come here?
03 He is going to go to the places he saw on TV.
04 which means he likes foreign cultures
05 was because of my mother that I won the award
06 His wife's beautiful golden hair was gone.
07 such a terrible thing
08 advise / should / to undo
09 (A) missed (B) a piece of cloth (C) real hair
10 (A) a gold arm ring (B) a pig
   (C) the hammer Mjolnir

01 '성내어, 화가 나서'는 부사이므로 angrily, '쉬운'은 '결정'이라는 명사를 수식하므로 형용사 easy, '기꺼이'는 부사이므로 happily라고 쓰는 것이 적절하다.

02 make는 사역동사로 쓰였으므로 목적격보어로 동사원형을 쓰는 것이 적절하다.

03 그는 TV에서 보았던 장소들을 가볼 것이라고 하였다.

04 Lucas가 평소 다양한 나라의 국제 라디오 방송을 온라인으로 청취하고, 외국인들과 문화에 관한 이야기를 나누는 것을 즐긴다는 내용으로 보아, 그가 외국 문화를 좋아한다는 결론을 내릴 수 있다. 동사의 수의 일치에 주의하여, 단어를 배열한다.

05 기자의 질문이 '수상의 제일 큰 공로자'에 대해 묻는 것이었으므로, 괄호에 나온 어머니와 관련된 답변을 해야 한다. 'because of my mother'를 'It ~ that' 구문으로 강조하는 문장을 쓰는 것이 적절하다.

06 '그의 아내의 아름다운 금발머리가 사라진 것'을 가리킨다.

07 'such+a+형용사+명사'의 순서로 쓰는 것이 적절하다. so terrible a thing도 가능하다.

08 You had better 동사원형 = I advise you to 부정사 = You should 동사원형 = It would be better for you to 부정사: ~해야 하다, ~하는 것이 좋다

09 Odin을 위한 보물은 목표물을 절대로 '빗나가지' 않는 창이었고, Frey를 위한 보물은 '천 조각'으로 변할 수 있는 큰 배였다. Thor를 위한 보물은 그의 아내를 위한 매끈하게 늘어진 금발머리였는데, Thor가 그 머리카락을 그의 아내의 머리에 얹었을 때 그것이 뿌리를 내려서 '진짜 머리카락'이 되었다.

10 Brokk와 그의 남동생은 Odin을 위해 '금팔찌'를, Frey를 위해 '돼지 한 마리'를, Thor를 위해 '묠니르라는 망치'를 만들었다.

|모범답안|

01 if I change the channel / not at all / watch a program about Norway / learning about Norway in class

02 (A) southeastern part   (B) Gujibong
   (C) singing and dancing   (D) six golden eggs
   (E) six Gayas   (F) King Kim Suro

단원별 모의고사 p.115~119

01 ⑤   02 take
03 (1) fell asleep immediately
   (2) completely dark outside
04 It's because he has to study for his exams.
05 ④   06 ④   07 (B)-(D)-(C)-(A)
08 ⑤   09 a new movie about Thor
10 ④   11 He wants to read Yuri's book.
12 if I play the piano
13 (1) They watched the movie *Frozen 2*, which is the
      second episode of *Frozen*
   (2) It was the Korean version of the OST of *Frozen
      2* which was sung by the singer TY.
14 ③
15 (1) Mom asked me to put the unused things in
      the boxes, and we will donate them to charity.
   (2) Mom asked me to put the unused things in the
      boxes, which we will donate to charity.
16 ④
17 (1) I brushed my teeth for myself, which Mom
      praised.
   (2) Jason's dog Brown is so smart that he can
      wash many dishes, which will surprise the
      world.
18 to show his gifts to the gods
19 (A) eight more gold rings   (B) faster
   (C) come back
20 ①   21 ⑤   22 ④   23 ④
24 ⑤   25 (A) six eggs   (B) six Gayas

01 모두 '형용사-부사'의 관계이지만 fast의 부사는 fast이다.
02 take a picture: 사진을 찍다, take care: 조심하다, take a
   look: 보다
03 fall asleep: 잠들다, completely: 완전히, outside: 바깥에
04 시험을 위해 공부해야 하기 때문이라고 하였다.
05 이유를 묻는 말이므로 ④번이 가장 적절하다.
06 'Do you mind if ~?'는 허락을 구하는 표현으로 'Certainly
   not.'이라고 답할 경우 허락에 응하는 것이 된다. 그러나 이어지
   는 문장에서는 주차가 안 된다고 하였으므로 대화의 내용이 어색
   하다.
07 (B) 의자를 써도 되느냐는 요청 (D) 거절하는 말 (C) 이에 알겠
   다고 답함 (A) 웨이터에게 의자를 더 가져다 달라고 말하라고 알
   려 줌

08 이어지는 말로 보아 요청에 응하는 말이 들어가는 것이 적절하
   다. 따라서 금지하는 답변인 ⑤번은 적절하지 않다.
09 토르에 관한 새 영화를 의미한다.
10 Jaden이 'I know him. He's my favorite online game
   character.'라고 하고 있다.
11 Jaden은 영화를 보러 가기 전에 유리가 읽고 있는 책을 읽고 싶
   다고 하였다.
12 친구에게 피아노를 연주해 보아도 되는지를 묻는 말을 쓰는 것
   이 적절하다. 'Do you mind if ~?'는 허락을 구할 때 쓰이는
   표현이다.
13 내용을 정확히 이해하고, 조건에 맞게 질문에 답하도록 한다. (1)
   관계대명사의 계속적 용법을 활용한다. (2) It ~ that 강조구문
   의 형식으로 영작하되 which를 반드시 사용해야 하기 때문에
   which를 놓치지 않아야 한다.
14 '계속적' 용법의 관계대명사이다. ①, ⑤번은 전치사의 목적어
   역할(한정적 용법), ②, ④번은 의문대명사 which이다.
15 and we will donate them = , which we will donate
16 'Philip이 그 욕망을 갖고 그 부자 노인을 도운 것은 아니었다.
   (부자 노인을 도왔지만, 그 욕망 때문은 아니었다)'라는 내용에
   맞게 'It wasn't ~ that'을 적절히 활용한다.
17 (1) for myself: 혼자서(남의 도움 없이) (2) so smart that ~:
   너무나 영리해서 그 결과 ~
18 show는 to를 사용하여 3형식으로 고친다.
19 Odin을 위한 보물은 아홉 번째 밤이 될 때마다 '8개의 금팔찌를
   더' 만들어 내는 금팔찌였고, Frey를 위한 보물은 어떤 말보다
   도 그의 마차를 '더 빨리' 끌 수 있는 돼지였다. Thor를 위한 보
   물은 묠니르라는 망치였는데, Thor가 그것을 던질 때마다 그것
   은 항상 그에게 '되돌아 올 것'이었고 어떤 것에 의해서도 부서지
   지 않을 것이었다.
20 ① It은 The first treasure was for Odin을 가리키고, 주격
   관계대명사 that이 이끄는 관계대명사절이 that 앞에 오는 명사
   a spear를 수식하고 있다.
21 Loki가 가장 마음에 들어 한 보물이 무엇이었는지는 대답할
   수 없다. ① It was a spear. ② It was a big ship. ③ For
   Thor. ④ Because they thought it would protect the
   gods from their enemies.
22 아내의 아름다운 금발머리가 사라졌기 때문에 '속상하다'고 하는
   것이 적절하다. upset: 속상한, ② 지루한, ③ 안도하는, 다행으
   로 여기는, ⑤ 무관심한
23 이유를 나타내는 접속사를 쓰고, 선행사가 the sons of Ivaldi
   이므로 대명사를 they로 쓰는 것이 적절하다.
24 위 글은 '가야의 건국 신화'이다. ① 우화, ② 논픽션(소설이나
   허구의 이야기가 아닌 전기·역사·사건 기록 따위), ③ 공상 소
   설, ④ 공상 과학 소설[영화]
25 김수로왕은 황금 상자에 담겨 하늘에서부터 내려온 '여섯 개의
   알들' 중 하나에서 태어났다. 12일 뒤에 여섯 개의 알들은 여섯
   명의 소년들로 변했고, 그들이 '여섯 가야'의 왕이 되었다. 김수
   로왕이 그들 중 가장 강했다.

22 정답 및 해설

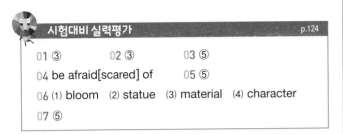

Plants That Feed Us

시험대비 실력평가
p.124

01 ③ 02 ③ 03 ⑤
04 be afraid[scared] of 05 ⑤
06 (1) bloom (2) statue (3) material (4) character
07 ⑤

01 주어진 단어는 반의어 관계에 있다. 모두 유의어지만 ③번은 반의어이다. ① 비슷한 ② 필수적인 ③ 진실 – 거짓 ④ 흔치 않은 ⑤ 이점

02 '소수의 사람들에 의해서만 알려진 사실이며 다른 누구에게도 말해지지 않는 어떤 것'은 '비밀(secret)'이다.

03 ⑤ composer라고 쓰는 것이 적절하다.

04 be scared of 혹은 be afraid of: ~을 두려워하다

05 각각 pilot, soak, crush, actor의 영영풀이이다. 따라서 tour가 적절하다.

06 bloom: (꽃을) 피우다, 피다, statue: 동상, material: 재료, 물질, character: 등장인물

07 '~ 옆에'라는 의미의 by는 교통수단과 함께 쓰여 '~로'라는 의미로도 쓰일 수 있으며 동명사와 함께 쓰이면 '~함으로써'라는 의미로도 쓰인다.

서술형 시험대비
p.125

01 inventor
02 (1) expect (2) statue (3) insect
03 (1) After graduation, I got a job with NASA as a researcher.
   (2) The interviewer asked me about my future plans.
   (3) I am proud of being a cartoonist.
04 (A) have (B) keep (C) take
05 (1) is good for (2) no longer (3) In addition
   (4) by making (5) poisonous material
06 inventor

01 동사에 '-er'이나 '-or'을 붙여서 명사를 만든 것이다. invent는 직업을 나타내는 명사로 쓰기 위하여 '-or'을 붙인다.

02 (1) 어떤 일이 일어날 것이라고 믿다 (2) 돌이나 금속 같은 단단한 재료로 만들어진 사람이나 동물의 이미지 (3) 여섯 개의 다리를 가진 파리나 개미 같은 작은 생물

03 researcher: 조사원, interviewer: 면접관, cartoonist: 만화가

04 have a fever: 열이 있다, have difficulty in Ving: V 하는데 어려움이 있다, keep ~ a secret: ~을 비밀로 하다, keep a diary: 일기를 쓰다, take medicine: 약을 먹다, take a walk: 산책하다

05 (1) be good for: ~에 유익하다 (2) no longer: 더 이상 ~가 아닌 (3) in addition: 게다가 (4) by Ving: V함으로써 (5) poisonous: 독성이 강한, material: 재료, 물질

06 에디슨이 롤모델이며 무언가를 발명하는 것을 좋아한다고 하였으므로 '발명가(inventor)'를 빈칸에 쓰는 것이 적절하다.

Conversation
교과서

핵심 Check
p.126~127

1 ④
2 What do you think I should do?

01 Bomi에게 약이 있는지 물어보는 것으로 보아 거기에 대한 대답으로 Bomi는 '왜? 무슨 문제가 있니?'라고 다시 물어보는 것이 적절하다. 'Where have you been?'은 '어디 갔다 왔니?'라는 뜻이다.

교과서 대화문 익히기

Check(√) True or False
p.128

1 F 2 T 3 F 4 T 5 T

교과서 확인학습
p.130~131

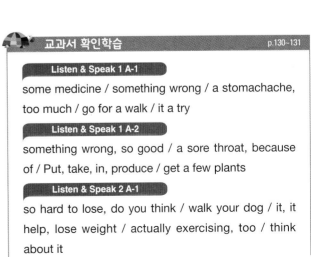

Listen & Speak 1 A-1

some medicine / something wrong / a stomachache, too much / go for a walk / it a try

Listen & Speak 1 A-2

something wrong, so good / a sore throat, because of / Put, take, in, produce / get a few plants

Listen & Speak 2 A-1

so hard to lose, do you think / walk your dog / it, it help, lose weight / actually exercising, too / think about it

How are, doing, growing / gotten, a few, so far, I should do / Where / In / need about, a day / move, over

is something wrong, quiet / a bit tired, little / something late / on, until, what I often do / that's why, before / getting worse, I should do / eating lots of carrots, rich in vitamin, keep, healthy / see

Is, wrong / a little, watched, for / why, red eyes, putting, over

wrong, worried / broke, plate, do you think / Tell, understand / hope, right

---

시험대비 기본평가
p.132

01 ④　　　　02 ③　　　　03 ③

04 She has watched a movie on her phone for two hours.

01 빈칸에는 안부를 묻는 말이 들어가는 것이 자연스럽다. 따라서 ④번이 적절하다.

02 밑줄 친 부분은 조언을 구하는 말이므로 ③번이 가장 적절하다.

03 눈이 충혈되었다는 것으로 보아 tired가 가장 적절하다.

04 소녀는 자신의 휴대전화로 두 시간 동안 영화를 보았다.

시험대비 실력평가
p.133~134

01 ③　　　　02 ③　　　　03 ④

04 It's because he has a stomachache.

05 ④　　　　06 ③　　　　07 ②

08 (C)–(A)–(D)–(B)

09 what should I do to say sorry to Mina?

10 She has the tomato pot in the kitchen.

11 ④　　　　12 ⑤

13 He watches a movie on his phone until late at night.

01 조언을 구하고 조언을 제공하는 대화를 나누고 있으므로 ③번이 가장 적절하다.

02 안부를 묻는 말에 '좋다'고 답하고 목이 아프다는 말이 이어지고 있으므로 어색하다.

03 밑줄 친 (A)는 시도해 보겠다는 의미로, 걷는 것이 어떠냐는 소녀의 조언을 시도해 보겠다는 말이다.

04 소년이 소녀에게 약이 있느냐고 물은 이유는 복통 때문이다.

---

05 (A)는 조언을 구하는 말이므로 ④번이 가장 적절하다.

06 help는 목적격보어로 to부정사나 동사원형을 취한다. 따라서 to lose 혹은 lose라고 쓰는 것이 적절하다.

07 소년의 문제에 소녀는 개를 산책시키라고 조언해 주고 있으므로 ②번을 답할 수 있다.

08 (C) 무슨 일이냐고 묻자 (A) 엄마가 가장 좋아하는 접시를 깼다며 조언을 구하자 (D) 엄마에게 사실대로 말씀드리라며 조언하고 (B) 이에 대한 답이 이어지는 것이 가장 자연스럽다.

09 'What should I do to ~?'는 조언을 구하는 표현이다. '미나에게 사과하기 위해서 무엇을 해야 할까?'라고 묻는 것이 적절하다.

10 소녀는 토마토 화분을 주방에 둔다고 하였다.

11 소년은 소녀에게 조언을 하고 있으므로 ④번이 대화의 내용과 일치한다.

12 눈을 건강하게 유지하는 데 도움을 주기 때문에 당근과 토마토를 먹으라고 권하는 것이 적절하다.

13 수호는 새벽 2시까지 휴대폰으로 영화를 본다고 하였으므로 수호가 요즈음에 종종 하는 것은 밤늦게까지 영화를 보는 것이라고 답할 수 있다.

서술형 시험대비
p.135

01 What do you think I should do?

02 (A) have　(B) take　(C) get

03 the fine dust, sore

04 She is likely to buy a few plants.

05 What's wrong with you?

06 It's because she has watched a movie on her phone for two hours.

07 (C)–(E)–(A)–(D)–(B)　　　08 is something wrong

01 의견을 묻는 말로 What do you think I should do?를 쓸 수 있다.

02 (A) '~가 아프다'고 말할 때에는 'have+병명'을 쓰는 것이 일반적이다. (B) 'take ~ in'은 '~을 흡수하다'는 의미이며, (C)에서 'get'은 '사다, 구하다'라는 의미로 쓰인다.

03 Jane은 미세먼지가 자신의 목을 아프게 한다고 생각한다.

04 식물을 몇 개 사야겠다고 하였다.

05 무슨 일이 있는지를 묻는 말이다. 'What's wrong with you?'와 그 의미가 같다.

06 소녀가 피곤한 이유는 휴대전화기로 두 시간 동안 영화를 봤기 때문이다.

07 (C) 약이 있냐고 물음 - (E) 무슨 문제가 있는지 되물음 - (A) 약이 필요한 이유를 설명 - (D) 조언 제공 - (B) 조언을 시도해 보겠다고 말함

08 슬퍼 보이는 친구에게 안부를 묻는 말이 들어가는 것이 적절하다. 'What's the matter?'라고 써도 무방하다.

1 (1) named (2) broken **2** (1) did (2) do

01 (1) using → used (2) called → call
(3) eats → eating (4) writing → written

02 ② **03** ②

04 (1) Most Americans did think that tomatoes were poisonous.
(2) The pictures taken by Lily were impressive.

01 (1) 당근이 전쟁에서 사용될 수도 있다는 수동이므로 used가 적절하다. (2) 강조의 조동사 뒤에는 동사 원형을 쓴다. (3) 능동의 현재분사가 뒤에서 꾸미는 것이 적절하다. (4) 라틴어로 쓰여진 편지이므로, written이 적절하다.

02 주어가 복수이므로 동사를 강조할 때 do를 써야 한다.

03 싫증을 느끼는 것은 능동이 아니라 수동의 과거분사를 써야 한다.

04 (1) 주어가 복수이므로 동사를 강조할 때 do를 써야 한다. (2) 명사를 뒤에서 꾸미는 과거분사의 활용에 유의하여, 단어를 배열한다.

01 ③ **02** ①

03 (1) were many people watching
(2) built by my grandfather is

04 ② **05** making → made **06** ⑤

07 ②

08 Potato juice mixed with honey makes your skin soft.

09 ③ **10** ② **11** ③

12 ①, ④, ⑤ **13** ④ **14** ⑤ **15** ④

16 (1) writing → written (2) mixing → mixed
(3) cry → crying

17 ④ **18** ①, ③, ⑤ **19** ③

20 (A) made (B) known (C) using (D) named
(E) meaning (F) covered

21 ② **22** invented, using

01 (1) 꽃을 꺾는 소년(능동) (2) 여행에 쓰인 돈(수동) (3) 두려워하는(수동) 등에 적절하게 분사를 활용한다.

02 첫 번째 빈칸은 동사 강조의 does이며, 두 번째 빈칸은 본동사이다. do the laundry: 빨래를 하다

03 분사가 명사의 뒤에서 꾸며주는 것을 적절히 활용한다. (1)은 watching the pet contest가 people을 꾸며주고(능동), (2)는 built by my grandfather가 the swimming pool을 뒤에서 꾸민다.(수동)

04 ② Be로 시작하는 명령문도 Do로 강조 가능하다. ① warned → warn, ③ changed → change, ④ believed → believe, ⑤ looks → look

05 베트남에서 제조된 셔츠이므로 과거분사가 적절하다.

06 '그는 잃어버린 아이를 정말로 찾아냈다.'라는 문장과 '잃어버린 아이를 찾을 수 있었다.'라는 문장은 다르다.

07 ②는 try의 목적어로 쓰인 동명사이고, 나머지는 모두 명사를 앞 또는 뒤에서 꾸며 주는 현재분사이다.

08 분사가 명사 뒤에서 꾸며주는 것을 활용한다. 수동이므로 mixed를 사용하고, 본동사는 makes를 쓴다.

09 첫 번째 빈칸은 강조의 does 또는 did를 쓸 수 있다. 두 번째 빈칸은 시제가 과거이기 때문에 did만 가능.

10 ⓐ 타는 불, ⓑ 노래하는 학생들 모두 '능동'의 의미를 갖고 있으며, 명사를 앞, 뒤에서 꾸며주고 있다.

11 강조의 did를 쓰면 동사는 원형이 와야 한다.

12 ① 토마토를 먹고 있는 소녀이므로 eats → eating ④ '거짓말을 하고 있었다'는 뜻의 과거진행형이므로 현재분사가 필요. lied → lying, ⑤ 그녀의 가족을 만난 것이면, meeting her family가, 그녀의 가족이 만난 사람들이면 meeting → met으로 하는 것이 적절하다.

13 11년 전 과거의 일이므로 does를 did로 바꿔야 한다.

14 ① 수동의 의미이므로, 과거분사 surrounded가 온다. ② 명사를 뒤에서 꾸미는 분사를 활용한다. 능동이므로 sat → sitting ③ using → used ④ 남겨진 케이크가 없는 것이므로 leaving → left가 적절하다.

15 과거 시제를 강조하는 'did+동사원형'을 이용한다.

16 (1) 쓰인 책(수동) (2) 꿀과 섞인 감자 주스(수동) (3) 우는 아기들(능동)

17 동사 강조의 do(does/did)를 찾는다.

18 ① 감동적인 장면들 touched → touching ③ 신나는 날 excited → exciting ⑤ 시간을 알려주는 shown → showing

19 ① do → does ② made → make ④ plays → play ⑤ called → call

20 (A) 만들어진 (B) ~로 알려진 (C) (당근)을 이용하여 (D) ~라고 이름 불리는 (E) ~를 의미하는 (F) ~로 덮인

21 동사 강조의 do(does/did)를 찾는다.

22 어법에 맞게 배열하면, 'This is a battery invented from the idea of using the characteristic of sunflowers.'이다. invented는 과거분사, using은 동명사이다.

01 (1) Sofia did find her missing cat.

   (2) Gordon does know many K-pop songs.

   (3) Grace did write these essays last week.

02 (1) girl standing across the street

   (2) played by the band on the stage

   (3) wearing a red shirt

03 (1) did build   (2) do think   (3) did write

04 (1) This is the thing placed on the wall.

   (2) Sarah is the one wearing glasses.

   (3) Mary is erasing the scores written on the board.

   (4) I do love Susan, the girl drinking water.

   (5) The news was really shocking.

05 (1) with the crying baby

   (2) the birds flying southwards

   (3) an illegally parked taxi

06 (A) sitting   (B) standing   (C) closed

07 (1) Alex himself called you yesterday.

   (2) It was you that Alex called yesterday.

   (3) Alex did call you yesterday.

   (4) It was yesterday that Alex called you.

08 As Ethan did feel a headache

09 (1) does   (2) hidden   (3) kill   (4) called

10 place a cup of crushed tomatoes

---

01 수와 시제 등에 유의하여 do/does/did를 활용하되 강조를 위해 사용한 do 뒤에는 본동사의 원형이 와야 한다.

02 명사의 뒤에서 꾸미는 분사 활용 (1) 서 있는 소녀(능동) (2) 연주되는 음악(수동) (3) 셔츠를 입은 사람(능동)

03 수와 시제 등에 유의하여 do를 활용하되 do 뒤에는 동사 원형이 와야 한다.

04 명사를 뒤에서 꾸며주는 분사를 활용한다. 능동/진행은 현재분사, 수동/완료는 과거분사를 쓴다. (1) 벽에 놓이는 물건 placed (2) 안경을 쓰고 있는 사람 wearing (3) 보드에 쓰여진 점수 written (4) 물을 마시는 소녀 drinking (5) 충격적인 뉴스 shocking

05 (1) 울고 있는 아기 (2) 남쪽으로 날아가고 있는 새들 (3) 불법으로 주차된 택시(부정관사 an에 유의한다)

06 (A) 능동 (B) 능동 (C) 'with+목적어' 뒤에 나오는 '현재분사/과거분사' 여부는 목적어의 '능동/수동'을 따진다. 목적어가 eyes이므로, 수동의 과거분사 closed가 적절하다.

07 (1) himself를 문미로 보내도 된다. (2) (대)명사와 부사는 'It ~ that 강조 구문'으로 강조 가능하다. (3) 'did+동사원형'으로 동사를 강조한다. (4) 부사 yesterday는 'It ~ that 강조 구문'으로 강조한다.

08 동사 강조의 'do'를 시제에 맞게 활용한다. 과거시제이므로 did를

쓰는 것에 유의한다.

09 (1) does로 강조 (2) 땅에 숨겨진 폭탄이므로 hide의 과거분사 hidden이 적절하다. (3) 강조의 did 뒤에는 원형동사 kill이 적절하다. (4) '~라고 불리는'이라는 표현은 call의 과거분사를 쓴다.

10 으깬 토마토가 되려면 crush의 과거분사형이 명사의 앞에서 수식하는 형태가 된다. 명령문이므로 place로 시작하는 것이 적절하다.

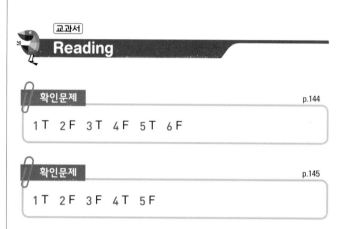

Reading

1 T   2 F   3 T   4 F   5 T   6 F

1 T   2 F   3 F   4 T   5 F

01 Hidden

02 Spinach

03 cartoon character

04 by eating spinach

05 became popular

06 the spinach capital, a statue

07 Although, does have

08 one of the ten healthiest foods

09 in a surprising way

10 also absorbs, from

11 hidden in the ground

12 with sensors on their leaves

13 soak up, light up

14 World War II

15 defeated, during, by using

16 keep, secret, an article

17 improved their night vision

18 than before

19 by eating

20 which does keep

21 may actually be used

22 turn, into

23 can even be used

24 has already been used

25 Scariest

26 are good for

27 Up until, poisonous

28 named, safe to eat

29 a basket of, watching

30 happened to

31 have enjoyed eating

32 no longer, scared of

33 keep, away from, place, crushed

34 come near

1 Hidden Stories about Plants

2 Popeye and the Great Spinach

3 Popeye is a world-famous cartoon character.

4 He gets his super power by eating spinach.

5 When Popeye became popular in the 1930s in the United States, a lot of children began to eat spinach.

6 Crystal City in Texas, which is called the spinach capital of the world, even built a statue of Popeye.

7 Although eating spinach will not give us super powers, spinach does have a lot of nutrients.

8 It is actually considered one of the ten healthiest foods on the planet.

9 Spinach can be used in a surprising way.

10 When it absorbs water, spinach also absorbs many other things from the soil.

11 Some scientists have used this characteristic of spinach to find bombs hidden in the ground.

12 They make special spinach plants with sensors on their leaves.

13 When these plants soak up traces from bombs, the sensors light up.

14 Carrots in World War II

15 In 1940, the Royal Air Force defeated German fighters during World War II by using a radar system.

16 The British government wanted to keep this technology a secret, so it published an article in the newspaper.

17 It said that British pilots improved their night vision because they ate a lot of carrots.

18 Everybody believed the story and began to eat a lot more carrots than before.

19 Can we really improve night vision by eating lots of carrots?

20 Not really, but carrots contain a lot of vitamin A, which does keep our eyes healthy.

21 In the future, carrots may actually be used in wars.

22 Scottish researchers have discovered a way to turn carrots into a very strong and light material.

23 It can even be used to make battleships.

24 This new material has already been used to make snowboards and bicycles.

25 Tomatoes, the Scariest Vegetables

26 We all know that tomatoes are good for our health.

27 Up until the 1800s, however, most Americans thought that tomatoes were poisonous.

28 In 1820, a man named Robert Johnson wanted to prove that tomatoes were safe to eat.

29 So, he ate a basket of tomatoes in front of many people watching him.

30 They all expected him to die, but nothing happened to him.

31 Ever since then, Americans have enjoyed eating tomatoes.

32 We are no longer afraid of tomatoes, but some insects are still scared of them.

33 If you want to keep insects away from your room, place a bowl of crushed tomatoes in a corner of your room.

34 Insects will not come near the tomatoes.

01 ④   02 ②   03 ④   04 ①

05 시금치가 물을 흡수할 때, 시금치는 흙으로부터 다른 많은 것들도 흡수하는 것

06 go out → light up   07 ④

08 the British government   09 ②

10 carrots may actually be used in wars

11 ②, ④   12 ③   13 ⑤   14 ③

15 (A) crushed tomatoes   (B) scared[afraid]

16 Some / ground   17 ②, ③, ④, ⑤

18 absorb   19 (A) called   (B) capital   (C) does

20 ③   21 He gets it by eating spinach.

22 tomatoes   23 died → didn't die   24 ④

01 ④번 다음 문장의 It에 주목한다. 주어진 문장의 spinach를 받고 있으므로 ④번이 적절하다.

02 ⓐ와 ②: 캐릭터, 등장인물, ① 성격, ③ 문자, ④ 특징, ⑤ 인격

03 시금치를 먹는 것이 우리에게 초인적인 힘을 주지는 않는다.

04 ⓐ absorb A from B: B로부터 A를 흡수하다, ⓑ with sensors on their leaves: 잎에 감지기가 있는

05 시금치의 이 특성은 바로 앞 문장의 내용을 가리킨다.

06 시금치의 특성을 사용하여 땅에 숨겨진 폭탄을 찾는다고 했기 때문에, 이 특별한 시금치가 폭탄의 흔적을 흡수하면 감지기가 '빛난다'고 해야 하므로 light up으로 고치는 것이 적절하다. go out: (불·전깃불이) 꺼지다, light up: (빛·색으로) 환하게 되다

07 본문 끝 부분에 '실제로 그렇지는 않지만(야간 시력을 높일 수는 없지만), 당근은 많은 비타민 A를 함유하는데, 그것은 정말로 우리 눈을 건강하게 유지해 준다.'라는 말이 있으므로, 야간 '시력'

이라고 하는 것이 적절하다. vision: 시력, 시야, ① (이전의 것·비슷한 종류의 다른 것들과 약간 다른) 판[형태], ② 촉각, ③ 청력 ⑤ 후각

08 '영국 정부'를 가리킨다.

09 이 글은 '영국 공군이 제2차 세계 대전에서 독일군을 패배시킨 레이더 시스템을 비밀로 하려고, 영국 비행사들이 당근을 많이 먹어 야간 시력이 좋아졌다는 신문 기사를 실었는데, 당근이 야간 시력을 높일 수는 없지만 실제로 많은 비타민 A를 함유하고 있어서 우리 눈을 건강하게 유지해 준다.'는 내용의 글이므로, 제목으로는 ②번 '제2차 세계대전에서의 당근'이 적절하다.

10 추측을 나타내는 조동사 may를 사용하여 수동태로 쓰는 것이 적절하다.

11 ⓑ와 ②, ④: 완료 용법, ① 계속 용법, ③ 경험 용법, ⑤ 결과 용법

12 스코틀랜드의 연구원들은 어떻게 당근을 매우 강하고 가벼운 물질로 바꾸는지는 대답할 수 없다. ① Yes. ② A way to turn carrots into a very strong and light material. ④ Yes. ⑤ Yes, it has already been used to make snowboards and bicycles.

13 앞에 나오는 내용과 상반되는 내용이 뒤에 이어지므로 however가 가장 적절하다.① 그 결과, ② 뿐만 아니라, 더욱이, ③ 즉, 말하자면 ④ 예를 들면

14 이 글은 '1820년에 Robert Johnson이 토마토가 먹기에 안전하다는 것을 증명하기 전까지는 대부분의 미국인들은 토마토에 독성이 있다고 생각했다는 것과 몇몇 곤충들은 여전히 토마토를 무서워한다.'는 내용의 글이므로, 주제로는 ③번 '토마토에 관한 근거 없는 믿음과 진실'이 적절하다. myth: (많은 사람들의) 근거 없는 믿음

15 몇몇 곤충들은 여전히 토마토를 '무서워해서' 토마토 가까이 오지 않을 것이므로, 만약 '으깬 토마토' 한 그릇을 방구석에 놓아두면 곤충들이 방에 들어오지 않게 할 수 있다.

16 시금치의 놀라운 용도는 '몇몇 과학자들이 시금치의 특성을 사용하여 땅에 숨겨진 폭탄을 찾는 것'을 가리킨다.

17 ⓑ와 ①: 부사적 용법, ②, ③, ⑤: 명사적 용법, ④: 형용사적 용법

18 soak up = absorb: 흡수하다, 빨아들이다

19 (A) 시금치 수도라고 '불린다'고 해야 하므로 called가 적절하다. (B) 시금치 '수도'라고 해야 하므로 capital이 적절하다. capital: 수도, capitol: 미국 국회 의사당, (C) 시금치가 정말로 많은 영양분을 가지고 있다는 것은 일반적인 사실에 해당하므로 현재시제로 쓰는 것이 적절하다.

20 ⓐ와 ①, ③, ④: 동명사, ②, ⑤: 현재분사

21 Popeye는 '시금치를 먹음으로써' 초인적인 힘을 얻는다.

22 '토마토'를 가리킨다.

23 Robert Johnson은 그를 지켜보는 많은 사람들 앞에서 한 바구니의 토마토를 먹었고, 모두 그가 죽을 것이라고 예상했

으나 '그에게는 아무 일도 일어나지 않았다.' against one's expectations: 예상과 달리

24 무슨 곤충들이 토마토를 무서워하는지는 알 수 없다. ① They thought that tomatoes were poisonous. ② He wanted to prove that tomatoes were safe to eat. ③ They have enjoyed eating tomatoes since Robert Johnson proved that they were safe to eat. ⑤ Insects will not come near the tomatoes.

서술형 시험대비
p.154~155

01 As → Although 또는 Though
02 actually considers → is actually considered
03 (A) cartoon character   (B) eating spinach
04 ⓐ be used   ⓑ hidden
05 ⓒ Some scientists   ⓓ special spinach plants
06 (A) sensors   (B) bombs
07 (A) defeated   (B) during   (C) healthy
08 World War Two 또는 the second World War
09 An article
10 (1) 영국 비행사들이 당근을 많이 먹어 야간 시력이 좋아졌다.
   (2) 당근은 많은 비타민 A를 함유하는데, 그것은 정말로 우리 눈을 건강하게 유지해 준다.
11 Ever since then, Americans have enjoyed eating tomatoes.
12 any longer[more]   13 crushing → crushed
14 Because he wanted to prove that tomatoes were safe to eat.

---

01 '비록' 시금치를 먹는 것이 우리에게 초인적인 힘을 주지는 않지만, 시금치는 정말로 많은 영양분을 가지고 있다고 해야 하므로, Although 또는 Though로 고치는 것이 적절하다.

02 '가장 건강한 식품 10개 중 하나로 여겨진다.'고 해야 하므로 수동태로 쓰는 것이 적절하다.

03 시금치를 먹음으로써 초인적인 힘을 얻는 Popeye는 세계적으로 유명한 만화 캐릭터다. Popeye 덕분에, 1930년대 미국의 많은 어린이들이 시금치를 먹기 시작했다. 동사 begin은 목적어로 to부정사와 동명사를 모두 다 사용할 수 있다.

04 ⓐ 시금치는 놀라운 용도로 '사용될 수 있다'고 해야 하므로, 수동태로 쓰는 것이 적절하다. ⓑ 땅에 '숨겨진' 폭탄이라고 해야 하므로 hidden으로 쓰는 것이 적절하다.

05 ⓒ '몇몇 과학자들' ⓓ '특별한 시금치'를 가리킨다.

06 시금치는 흙으로부터 물뿐만 아니라 다른 많은 것들도 흡수한다. 잎에 '감지기'가 있는 특별한 시금치가 폭탄의 흔적을 흡수하면, 감지기가 빛나서 땅속에 있는 '폭탄'을 찾도록 도와준다.

07 (A) 영국 공군이 독일군을 '패배시킨' 것이므로 defeated가 적

절하다. (B) '제2차 세계 대전에서'라고 해야 하므로 during이 적절하다. during+기간을 나타내는 명사, while+주어+동사, (C) keep의 목적격보어에 해당하기 때문에 형용사 healthy가 적절하다.

08 'World War+기수', 또는 'the 서수+World War'로 읽는 것이 적절하다.

09 신문의 '기사'를 가리킨다.

10 영국 공군이 제2차 세계 대전에서 독일군을 패배시킨 레이더 시스템을 비밀로 하려고, '영국 비행사들이 당근을 많이 먹어 야간 시력이 좋아졌다'는 신문 기사를 실었는데, 당근이 야간 시력을 높일 수는 없지만 '실제로 많은 비타민 A를 함유하고 있어서 우리 눈을 건강하게 유지해 준다.'

11 과거의 일이 현재까지 영향을 미쳐 현재와 관련이 있을 때 사용하는 현재완료시제로 쓰는 것이 적절하다.

12 no longer = not ~ any longer[more]: 더 이상 … 아닌

13 토마토가 으깨지는 것이므로 crushed가 적절하다.

14 토마토가 먹기에 안전하다는 것을 증명하기를 원했기 때문이다.

p.157~161

영역별 핵심문제

01 ⑤   02 ③

03 (1) The magician turned the hat into a rabbit.
    (2) What do you advise me to do?
    (3) Why don't you get some fresh air?

04 ③   05 ③

06 (1) the director, the actor, surprising
    (2) visitors were scared of

07 ③   08 ⑤번 → a few   09 ⑤

10 ②   11 move it over to the window

12 ③   13 ③   14 ④   15 ①

16 (1) ate a basket of tomatoes in front of many
       people watching him
    (2) did eat a basket of tomatoes in front of many
       people who[that] were watching him

17 ④   18 ②, ⑤   19 (1) did   (2) found

20 ③   21 ③   22 ②, ⑤

23 wanting to prove that tomatoes were safe to eat
   was Robert Johnson

24 ③

25 It is actually considered one of the ten healthiest
   foods on the planet.

26 (A) spinach   (B) nutrients   (C) healthiest

27 ②   28 a radar system   29 ④

01 모두 유의어이지만 ⑤번은 반의어로 '이기다 – 굴복하다'라는 의미로 쓰인다.

02 각각 ① interviewer ② meal ③ nutrient ④ ingredient

⑤ flavor를 풀이한 말이다.

03 (1) turn A into B: A를 B로 바꾸다 (2) advise+목적어+to V: 목적어가 V하도록 조언하다 (3) get some fresh air: 신선한 공기를 마시다

04 trace는 '흔적'이라는 명사와 '추적하다'라는 의미의 동사로 쓰인다. 따라서 ③번이 가장 적절하다.

05 주어진 문장의 밑줄 친 부분은 '수도'라는 의미로 쓰였다. capital은 그 외에도 '자본', '대문자의'라는 의미로도 쓰인다.

06 (1) '놀라운'이라는 의미로 쓰이는 것은 surprising이다. (2) '~을 두려워하다'는 'be scared of' 혹은 'be afraid of'를 쓴다.

07 자신의 잘못에 대한 조언을 구하는 말이 들어가는 것이 적절하다.

08 셀 수 있는 명사를 수식하는 'a few'를 쓰는 것이 적절하다.

09 소년은 소녀에게 방 안에 식물을 두라고 권하고 있다.

10 주어진 문장은 조언을 구하는 말이다. 지금까지 토마토를 몇 개밖에 수확하지 못했다는 말을 하며 조언을 구하는 말을 하는 것이 가장 자연스럽다.

11 해석: 토마토 화분이 충분한 햇빛을 얻도록, 소녀는 화분을 창가로 옮길 것이다.

12 소년의 조언에 알겠다며 고마움을 표시하고 있으므로, 한 번 시도해 보겠다는 ③번이 가장 적절하다.

13 ① Popeye라고 '이름이 불리는' 것이므로 named가 적절하다. ② 그 농부들에 의해 '길러진 채소들'이 되어야 하므로 grown을 써야 한다. ④ 비타민 A를 '함유하고 있는' 것이므로 containing이 적절하다. ⑤ 파티에 '초대 받은 사람들'이므로 invited가 적절하다.

14 ① Vegetables가 복수이므로 do make가 적절하다. ② does say가 적절하다 ③ be동사와 상태를 나타내는 look 본동사가 같이 쓰였다. is를 생략하거나 does look으로 강조한다. ⑤ 과거동사 met을 강조할 때는 did meet이 적절하다.

15 첫 번째 문장에서 '사용될 것(수동)'을 뜻하므로 used가 적절하다. 두 번째 문장에서 '두려워하는'(수동)의 내용이므로 scared가 적절하다. be scary of로는 표현하지 않는다.

16 (1) 과거시제이므로 ate를 써야 하고, 명사를 뒤에서 꾸미는 현재분사 watching에 유의하여 영작한다. (2) ate의 강조는 did eat이며, 명사를 뒤에서 수식하는 분사의 앞에 '관계대명사+be동사'를 넣을 수 있다. who를 that으로 써도 된다.

17 do some laundry는 '빨래를 하다'라는 뜻으로 do는 본동사이다. 다른 문장들의 do는 강조를 위해 사용되었다.

18 ② be busy ~ing는 '~하느라 바쁘다'라는 뜻의 동명사의 관용적 표현이며, ⑤는 전치사 by의 목적어로 쓰인 동명사이다. 다른 문장들에서는 모두 현재분사로 사용되었다.

19 (1) 책 '어린 완자'는 3인칭 단수이고, 동사원형 make가 쓰였으므로, 강조의 does 또는 did가 가능하지만, 시제가 과거이므로 did가 적절하다. (2) 이집트의 Giza에서 발견된 pyramids(수동)이므로, 과거분사 found가 적절하다.

20 'with+A+형용사/분사' 형태는 A의 능동/수동 여부에 따라 현재분사 또는 과거분사를 활용한다. ③ with one's legs crossed '다리를 꼰 채로', crossing은 부적절하다.

21 ① (A) 강조 (B) 본동사 ② (A) 본동사 (B) 강조 ③ (A) 강조 (B) 강조 ④ (A) 본동사 (B) 강조 ⑤ (A) 의문문을 만드는 조동사 (B) 본동사

22 ② do likes → does like 또는 likes가 적절하다. ⑤ 강조의 did 뒤에는 동사 원형을 써야 한다.

23 분사가 명사의 앞, 뒤에서 꾸미는 것을 적절히 활용하여 영작한다.

24 ⓐ와 ③: 수도, ① 자본의(형용사), investment: 투자, ② 대문자, ④ 자본금, 자금, ⑤ 사형에 처해야 할(형용사), sentence: 선고하다

25 one of the ten healthiest foods: 가장 건강한 식품 10개 중 하나, 수량형용사 ten을 성상 형용사(사물의 성질, 상태, 종류를 나타내는 형용사) healthiest보다 먼저 쓰는 것이 적절하다.

26 '시금치'를 먹는 것으로 우리가 초인적인 힘을 얻지는 못하지만, 시금치는 정말로 많은 '영양분'을 가지고 있다. 실제로 사람들은 그것을 지구상에서 '가장 건강한' 식품 10개 중 하나로 여긴다.

27 주어진 문장의 It에 주목한다. ②번 앞 문장의 an article을 받고 있으므로 ②번이 적절하다.

28 '레이더 시스템'을 가리킨다.

29 실제로 당근을 많이 먹어서 야간 시력을 높일 수 있는 것은 아니라고 했다.

단원별 예상문제

01 ③　　　　**02** ⑤　　　　**03** ③

04 Do you still keep in touch with your friends?

05 (D)–(A)–(C)–(B)　　　　**06** ⑤

07 What about telling her the truth?

08 It's because he broke his mom's favorite plate.

09 ④　　　　**10** ⑤　　　　**11** ③, ⑤, ⑦

12 ①, ②, ⑥, ⑦　　　　**13** ③

14 ①, ③

15 eating spinach won't give us super powers, spinach does have a lot of nutrients

16 Although eating spinach will not give super powers to us

17 ⑤

18 (1) 시금치를 먹으면 초인적인 힘을 얻는다.
(2) 시금치는 정말로 많은 영양분을 가지고 있고, 실제로 지구상에서 가장 건강한 식품 10개 중 하나로 여겨진다.

19 making → make

20 (A) strong and light　(B) carrots

21 ③　　　　**22** ④

23 a man named Robert Johnson wanted to prove that tomatoes were safe to eat

24 ②　　　　**25** ①

26 (1) 혈압을 낮춰 심장을 건강하게 유지시켜 준다.
(2) 피부 문제를 해결해 준다.
(3) 살이 빠지도록 도와준다.

01 ①, ②, ④, ⑤는 동사에 '-er'이나 '-or'을 붙여서 사람을 나타내는 명사로 쓰였으나 cooker는 '주방기구'의 뜻으로 사람을 나타내지 않는다.

02 keep away from: ~으로부터 멀어지다

03 '책, 연극, 영화 등에 등장하는 사람'은 '등장인물(character)'이다.

04 keep in touch (with): (~와) 연락하고 지내다

05 (D) 무슨 문제가 있냐고 물음 - (A) 자신의 문제를 말함 - (C) 조언을 제시함 - (B) 조언을 받아들임

06 조언을 구하는 말이 들어가는 것이 자연스러우므로 ⑤번은 적절하지 않다.

07 What about ~?: ~하는 것이 어때?

08 소년이 걱정스러워 보였던 이유는 그의 엄마가 가장 좋아하는 그릇을 깨트려서이다.

09 보미는 소년이 왜 약을 달라고 하는지 궁금해 하고 있으므로 ④번이 대화 내용과 일치한다.

10 Make sure는 that절을 이끈다. 따라서 'Make sure that you take it to the police station.'이라고 말하는 것이 적절하다.

11 명사를 꾸미는 분사가 다른 어구와 결합해서 뒤에서 꾸밀 때는 '관계대명사+be동사'가 생략된 것으로 볼 수 있다. 그러므로, 명사를 앞에서 꾸미거나 서술적 용법으로 사용된 분사를 찾으면, '관계대명사+be동사'가 생략된 것이 아닌 경우에 해당한다. ③, ⑦번은 서술적 용법으로, ⑤번은 명사 앞에서 수식하는 분사로 사용되었다.

12 ① are와 make 두 개의 동사가 같이 쓰였다. make만 쓰거나 강조의 do make로 하는 것이 적절하다. ②, ⑥ 강조의 do/does/did 뒤에는 원형동사를 써야 한다. ⑦ 'It ~ that 강조 구문'의 동사는 is와 was 둘 뿐이다.

13 ③번은 전치사의 목적어로 쓰인 동명사이다. 그 외에는 모두 명사의 뒤에서 꾸미는 분사로 사용되었다.

14 분사의 역할이 아니라 종류가 다른 두 개를 찾는 문제이다. ①, ③번만 과거분사로서 ① abandoned dogs, ③ make himself understood이며, 나머지는 모두 현재분사를 써야 한다. ③ smoke coming out, ④ kept him waiting, ⑤ the boy smiling at her

15 has를 강조할 때는 does have로 한다.

16 give는 to를 사용하여 3형식으로 고친다.

17 ⓑ와 ⑤: 강조의 조동사, ① 부정문의 조동사, ② 부사(구) 따위가 문두에 오면서 어순이 도치되는 경우에 쓰이는 조동사, ③

30 정답 및 해설

~을 하다(본동사), ④ 의문문의 조동사

18 비록 시금치를 먹는 것이 우리에게 초인적인 힘을 주지는 않지만, 시금치는 정말로 많은 영양분을 가지고 있고, 이것은 실제로 지구상에서 가장 건강한 식품 10개 중 하나로 여겨진다.

19 '전함을 만드는 데 사용될 수도 있다'라고 해야 하므로 to부정사의 부사적 용법(목적)이 되도록, make로 고치는 것이 적절하다. be used to ~ing: ~하는 데 익숙하다

20 그것은 스코틀랜드의 연구원들에 의해 '당근'을 재료로 하여 만들어진 매우 '강하고 가벼운' 물질이다.

21 이 글은 '미래에는, 당근이 실제로 전쟁에 이용될지도 모른다.'는 내용의 글이므로, 주제로는 ③번 '미래에 전쟁에서의 당근의 용도'가 적절하다.

22 주어진 문장의 They에 주목한다. ④번 앞 문장의 many people을 받고 있으므로 ④번이 적절하다.

23 safe to eat: 먹기에 안전한

24 1800년대까지 대부분의 미국인들은 토마토에 '독성이 있다'고 생각했다.

25 앞에 나오는 내용에 추가하는 내용이 뒤에 이어지므로 In addition이 가장 적절하다. ② 그러므로, ④ 그에 반해서

26 (3) 오랜 시간 동안 허기를 느끼지 않고 배부른 상태를 유지하게 하여 살이 빠지도록 도와준다. stay full: 허기를 느끼지 않고 배부른 상태를 유지하다

서술형 실전문제   p.166~167

01 It is so hard to lose weight.

02 lose weight   03 is something wrong

04 ⓐ surprising   ⓑ leaving   ⓒ eating   ⓓ covered
　 ⓔ written   ⓕ eating
　 이유: ⓒ와 ⓕ 두 개는 동명사이고, 나머지는 모두 분사이다.

05 (1) British pilots did eat a lot of carrots.
　 (2) Do place a bowl of crushed tomatoes in a corner of your room.
　 (3) People in Hong Kong do love freedom.

06 which does keep our eyes healthy

07 to die

08 (A) named   (B) watching   (C) happened

09 (1) 토마토에 독성이 있다.
　 (2) 토마토를 먹는 것을 즐겼다.

10 The British government wanted to keep this technology a secret, so it published an article in the newspaper.

11 British pilots improved their night vision because they ate a lot of carrots.

01 가주어 It과 진주어 to부정사구를 이용하여 문장을 쓸 수 있다. lose weight: 몸무게를 줄이다

02 소녀가 소년에게 개를 매일 산책시키라고 제안한 이유는 그렇게 하는 것이 소년이 살을 빼도록 도움을 줄 것이라고 생각하기 때문이다.

03 엄마에게 무슨 문제가 있는지 묻는 말이 들어가는 것이 적절하다. 'what's the matter'를 써도 좋다.

04 ⓐ '놀라운 방법'(능동) ⓑ '7시에 출발하는 기차'(능동) ⓒ '먹음'으로써, 전치사의 목적어로 쓰인 동명사 ⓓ '담쟁이로 덮인 건물 벽'(수동) ⓔ '에머슨에 의해 쓰여진 시'(수동) ⓕ '먹는 것'을 즐겨왔다. enjoy의 목적어로 쓰인 동명사

05 (1) 과거 시제이므로 did eat이 적절하다. (2) 명령문의 강조는 동사 앞에 Do를 쓴다. (3) 주어가 복수이고 현재시제이므로 do love로 강조한다.

06 선행사 vitamin A를 받으며, 접속사 역할까지 하는 관계대명사 which를 사용하고, 동사 keep을 강조하는 does를 이용해서 알맞게 배열한다.

07 expect+목적어+to부정사

08 (A) Robert Johnson이라는 '이름의(~라고 이름 지어진)' 남자라고 해야 하므로 named가 적절하다. (B) 그를 '지켜보는' 많은 사람들이라고 해야 하므로 watching이 적절하다. (C) happen은 수동태로 만들 수 없으므로 happened가 적절하다.

09 1800년대까지 대부분의 미국인들은 토마토에 독성이 있다고 생각했지만, Robert Johnson이 토마토가 먹기에 안전하다는 것을 증명한 이후로, 미국인들은 토마토를 먹는 것을 즐겼다.

10 keep+목적어+목적격보어: ~을 …한 상태로 유지시키다

11 영국 정부가 신문에 낸 기사의 내용을 가리킨다.

창의사고력 서술형 문제   p.168

|모범답안|

01 growing well, she has gotten only a few tomatoes, her advice, where she has the pot, in the kitchen, tomato plants need about 7 hours of sunlight a day, she will move the pot over to the window

02 (1) Unlike the man presenting the plan, the boss is sleeping in a chair.
　 (2) Unlike my sister reading a book on the sofa, I am cleaning the table.

03 (A) your health   (B) lower blood pressure
　 (C) skin problems   (D) soft and clear

단원별 모의고사   p.169~173

01 ④   02 ④   03 ④

04 (C)–(A)–(E)–(D)–(B)

05 ④　　　　06 fine dust, put some plants

07 ⑤　　　　08 ③

09 What do you think I should do?　　　10 ③

11 It's because they are rich in vitamin A, so they'll keep Suho's eyes healthy.

12 ⑤　　　　13 ⑤　　　　14 ③, ⑥　　　　15 ③

16 (1) This new material has already been used to make bicycles.

　　(2) Some scientists have used this characteristic of spinach to find bombs hidden in the ground.

17 ⑤

18 real person → world-famous cartoon character

19 spinach　　　　20 does keep

21 ②　　　　22 and it

23 ⓐ eighteen hundreds　ⓑ eighteen twenty

24 ①, ②, ④　25 ④　　　26 ②　　　27 ③, ⑤

28 By lowering blood pressure.

29 Garlic tea which[that] is mixed with honey makes you get better faster.

01 ① keep ~ a secret: ~을 비밀로 하다 ② keep away: 멀리하다 ③ keep in touch: 연락하다 ④ make use of: ~을 이용하다 ⑤ keep the change: 잔돈을 가지다

02 주어진 단어는 '명사-명사(행위자)'의 관계에 있다. ④번은 '형용사-명사'의 연결이다. economic: 경제의, 경제성이 있는 economist: 경제학자

03 defeat은 '~를 패배시키다'라는 의미이므로 '전투에서 이기는 것에 성공하지 못하다'는 적절한 풀이가 아니다.

04 (C) 체중을 줄이는 것이 힘들다고 말하며 조언을 요청함 (A) 개를 산책시키라고 조언함 (E) 그것이 어떻게 체중을 줄이는데 도움이 되는지 되물음 (D) 이에 대한 설명 (B) 생각해 보겠다고 말함

05 빈칸에는 상대를 걱정하며 안부를 묻는 말이 들어가는 것이 적절하다. ④번은 무엇을 잘못했는지를 묻는 말이다.

06 소녀는 미세먼지 때문에 목이 아프다고 생각하고, 이에 소년은 방 안에 식물을 두라고 조언하고 있다.

07 돈을 저축할 수 없다고 말하며 조언을 요청하고 있으므로 더 많은 옷을 사라는 조언은 적절하지 않다.

08 모두 선생님에게 도움을 요청하라는 의미이지만 ③번은 선생님이 너에게 도움을 요청하는 것을 확실히 하라는 의미이다.

09 조언을 구하는 말로 자주 쓰이는 표현은 'What do you think I should do?'이다.

10 새벽 2시까지 휴대 전화로 영화를 본 결과 눈이 충혈된 것이므로 'that's why'라고 쓰는 것이 적절하다.

11 Anna가 수호에게 당근과 토마토를 많이 먹어 보라고 한 이유는 그것들에 비타민 A가 많아서 눈을 건강하게 유지해 줄 것이기

때문이다.

12 수호가 휴대전화로 영화를 얼마나 오래 보는지 위 글을 읽고 답할 수 없다.

13 ⑤ included → including

14 ③, ⑥번이 주어진 문장의 밑줄 친 does와 같은 용법인 동사를 강조하는 do/did로 사용되었다. ①, ②, ④번은 모두 조동사로서 각각 ① 의문문, ② 부정문, ④ 명령문을 만들기 위해 사용됐다. ⑤, ⑦번은 본동사로 쓰였다.

15 ③번은 containing(현재분사)이 들어가야 하지만 주어진 문장과 나머지는 모두 수동의 의미로 명사를 뒤에서 꾸미는 과거분사가 들어가야 한다. *repellent: 방충제

16 (1) used는 과거분사의 서술 용법으로, (2) hidden은 과거분사의 한정 용법으로 명사 뒤에서 꾸미는 역할이다.

17 ⑤번만 현재완료시제에 사용되어 동사의 일부가 되었다. 나머지는 모두 형용사적 용법으로 사용된 과거분사이다. *crush: 즙음료

18 Popeye는 세계적으로 유명한 '만화 캐릭터'다.

19 '시금치'를 가리킨다.

20 조동사 does를 사용하여 고치는 것이 적절하다.

21 (A)와 ②: (신문·잡지의) 글, 기사, ① (같은 종류의 물건 중) 한 개, 한 가지, ③, ⑤: 물품, 물건, ④ (조약·계약 등의) 조항, 소목

22 계속적 용법의 관계대명사 = 접속사+대명사

23 연도는 두 단위씩 끊어서 읽는 것이 적절하다. 단, 2000년이 넘어가면 'two thousand+나머지 숫자'로 읽는 것이 적절하다. ⓐ의 경우는 끝부분을 hundreds로 읽으면 된다.

24 ⓒ와 ③, ⑤: 부사적 용법, ①, ④: 명사적 용법, ②: 형용사적 용법

25 이 글은 '요즘 우리는 토마토를 두려워하지 않지만, 1800년대까지 대부분의 미국인들은 토마토에 독성이 있다고 생각했고, 몇몇 곤충들은 여전히 그것을 무서워한다.'는 내용의 글이므로, 제목으로는 ④번 '토마토, 가장 무서운 채소'가 적절하다.

26 1800년대까지 대부분의 미국인들은 토마토에 '독성이 있다'고 생각했지만, Robert Johnson이 토마토가 먹기에 '안전하다'는 것을 증명하기를 원했다고 하는 것이 문맥상 적절하다. ① harmless: 해가 없는, ③ precious: 귀중한, harmful: 해로운, ⑤ evil: 사악한

27 ⓒ와 ①, ②, ④: 계속 용법, ③, ⑤ 경험 용법

28 '혈압을 낮춤으로써' 심장을 건강하게 유지시켜 준다.

29 mixed 앞에 주격 관계대명사(which/that)와 be동사가 생략되어 있다.

교과서 파헤치기

Lesson 1

단어 TEST Step 1

p.02

01 해양의	02 입양하다	03 멸종 위기의
04 고치다	05 세대	06 탁아소, 보육원
07 전달하다, 배달하다		08 실제로
09 가르치다, 교육하다		10 목구멍, 목
11 다양한, 여러 가지의		12 표현
13 서평	14 고무	15 이웃, 근처
16 번역하다	17 모으다, 수집하다	18 기르다
19 ~임에도 불구하고, 비록 ~이지만		20 아마도
21 줄이다	22 유출	23 기부하다, 기증하다
24 자선단체, 자선	25 구조, 구출	26 전문가
27 공급	28 십 대, 청소년	29 비영리 단체
30 일어나다, 발생하다		31 쓰레기
32 자원봉사자; 자원하다		33 만
34 서명	35 ~으로 죽다	
36 (곤경, 어려움 등을) 만나다[겪다]		37 ~할 수 있다
38 토하다	39 ~ 이외에, ~에 더하여	
40 고장나다	41 ~으로 뒤덮여 있다	
42 A를 B에게 읽어주다		43 도움을 청하다

단어 TEST Step 2

p.03

01 charity	02 specialist	03 various
04 occur	05 waste	06 marine
07 collect	08 probably	09 donate
10 supply	11 reduce	12 throat
13 deliver	14 translate	15 spill
16 neighborhood	17 although	18 fix
19 generation	20 actually	21 raise
22 endangered	23 rescue	24 adopt
25 expression	26 educate	27 signature
28 gulf	29 rubber	30 child-care center
31 mayonnaise	32 teenager	33 volunteer
34 parking space	35 die from	36 any longer
37 read A to B	38 throw up	39 be covered with
40 break down	41 run into	42 in addition to
43 share A with B		

단어 TEST Step 3

p.04

1 occur, 일어나다, 발생하다 2 endangered, 멸종 위기의
3 gulf, 만 4 fix, 고치다 5 rescue, 구조, 구출
6 educate, 가르치다, 교육하다 7 marine, 해양의
8 raise, 기르다 9 expression, 표현
10 translate, 번역하다 11 reduce, 줄이다
12 deliver, 전달하다, 배달하다 13 signature, 서명
14 specialist, 전문가 15 donate, 기부하다, 기증하다
16 charity, 자선단체

대화문 TEST Step 1

p.05~07

Listen & Speak 1 A
1. doing this weekend / thinking of doing, volunteer work / What / probably read, to / sounds, join / course
2. are you, to read, review homework / thinking, young leaders / have, perfect book / lend / bring

Listen & Speak 1 B
1. What's, this year / thinking, every weekend
2. What's, plan / thinking of, how to
3. What's, plan for / thinking of taking, lessons

Listen & Speak 2 A
1. a, there, to / want me to / a few minutes
2. What can I do / ask, to make, parking space / want me to help, collect signatures / a lot

Listen & Speak 2 B
1. broke down / want me to fix
2. bring / share, umbrella with
3. This, too heavy / want me to help, carry
4. arm / want me to take

Communicate A
you don't, any longer / I'm thinking of sending, told me that, to read / aren't / about translating, into / Translating / Do you want me to help you / run into, difficult, expressions, for help / that we, help

Communicate B
thinking of learning / Are you thinking, to dance / I'm thinking of learning / want me to teach

Progress Check 1
What are, doing / I'm thinking of, bike ride / Can, join / Let's, in front of

Progress Check 2
Can we, for / don't / want me to go, get / blueberry syrup, too

Listen & Speak 1 A

1. G: What are you doing this weekend?

B: I'm thinking of doing some volunteer work at the child-care center.

G: What would you do there?

B: I would probably read some books to the children.

G: That sounds interesting. Can I join you?

B: Of course.

2. B: What are you going to read for the book review homework?

G: I'm thinking of reading a book about young leaders.

B: Good idea. I have the perfect book for you.

G: Oh, could you lend it to me?

B: Sure. I'll bring it tomorrow.

Listen & Speak 1 B

1. A: What's your plan for this year?

B: I'm thinking of watching a movie every weekend.

2. A: What's your plan for this year?

B: I'm thinking of learning how to play baduk.

3. A: What's your plan for this year?

B: I'm thinking of taking swimming lessons.

Listen & Speak 2 A

1. G: Dad, I'm a bit hungry. Is there anything to eat?

M: Do you want me to cook tteokbokki for you?

G: That'd be great. I love tteokbokki.

M: O.K. Give me a few minutes.

2. B: Sujin, can you help us?

G: Sure. What can I do for you?

B: We're going to ask the school to make a parking space for bicycles.

G: That's a great idea. Do you want me to help you collect signatures from students?

B: That would help us a lot. Thanks!

Listen & Speak 2 B

1. A: My bike broke down.

B: Do you want me to fix it?

A: Yes, please.

2. A: I didn't bring an umbrella.

B: Do you want me to share my umbrella with you?

A: Yes, please.

3. A: This box is too heavy.

B: Do you want me to help you carry it?

A: Yes, please.

4. A: My arm is too short.

B: Do you want me to take a picture of you?

A: Yes, please.

Communicate A

Suho: Anna, do you have any children's books you don't read any longer?

Anna: Sure. Why?

Suho: I'm thinking of sending some books to children in Africa. My aunt told me that they need books to read.

Anna: Good idea, Suho! Wait, aren't your books in Korean?

Suho: Oh, that's a problem.

Anna: Well, how about translating them into English?

Suho: Translating? That's a great idea, Anna.

Anna: Do you want me to help you?

Suho: Sure. If we run into any difficult expressions, let's ask our English teacher for help.

Anna: O.K. It's really great that we can help the children in Africa.

Communicate B

A: (춤추는 동작을 한다.)

B: Are you thinking of learning taekwondo?

A: No.

C: Are you thinking of learning to dance?

A: Yes. I'm thinking of learning K-pop dancing.

C: Do you want me to teach you?

A: Sure. That'd be great.

Progress Check 1

B: What are you doing this weekend?

G: I'm thinking of going for a bike ride.

B: Sounds good. Can I join you?

G: Sure. Let's meet in front of the park at ten.

B: O.K.

Progress Check 2

M: Can we have pancakes for breakfast?

W: Sure. Oh, we don't have any eggs.

M: Do you want me to go to the store and get some?

W: Thanks, Mike. Can you get blueberry syrup, too?

M: Sure.

01 Teens, Action

02 making, world, better place

03 For example, in saving

04 Although, have, made, difference

05 How, able to   06 Let's hear from

07 When, little, each adopted

08 raise, at home

09 donated to, charity, protects

10 protect, might, able, near

11 became interested in, endangered

12 later, created, non-profit organization

13 generation, so, named, organization

14 studied endangered, educated, friends

15 terrible oil spill occurred

16 completely covered with, dying

17 had to do

18 rescue supplies, as, neighborhood

19 deliver what, collected, save

20 While, working, something, useful

21 into, throat, threw up   22 wat, get, out of

23 be used to save

24 last, marine life specialist

25 waste, dangerous, than, spills

26 die from eating, waste

27 created, educational, how, reduce

28 addition, continues, various, save

29 Although, making, big difference

30 What, change, take, step

01 in Action   02 Many, a better place

03 For example, in saving animals

04 Although, teenagers, have actually made a difference

05 How, able to   06 Let's hear from

07 little sister, each adopted 08 raise, at home

09 donated to a charity, protects, South Africa

10 might not be able to see cheetahs

11 became interested in, other endangered animals

12 A few years, created a non-profit organization

13 the next generation, be able to

14 endangered animals, educated our friends

15 a terrible oil spill occurred

16 were completely covered with oil, were dying

17 had to do

18 collecting, animal rescue supplies, in our
     neighborhood

19 later, what we collected, to save the animals

20 while, working, something very useful

21 put, into, threw up   22 get, out of

23 could be used to save   24 marine life specialist

25 more dangerous, than oil spils

26 die from eating plastic waste

27 created an educational project, how to reduce

28 In addition to, projects to save

29 Although, making a big difference

30 What, take that first step

1 활약하는 십 대들

2 많은 젊은 사람들이 세상을 더 좋은 곳으로 만들고 있다.

3 예를 들어, Carter Ries와 Olivia Ries는 동물을 구하는 일에 리더가 되어 왔다.

4 비록 그들은 십 대일 뿐이지만, 실제로 세상에 변화를 일으켜 왔다.

5 그들은 어떻게 그것을 할 수 있었을까?

6 Carter의 이야기를 들어보자.

7 내가 다섯 살이었을 때, 나의 여동생 Olivia와 나는 각자 치타를 입양했다.

8 우리가 치타를 집에서 길렀을까?

9 아니, 우리는 남아프리카 공화국에 있는 야생 치타를 보호하는 자선단체에 기부했다.

10 부모님께서는 우리에게 우리가 그들을 보호하지 않으면, 가까운 미래에 치타를 볼 수 없을지도 모른다고 말씀하셨다.

11 우리는 곧 다른 멸종 위기의 동물들을 도와주는 것에 관심을 갖게 되었다.

12 몇 년 후에, 부모님의 도움으로, 우리는 그들을 보호하기 위해 비영리 단체를 만들었다.

13 우리는 다음 세대가 이러한 동물들을 볼 수 있기를 원했기에, 우리 단체를 One More Generation이라고 이름 붙였다.

14 우리는 또한 멸종 위기의 동물들을 연구했고 친구들에게 그들에 대해 가르쳐 주었다.

15 그러던 어느 날, 끔찍한 석유 유출 사건이 멕시코만에서 발생했다.

16 많은 해양 동물들이 완전히 기름을 뒤집어썼고, 죽어가고 있었다.

17 우리는 무엇인가를 해야만 했다.

18 우리는 애완동물 수송용 우리와 고무장갑과 같은 동물 구조 물품들을 동네의 모든 사람으로부터 모으기 시작했다.

19 4개월 후에, 우리 가족은 우리가 모았던 것들을 전달하기 위해서 멕시코만으로 운전해 갔으며 동물들을 구하는 일을 도왔다.

20 거기서 일하는 동안에, 우리는 매우 유용한 것을 배웠다.

21 마요네즈를 거북이의 목구멍에 집어넣으면, 거북이가 토했다.

22 그런 식으로, 우리는 거북이들에게서 기름을 빼낼 수 있었다.

23 나는 마요네즈가 동물을 구하는 데 사용될 수 있다는 것을 전혀 알지 못했다!

24 마지막 날에, 우리는 해양 생물 전문가를 만났다.

25 그녀는 우리에게 석유 유출보다 플라스틱 쓰레기가 해양 동물에게 더 위험하다고 말했다.

26 많은 해양 동물과 바다 새들이 플라스틱 쓰레기를 먹어서 죽는다.

27 집으로 돌아온 후, 우리는 플라스틱 쓰레기를 줄일 수 있는 방법에 관한 교육 프로젝트를 만들었다.

28 이것 외에도, 우리 단체는 동물들을 구하기 위한 다양한 프로젝트들을 계속하고 있다.

29 비록 우리는 작은 것부터 시작했지만, 큰 변화를 만들어 내고 있는 중이다.

30 당신이 오늘 하는 일이 세상을 바꿀 수 있기에, 첫발을 내디뎌라!

본문 TEST Step 4-Step 5

p.17~20

1 Teens in Action

2 Many young people are making the world a better place.

3 For example, Carter and Olivia Ries have become leaders in saving animals.

4 Although they are only teenagers, they have actually made a difference in the world.

5 How were they able to do that?

6 Let's hear from Carter.

7 When I was five, my little sister Olivia and I each adopted a cheetah.

8 Did we raise cheetahs at home?

9 No, we donated to a charity that protects wild cheetahs in South Africa.

10 Our parents told us that if we did not protect them, we might not be able to see cheetahs in the near future.

11 We soon became interested in helping other endangered animals..

12 A few years later, with help from our parents, we created a non-profit organization to protect them.

13 We wanted the next generation to be able to see these animals, so we named our organization One More Generation.

14 We also studied endangered animals and educated our friends about them.

15 Then one day, a terrible oil spill occurred in the Gulf of Mexico.

16 A lot of sea animals were completely covered with oil, and they were dying.

17 We had to do something.

18 We started collecting animal rescue supplies such as pet carrying cages and rubber gloves from everyone in our neighborhood.

19 Four months later, our family drove to the Gulf of Mexico to deliver what we collected and helped to save the animals.

20 While we were working there, we learned something very useful.

21 When we put mayonnaise into a turtle's throat, the turtle threw up.

22 That way, we were able to get oil out of turtles.

23 I never knew mayonnaise could be used to save animals!

24 On our last day, we met a marine life specialist.

25 She told us that plastic waste is more dangerous to sea animals than oil spills are.

26 A lot of sea animals and sea birds die from eating plastic waste.

27 After we came home, we created an educational project about how to reduce plastic waste.

28 In addition to this, our organization continues to do various projects to save animals.

29 Although we started small, we are making a big difference.

30 What you do today can change the world, so take that first step!

구석구석지문 TEST Step 1

p.21

After You Read B

1. Why don't you join
2. What, that
3. non-profit organization, protects endangered
4. does, mean
5. generation to be able to see
6. organization, join

Link Science - Share

1. white V-shape on their chests
2. mostly live in forests
3. become endangered because, hunt, body parts, destroy forests
4. what you can do
5. use less, to protect forests
6. should not buy, black bear products

Write

1. one, most serious environmental problems

2. Although, make, convenient, a lot of smoke, pollutes

3. big problem

4. what we can do

5. take the bus, subway

6. buy local products, do not need to be shipped

7. Even simple actions like

단어 TEST Step 1 　　　　　　　　p.23

01 받아들이다, 수락하다	02 보물
03 꽃이 피다, 꽃을 피우다	
04 만들어 내다, 제조하다	05 빌리다
06 신비로운　07 모험	08 신화
09 난쟁이　10 단언하다, 돈을 걸다	
11 금빛의　12 거인	
13 수확, 추수; 수확하다, 거둬들이다	
14 대장장이, 금속 세공인	15 원상태로 돌리다
16 왕국, 왕조　17 게다가	18 시
19 마차, 객차　20 도전, 결투 신청	21 선택하다
22 귀중한, 값어치 있는	23 적, 적군
24 증명하다　25 마법 같은	26 해산물
27 지혜, 슬기, 현명함　28 즉시, 곧	
29 결정, 판결　30 지키다, 보호하다	31 창
32 주문하다　33 조절하다	34 장난, 묘기
35 ~에 관심이 많다　36 포기하다	37 ~로 되다
38 ~을 생각해 내다　39 ~하는 편이 더 낫다	
40 그렇다면, 그런 경우에는	41 ~로 유명하다
42 잠들다　43 함께 가다, 동행하다	

구석구석지문 TEST Step 2 　　　　　　　p.22

After You Read B

1. A: Why don't you join One More Generation?

2. B: What is that?

3. A: It is a non-profit organization that protects endangered animals.

4. B: What does One More Generation mean?

5. A: The organization wants the next generation to be able to see those animals.

6. B: That's a great organization. I'll join it.

Link Science - Share

1. Asian black bears have a white V-shape on their chests.

2. They mostly live in forests in Asia.

3. They've become endangered because people hunt them for their body parts and destroy forests.

4. We'll tell you what you can do for them.

5. First, use less paper to protect forests.

6. Second, you should not buy any Asian black bear products.

Write

1. Air pollution is one of the most serious environmental problems these days.

2. Although cars make our lives convenient, they produce a lot of smoke that pollutes the air.

3. That is a big problem.

4. Here is what we can do.

5. We can take the bus or subway more.

6. We can also buy local products because they do not need to be shipped very far.

7. Even simple actions like these can help.

단어 TEST Step 2 　　　　　　　　p.24

01 adventure	02 wisdom	03 carriage
04 challenge	05 harvest	06 accept
07 spear	08 choose	09 poem
10 miss	11 powerful	12 moreover
13 control	14 decision	15 dwarf
16 bloom	17 decide	18 produce
19 treasure	20 magical	21 mind
22 protect	23 enemy	24 hammer
25 immediately	26 kingdom	27 giant
28 mysterious	29 myth	30 precious
31 trick	32 undo	33 prove
34 seafood	35 fall asleep	36 had better ~
37 come up with ~		38 of one's own
39 take root	40 be famous for ~	
41 give up	42 in that case	43 turn into ~

1 bloom, 꽃이 피다　2 order, 주문하다　3 treasure, 보물

4 elf, 요정　5 smith, 대장장이　6 seafood, 해산물

7 carriage, 마차, 수레　8 enemy, 적　9 spear, 창

10 trick, 장난, 속임수　11 choose, 선택하다

12 bet, 돈을 걸다　13 challenge, 도전

14 hammer, 망치　15 throw, 던지다　16 wisdom, 지혜

Listen & Speak 1 A-1

it, to visit / is, always wanted to come to / What made / into, going to go to, I saw / Have

Listen & Speak 1 A-2

the worst month of / What makes, say / blooming, have to stay inside / what you mean

Listen & Speak 2 A-1

if I change / not at all / need to watch, about / Why / learning about, in class / see

Listen & Talk 2 A-2

mind if I open / have a cold, pretty windy / problem, Would you like, good for / would be

Communicate A

doing / reading, on, into them these days / What, like them / interesting, lots of / any good / about, famous god / favorite, character / In that case, go see / if I borrow, finished, it before / at all, like this book, too

Progress Check 1

of the year / makes, say / cold, flowers are blooming / because, in April / throw, a party

Progress Check 2

mind if I take, more / waiting for, soon / Never mind / ask, to bring

Listen & Speak 1 A-1

W: Is it your first time to visit Korea, Mike?

M: Yes, it is. I've always wanted to come to Seoul.

W: What made you come here?

M: I'm really into Korean TV shows. I'm going to go to the places I saw on TV.

W: Have fun!

Listen & Speak 1 A-2

B: April is the worst month of the year.

G: What makes you say so?

B: Flowers are blooming, but I have to stay inside to study for my exams.

G: Oh, I know what you mean.

Listen & Speak 2 A-1

G: Dad, do you mind if I change the channel?

M: No, not at all.

G: Thank you. I need to watch a program about Norway.

M: Norway? Why?

G: Well, we're learning about Norway in class.

M: Oh, I see.

Listen & Talk 2 A-2

M: Jane, do you mind if I open the window?

W: Sorry, but I have a cold, and it's pretty windy today.

M: O.K. No problem. Would you like some hot tea? It'd be good for your cold.

W: That would be great. Thanks.

Communicate A

Jaden: Hi, Yuri, What're you doing?

Yuri: Hi, Jaden. I'm reading a book on Norse myths. I'm really into them these days.

Jaden: What makes you like them so much?

Yuri: The stories are very interesting, and there are lots of movies about Norse myths.

Jaden: Are they any good?

Yuri: Yes. There's actually a new movie about Thor, a famous god in Norse myths.

Jaden: Oh, I know him. He's my favorite online game character.

Yuri: In that case, we should go see the movie together.

Jaden: Do you mind if I borrow your book when you're finished? I want to read it before we see the movie.

Yuri: No, not at all. I'm sure you'll like this book, too.

Progress Check 1

B: April is the best month of the year.

G: What makes you say so?

B: The weather is not cold, and flowers are blooming.

G: I love April because my birthday is in April.

B: Really? We should throw you a party.

Progress Check 2

M: Excuse me, do you mind if I take this chair? We need one more.

W: I'm sorry, but I'm waiting for my friend. She'll be here soon.

M: Oh, I see. Never mind.

W: You can ask the waiter to bring more chairs.

01 Treasures, Three Gods
02 Important Norse
03 highest, gave up, wisdom
04 the strongest god
05 god, harvest, controls, weather
06 plays tricks on others
07 woke, something, wrong
08 wife's, was gone
09 such a terrible thing
10 found, who was drinking
11 better undo what, angrily
12 was scared
13 promised, would get, wife
14 only, sons, fine golden
15 heard, finest smiths, true
16 It is, who, replied
17 making three treasures
18 make treasures better than
19 Of course, answered
20 should, make, treasures for
21 decide on, treasure
22 one, had to be
23 to work immediately
24 went to see
25 are making, for, said
26 bet, as fine as
27 became, accepted, challenge
28 produced, of their own
29 with all the treasures
30 came along
31 showed, treasures from, sons
32 for, only one eye
33 spear, missed, target
34 turn into, piece, cloth
35 was for
36 third treasure, for
37 showed, flowing golden hair
38 put, on, took root
39 turn, show, gifts
40 eight more, every ninth
41 gave Frey, pig
42 pull, carriage faster, any
43 My third treasure
44 hammer, which, love
45 throw, come back
46 Moreover, nothing, break
47 decision, choose, greatest treasure
48 It, gods liked most
49 thought, protect, from, enemies
50 the better smiths
51 proved, wrong, precious treasures

01 Treasures, Gods
02 Important Norse
03 highest, gave up
04 the strongest god of
05 harvest, controls the weather
06 plays tricks on
07 something was wrong
08 golden, was gone
09 such a terrible thing
10 found, who was drinking
11 You'd better undo, angrily
12 scared
13 promised, would get
14 fine golden hair
15 the finest smiths, true
16 it is, who, replied
17 three treasures
18 treasures better than theirs
19 Of course, answered
20 make, for them
21 decide on, best treasure
22 one of, had to be
23 to work immediately
24 went to see
25 are making, for
26 I bet, as fine as theirs
27 angry, accepted the challenge
28 of their own
29 with all the treasures
30 came along
31 showed, from
32 for, only one eye
33 It was, that, missed
34 turn into, piece of cloth
35 for
36 The third treasure
37 flowing golden hair
38 put, on, took root, became real hair
39 Brokk's turn, gifts
40 eight more, every ninth night
41 Frey a pig
42 faster than any horse
43 My third treasure
44 hammer, which
45 come back to
46 Moreover, break it
47 the greatest treasure
48 the three gods liked most
49 protect, from, enemies
50 the better smiths
51 proved, wrong, precious treasures

1 세 명의 신을 위한 보물

2 북유럽 신화의 주요 신들

3 Odin은 가장 높은 신이며, 지혜를 위해 한쪽 눈을 포기했다.

4 Thor는 Odin의 아들이며 모든 신들 중에서 가장 강한 신이다.

5 Frey는 수확의 신으로 날씨를 다스린다.

6 Loki는 다른 신들에게 농간을 부리는 신이다.

7 Thor는 잠에서 깨어 즉시 무엇인가가 잘못되었다는 것을 알았다.

8 그의 아내의 아름다운 금발머리가 사라졌다.

9 그는 오직 Loki만이 이런 끔찍한 일을 할 수 있다는 것을 알고 있었다.

10 Thor는 곧 Loki를 찾았는데, 그는 집에서 술을 마시고 있었다.

11 "네가 한 짓을 되돌려 놓는 것이 좋을 거야. 그렇지 않으면 후회하게 될 거다." Thor는 노하여 Loki에게 말했다.

12 Loki는 겁이 났다.

13 그는 Thor의 아내를 위해 금발머리를 얻어 오겠다고 약속했다.

14 Loki는 Ivaldi의 아들들만이 훌륭한 금발머리를 만들 수 있다는 것을 알고 있었다.

15 그는 그들에게 가서 "내가 듣기로 Brokk와 그의 남동생이 가장 훌륭한 대장장이라고 하던데. 그것이 사실인가?"라고 말했다.

16 "아니요, 가장 훌륭한 대장장이는 바로 우리들이요." Ivaldi의 아들들이 대답했다.

17 "그들은 Odin과 Thor와 Frey를 위해서 보물을 만들고 있네." Loki는 말했다.

18 "너희들이 그들의 보물보다 더 나은 보물을 만들 수 있다고 생각하는가?"

19 "물론 할 수 있소." 그들이 대답했다.

20 "좋아, 그러면 너희도 그들을 위해 세 개의 보물을 만들어야 한다." Loki가 말했다.

21 "그 신들이 가장 훌륭한 보물을 결정할 것이다."

22 Loki는 또한 그들에게 보물 중 하나는 금발머리이어야 한다고 말했다.

23 그들은 즉시 일에 착수했다.

24 Loki는 그 다음에 Brokk와 그의 남동생을 보러 갔다.

25 "Ivaldi의 아들들이 Odin과 Thor, 그리고 Frey를 위해 세 개의 보물을 만들고 있어." Loki가 말했다.

26 "너희들은 절대 그들의 보물만큼 훌륭한 보물을 만들 수 없다는 것을 내 장담하지."

27 Brokk는 화가 나서 그 도전을 받아들였다.

28 그와 그의 남동생은 그들만의 세 가지 보물을 만들었다.

29 Loki는 모든 보물을 가지고 세 신을 만나러 갔다.

30 Brokk가 같이 갔다.

31 Loki는 그들에게 Ivaldi의 아들들이 만든 보물들을 보여 주었다.

32 첫 번째 보물은 Odin을 위한 것으로, 그는 눈이 한쪽밖에 없었다.

33 그것은 목표물을 절대로 빗나가지 않는 창이었다.

34 두 번째 보물은 천 조각으로 변할 수 있는 큰 배였다.

35 그것은 Frey를 위한 것이었다.

36 세 번째 보물은 Thor를 위한 것이었다.

37 Loki는 Thor에게 그의 아내를 위한 매끈하게 늘어진 금발머리를 보여 주었다.

38 Thor가 그 머리카락을 그의 아내의 머리에 얹었더니 그것이 뿌리를 내려서 진짜 머리카락이 되었다.

39 이제 Brokk가 신들에게 그의 선물들을 보여 줄 차례였다.

40 그는 Odin에게 아홉 번째 밤이 될 때마다 8개의 금팔찌를 더 만들어 내는 금팔찌를 주었다.

41 그러고 나서 Brokk는 Frey에게 돼지를 한 마리 주었다.

42 그것은 어떤 말보다도 그의 마차를 더 빨리 끌 수 있었다.

43 "나의 세 번째 보물은 당신을 위한 것입니다. Thor." Brokk가 말했다.

44 "이것은 묠니르라는 망치인데 당신은 마음에 드실 겁니다.

45 그것을 던지면, 그것은 항상 당신에게 되돌아 올 것입니다.

46 게다가, 그 무엇도 이것을 부술 수 없지요."

47 가장 훌륭한 보물을 선택하는 것은 쉬운 결정이었다.

48 세 명의 신들이 가장 마음에 든 것은 묠니르였다.

49 그들은 그 망치가 신들을 그들의 적들로부터 보호해 줄 것이라고 생각했다.

50 "Brokk와 그의 남동생이 더 훌륭한 대장장이야." Odin이 말했다.

51 Brokk는 Loki가 틀렸다는 것을 증명해 냈고, 세 신들은 이제 소중한 보물을 가지게 되었다.

1 Treasures for Three Gods

2 Important Norse Gods

3 Odin, who is the highest god, gave up his eye for wisdom.

4 Thor is Odin's son and the strongest god of all.

5 Frey, who is the god of the harvest, controls the weather.

6 Loki is a god who plays tricks on others.

7 Thor woke and knew immediately something was wrong.

8 His wife's beautiful golden hair was gone.

9 He knew only Loki could do such a terrible thing.

10 Thor soon found Loki, who was drinking at home.

11 "You'd better undo what you did, or you'll be sorry," Thor said angrily to Loki.

12 Loki was scared.

13 He promised that he would get golden hair for Thor's wife.

14 Loki knew only the sons of Ivaldi could make fine golden hair.

15 He went to them and said, "I heard Brokk and his brother are the finest smiths. Is that true?"

16 "No, it is we who are the finest smiths," the sons of Ivaldi replied.

17 "They're making three treasures for Odin, Thor, and Frey," said Loki.

18 "Do you think you can make treasures better than theirs?"

19 "Of course we can," they answered.

20 "O.K., then you should also make three treasures for them," said Loki.

21 "The gods will decide on the best treasure."

22 Loki also told them that one of the treasures had to be golden hair.

23 They went to work immediately.

24 Loki then went to see Brokk and his brother.

25 "Ivaldi's sons are making three treasures for Odin, Thor, and Frey," said Loki.

26 "I bet that you can never make treasures as fine as theirs."

27 Brokk became angry and accepted the challenge.

28 He and his brother produced three treasures of their own.

29 Loki went to see the three gods with all the treasures.

30 Brokk came along.

31 Loki showed them the treasures from Ivaldi's sons.

32 The first treasure was for Odin, who had only one eye.

33 It was a spear that never missed its target.

34 The second treasure was a big ship that could turn into a piece of cloth.

35 It was for Frey.

36 The third treasure was for Thor.

37 Loki showed Thor the flowing golden hair for his wife.

38 Thor put the hair on his wife's head, and it took root and became real hair.

39 It was now Brokk's turn to show the gods his gifts.

40 He gave Odin a gold arm ring that produced eight more gold rings every ninth night.

41 Brokk then gave Frey a pig.

42 It could pull his carriage faster than any horse.

43 "My third treasure is for you, Thor," said Brokk.

44 "This is the hammer Mjolnir, which you'll love.

45 If you throw it, it'll always come back to you.

46 Moreover, nothing can ever break it."

47 It was an easy decision to choose the greatest treasure.

48 It was Mjolnir that the three gods liked most.

49 They thought the hammer would protect the gods from their enemies.

50 "Brokk and his brother," said Odin, "are the better smiths."

51 Brokk proved that Loki was wrong, and the three gods now had precious treasures.

After You Read A

1. took, golden hair, so, became angry at

2. promised to get golden hair

3. asked, to make three treasures for

4. had, produce three treasures for the gods

5. bet, would make better treasures

6. showed, three gods, treasures from

7. spear, big ship, golden hair

8. The treasures from, were, gold arm ring, and a hammer

9. liked the summer most

10. their own precious treasures

Link Create

1. have, been, who, the strongest god

2. few days, just for fun, became angry at

3. came up with, to get, back

4. to make fine golden hair

Culture Project

1. Strongest Gods and Heroes

2. who, is famous for his many adventures

3. Brave and powerful, wore, lion's skin as a coat

4. also fought, many-headed

5. who, Miss, the strongest hero

After You Read A

1. (1) Loki took the beautiful golden hair of Thor's wife, so Thor became angry at him.
2. Loki promised to get golden hair for Thor's wife.
3. (2) Loki asked the sons of Ivaldi to make three treasures for Odin, Thor, and Frey.
4. He also had Brokk and his brother produce three treasures for the gods.
5. Loki bet that Ivaldi's sons would make better treasures.
6. (3) Loki showed the three gods the treasures from Ivaldi's sons.
7. They were a spear, a big ship, and golden hair.
8. The treasures from Brokk and his brother were a gold arm ring, a pig, and a hammer.
9. (4) The gods liked the summer most.
10. They each had their own precious treasures.

Link Create

1. I have always been friends with Sif, who is the wife of the strongest god.
2. A few days ago, I cut her golden hair just for fun, and her husband became angry at me.
3. I came up with a good idea to get her hair back.
4. I asked the sons of Ivaldi to make fine golden hair.

Culture Project

1. The Strongest Gods and Heroes in the World
2. Hercules, who was the son of Zeus, is famous for his many adventures.
3. Brave and powerful Hercules killed the Nemean lion and wore the lion's skin as a coat.
4. He also fought the many-headed Hydra.
5. I think who is Hercules Miss is the strongest hero in the world.

Lesson 3

01 증명하다	02 흡수하다	03 출판하다
04 꽃을 피우다	05 수도	06 비밀
07 실제로	08 해결하다	09 발견하다
10 담그다, 적시다	11 지우다	12 기대하다
13 시금치	14 향하다	
15 물리치다, 패배시키다		16 등장인물
17 조각상, 동상	18 기사, 논문	19 전함
20 정부, 국가	21 콩	22 숨겨진
23 고려하다, 여기다	24 일어나다	25 숨다, 숨기다
26 특성, 특징; 특징적인		
27 개선하다, 향상시키다		28 낮추다
29 포함하다, 담고 있다		30 영양소, 영양분
31 세계적으로 유명한		32 으스러뜨리다
33 흔적; 추적하다	34 유독한, 독성의	35 살을 빼다
36 흡수하다, 빨아들이다		
37 ~을 …로부터 멀리하다		38 A를 B로 바꾸다
39 더 이상 ~가 아닌	40 ~을 무서워하다	41 시도해 보다
42 비밀을 지키다	43 게다가	

01 absorb	02 article	03 battleship
04 bloom	05 capital	06 character
07 expect	08 consider	09 defeat
10 characteristic	11 crush	12 poisonous
13 contain	14 hide	15 publish
16 statue	17 improve	18 lower
19 truth	20 trace	21 spinach
22 material	23 hidden	24 nutrient
25 prove	26 world-famous	27 soak
28 planet	29 vision	30 secret
31 solve	32 cartoon	33 researcher
34 government	35 stay full	36 in addition
37 be good for	38 lose weight	39 keep a secret
40 no longer	41 soak up	42 give it a try
43 take medicine		

1 character, 등장인물   2 cartoon, 만화   3 hide, 숨기다
4 prove, 증명하다   5 insect, 곤충   6 publish, 출판하다
7 soak, 담그다, 적시다   8 carrot, 당근   9 spinach, 시금치

10 battleship, 전함　11 secret, 비밀
12 nutrient, 영양분　13 statue, 동상　14 bean, 콩
15 trace, 흔적　16 snowboard, 스노보드

대화문 TEST Step 1

p.50~51

Listen & Speak 1 A-1

some medicine / something wrong / a stomachache, too much / Why don't, go for a walk / it a try

Listen & Speak 1 A-2

something wrong, look so good / a sore throat, because of, these days / Put, take, in, produce fresh air / get a few plants

Listen & Speak 2 A-1

so hard to lose weight, do you think / walk your dog / it, it help, lose weight / When, walk, actually exercising, too / think about it

Listen & Talk 2 A-2

How are, doing, growing / gotten, a few, so far, I should do / Where / In / need about, a day / move, over

Communicate A

is something wrong, quiet / a bit tired, little / something late / on, until, what I often do these days / that's why, before midnight / getting worse, I should do / eating lots of carrots, rich in vitamin, keep, healthy / see

Progress Check 1

Is, wrong / a little tired, watched, for two hours / why, red eyes, putting, over

Progress Check 2

wrong, look worried / broke, plate, do you think / Tell, truth, understand / hope, right

대화문 TEST Step 2

p.52~53

Listen & Speak 1 A-1

B: Bomi, do you have some medicine?

G: Why? Is something wrong?

B: I have a stomachache. I think I ate too much for lunch.

G: Why don't you go for a walk?

B: O.K. I'll give it a try.

Listen & Speak 1 A-2

B: Is something wrong? You don't look so good.

G: I have a sore throat. I think it's because of the fine dust these days.

B: Put some plants in your room. They take bad air in and produce fresh air.

G: Really? I'll get a few plants right away.

Listen & Speak 2 A-1

B: It's so hard to lose weight. What do you think I should do?

G: Well, why don't you walk your dog every day?

B: My dog would love it, but would it help me lose weight?

G: Sure. When you walk your dog, you're actually exercising, too.

B: O.K. I'll think about it.

Listen & Talk 2 A-2

B: How are your tomatoes doing? Are they growing well?

G: No. I've gotten only a few tomatoes so far. What do you think I should do?

B: Where do you have the pot?

G: In the kitchen.

B: Well, tomato plants need about 7 hours of sunlight a day.

G: Oh, I see. I'll move the pot over to the window.

Communicate A

Anna: Suho, is something wrong? You're very quiet today.

Suho: I'm just a bit tired. I slept very little last night.

Anna: Did you do something late last night?

Suho: Yes, I watched a movie on my phone until 2 a.m. That's what I often do these days.

Anna: Oh, that's why you have red eyes. You should go to bed before midnight for your health.

Suho: I think my eyes are getting worse. What do you think I should do?

Anna: Try eating lots of carrots and tomatoes. They're rich in vitamin A, so they'll keep your eyes healthy.

Suho: I see. Thank you, Anna.

Progress Check 1

B: Is something wrong?

G: I'm just a little tired. I've watched a movie on my phone for two hours.

B: That's why you have red eyes. Try putting a warm towel over your eyes.

G: O.K. Thanks.

Progress Check 2

G: What's wrong? You look worried.

B: Well, I broke my mom's favorite plate. What do you think I should do?

G: Tell her the truth. She will understand.

B: I hope you're right.

본문 TEST Step 1

p.54~55

01 Hidden, Plants   02 Great Spinach

03 world-famous cartoon character

04 gets, by eating spinach

05 When, became popular, lot

06 called, capital, built, statue

07 Although, powers, spinach, nutrients

08 considered, healthiest foods, planet

09 used, surprising way

10 When, absorbs, other, soil

11 characteristic, bombs hidden, ground

12 with sensors on, leaves   13 soak, bombs, light up

14 World War II

15 defeated, during, by using

16 keep, secret, published, article

17 said, improved, vision, ate

18 believed, lot, than before

19 improve, by eating, carrots

20 contain, vitamin, keep, healthy

21 future, may, used, wars

22 discovered, turn, into, light

23 even be used, battleships

24 has already been used   25 Scariest Vegetables

26 are good for, health

27 Up until, however, poisonous

28 named, prove, safe, eat

29 ate, basket, front, watching

30 expected, nothing happened to

31 since, have enjoyed eating

32 no longer, scared of

33 keep, away, place, crushed

34 Insects, come near

본문 TEST Step 2

p.56~57

01 Hidden, Plants   02 Spinach

03 world-famous cartoon character

04 by eating spinach

05 became popular, a lot of

06 which, the spinach capital, a statue

07 Although eating, does have, nutrients

08 one of the ten healthiest foods

09 in a surprising way

10 When, absorbs, also absorbs, from

11 to find, hidden in the ground

12 with sensors on their leaves

13 soak up traces, light up   14 World War II

15 defeated, during, by using

16 keep, secret, published an article

17 improved their night vision because

18 a lot, than before

19 improve, by eating

20 which does keep, healthy

21 may actually be used

22 turn, into, light material   23 can even be used

24 has already been used   25 Scariest

26 are good for

27 Up until, however, poisonous

28 named, to prove, safe to eat

29 a basket of, in front of, watching

30 happened to

31 since, have enjoyed eating

32 no longer, scared of

33 keep, away from, place, crushed

34 come near

본문 TEST Step 3

p.58~59

1 식물에 대한 숨겨진 이야기

2 Popeye와 위대한 시금치

3 Popeye는 세계적으로 유명한 만화 캐릭터다.

4 그는 시금치를 먹음으로써 초인적인 힘을 얻는다.

5 Popeye가 1930년대 미국에서 인기를 얻었을 때, 많은 어린이들이 시금치를 먹기 시작했다.

6 텍사스의 크리스털 시티는 세계의 시금치 수도라고 불리는데, 이곳에서는 Popeye의 동상을 세우기까지 했다.

7 비록 시금치를 먹는 것이 우리에게 초인적인 힘을 주지는 않지만, 시금치는 정말로 많은 영양분을 가지고 있다.

8 이것은 실제로 지구상에서 가장 건강한 식품 10개 중 하나로 여겨진다.

9 시금치는 놀라운 용도로 사용될 수 있다.

10 그것이 물을 흡수할 때, 시금치는 흙으로부터 다른 많은 것들도 흡수한다.

11 몇몇 과학자들은 시금치의 이 특성을 땅에 숨겨진 폭탄을 찾는 데 사용했다.

12 그들은 잎에 감지기가 있는 특별한 시금치를 만든다.

13 이 식물들이 폭탄의 흔적을 흡수하면, 감지기가 빛난다.

14 제2차 세계대전에서의 당근

15 1940년, 영국 공군은 제2차 세계 대전에서 레이더 시스템을 사용해 독일군을 패배시켰다.

16 영국 정부는 이 기술을 비밀로 하기를 원했기 때문에, 신문에 기사를 하나 냈다.

17 그것은 영국 비행사들이 당근을 많이 먹어 야간 시력이 좋아졌다는 내용이었다.

18 모두가 그 이야기를 믿었고 전보다 훨씬 많은 당근을 먹기 시작했다.

19 우리는 정말 당근을 많이 먹어서 야간 시력을 높일 수 있을까?

20 실제로 그렇지는 않지만, 당근은 많은 비타민 A를 함유하는데, 그것은 정말로 우리 눈을 건강하게 유지해 준다.

21 미래에는, 당근이 실제로 전쟁에 이용될지도 모른다.

22 스코틀랜드의 연구원들은 당근을 매우 강하고 가벼운 물질로 바꾸는 방법을 발견했다.

23 그것은 심지어 전함을 만드는 데 사용될 수도 있다.

24 이 새로운 소재는 이미 스노보드와 자전거를 만드는 데 사용되었다.

25 토마토, 가장 무서운 채소

26 우리는 모두 토마토가 건강에 좋다는 것을 안다.

27 그러나, 1800년대까지 대부분의 미국인들은 토마토에 독성이 있다고 생각했다.

28 1820년에, Robert Johnson이라는 이름의 남자가 토마토가 먹기에 안전하다는 것을 증명하기를 원했다.

29 그래서, 그는 그를 지켜보는 많은 사람들 앞에서 한 바구니의 토마토를 먹었다.

30 그들은 모두 그가 죽을 것이라고 예상했으나 그에게는 아무 일도 일어나지 않았다.

31 그 이후로, 미국인들은 토마토를 먹는 것을 즐겼다.

32 우리는 더 이상 토마토를 두려워하지 않지만, 몇몇 곤충들은 여전히 그것을 무서워한다.

33 만약 곤충들이 방에 들어오지 않게 하고 싶다면, 으깬 토마토 한 그릇을 방구석에 놓아 두어라.

34 곤충들은 토마토 가까이 오지 않을 것이다.

본문 TEST Step 4~Step 5

1 Hidden Stories about Plants

2 Popeye and the Great Spinach

3 Popeye is a world-famous cartoon character.

4 He gets his super power by eating spinach.

5 When Popeye became popular in the 1930s in the United States, a lot of children began to eat spinach.

6 Crystal City in Texas, which is called the spinach capital of the world, even built a statue of Popeye.

7 Although eating spinach will not give us super powers, spinach does have a lot of nutrients.

8 It is actually considered one of the ten healthiest foods on the planet.

9 Spinach can be used in a surprising way.

10 When it absorbs water, spinach also absorbs many other things from the soil.

11 Some scientists have used this characteristic of spinach to find bombs hidden in the ground.

12 They make special spinach plants with sensors on their leaves.

13 When these plants soak up traces from bombs, the sensors light up.

14 Carrots in World War II

15 In 1940, the Royal Air Force defeated German fighters during World War II by using a radar system.

16 The British government wanted to keep this technology a secret, so it published an article in the newspaper.

17 It said that British pilots improved their night vision because they ate a lot of carrots.

18 Everybody believed the story and began to eat a lot more carrots than before.

19 Can we really improve night vision by eating lots of carrots?

20 Not really, but carrots contain a lot of vitamin A, which does keep our eyes healthy.

21 In the future, carrots may actually be used in wars.

22 Scottish researchers have discovered a way to turn carrots into a very strong and light material.

23 It can even be used to make battleships.

24 This new material has already been used to make snowboards and bicycles.

25 Tomatoes, the Scariest Vegetables

26 We all know that tomatoes are good for our health.

27 Up until the 1800s, however, most Americans thought that tomatoes were poisonous.

28 In 1820, a man named Robert Johnson wanted to prove that tomatoes were safe to eat.

29 So, he ate a basket of tomatoes in front of many people watching him.

30 They all expected him to die, but nothing happened to him.

31 Ever since then, Americans have enjoyed eating tomatoes.

32 We are no longer afraid of tomatoes, but some insects are still scared of them.

33 If you want to keep insects away from your room, place a bowl of crushed tomatoes in a corner of your room.

34 Insects will not come near the tomatoes.

구석구석지문 TEST Step 1 p.64

Inventions from Plants

1. good way to produce
2. battery invented from, of using, characteristic of sunflowers
3. Like, faces, during the day, more electricity than other batteries

After You Read A Read and Match

1. Spinach
2. secret, super power
3. one of the ten healthiest foods
4. with, to find bombs hidden
5. Carrots
6. to make snowboards
7. into, light material
8. which keeps our eyes healthy
9. Tomatoes
10. keeping insects away
11. poisonous until

Write

1. are good for
2. keep your heart healthy, lower blood pressure
3. solve your skin problems
4. mixed with, makes, soft, clear
5. In addition, help, lose weight
6. stay full for a long time
7. help, stay healthy

구석구석지문 TEST Step 2 p.65

Inventions from Plants

1. The Sunflower Battery is a good way to produce energy.
2. It is a battery invented from the idea of using the characteristic of sunflowers.
3. Like sunflowers, it faces the sun during the day, so it produces more electricity than other batteries.

After You Read A Read and Match

1. 1. Spinach
2. • the secret of Popeye's super power

---

3. • one of the ten healthiest foods on the planet
4. • used with sensors to find bombs hidden in the ground
5. 2. Carrots
6. • used to make snowboards and bicycles
7. • made into a very strong and light material
8. • containing a lot of vitamin A, which keeps our eyes healthy
9. 3. Tomatoes
10. • good for keeping insects away
11. • considered poisonous until the 1800s

Write

1. Potatoes are good for your health.
2. They keep your heart healthy because they lower blood pressure.
3. They also solve your skin problems.
4. Potato juice mixed with honey makes your skin soft and clear.
5. In addition, they help you lose weight.
6. If you eat potatoes, you will stay full for a long time.
7. Potatoes help you stay healthy in many ways.

MEMO

MEMO

적중100

영어 기출 문제집

정답 및 해설

미래 | 최연희